MARCUS AURELIUS

MEDITATIONS

THE ORIGINAL ANCIENT GREEK TEXT
WITH ENGLISH TRANSLATION

CONSTANTIN VAUGHN

Erebus Society

First published in Great Britain in 2017
by Erebus Society

First Edition

Editor: Constantin Vaughn

ISBN: 978-0-9933284-4-2

TABLE OF CONTENTS

BOOK ONE

I. Of my grandfather Verus I have learned to be gentle and meek, and to re-frain from all anger and passion. From the fame and memory of him that begot me I have learned both shamefastness and manlike behaviour. Of my mother I have learned to be religious, and bountiful; and to forbear, not only to do, but to intend any evil; to content myself with a spare diet, and to fly all such excess as is incidental to great wealth. Of my greatgrandfather, both to frequent public schools and auditories, and to get me good and able teachers at home; and that I ought not to think much, if upon such occasions, I were at excessive charges.

II. Of him that brought me up, not to be fondly addicted to either of the two great factions of the coursers in the circus, called Prasini, and Veneti: nor in the amphitheatre partially to favour any of the gladiators, or fencers, as either the Parmularii, or the Secutores. Moreover, to endure labour; nor to need many things; when I have anything to do, to do it myself rather than by others; not to meddle with many businesses; and not easily to admit of any slander.

III. Of Diognetus, not to busy myself about vain things, and not easily to believe those things, which are commonly spoken, by such as take upon them to work wonders, and by sorcerers, or prestidigitators, and impostors; concerning the power of charms, and their driving out of demons, or evil spirits; and the like. Not to keep quails for the game; nor to be mad after such things. Not to be of-fended with other men's liberty of speech, and to apply myself unto philosophy. Him also I must thank, that ever I heard first Bacchius, then Tandasis and Mar-cianus, and that I did write dialogues in my youth; and that I took liking to the philosophers' little couch and skins, and such other things, which by the Grecian discipline are proper to those who profess philosophy.

IV. To Rusticus I am beholding, that I first entered into the conceit that my life wanted some redress and cure. And then, that I did not fall into the ambition of ordinary sophists, either to write tracts concerning the common theorems, or to exhort men unto virtue and the study of philosophy by public orations; as also that I never by way of ostentation did affect to show myself an active able man, for any kind of bodily exercises. And that I gave over the study of rhetoric and poetry, and of elegant neat language. That I did not use to walk about the house in my long robe, nor to do any such things. Moreover I learned of him to write letters without any affectation, or curiosity; such as that was, which by him was written to my mother from Sinuessa: and to be easy and ready to be recon-ciled, and well pleased again with them that had offended me, as soon as any of them would be content to seek unto me again. To read with diligence; not to rest satisfied with a light and superficial knowledge, nor quickly to assent to things commonly spoken of: whom also I must thank that ever I lighted upon Epictetus his Hypomnemata, or moral commentaries and common-factions: which also he gave me of his own.

V. From Apollonius, true liberty, and unvariable steadfastness, and not to regard anything at all, though never so little, but right and reason: and always, whether in the sharpest pains, or after the loss of a child, or in long diseases, to be still the same man; who also was a present and visible example unto me, that it was possible for the same man to be both vehement and remiss: a man not subject to be vexed, and offended with the incapacity of his scholars and auditors in his lectures and expositions; and a true pattern of a man who of all his good gifts and faculties, least esteemed in himself, that his excellent skill and ability to teach and persuade others the common theorems and maxims of the Stoic philosophy. Of him also I learned how to receive favours and kindnesses (as commonly they are accounted:) from friends, so that I might not become obnoxious unto them, for them, nor more yielding upon occasion, than in right I ought; and yet so that I should not pass them neither, as an unsensible and unthankful man.

VI. Of Sextus, mildness and the pattern of a family governed with paternal affection; and a purpose to live according to nature: to be grave without affectation: to observe carefully the several dispositions of my friends, not to be offended with idiots, nor unseasonably to set upon those that are carried with the vulgar opinions, with the theorems, and tenets of philosophers: his conversation being an example how a man might accommodate himself to all men and companies; so that though his company were sweeter and more pleasing than any flatterer's cogging and fawning; yet was it at the same time most respected and reverenced: who also had a proper happiness and faculty, rationally and methodically to find out, and set in order all necessary determinations and instructions for a man's life. A man without ever the least appearance of anger, or any other passion; able at the same time most exactly to observe the Stoic Apathia, or unpassionateness, and yet to be most tenderhearted: ever of good credit; and yet almost without any noise, or rumour: very learned, and yet making little show.

VII. From Alexander the Grammarian, to be unreprovable myself, and not reproachfully to reprehend any man for a barbarism, or a solecism, or any false pronunciation, but dextrously by way of answer, or testimony, or confirmation of the same matter (taking no notice of the word) to utter it as it should have been spoken; or by some other such close and indirect admonition, hansomely and civilly to tell him of it.

VIII. Of Fronto, to how much envy and fraud and hypocrisy the state of a tyrannous king is subject unto, and how they who are commonly called nobly born, are in some sort incapable, or void of natural affection.

IX. Of Alexander the Platonic, not often nor without great necessity to say, or to write to any man in a letter, 'I am not at leisure'; nor in this manner still to put off those duties, which we owe to our friends and acquaintances (to every one in his kind) under pretence of urgent affairs.

X. Of Catulus, not to contemn any friend's expostulation, though unjust, but to strive to reduce him to his former disposition: freely and heartily to speak well of all my masters upon any occasion, as it is reported of Domitius, and Athenodotus: and to love my children with true affection.

XI. From my brother Severus, to be kind and loving to all them of my house and family; by whom also I came to the knowledge of Thrasea and Helvidius, and Cato, and Dio, and Brutus. He it was also that did put me in the first conceit and desire of an equal commonwealth, administered by justice and equality; and of a kingdom wherein should be regarded nothing more than the good and welfare of the subjects. Of him also, to observe a constant tenor, (not interrupted, with any other cares and distractions,) in the study and esteem of philosophy: to be bountiful and liberal in the largest measure; always to hope the best; and to be confident that my friends love me. In whom I moreover observed open dealing towards those whom he reproved at any time, and that his friends might without all doubt or much observation know what he would, or would not, so open and plain was he.

XII. From Claudius Maximus, in all things to endeavour to have power of myself, and in nothing to be carried about; to be cheerful and courageous in all sudden chances and accidents, as in sicknesses: to love mildness, and moderation, and gravity: and to do my business, whatsoever it be, thoroughly, and without querulousness. Whatsoever he said, all men believed him that as he spake, so he thought, and whatsoever he did, that he did it with a good intent. His manner was, never to wonder at anything; never to be in haste, and yet never slow: nor to be perplexed, or dejected, or at any time unseemly, or excessively to laugh: nor to be angry, or suspicious, but ever ready to do good, and to forgive, and to speak truth; and all this, as one that seemed rather of himself to have been straight and right, than ever to have been rectified or redressed; neither was there any man that ever thought himself undervalued by him, or that could find in his heart, to think himself a better man than he. He would also be very pleasant and gracious.

XIII. In my father, I observed his meekness; his constancy without wavering in those things, which after a due examination and deliberation, he had determined. How free from all vanity he carried himself in matter of honour and dignity, his laboriousness and assiduity, his readiness to hear any man, that had aught to say tending to any common good: how generally and impartially he would give every man his due; his skill and knowledge, when rigour or extremity, or when remissness or moderation was in season; how he did abstain from all unchaste love of youths; his moderate condescending to other men's occasions as an ordinary man, neither absolutely requiring of his friends, that they should wait upon him at his ordinary meals, nor that they should of necessity accompany him in his journeys; and that whensoever any business upon some necessary occasions was to be put off and omitted before it could be ended, he was ever found when he went about it again, the same man that he was before. His accurate examination of things in consultations, and patient hearing of others. He would not hastily give over the search of the matter, as one easy to be satisfied with sudden notions and apprehensions. His care to preserve his friends; how neither at any time he would carry himself towards them with disdainful neglect, and grow weary of them; nor yet at any time be madly fond of them. His contented mind in all things, his cheerful countenance, his care to foresee things afar off, and to take order for the least, without any noise or clamour. Moreover how all acclamations and flattery were repressed by him: how carefully he observed all things necessary to the government, and kept an account of the common expenses, and how patiently he did abide that he was reprehended by some for this his strict and rigid kind of dealing. How he was neither a superstitious worshipper of the gods, nor an ambitious pleaser of men, or studious of popular applause; but sober in all things, and everywhere observant of that which was fitting; no affecter of novelties: in those things which conduced to his ease and convenience, (plenty whereof his fortune did afford him,) without pride and bragging, yet with all freedom and liberty: so that as he did freely enjoy them without any anxiety or affectation when they were present; so when absent, he found no want of them. Moreover, that he was never commended by any man, as either a learned acute man, or an obsequious officious man, or a fine orator; but as a ripe mature man, a perfect sound man; one that could not endure to be flattered; able to govern both himself and others. Moreover, how much he did honour all true philosophers, without upbraiding those that were not so; his sociableness, his gracious and delightful conversation, but never unto satiety; his care of his body within bounds and measure, not as one that desired to live long, or overstudious of neatness, and elegancy; and yet not as one that did not regard it: so that through his own care and providence, he seldom needed any inward physic, or outward applications: but especially how ingeniously he would yield to any that had obtained any peculiar faculty, as either eloquence, or the knowledge of the laws, or of ancient customs, or the like; and how he concurred with them, in his best care and endeavour that every one of them might in his kind, for that wherein he excelled, be regarded and esteemed: and although he did all things carefully after the ancient customs of his forefathers, yet even of this was he not desirous that men should take notice, that he did imitate ancient customs. Again, how he was not easily moved and tossed up and down, but loved to be constant, both in the same places and businesses; and how after his great fits of headache he would return fresh and vigorous to his wonted affairs. Again, that secrets he neither had many, nor often, and such only as concerned public matters: his discretion and moderation, in exhibiting of the public sights and shows for the pleasure and pastime of the people: in public buildings. congiaries, and the like. In all these things, having a respect unto men only as men, and to the equity of the things themselves, and not unto the glory that might follow. Never wont to use the baths at unseasonable hours; no builder; never curious, or solicitous, either about his meat, or about the workmanship, or colour of his clothes, or about anything that belonged to external beauty. In all his conversation, far from all inhumanity, all boldness, and incivility, all greediness and impetuosity; never doing anything with such earnestness, and intention, that a man could say of him, that he did sweat about it: but contrariwise, all things distinctly, as at leisure; without trouble; orderly, soundly, and agreeably. A man might have applied that to him, which is recorded of Socrates, that he knew how to want, and to enjoy those things, in the want whereof, most men show themselves weak; and in the fruition, intemperate: but to hold out firm and constant, and to keep within the compass of true moderation and sobriety in either estate, is proper to a man, who hath a perfect and invincible soul; such as he showed himself in the sickness of Maximus.

XIV. From the gods I received that I had good grandfathers, and parents, a good sister, good masters, good domestics, loving kinsmen, almost all that I have; and that I never through haste and rashness transgressed against any of them, not-withstanding that my disposition was such, as that such a thing (if occasion had been) might very well have been committed by me, but that It was the mercy of the gods, to prevent such a concurring of matters and occasions, as might make me to incur this blame. That I was not long brought up by the concubine of my father; that I preserved the flower of my youth. That I took not upon me to be a man before my time, but rather put it off longer than I needed. That I lived under the government of my lord and father, who would take away from me all pride and vainglory, and reduce me to that conceit and opinion that it was not impossible for a prince to live in the court without a troop of guards and followers, extraordinary apparel, such and such torches and statues, and other like particulars of state and magnificence; but that a man may reduce and contract himself almost to the state of a private man, and yet for all that not to become the more base and remiss in those public matters and affairs, wherein power and authority is requisite. That I have had such a brother, who by his own example might stir me up to think of myself; and by his respect and love, delight and please me. That I have got ingenuous children, and that they were not born distorted, nor with any other natural deformity. That I was no great proficient in the study of rhetoric and poetry, and of other faculties, which perchance I might have dwelt upon, if I had found myself to go on in them with success. That I did by times prefer those, by whom I was brought up, to such places and dignities, which they seemed unto me most to desire; and that I did not put them off with hope and expectation, that (since that they were yet but young) I would do the same hereafter. That I ever knew Apollonius and Rusticus, and Maximus. That I have had occasion often and effectually to consider and meditate with myself, concerning that life which is according to nature, what the nature and manner of it is: so that as for the gods and such suggestions, helps and inspirations, as might be expected from them, nothing did hinder, but that I might have begun long before to live according to nature; or that even now that I was not yet partaker and in present possession of that life, that I myself (in that I did not observe those inward motions, and suggestions, yea and almost plain and apparent instructions and admonitions of the gods,) was the only cause of it. That my body in such a life, hath been able to hold out so long. That I never had to do with Benedicta and Theodotus, yea and afterwards when I fell into some fits of love, I was soon cured. That having been often displeased with Rusticus, I never did him anything for which afterwards I had occasion to repent. That it being so that my mother was to die young, yet she lived with me all her latter years. That as often as I had a purpose to help and succour any that either were poor, or fallen into some present necessity, I never was answered by my officers that there was not ready money enough to do it; and that I myself never had occasion to require the like succour from any other. That I have such a wife, so obedient, so loving, so ingenuous. That I had choice of fit and able men, to whom I might commit the bringing up of my children. That by dreams I have received help, as for other things, so in particular, how I might stay my casting of blood, and cure my dizziness, as that also that happened to thee in Cajeta, as unto Chryses when he prayed by the seashore. And when I did first apply myself to philosophy, that I did not fall into the hands of some sophists, or spent my time either in reading the manifold volumes of ordinary philosophers, nor in practising myself in the solution of arguments and fallacies, nor dwelt upon the studies of the meteors, and other natural curiosities. All these things without the assistance of the gods, and fortune, could not have been.

8

XV. In the country of the Quadi at Granua, these. Betimes in the morning say to thyself, This day I shalt have to do with an idle curious man, with an unthankful man, a railer, a crafty, false, or an envious man; an unsociable uncharitable man. All these ill qualities have happened unto them, through ignorance of that which is truly good and truly bad. But I that understand the nature of that which is good, that it only is to be desired, and of that which is bad, that it only is truly odious and shameful: who know moreover, that this transgressor, whosoever he be, is my kinsman, not by the same blood and seed, but by participation of the same reason, and of the same divine particle; How can I either be hurt by any of those, since it is not in their power to make me incur anything that is truly reproachful? or angry, and ill affected towards him, who by nature is so near unto me? for we are all born to be fellow-workers, as the feet, the hands, and the eyelids; as the rows of the upper and under teeth: for such therefore to be in opposition, is against nature; and what is it to chafe at, and to be averse from, but to be in opposition?

XVI. Whatsoever I am, is either flesh, or life, or that which we commonly call the mistress and overruling part of man; reason. Away with thy books, suffer not thy mind any more to be distracted, and carried to and fro; for it will not be; but as even now ready to die, think little of thy flesh: blood, bones, and a skin; a pretty piece of knit and twisted work, consisting of nerves, veins and arteries; think no more of it, than so. And as for thy life, consider what it is; a wind; not one constant wind neither, but every moment of an hour let out, and sucked in again. The third, is thy ruling part; and here consider; Thou art an old man; suffer not that excellent part to be brought in subjection, and to become slavish: suffer it not to be drawn up and down with unreasonable and unsociable lusts and motions, as it were with wires and nerves; suffer it not any more, either to repine at anything now present, or to fear and fly anything to come, which the destiny hath appointed thee.

XVII. Whatsoever proceeds from the gods immediately, that any man will grant totally depends from their divine providence. As for those things that are commonly said to happen by fortune, even those must be conceived to have dependence from nature, or from that first and general connection, and concatenation of all those things, which more apparently by the divine providence are administered and brought to pass. All things flow from thence: and whatsoever it is that is, is both necessary, and conducing to the whole (part of which thou art), and whatsoever it is that is requisite and necessary for the preservation of the general, must of necessity for every particular nature, be good and behoveful. And as for the whole, it is preserved, as by the perpetual mutation and conversion of the simple elements one into another, so also by the mutation, and alteration of things mixed and compounded. Let these things suffice thee; let them be always unto thee, as thy general rules and precepts. As for thy thirst after books, away with it with all speed, that thou die not murmuring and complaining, but truly meek and well satisfied, and from thy heart thankful unto the gods.

ΒΙΒΛΙΟ ΠΡΩΤΟ

Meditations

1.Παρὰ τοῦ πάππου Οὐήρου τὸ καλόηθες καὶ ἀόργητον.

2.Παρὰ τῆς δόξης καὶ μνήμης τῆς περὶ τοῦ γεννήσαντος τὸ αἰδῆμον καὶ ἀρρενικόν.

3.Παρὰ τῆς μητρὸς τὸ θεοσεβὲς καὶ μεταδοτικὸν καὶ ἀφεκτικὸν οὐ μόνον τοῦ κακοποιεῖν, ἀλλὰ καὶ τοῦ ἐπὶ ἐννοίας γίνεσθαι τοιαύτης· ἔτι δὲ τὸ λιτὸν κατὰ τὴν δίαιταν καὶ πόρρω τῆς πλουσιακῆς διαγωγῆς.

4.Παρὰ τοῦ προπάππου τὸ μὴ εἰς δημοσίας διατριβὰς φοιτῆσαι καὶ τὸ ἀγαθοῖς διδασκάλοις κατ᾿ οἶκον χρήσασθαι καὶ τὸ γνῶναι ὅτι εἰς τὰ τοιαῦτα δεῖ ἐκτενῶς ἀναλίσκειν.

5.Παρὰ τοῦ τροφέως τὸ μήτε Πρασιανὸς ἢ Βενετιανὸς μήτε Παλμουλάριος ἢ Σκουτάριος γενέσθαι· καὶ τὸ φερέπονον καὶ ὀλιγοδεές· καὶ τὸ αὐτουργικὸν καὶ ἀπολύπραγμον· καὶ τὸ δυσπρόςδεκτον διαβολῆς.

6.Παρὰ Διογνήτου τὸ ἀκενόσπουδον· καὶ τὸ ἀπιστητικὸν τοῖς ὑπὸ τῶν τερατευομένων καὶ γοήτων περὶ ἐπῳδῶν καὶ [περὶ] δαιμόνων ἀποπομπῆς καὶ τῶν τοιούτων λεγομένοις· καὶ τὸ μὴ ὀρτυγοκοπεῖν μηδὲ περὶ τὰ τοιαῦτα ἐπτοῆσθαι· καὶ τὸ ἀνέχεσθαι παρρησίας· καὶ τὸ οἰκειωθῆναι φιλοσοφίᾳ καὶ τὸ ἀκοῦσαι πρῶτον μὲν Βακχείου, εἶτα Τανδάσιδος καὶ Μαρκιανοῦ· καὶ τὸ γράψαι διαλόγους ἐν παιδί· καὶ τὸ σκίμποδος καὶ δορᾶς ἐπιθυμῆσαι καὶ ὅσα τοιαῦτα τῆς Ἑλληνικῆς ἀγωγῆς ἐχόμενα.

7.Παρὰ Ῥουστίκου τὸ λαβεῖν φαντασίαν τοῦ χρήζειν διορθώσεως καὶ θεραπείας τοῦ ἤθους· καὶ τὸ μὴ ἐκτραπῆναι εἰς ζῆλον σοφιστικόν, μηδὲ τὸ συγγράφειν περὶ τῶν θεωρημάτων, ἢ προτρεπτικὰ λογάρια διαλέγεσθαι, ἢ φαντασιοπλήκτως τὸν ἀσκητικὸν ἢ τὸν εὐεργετικὸν ἄνδρα ἐπιδείκνυσθαι· καὶ τὸ ἀποστῆναι ῥητορικῆς καὶ ποιητικῆς καὶ ἀστειολογίας· καὶ τὸ μὴ ἐν στολίῳ κατ᾿ οἶκον περιπατεῖν μηδὲ τὰ τοιαῦτα ποιεῖν· καὶ τὸ τὰ ἐπιστόλια ἀφελῶς γράφειν, οἷον τὸ ὑπ᾿ αὐτοῦ τούτου ἀπὸ Σινοέσσης τῇ μητρί μου γραφέν· καὶ τὸ πρὸς τοὺς χαλεπήναντας καὶ πλημμελήσαντας εὐανακλήτως καὶ εὐδιαλλάκτως, ἐπειδὰν τάχιστα αὐτοὶ ἐπανελθεῖν ἐθελήσωσι, διακεῖσθαι· καὶ τὸ ἀκριβῶς ἀναγινώσκειν καὶ μὴ ἀρκεῖσθαι περινοοῦντα ὁλοσχερῶς μηδὲ τοῖς περιλαλοῦσι ταχέως συγκατατίθεσθαι· καὶ τὸ ἐντυχεῖν τοῖς Ἐπικτητείοις ὑπομνήμασιν, ὧν οἴκοθεν μετέδωκεν.

8.Παρὰ Ἀπολλωνίου τὸ ἐλεύθερον καὶ ἀναμφιβόλως ἀκύβευτον καὶ πρὸς μηδὲν ἄλλο ἀποβλέπειν μηδὲ ἐπ ὀλίγον ἢ πρὸς τὸν λόγον· καὶ τὸ ἀεὶ ὅμοιον, ἐν ἀλγηδόσιν ὀξείαις, ἐν ἀποβολῇ τέκνου, ἐν μακραῖς νόσοις· καὶ τὸ ἐπὶ παραδείγματος ζῶντος ἰδεῖν ἐναργῶς ὅτι δύναται ὁ αὐτὸς σφοδρότατος εἶναι καὶ ἀνειμένος· καὶ τὸ ἐν ταῖς ἐξηγήσεσι μὴ δυσχεραντικόν· καὶ τὸ ἰδεῖν ἄνθρωπον σαφῶς ἐλάχιστον τῶν ἑαυτοῦ καλῶν ἡγούμενον τὴν ἐμπειρίαν καὶ τὴν ἐντρέχειαν τὴν περὶ τὸ παραδιδόναι τὰ θεωρήματα· καὶ τὸ μαθεῖν πῶς δεῖ λαμβάνειν τὰς δοκούσας χάριτας παρὰ φίλων, μήτε ἐξηττώμενον διὰ ταῦτα μήτε ἀναισθήτως παραπέμποντα.

9.Παρὰ Σέξτου τὸ εὐμενές· καὶ τὸ παράδειγμα τοῦ οἴκου τοῦ πατρονομουμένου· καὶ τὴν ἔννοιαν τοῦ κατὰ φύσιν ζῆν· καὶ τὸ σεμνὸν ἀπλάστως· καὶ τὸ στοχαστικὸν τῶν φίλων κηδεμονικῶς· καὶ τὸ ἀνεκτικὸν τῶν ἰδιωτῶν καὶ τῶν ἀθεωρητὶ οἰομένων· καὶ τὸ πρὸς πάντας εὐάρμοστον, ὥστε κολακείας μὲν πάσης προσηνεστέραν εἶναι τὴν ὁμιλίαν αὐτοῦ, αἰδεσιμώτατον δὲ αὐτοῖς ἐκείνοις παρ᾽ αὐτὸν ἐκεῖνον τὸν καιρὸν εἶναι· καὶ τὸ καταληπτικῶς καὶ ὁδῷ ἐξευρετικόν τε καὶ τακτικὸν τῶν εἰς βίον ἀναγκαίων δογμάτων· καὶ τὸ μηδὲ ἔμφασίν ποτε ὀργῆς ἢ ἄλλου τινὸς πάθους παρασχεῖν, ἀλλὰ ἅμα μὲν ἀπαθέστατον εἶναι, ἅμα δὲ φιλοστοργότατον· καὶ τὸ εὔφημον ἀψοφητὶ καὶ τὸ πολυμαθὲς ἀνεπιφάντως.

10.Παρὰ Ἀλεξάνδρου τοῦ γραμματικοῦ τὸ ἀνεπίπληκτον καὶ τὸ μὴ ὀνειδιστικῶς ἐπιλαμβάνεσθαι τῶν βάρβαρον ἢ σόλοικόν τι ἢ ἀπηχὲς προενεγκαμένων, ἀλλ ἐπιδεξίως αὐτὸ μόνον ἐκεῖνο ὃ ἔδει εἰρῆσθαι προφέρεσθαι ἐν τρόπῳ ἀποκρίσεως ἢ συνεπιμαρτυρήσεως ἢ συνδιαλήψεως περὶ αὐτοῦ τοῦ πράγματος, οὐχὶ περὶ τοῦ ῥήματος, ἢ δί ἑτέρας τινὸς τοιαύτης ἐμμελοῦς παρυπομνήσεως.

11.Παρὰ Φρόντωνος τὸ ἐπιστῆσαι οἵα ἡ τυραννικὴ βασκανία καὶ ποικιλία καὶ ὑπόκρισις, καὶ ὅτι ὡς ἐπίπαν οἱ καλούμενοι οΡτοι παρ᾽ ἡμῖν εὐπατρίδαι ἀστοργότεροί πως εἰσί.

12.Παρὰ Ἀλεξάνδρου τοῦ Πλατωνικοῦ τὸ μὴ πολλάκις μηδὲ χωρὶς ἀνάγκης λέγειν πρός τινα ἢ ἐν ἐπιστολῇ γράφειν ὅτι ἄσχολός εἰμι, μηδὲ διὰ τοιούτου τρόπου συνεχῶς παραιτεῖσθαι τὰ κατὰ τὰς πρὸς τοὺς συμβιοῦντας σχέσεις καθήκοντα, προβαλλόμενον τὰ περιεστῶτα πράγματα.

13.Παρὰ Κατούλου τὸ μὴ ὀλιγώρως ἔχειν φίλου αἰτιωμένου τι, κἂν τύχῃ ἀλόγως αἰτιώμενος, ἀλλὰ πειρᾶσθαι [καὶ] ἀποκαθιστάναι ἐπὶ τὸ σύνηθες· καὶ τὸ περὶ τῶν διδασκάλων ἐκθύμως εὔφημον, οἷα τὰ περὶ Δομετίου καὶ Ἀθηνοδότου ἀπομνημονευόμενα· καὶ τὸ περὶ τὰ τέκνα ἀληθινῶς ἀγαπητικόν.

14.Παρὰ Σευήρου τὸ φιλοίκειον καὶ φιλάληθες καὶ φιλοδίκαιον· καὶ τὸ δι᾽ αὐτὸν
γνῶναι Θρασέαν, Ἐλβίδιον, Κάτωνα, Δίωνα, Βροῦτον· καὶ φαντασίαν λαβεῖν
πολιτείας ἰσονόμου, κατ᾽ ἰσότητα καὶ ἰσηγορίαν διοικουμένης, καὶ βασιλείας
τιμώσης πάντων μάλιστα τὴν ἐλευθερίαν τῶν ἀρχομένων· καὶ ἔτι παρ᾽ αὐτοῦ
τὸ ὁμαλὲς καὶ εὔτονον ἐν τῇ τιμῇ τῆς φιλοσοφίας· καὶ τὸ εὐποιητικὸν καὶ τὸ
εὐμετάδοτον ἐκτενῶς καὶ τὸ εὔελπι· καὶ τὸ πιστευτικὸν περὶ τοῦ ὑπὸ τῶν φίλων
φιλεῖσθαι, καὶ τὸ ἀνεπίκρυπτον πρὸς τοὺς καταγνώσεως ὑπ᾽ αὐτοῦ τυγχάνοντας,
καὶ τὸ μὴ δεῖσθαι στοχασμοῦ τοὺς φίλους αὐτοῦ περὶ τοῦ τί θέλει ἢ τί οὐ θέλει,
ἀλλὰ δῆλον εἶναι.

15.Παρὰ Μαξίμου τὸ κρατεῖν ἑαυτοῦ καὶ κατὰ μηδὲν περίφορον εἶναι· καὶ τὸ
εὔθυμον ἔν τε ταῖς ἄλλαις περιστάσεσι καὶ ἐν ταῖς νόσοις· καὶ τὸ εὔκρατον
τοῦ ἤθους καὶ μειλίχιον καὶ γεραρόν· καὶ τὸ οὐ σχετλίως κατεργαστικὸν τῶν
προκειμένων· καὶ τὸ πάντας αὐτῷ πιστεύειν περὶ ὧν λέγοι ὅτι οὕτως φρονεῖ, καὶ
περὶ ὧν πράττοι ὅτι οὐ κακῶς πράττει. καὶ τὸ ἀθαύμαστον καὶ ἀνέκπληκτον καὶ
μηδαμοῦ ἐπειγόμενον ἢ ὀκνοῦν ἢ ἀμηχανοῦν ἢ κατηφὲς ἢ προσσεσηρός, ἢ πάλιν
θυμούμενον ἢ ὑφορώμενον· καὶ τὸ εὐεργετικὸν καὶ τὸ συγγνωμονικὸν καὶ τὸ
ἀψευδές· καὶ τὸ ἀδιαστρόφου μᾶλλον ἢ διορθουμένου φαντασίαν παρέχειν· καὶ
ὅτι οὔτε ᾠήθη ἄν ποτέ τις ὑπερορᾶσθαι ὑπ᾽ αὐτοῦ οὔτε ὑπέμεινεν ἂν κρείττονα
αὐτοῦ αὑτὸν ὑπολαβεῖν· καὶ τὸ εὔχαρι ἐν τ ..

16.Παρὰ τοῦ πατρὸς τὸ ἥμερον καὶ μενετικὸν ἀσαλεύτως ἐπὶ τῶν ἐξητασμένως
κριθέντων· καὶ τὸ ἀκενόδοξον περὶ τὰς δοκούσας τιμάς· καὶ τὸ φιλόπονον
καὶ ἐνδελεχές· καὶ τὸ ἀκουστικὸν τῶν ἐχόντων τι κοινωφελὲς εἰσφέρειν· καὶ
τὸ ἀπαρατρέπτως [εἰς] τοῦ κατ᾽ ἀξίαν ἀπονεμητικὸν ἑκάστῳ· καὶ τὸ ἔμπειρον
ποῦ μὲν χρεία ἐντάσεως, ποῦ δὲ ἀνέσεως· καὶ τὸ παῦσαι τὰ περὶ τοὺς ἔρωτας
τῶν μειρακίων· καὶ ἡ κοινονοημοσύνη καὶ τὸ ἐφεῖσθαι τοῖς φίλοις μήτε
συνδειπνεῖν αὐτῷ πάντως μήτε συναποδημεῖν ἐπάναγκες, ἀεὶ δὲ ὅμοιον αὐτὸν
καταλαμβάνεσθαι ὑπὸ τῶν διὰ χρείας τινὰς ἀπολειφθέντων· καὶ τὸ ζητητικὸν
ἀκριβῶς ἐν τοῖς συμβουλίοις καὶ ἐπίμονον, † ἀλλ᾽ οὐ τό· προαπέστη τῆς ἐρεύνης,
ἀρκεσθεὶς ταῖς προχείροις φαντασίαις· καὶ τὸ διατηρητικὸν τῶν φίλων καὶ
μηδαμοῦ ἁψίκορον μηδὲ ἐπιμανές· καὶ τὸ αὔταρκες ἐν παντὶ καὶ τὸ φαιδρόν·
καὶ τὸ πόρρωθεν προνοητικὸν καὶ τῶν ἐλαχίστων προδιοικητικὸν ἀτραγῴδως·
καὶ τὸ τὰς ἐπιβοήσεις καὶ πᾶσαν κολακείαν ἐπ᾽ αὐτοῦ ‹συ›σταλῆναι· καὶ τὸ
φυλακτικὸν ἀεὶ τῶν ἀναγκαίων τῇ ἀρχῇ καὶ ταμιευτικὸν τῆς χορηγίας καὶ
ὑπομενετικὸν τῆς ἐπὶ τῶν τοιούτων τινῶν καταιτιάσεως· καὶ τὸ μήτε περὶ θεοὺς
δεισίδαιμον μήτε περὶ ἀνθρώπους δημοκοπικὸν ἢ ἀρεσκευτικὸν ἢ ὀχλοχαρές,
ἀλλὰ νῆφον ἐν πᾶσι καὶ βέβαιον καὶ μηδαμοῦ ἀπειρόκαλον μηδὲ καινοτόμον·
καὶ τὸ τοῖς εἰς εὐμάρειαν βίου φέρουσί τι, ὧν ἡ τύχη παρεῖχε δαψίλειαν,
χρηστικὸν ἀτύφως ἅμα καὶ ἀπροφασίστως, ὥστε παρόντων μὲν ἀνεπιτηδεύτως
ἅπτεσθαι, ἀπόντων δὲ μὴ δεῖσθαι· καὶ τὸ μηδ᾽ ἂν τινα εἰπεῖν μήτε ὅτι σοφιστὴς

μήτε ὅτι οὐερνάκλος μήτε ὅτι σχολαστικός, ἀλλ ὅτι ἀνὴρ πέπειρος, τέλειος, ἀκολάκευτος, προεστάναι δυνάμενος καὶ τῶν ἑαυτοῦ καὶ ἄλλων. πρὸς τούτοις δὲ καὶ τὸ τιμητικὸν τῶν ἀληθῶς φιλοσοφούντων, τοῖς δὲ ἄλλοις οὐκ ἐξονειδιστικὸν οὐδὲ μὴν εὐπαράγωγον ὑπ αὐτῶν· ἔτι δὲ τὸ εὐόμιλον καὶ εὔχαρι οὐ κατακόρως· καὶ τὸ τοῦ ἰδίου σώματος ἐπιμελητικὸν ἐμμέτρως, οὔτε ὡς ἄν τις φιλόζωος οὔτε πρὸς καλλωπισμὸν οὔτε μὴν ὀλιγώρως, ἀλλ ὥστε διὰ τὴν ἰδίαν προσοχὴν εἰς ὀλίγιστα ἰατρικῆς χρήζειν ἢ φαρμάκων καὶ ἐπιθεμάτων [ἐκτός]· μάλιστα δὲ τὸ παραχωρητικὸν ἀβασκάνως τοῖς δύναμίν τινα κεκτημένοις, οἷον τὴν φραστικὴν ἢ τὴν ἐξ ἱστορίας νόμων ἢ ἐθῶν ἢ ἄλλων τινῶν πραγμάτων, καὶ συσπουδαστικὸν αὐτοῖς, ἵνα ἕκαστοι κατὰ τὰ ἴδια προτερήματα εὐδοκιμῶσι· πάντα δὲ κατὰ τὰ πάτρια πράσσων, οὐδὲ αὐτὸ τοῦτο ἐπιτηδεύων φαίνεσθαι, τὸ τὰ πάτρια φυλάσσειν. ἔτι δὲ τὸ μὴ εὐμετακίνητον καὶ ῥιπταστικόν, ἀλλὰ καὶ τόποις καὶ πράγμασι τοῖς αὐτοῖς ἐνδιατριπτικόν· καὶ τὸ μετὰ τοὺς παροξυσμοὺς τῆς κεφαλαλγίας νεαρὸν εὐθὺς καὶ ἀκμαῖον πρὸς τὰ συνήθη ἔργα· καὶ τὸ μὴ εἶναι αὐτῷ πολλὰ τὰ ἀπόρρητα, ἀλλ ὀλίγιστα καὶ σπανιώτατα καὶ ταῦτα ὑπὲρ τῶν κοινῶν μόνον· καὶ τὸ ἔμφρον καὶ μεμετρημένον ἔν τε θεωριῶν ἐπιτελέσει καὶ ἔργων κατασκευαῖς καὶ διανομαῖς καὶ τοῖς τοιούτοις, ‹ὡς› ἀνθρώπου πρὸς αὐτὸ τὸ δέον πραχθῆναι δεδορκότος, οὐ πρὸς τὴν ἐπὶ τοῖς πραχθεῖσιν εὐδοξίαν. οὐκ ἦν ἀωρὶ λούστης, οὐχὶ φιλοικοδόμος, οὐ περὶ τὰς ἐδωδὰς ἐπινοητής, οὐ περὶ ἐσθήτων ὕφας καὶ χρόας, οὐ περὶ σωμάτων ὥρας. ἡ ἀπὸ Λωρίου στολὴ ἀνάγουσα ἀπὸ τῆς κάτω ἐπαύλεως· καὶ τῶν ἐν Λανουβίῳ τὰ πολλά· τῷ τελώνῃ ἐν Τούσκλοις παραιτουμένῳ ὡς ἐχρήσατο καὶ πᾶς ὁ τοιοῦτος τρόπος. οὐδὲν ἀπηνὲς οὐδὲ μὴν ἀδυσώπητον οὐδὲ λάβρον οὐδὲ ὥστ ἄν τινα εἰπεῖν ποτε· "ἕως ἱδρῶτος"· ἀλλὰ πάντα διειλημμένα λελογίσθαι ὡς ἐπὶ σχολῆς, ἀταράχως, τεταγμένως, ἐρρωμένως, συμφώνως ἑαυτοῖς. ἐφαρμόσειε δ ἂν αὐτῷ τὸ περὶ τοῦ Σωκράτους μνημονευόμενον, ὅτι καὶ ἀπέχεσθαι καὶ ἀπολαύειν ἐδύνατο τούτων, ὧν πολλοὶ πρός τε τὰς ἀποχὰς ἀσθενῶς καὶ πρὸς τὰς ἀπολαύσεις ἐνδοτικῶς ἔχουσι. τὸ δὲ ἰσχύειν καὶ ἔτι καρτερεῖν καὶ ἐννήφειν ἑκατέρῳ ἀνδρός ἐστιν ἄρτιον καὶ ἀήττητον ψυχὴν ἔχοντος, οἷον ἐν τῇ νόσῳ τὴν Μαξίμου.

17.Παρὰ τῶν θεῶν τὸ ἀγαθοὺς πάππους, ἀγαθοὺς γονέας, ἀγαθὴν ἀδελφήν, ἀγαθοὺς διδασκάλους, ἀγαθοὺς οἰκείους, συγγενεῖς, φίλους, σχεδὸν ἅπαντα ἔχειν· καὶ ὅτι περὶ οὐδένα αὐτῶν προέπεσον πλημμελῆσαί τι, καίτοι διάθεσιν ἔχων τοιαύτην, ἀφ ἧς, εἰ ἔτυχε, κἂν ἔπραξά τι τοιοῦτον· τῶν θεῶν δὲ εὐποιία τὸ μηδεμίαν συνδρομὴν πραγμάτων γενέσθαι, ἥτις ἔμελλέ με ἐλέγξειν. καὶ τὸ μὴ ἐπὶ πλέον τραφῆναι παρὰ τῇ παλλακῇ τοῦ πάππου καὶ τὸ τὴν ὥραν διασῶσαι καὶ τὸ μὴ πρὸ ὥρας ἀνδρωθῆναι, ἀλλ ἔτι καὶ ἐπιλαβεῖν τοῦ χρόνου. τὸ ἄρχοντι καὶ πατρὶ ὑποταχθῆναι, ὃς ἔμελλε πάντα τὸν τῦφον ἀφαιρήσειν μου καὶ εἰς ἔννοιαν ἄξειν τοῦ ὅτι δυνατόν ἐστιν ἐν αὐλῇ βιοῦντα μήτε δορυφορήσεων χρῄζειν μήτε ἐσθήτων σημειωδῶν μήτε λαμπάδων καὶ ἀνδριάντων ‹καὶ› τοιῶνδέ τινων [καὶ] τοῦ ὁμοίου κόμπου, ἀλλ ἔξεστιν ἐγγυτάτω ἰδιώτου συστέλλειν ἑαυτὸν καὶ μὴ διὰ τοῦτο ταπεινότερον ἢ ῥᾳθυμότερον ἔχειν πρὸς τὰ ὑπὲρ τῶν κοινῶν ἡγεμονικῶς πραχθῆναι δέοντα. τὸ ἀδελφοῦ τοιούτου τυχεῖν, δυναμένου μὲν διὰ ἤθους ἐπεγεῖραί με πρὸς ἐπιμέλειαν ἐμαυτοῦ, ἅμα δὲ καὶ τιμῇ καὶ στοργῇ εὐφραίνοντός με· τὸ παιδία μοι ἀφυῆ μὴ γενέσθαι μηδὲ κατὰ τὸ σωμάτιον διάστροφα. τὸ μὴ ἐπὶ πλέον με προκόψαι ἐν ῥητορικῇ καὶ ποιητικῇ καὶ τοῖς ἄλλοις ἐπιτηδεύμασιν, ἐν οἷς ἴσως ἂν κατεσχέθην, εἰ ᾐσθόμην ἐμαυτὸν εὐόδως προϊόντα. τὸ φθάσαι τοὺς τροφέας ἐν ἀξιώματι καταστῆσαι, οὗ δὴ ἐδόκουν μοι ἐπιθυμεῖν, καὶ μὴ ἀναβαλέσθαι ἐλπίδι τοῦ με, ἐπεὶ νέοι ἔτι ἦσαν, ὕστερον αὐτὸ πράξειν. τὸ γνῶναι Ἀπολλώνιον, Ῥούστικον, Μάξιμον. τὸ φαντασθῆναι περὶ τοῦ κατὰ φύσιν βίου ἐναργῶς καὶ πολλάκις οἷός τίς ἐστιν, ὥστε, ὅσον ἐπὶ τοῖς θεοῖς καὶ ταῖς ἐκεῖθεν διαδόσεσι καὶ συλλήψεσι καὶ ἐπιπνοίαις, μηδὲν κωλύειν ἤδη κατὰ φύσιν ζῆν με, ἀπολείπεσθαι δέ τι ἔτι τούτου παρὰ τὴν ἐμὴν αἰτίαν καὶ παρὰ τὸ μὴ διατηρεῖν τὰς ἐκ τῶν θεῶν ὑπομνήσεις καὶ μονονουχὶ διδασκαλίας· τὸ ἀντισχεῖν μοι τὸ σῶμα ἐπὶ τοσοῦτον ἐν τοιούτῳ βίῳ· τὸ μήτε Βενεδίκτης ἅψασθαι μήτε Θεοδότου, ἀλλὰ καὶ ὕστερον ἐν ἐρωτικοῖς πάθεσι γενόμενον ὑγιᾶναι· τὸ χαλεπήναντα πολλάκις Ῥουστίκῳ μηδὲν πλέον πρᾶξαι, ἐφ' ᾧ ἂν μετέγνων· τὸ μέλλουσαν νέαν τελευτᾶν τὴν τεκοῦσαν ὅμως οἰκῆσαι μετ' ἐμοῦ τὰ τελευταῖα ἔτη. τὸ ὁσάκις ἐβουλήθην ἐπικουρῆσαί τινι πενομένῳ ἢ εἰς ἄλλο τι χρῄζοντι, μηδέποτε ἀκοῦσαί με ὅτι οὐκ ἔστι μοι χρήματα, ὅθεν γένηται, καὶ τὸ αὐτῷ ἐμοὶ χρείαν ὁμοίαν, ὡς παρ' ἑτέρου μεταλαβεῖν, μὴ συμπεσεῖν· τὸ τὴν γυναῖκα τοιαύτην εἶναι, οὕτωσὶ μὲν πειθήνιον, οὕτω δὲ φιλόστοργον, οὕτω δὲ ἀφελῆ· τὸ ἐπιτηδείων τροφέων εἰς τὰ παιδία εὐπορῆσαι. τὸ δι' ὀνειράτων βοηθήματα δοθῆναι ἄλλα τε καὶ ὡς μὴ πτύειν αἷμα καὶ μὴ ἰλιγγιᾶν, καὶ τὸ τοῦ ἐν Καιήτῃ "ὥσπερ χρῇς"· ‹τὸ› ὅπως ἐπεθύμησα φιλοσοφίας, μὴ ἐμπεσεῖν εἴς τινα σοφιστὴν μηδὲ ἀποκαθίσαι ἐπὶ τοῦ συγγραφᾶς ἢ συλλογισμοὺς ἀναλύειν ἢ περὶ τὰ μετεωρολογικὰ καταγίνεσθαι. πάντα γὰρ ταῦτα "θεῶν βοηθῶν καὶ τύχης δεῖτα".

BOOK TWO

I. Remember how long thou hast already put off these things, and how often a certain day and hour as it were, having been set unto thee by the gods, thou hast neglected it. It is high time for thee to understand the true nature both of the world, whereof thou art a part; and of that Lord and Governor of the world, from whom, as a channel from the spring, thou thyself didst flow: and that there is but a certain limit of time appointed unto thee, which if thou shalt not make use of to calm and allay the many distempers of thy soul, it will pass away and thou with it, and never after return.

II. Let it be thy earnest and incessant care as a Roman and a man to perform whatsoever it is that thou art about, with true and unfeigned gravity, natural affection, freedom and justice: and as for all other cares, and imaginations, how thou mayest ease thy mind of them. Which thou shalt do; if thou shalt go about every action as thy last action, free from all vanity, all passionate and wilful aberration from reason, and from all hypocrisy, and self-love, and dislike of those things, which by the fates or appointment of God have happened unto thee. Thou seest that those things, which for a man to hold on in a prosperous course, and to live a divine life, are requisite and necessary, are not many, for the gods will require no more of any man, that shall but keep and observe these things.

III. Do, soul, do; abuse and contemn thyself; yet a while and the time for thee to respect thyself, will be at an end. Every man's happiness depends from himself, but behold thy life is almost at an end, whiles affording thyself no respect, thou dost make thy happiness to consist in the souls, and conceits of other men.

IV. Why should any of these things that happen externally, so much distract thee? Give thyself leisure to learn some good thing, and cease roving and wandering to and fro. Thou must also take heed of another kind of wandering, for they are idle in their actions, who toil and labour in this life, and have no certain scope to which to direct all their motions, and desires.

V. For not observing the state of another man's soul, scarce was ever any man known to be unhappy. Tell whosoever they be that intend not, and guide not by reason and discretion the motions of their own souls, they must of necessity be unhappy.

VI. These things thou must always have in mind: What is the nature of the universe, and what is mine—in particular: This unto that what relation it hath: what kind of part, of what kind of universe it is: And that there is nobody that can hinder thee, but that thou mayest always both do and speak those things which are agreeable to that nature, whereof thou art a part.

VII. Theophrastus, where he compares sin with sin (as after a vulgar sense such things I grant may be compared:) says well and like a philosopher, that those sins are greater which are committed through lust, than those which are committed through anger. For he that is angry seems with a kind of grief and close contraction of himself, to turn away from reason; but he that sins through lust, being overcome by pleasure, doth in his very sin bewray a more impotent, and unmanlike disposition. Well then and like a philosopher doth he say, that he of the two is the more to be condemned, that sins with pleasure, than he that sins with grief. For indeed this latter may seem first to have been wronged, and so in some manner through grief thereof to have been forced to be angry, whereas he who through lust doth commit anything, did of himself merely resolve upon that action.

VIII. Whatsoever thou dost affect, whatsoever thou dost project, so do, and so project all, as one who, for aught thou knowest, may at this very present depart out of this life. And as for death, if there be any gods, it is no grievous thing to leave the society of men. The gods will do thee no hurt, thou mayest be sure. But if it be so that there be no gods, or that they take no care of the world, why should I desire to live in a world void of gods, and of all divine providence? But gods there be certainly, and they take care for the world; and as for those things which be truly evil, as vice and wickedness, such things they have put in a man's own power, that he might avoid them if he would: and had there been anything besides that had been truly bad and evil, they would have had a care of that also, that a man might have avoided it. But why should that be thought to hurt and prejudice a man's life in this world, which cannot any ways make man himself the better, or the worse in his own person? Neither must we think that the nature of the universe did either through ignorance pass these things, or if not as ignorant of them, yet as unable either to prevent, or better to order and dispose them. It cannot be that she through want either of power or skill, should have committed such a thing, so as to suffer all things both good and bad, equally and promiscuously, to happen unto all both good and bad. As for life therefore, and death, honour and dishonour, labour and pleasure, riches and poverty, all these things happen unto men indeed, both good and bad, equally; but as things which of themselves are neither good nor bad; because of themselves, neither shameful nor praiseworthy.

22

IX. Consider how quickly all things are dissolved and resolved: the bodies and substances themselves, into the matter and substance of the world: and their memories into the general age and time of the world. Consider the nature of all worldly sensible things; of those especially, which either ensnare by pleasure, or for their irksomeness are dreadful, or for their outward lustre and show are in great esteem and request, how vile and contemptible, how base and corruptible, how destitute of all true life and being they are.

X. It is the part of a man endowed with a good understanding faculty, to consider what they themselves are in very deed, from whose bare conceits and voices, honour and credit do proceed: as also what it is to die, and how if a man shall consider this by itself alone, to die, and separate from it in his mind all those things which with it usually represent themselves unto us, he can conceive of it no otherwise, than as of a work of nature, and he that fears any work of nature, is a very child. Now death, it is not only a work of nature, but also conducing to nature.

XI. Consider with thyself how man, and by what part of his, is joined unto God, and how that part of man is affected, when it is said to be diffused. There is nothing more wretched than that soul, which in a kind of circuit compasseth all things, searching (as he saith) even the very depths of the earth; and by all signs and conjectures prying into the very thoughts of other men's souls; and yet of this, is not sensible, that it is sufficient for a man to apply himself wholly, and to confine all his thoughts and cares to the tendance of that spirit which is within him, and truly and really to serve him. His service doth consist in this, that a man keep himself pure from all violent passion and evil affection, from all rashness and vanity, and from all manner of discontent, either in regard of the gods or men. For indeed whatsoever proceeds from the gods, deserves respect for their worth and excellency; and whatsoever proceeds from men, as they are our kinsmen, should by us be entertained, with love, always; sometimes, as proceeding from their ignorance, of that which is truly good and bad, (a blindness no less, than that by which we are not able to discern between white and black:) with a kind of pity and compassion also.

XII. If thou shouldst live three thousand, or as many as ten thousands of years, yet remember this, that man can part with no life properly, save with that little part of life, which he now lives: and that which he lives, is no other, than that which at every instant he parts with. That then which is longest of duration, and that which is shortest, come both to one effect. For although in regard of that which is already past there may be some inequality, yet that time which is now present and in being, is equal unto all men. And that being it which we part with whensoever we die, it doth manifestly appear, that it can be but a moment of time, that we then part with. For as for that which is either past or to come, a man cannot be said properly to part with it. For how should a man part with that which he hath not? These two things therefore thou must remember. First, that all things in the world from all eternity, by a perpetual revolution of the same times and things ever continued and renewed, are of one kind and nature; so that whether for a hundred or two hundred years only, or for an infinite space of time, a man see those things which are still the same, it can be no matter of great moment. And secondly, that that life which any the longest liver, or the shortest liver parts with, is for length and duration the very same, for that only which is present, is that, which either of them can lose, as being that only which they have; for that which he hath not, no man can truly be said to lose.

XIII. Remember that all is but opinion and conceit, for those things are plain and apparent, which were spoken unto Monimus the Cynic; and as plain and apparent is the use that may be made of those things, if that which is true and serious in them, be received as well as that which is sweet and pleasing.

XIV. A man's soul doth wrong and disrespect itself first and especially, when as much as in itself lies it becomes an aposteme, and as it were an excrescency of the world, for to be grieved and displeased with anything that happens in the world, is direct apostacy from the nature of the universe; part of which, all particular natures of the world, are. Secondly, when she either is averse from any man, or led by contrary desires or affections, tending to his hurt and prejudice; such as are the souls of them that are angry. Thirdly, when she is overcome by any pleasure or pain. Fourthly, when she doth dissemble, and covertly and falsely either doth or saith anything. Fifthly, when she doth either affect or endeavour anything to no certain end, but rashly and without due ratiocination and consideration, how consequent or inconsequent it is to the common end. For even the least things ought not to be done, without relation unto the end; and the end of the reasonable creatures is, to follow and obey him, who is the reason as it were, and the law of this great city, and ancient commonwealth.

XV. The time of a man's life is as a point; the substance of it ever flowing, the sense obscure; and the whole composition of the body tending to corruption. His soul is restless, fortune uncertain, and fame doubtful; to be brief, as a stream so are all things belonging to the body; as a dream, or as a smoke, so are all that belong unto the soul. Our life is a warfare, and a mere pilgrimage. Fame after life is no better than oblivion. What is it then that will adhere and follow? Only one thing, philosophy. And philosophy doth consist in this, for a man to preserve that spirit which is within him, from all manner of contumelies and injuries, and above all pains or pleasures; never to do anything either rashly, or feignedly, or hypocritically: wholly to depend from himself and his own proper actions: all things that happen unto him to embrace contentedly, as coming from Him from whom he himself also came; and above all things, with all meekness and a calm cheerfulness, to expect death, as being nothing else but the resolution of those elements, of which every creature is composed. And if the elements themselves suffer nothing by this their perpetual conversion of one into another, that disso-lution, and alteration, which is so common unto all, why should it be feared by any? Is not this according to nature? But nothing that is according to nature can be evil, whilst I was at Carnuntzim.

ΒΙΒΛΙΟ ΔΕΥΤΕΡΟ

❖ Meditations ❖

[Τὰ ἐν Κουάδοις πρὸς τῷ Γρανούᾳ α′]

1. Ἕωθεν προλέγειν ἑαυτῷ· συντεύξομαι περιέργῳ, ἀχαρίστῳ, ὑβριστῇ, δολερῷ, βασκάνῳ, ἀκοινωνήτῳ· πάντα ταῦτα συμβέβηκεν ἐκείνοις παρὰ τὴν ἄγνοιαν τῶν ἀγαθῶν καὶ κακῶν. ἐγὼ δὲ τεθεωρηκὼς τὴν φύσιν τοῦ ἀγαθοῦ ὅτι καλόν, καὶ τοῦ κακοῦ ὅτι αἰσχρόν, καὶ τὴν αὐτοῦ τοῦ ἁμαρτάνοντος φύσιν ὅτι μοι συγγενής, οὐχὶ αἵματος ἢ σπέρματος τοῦ αὐτοῦ ἀλλὰ νοῦ καὶ θείας ἀπομοίρας μέτοχος, οὔτε βλαβῆναι ὑπό τινος αὐτῶν δύναμαι· αἰσχρῷ γάρ με οὐδεὶς περιβαλεῖ· οὔτε ὀργίζεσθαι τῷ συγγενεῖ δύναμαι οὔτε ἀπέχθεσθαι αὐτῷ. γεγόναμεν γὰρ πρὸς συνεργίαν ὡς πόδες, ὡς χεῖρες, ὡς βλέφαρα, ὡς οἱ στοῖχοι τῶν ἄνω καὶ τῶν κάτω ὀδόντων. τὸ οὖν ἀντιπράσσειν ἀλλήλοις παρὰ φύσιν· ἀντιπρακτικὸν δὲ τὸ ἀγανακτεῖν καὶ ἀποστρέφεσθαι.

2. Ὅ τί ποτε τοῦτό εἰμι, σαρκία ἐστὶ καὶ πνευμάτιον καὶ τὸ ἡγεμονικόν. τῶν μὲν σαρκίων καταφρόνησον· λύθρος καὶ ὀστάρια καὶ κροκύφαντος, ἐκ νεύρων, φλεβίων, ἀρτηριῶν πλεγμάτιον. θέασαι δὲ καὶ τὸ πνεῦμα ὁποῖόν τί ἐστιν· ἄνεμος, οὐδὲ ἀεὶ τὸ αὐτό, ἀλλὰ πάσης ὥρας ἐξεμούμενον καὶ πάλιν ῥοφούμενον. τρίτον οὖν ἐστι τὸ ἡγεμονικόν. ἄφες τὰ βιβλία· μηκέτι σπῶ· οὐ δέδοται. ἀλλ᾽ ὡς ἤδη ἀποθνήσκων ὧδε ἐπινοήθητι· γέρων εἶ· μηκέτι τοῦτο ἐάσῃς δουλεῦσαι, μηκέτι καθ᾽ ὁρμὴν ἀκοινώνητον νευροσπαστηθῆναι, μηκέτι τὸ εἱμαρμένον ἢ παρὸν δυσχερᾶναι ἢ μέλλον ὑπιδέσθαι.

3. Τὰ τῶν θεῶν προνοίας μεστά. τὰ τῆς τύχης οὐκ ἄνευ φύσεως ἢ συγκλώσεως καὶ ἐπιπλοκῆς τῶν προνοίᾳ διοικουμένων. πάντα ἐκεῖθεν ῥεῖ· πρόσεστι δὲ τὸ ἀναγκαῖον καὶ τὸ τῷ ὅλῳ κόσμῳ συμφέρον, οὗ μέρος εἶ. παντὶ δὲ φύσεως μέρει ἀγαθόν, ὃ φέρει ἡ τοῦ ὅλου φύσις καὶ ὃ ἐκείνης ἐστὶ σωστικόν. σῴζουσι δὲ κόσμον, ὥσπερ αἱ τῶν στοιχείων, οὕτως καὶ αἱ τῶν συγκριμάτων μεταβολαί. ταῦτά σοι ἀρκείτω· ἀεὶ δόγματα ἔστω. τὴν δὲ τῶν βιβλίων δίψαν ῥῖψον, ἵνα μὴ γογγύζων ἀποθάνῃς, ἀλλὰ ἵλεως ἀληθῶς καὶ ἀπὸ καρδίας εὐχάριστος τοῖς θεοῖς.

4. Μέμνησο ἐκ πόσου ταῦτα ἀναβάλλῃ καὶ ὁποσάκις προθεσμίας λαβὼν παρὰ τῶν θεῶν οὐ χρᾷ αὐταῖς. δεῖ δὲ ἤδη ποτὲ αἰσθέσθαι τίνος κόσμου μέρος εἶ καὶ τίνος διοικοῦντος τὸν κόσμον ἀπόρροια ὑπέστης καὶ ὅτι ὅρος ἐστί σοι περιγεγραμμένος τοῦ χρόνου, ᾧ ἐὰν εἰς τὸ ἀπαιθριάσαι μὴ χρήσῃ, οἰχήσεται καὶ οἰχήσῃ καὶ αὖθις οὐκ ἐξέσται.

29

5. Πάσης ὥρας φρόντιζε στιβαρῶς ὡς Ῥωμαῖος καὶ ἄρρην τὸ ἐν χερσὶ μετὰ τῆς ἀκριβοῦς .. καὶ ἀπλάστου σεμνότητος καὶ φιλοστοργίας καὶ ἐλευθερίας καὶ δικαιότητος πράσσειν καὶ σχολὴν ἑαυτῷ ἀπὸ πασῶν τῶν ἄλλων φαντασιῶν πορίζειν. ποριεῖς δέ, ἂν ὡς ἐσχάτην τοῦ βίου ἑκάστην πρᾶξιν ἐνεργῇς, ἀπηλλαγμένος πάσης εἰκαιότητος καὶ ἐμπαθοῦς ἀποστροφῆς ἀπὸ τοῦ αἱροῦντος λόγου καὶ ὑποκρίσεως καὶ φιλαυτίας καὶ δυσαρεστήσεως πρὸς τὰ συμμεμοιραμένα. ὁρᾷς πῶς ὀλίγα ἐστίν, ὧν κρατήσας τις δύναται εὔρουν καὶ θεουδῆ βιῶσαι βίον· καὶ γὰρ οἱ θεοὶ πλέον οὐδὲν ἀπαιτήσουσι παρὰ τοῦ ταῦτα φυλάσσοντος.

6. Ὑβρίζεις, ὑβρίζεις ἑαυτήν, ὦ ψυχή· τοῦ δὲ τιμῆσαι σεαυτὴν οὐκέτι καιρὸν ἕξεις· ἀκαριαῖος ὁ βίος ἑκάστῳ, οῦτος δέ σοι σχεδὸν διήνυσται, μὴ αἰδουμένη σεαυτήν, ἀλλ ἐν ταῖς ἄλλων ψυχαῖς τιθεμένη τὴν σὴν εὐμοιρίαν.

7. Περισπᾷ τί σε τὰ ἔξωθεν ἐμπίπτοντα; καὶ σχολὴν πάρεχε σεαυτῷ τοῦ προσμανθάνειν ἀγαθόν τι καὶ παῦσαι ῥεμβόμενος. ἤδη δὲ καὶ τὴν ἑτέραν περιφορὰν φυλακτέον· ληροῦσι γὰρ καὶ διὰ πράξεων οἱ κεκμηκότες τῷ βίῳ καὶ μὴ ἔχοντες σκοπόν, ἐφ ὃν πᾶσαν ὁρμὴν καὶ καθάπαξ φαντασίαν ἀπευθύνουσιν.

8. Παρὰ μὲν τὸ μὴ ἐφιστάνειν, τί ἐν τῇ ἄλλου ψυχῇ γίνεται, οὐ ῥαδίως τις ὤφθη κακοδαιμονῶν· τοὺς δὲ τοῖς τῆς ἰδίας ψυχῆς κινήμασι μὴ παρακολουθοῦντας ἀνάγκη κακοδαιμονεῖν.

9. Τούτων ἀεὶ μεμνῆσθαι, τίς ἡ τῶν ὅλων φύσις καὶ τίς ἡ ἐμὴ καὶ πῶς αὕτη πρὸς ἐκείνην ἔχουσα καὶ ὁποῖόν τι μέρος ὁποίου τοῦ ὅλου οὖσα καὶ ὅτι οὐδεὶς ὁ κωλύων τὰ ἀκόλουθα τῇ φύσει, ἧς μέρος εἶ, πράσσειν τε ἀεὶ καὶ λέγειν.

10. Φιλοσόφως ὁ Θεόφραστος ἐν τῇ συγκρίσει τῶν ἁμαρτημάτων, ὡς ἄν τις κοινότερον τὰ τοιαῦτα συγκρίνειε, φησὶ βαρύτερα εἶναι τὰ κατ ἐπιθυμίαν πλημμελούμενα τῶν κατὰ θυμόν. ὁ γὰρ θυμούμενος μετά τινος λύπης καὶ λεληθυίας συστολῆς φαίνεται τὸν λόγον ἀποστρεφόμενος· ὁ δὲ κατ ἐπιθυμίαν ἁμαρτάνων, ὑφ ἡδονῆς ἡττώμενος ἀκολαστότερός πως φαίνεται καὶ θηλύτερος ἐν ταῖς ἁμαρτίαις. ὀρθῶς οὖν καὶ φιλοσοφίας ἀξίως ἔφη μείζονος ἐγκλή ματος ἔχεσθαι τὸ μεθ ἡδονῆς ἁμαρτανόμενον ἤπερ τὸ μετὰ λύπης· ὅλως τε ὁ μὲν προηδικημένῳ μᾶλλον ἔοικε καὶ διὰ λύπης ἠναγκασμένῳ θυμωθῆναι· ὁ δὲ αὐτόθεν πρὸς τὸ ἀδικεῖν ὥρμηται, φερόμενος ἐπὶ τὸ πρᾶξαί τι κατ ἐπιθυμίαν.

11. Ὡς ἤδη δυνατοῦ ὄντος ἐξιέναι τοῦ βίου, οὕτως ἕκαστα ποιεῖν καὶ λέγειν καὶ διανοεῖσθαι. τὸ δὲ ἐξ ἀνθρώπων ἀπελθεῖν, εἰ μὲν θεοὶ εἰσίν, οὐδὲν δεινόν·

κακῷ γάρ σε οὐκ ἂν περιβάλοιεν· εἰ δὲ ἤτοι οὐκ εἰσὶν ἢ οὐ μέλει αὐτοῖς τῶν ἀνθρωπείων, τί μοι ζῆν ἐν κόσμῳ κενῷ θεῶν ἢ προνοίας κενῷ; ἀλλὰ καὶ εἰσὶ καὶ μέλει αὐτοῖς τῶν ἀνθρωπείων καὶ τοῖς μὲν κατ ἀλήθειαν κακοῖς ἵνα μὴ περιπίπτῃ ὁ ἄνθρωπος, ἐπ αὐτῷ τὸ πᾶν ἔθεντο· τῶν δὲ λοιπῶν εἴ τι κακὸν ἦν, καὶ τοῦτο ἂν προείδοντο, ἵνα ἐπὶ παντὶ ᾖ τὸ μὴ περιπίπτειν αὐτῷ. (ὃ δὲ χείρω μὴ ποιεῖ ἄνθρωπον, πῶς ἂν τοῦτο βίον ἀνθρώπου χείρω ποιήσειεν;) οὔτε δὲ κατ ἄγνοιαν οὔτε εἰδυῖα μέν, μὴ δυναμένη δὲ προφυλάξασθαι ἢ διορθώσασθαι ταῦτα ἡ τῶν ὅλων φύσις παρεῖδεν ἄν, οὔτ ἂν τηλικοῦτον ἥμαρτεν ἤτοι παρ ἀδυναμίαν ἢ παρ ἀτεχνίαν, ἵνα τὰ ἀγαθὰ καὶ τὰ κακὰ ἐπίσης τοῖς τε ἀγαθοῖς ἀνθρώποις καὶ τοῖς κακοῖς πεφυρμένως συμβαίνῃ. θάνατος δέ γε καὶ ζωή, δόξα καὶ ἀδοξία, πόνος καὶ ἡδονή, πλοῦτος καὶ πενία, πάντα ταῦτα ἐπίσης συμβαίνει ἀνθρώπων τοῖς τε ἀγαθοῖς καὶ τοῖς κακοῖς, οὔτε καλὰ ὄντα οὔτε αἰσχρά. οὔτ ἄρ ἀγαθὰ οὔτε κακά ἐστι.

12. Πῶς πάντα ταχέως ἐναφανίζεται, τῷ μὲν κόσμῳ αὐτὰ τὰ σώματα, τῷ δὲ αἰῶνι αἱ μνῆμαι αὐτῶν· οἷά ἐστι τὰ αἰσθητὰ πάντα καὶ μάλιστα τὰ ἡδονῇ δελεάζοντα ἢ τῷ πόνῳ φοβοῦντα ἢ τῷ τύφῳ διαβεβοημένα, πῶς εὐτελῆ καὶ εὐκαταφρόνητα καὶ ῥυπαρὰ καὶ εὔφθαρτα καὶ νεκρά· - νοερᾶς δυνάμεως ἐφιστάναι. τί εἰσιν οῥτοι, ὧν αἱ ὑπολήψεις καὶ αἱ φωναὶ τὴν εὐδοξίαν ‹καὶ τὴν ἀδοξίαν παρέχουσι›. τί ἐστι τὸ ἀποθανεῖν, καὶ ὅτι, ἐάν τις αὐτὸ μόνον ἴδῃ καὶ τῷ μερισμῷ τῆς ἐννοίας διαλύσῃ τὰ ἐμφανταζόμενα αὐτῷ, οὐκέτι ἄλλο τι ὑπολήψεται αὐτὸ εἶναι ἢ φύσεως ἔργον· φύσεως δὲ ἔργον εἴ τις φοβεῖται, παιδίον ἐστί· τοῦτο μέντοι οὐ μόνον φύσεως ἔργον ἐστίν, ἀλλὰ καὶ συμφέρον αὐτῇ. πῶς ἅπτεται θεοῦ ἄνθρωπος καὶ κατὰ τί ἑαυτοῦ μέρος καὶ ὅταν πῶς [ἔχῃ] διακέηται τὸ τοῦ ἀνθρώπου τοῦτο μόριον.

13. Οὐδὲν ἀθλιώτερον τοῦ πάντα κύκλῳ ἐκπεριερχομένου καὶ "τὰ νέρθεν γᾶς (φησὶν) ἐρευνῶντος" καὶ τὰ ἐν ταῖς ψυχαῖς τῶν πλησίον διὰ τεκμάρσεως ζητοῦντος, μὴ αἰσθομένου δέ, ὅτι ἀρκεῖ πρὸς μόνῳ τῷ ἔνδον ἑαυτοῦ δαίμονι εἶναι καὶ τοῦτον γνησίως θεραπεύειν. θεραπεία δὲ αὐτοῦ, καθαρὸν πάθους διατηρεῖν καὶ εἰκαιότητος καὶ δυσαρεστήσεως τῆς πρὸς τὰ ἐκ θεῶν καὶ ἀνθρώπων γινόμενα. τὰ μὲν γὰρ ἐκ θεῶν αἰδέσιμα δι ἀρετήν· τὰ δὲ ἐξ ἀνθρώπων φίλα διὰ συγγένειαν, ἔστι δὲ ὅτε καὶ τρόπον τινὰ ἐλεεινὰ δι ἄγνοιαν ἀγαθῶν καὶ κακῶν· οὐκ ἐλάττων ἡ πήρωσις αὕτη τῆς στερισκούσης τοῦ διακρίνειν τὰ λευκὰ καὶ μέλανα.

14. Κἂν τρὶς χίλια ἔτη βιώσεσθαι μέλλῃς, καὶ τοσαυτάκις μύρια, ὅμως μέμνησο ὅτι οὐδεὶς ἄλλον ἀποβάλλει βίον ἢ τοῦτον ὃν ζῇ, οὐδὲ ἄλλον ζῇ ἢ ὃν ἀποβάλλει. εἰς ταὐτὸν οὖν καθίσταται τὸ μήκιστον τῷ βραχυτάτῳ. τὸ γὰρ παρὸν πᾶσιν ἴσον καὶ τὸ ἀπολλύμενον οὖν ἴσον καὶ τὸ ἀποβαλλόμενον οὕτως ἀκαριαῖον

ἀναφαίνεται. οὔτε γὰρ τὸ παρῳχηκὸς οὔτε τὸ μέλλον ἀποβάλοι ἄν τις· ὃ γὰρ οὐκ ἔχει, πῶς ἄν τις τοῦτο αὐτοῦ ἀφέλοιτο; τούτων οὖν τῶν δύο ἀεὶ μεμνῆσθαι· ἑνὸς μέν, ὅτι πάντα ἐξ ἀιδίου ὁμοειδῆ καὶ ἀνακυκλούμενα καὶ οὐδὲν διαφέρει, πότερον ἐν ἑκατὸν ἔτεσιν ἢ ἐν διακοσίοις ἢ ἐν τῷ ἀπείρῳ χρόνῳ τὰ αὐτά τις ὄψεται· ἑτέρου δέ, ὅτι καὶ ὁ πολυχρονιώτατος καὶ ὁ τάχιστα τεθνηξόμενος τὸ ἴσον ἀποβάλλει. τὸ γὰρ παρόν ἐστι μόνον οὗ στερίσκεσθαι μέλλει, εἴπερ γε ἔχει καὶ τοῦτο μόνον καὶ ὃ μὴ ἔχει τις οὐκ ἀποβάλλει.

15. Ὅτι πᾶν ὑπόληψις. δῆλα μὲν γὰρ τὰ πρὸς τὸν Κυνικὸν Μόνιμον λεγόμενα· δῆλον δὲ καὶ τὸ χρήσιμον τοῦ λεγομένου, ἐάν τις αὐτοῦ τὸ νόστιμον μέχρι τοῦ ἀληθοῦς δέχηται.

16. Ὑβρίζει ἑαυτὴν ἡ τοῦ ἀνθρώπου ψυχὴ μάλιστα μέν, ὅταν ἀπόστημα καὶ οἷον φῦμα τοῦ κόσμου, ὅσον ἐφ᾽ ἑαυτῇ, γένηται· τὸ γὰρ δυσχεραίνειν τινὶ τῶν γινομένων ἀπόστασίς ἐστι τῆς φύσεως, ⟨ὑφ᾽⟩ ἧς ἐν μέρει ἕκασται τῶν λοιπῶν φύσεις περιέχονται. ἔπειτα δέ, ὅταν ἄνθρωπόν τινα ἀποστραφῇ ἢ καὶ ἐναντία φέρηται ὡς βλάψουσα, οἷαί εἰσιν αἱ τῶν ὀργιζομένων. τρίτον ὑβρίζει ἑαυτήν, ὅταν ἡσσᾶται ἡδονῆς ἢ πόνου. τέταρτον, ὅταν ὑποκρίνηται καὶ ἐπιπλάστως καὶ ἀναλήθως τι ποιῇ ἢ λέγῃ. πέμπτον, ὅταν πρᾶξίν τινα ἑαυτῆς καὶ ὁρμὴν ἐπ᾽ οὐδένα σκοπὸν ἀφιῇ, ἀλλ᾽ εἰκῇ καὶ ἀπαρακολουθήτως ὁτιοῦν ἐνεργῇ, δέον καὶ τὰ μικρότατα κατὰ τὴν ἐπὶ τὸ τέλος ἀναφορὰν γίνεσθαι· τέλος δὲ λογικῶν ζῴων τὸ ἕπεσθαι τῷ τῆς πόλεως καὶ πολιτείας τῆς πρεσβυτάτης λόγῳ καὶ θεσμῷ.

17. Τοῦ ἀνθρωπίνου βίου ὁ μὲν χρόνος στιγμή, ἡ δὲ οὐσία ῥέουσα, ἡ δὲ αἴσθησις ἀμυδρά, ἡ δὲ ὅλου τοῦ σώματος σύγκρισις εὔσηπτος, ἡ δὲ ψυχὴ ῥεμβός, ἡ δὲ τύχη δυστέκμαρτον, ἡ δὲ φήμη ἄκριτον· συνελόντι δὲ εἰπεῖν, πάντα τὰ μὲν τοῦ σώματος ποταμός, τὰ δὲ τῆς ψυχῆς ὄνειρος καὶ τῦφος, ὁ δὲ βίος πόλεμος καὶ ξένου ἐπιδημία, ἡ δὲ ὑστεροφημία λήθη. τί οὖν τὸ παραπέμψαι δυνάμενον; ἓν καὶ μόνον φιλοσοφία· τοῦτο δὲ ἐν τῷ τηρεῖν τὸν ἔνδον δαίμονα ἀνύβριστον καὶ ἀσινῆ, ἡδονῶν καὶ πόνων κρείττονα, μηδὲν εἰκῇ ποιοῦντα μηδὲ διεψευσμένως καὶ μεθ᾽ ὑποκρίσεως, ἀνενδεῆ τοῦ ἄλλον ποιῆσαί τι ἢ μὴ ποιῆσαι· ἔτι δὲ τὰ συμβαίνοντα καὶ ἀπονεμόμενα δεχόμενον ὡς ἐκεῖθέν ποθεν ἐρχόμενα, ὅθεν αὐτὸς ἦλθεν· ἐπὶ πᾶσι δὲ τὸν θάνατον ἵλεῳ τῇ γνώμῃ περιμένοντα ὡς οὐδὲν ἄλλο ἢ λύσιν τῶν στοιχείων, ἐξ ὧν ἕκαστον ζῷον συγκρίνεται. εἰ δὲ αὐτοῖς τοῖς στοιχείοις μηδὲν δεινὸν ἐν τῷ ἕκαστον διηνεκῶς εἰς ἕτερον μεταβάλλειν, διὰ τί ὑπίδηταί τις τὴν πάντων μεταβολὴν καὶ διάλυσιν; κατὰ φύσιν γάρ· οὐδὲν δὲ κακὸν κατὰ φύσιν.

BOOK THREE

I. A man must not only consider how daily his life wasteth and decreaseth, but this also, that if he live long, he cannot be certain, whether his understanding shall continue so able and sufficient, for either discreet consideration, in matter of businesses; or for contemplation: it being the thing, whereon true knowledge of things both divine and human, doth depend. For if once he shall begin to dote, his respiration, nutrition, his imaginative, and appetitive, and other natural faculties, may still continue the same: he shall find no want of them. But how to make that right use of himself that he should, how to observe exactly in all things that which is right and just, how to redress and rectify all wrong, or sudden apprehensions and imaginations, and even of this particular, whether he should live any longer or no, to consider duly; for all such things, wherein the best strength and vigour of the mind is most requisite; his power and ability will be past and gone. Thou must hasten therefore; not only because thou art every day nearer unto death than other, but also because that intellective faculty in thee, whereby thou art enabled to know the true nature of things, and to order all thy actions by that knowledge, doth daily waste and decay: or, may fail thee before thou die.

II. This also thou must observe, that whatsoever it is that naturally doth happen to things natural, hath somewhat in itself that is pleasing and delightful: as a great loaf when it is baked, some parts of it cleave as it were, and part asunder, and make the crust of it rugged and unequal, and yet those parts of it, though in some sort it be against the art and intention of baking itself, that they are thus cleft and parted, which should have been and were first made all even and uniform, they become it well nevertheless, and have a certain peculiar property, to stir the appetite. So figs are accounted fairest and ripest then, when they begin to shrink, and wither as it were. So ripe olives, when they are next to putrefaction, then are they in their proper beauty. The hanging down of grapes—the brow of a lion, the froth of a foaming wild boar, and many other like things, though by themselves considered, they are far from any beauty, yet because they happen naturally, they both are comely, and delightful; so that if a man shall with a profound mind and apprehension, consider all things in the world, even among all those things which are but mere accessories and natural appendices as it were, there will scarce appear anything unto him, wherein he will not find matter of pleasure and delight. So will he behold with as much pleasure the true rictus of wild beasts, as those which by skilful painters and other artificers are imitated. So will he be able to perceive the proper ripeness and beauty of old age, whether in man or woman: and whatsoever else it is that is beautiful and alluring in whatsoever is, with chaste and continent eyes he will soon find out and discern.

35

Those and many other things will he discern, not credible unto every one, but unto them only who are truly and familiarly acquainted, both with nature itself, and all natural things.

III. Hippocrates having cured many sicknesses, fell sick himself and died. The Chaldeans and Astrologians having foretold the deaths of divers, were afterwards themselves surprised by the fates. Alexander and Pompeius, and Caius Caesar, having destroyed so many towns, and cut off in the field so many thousands both of horse and foot, yet they themselves at last were fain to part with their own lives. Heraclitus having written so many natural tracts concerning the last and general conflagration of the world, died afterwards all filled with water within, and all bedaubed with dirt and dung without. Lice killed Democritus; and Socrates, another sort of vermin, wicked ungodly men. How then stands the case? Thou hast taken ship, thou hast sailed, thou art come to land, go out, if to another life, there also shalt thou find gods, who are everywhere. If all life and sense shall cease, then shalt thou cease also to be subject to either pains or pleasures; and to serve and tend this vile cottage; so much the viler, by how much that which ministers unto it doth excel; the one being a rational substance, and a spirit, the other nothing but earth and blood.

IV. Spend not the remnant of thy days in thoughts and fancies concerning other men, when it is not in relation to some common good, when by it thou art hindered from some other better work. That is, spend not thy time in thinking, what such a man doth, and to what end: what he saith, and what he thinks, and what he is about, and such other things or curiosities, which make a man to rove and wander from the care and observation of that part of himself, which is rational, and overruling. See therefore in the whole series and connection of thy thoughts, that thou be careful to prevent whatsoever is idle and impertinent: but especially, whatsoever is curious and malicious: and thou must use thyself to think only of such things, of which if a man upon a sudden should ask thee, what it is that thou art now thinking, thou mayest answer This, and That, freely and boldly, that so by thy thoughts it may presently appear that in all thee is sincere, and peaceable; as becometh one that is made for society, and regards not pleasures, nor gives way to any voluptuous imaginations at all: free from all contentiousness, envy, and suspicion, and from whatsoever else thou wouldest blush to confess thy thoughts were set upon. He that is such, is he surely that doth not put off to lay hold on that which is best indeed, a very priest and minister of the gods, well acquainted and in good correspondence with him especially that is seated and placed within himself, as in a temple and sacrary: to whom also he keeps and preserves himself unspotted by pleasure, undaunted by pain; free from any manner of wrong, or contumely, by himself offered unto himself: not capable of any evil from others: a wrestler of the best sort, and for the highest prize, that he may not be cast down by any passion or affection of his own; deeply dyed and drenched in righteousness, embracing and accepting with his whole heart whatsoever either happeneth or is allotted unto him. One who not often, nor without some great necessity tending to some public good, mindeth what any other, either speaks, or doth, or purposeth: for those things only that are in his own power, or that are truly his own, are the objects of his employments, and his thoughts are ever taken up with those things, which of the whole universe are by the fates or Providence destinated and appropriated unto himself. Those things that are his own, and in his own power, he himself takes order, for that they be good: and as for those that happen unto him, he believes them to be so. For that lot and portion which is assigned to every one, as it is unavoidable and neces-sary, so is it always profitable. He remembers besides that whatsoever partakes of reason, is akin unto him, and that to care for all men generally, is agreeing to the nature of a man: but as for honour and praise, that they ought not generally to be admitted and accepted of from all, but from such only, who live according to nature. As for them that do not, what manner of men they be at home, or abroad; day or night, how conditioned themselves with what manner of condi-tions, or with men of what conditions they moil and pass away the time together, he knoweth, and remembers right well, he therefore regards not such praise and approbation, as proceeding from them, who cannot like and approve themselves.

V. Do nothing against thy will, nor contrary to the community, no without due examination, nor with reluctancy. Affect not to set out thy thoughts with curious neat language. Be neither a great talker, nor a great undertaker. Moreover, let thy God that is in thee to rule over thee, find by thee, that he hath to do with a man; an aged man; a sociable man; a Roman; a prince; one that hath ordered his life, as one that expecteth, as it were, nothing but the sound of the trumpet, sounding a retreat to depart out of this life with all expedition. One who for his word or actions neither needs an oath, nor any man to be a witness.

VI. To be cheerful, and to stand in no need, either of other men's help or atten-dance, or of that rest and tranquillity, which thou must be beholding to others for. Rather like one that is straight of himself, or hath ever been straight, than one that hath been rectified.

VII. If thou shalt find anything in this mortal life better than righteousness, than truth, temperance, fortitude, and in general better than a mind contented both with those things which according to right and reason she doth, and in those, which without her will and knowledge happen unto thee by the providence; if I say, thou canst find out anything better than this, apply thyself unto it with thy whole heart, and that which is best wheresoever thou dost find it, enjoy freely. But if nothing thou shalt find worthy to be preferred to that spirit which is within thee; if nothing better than to subject unto thee thine own lusts and desires, and not to give way to any fancies or imaginations before thou hast duly considered of them, nothing better than to withdraw thyself (to use Socrates his words) from all sensuality, and submit thyself unto the gods, and to have care of all men in general: if thou shalt find that all other things in comparison of this, are but vile, and of little moment; then give not way to any other thing, which being once though but affected and inclined unto, it will no more be in thy power without all distraction as thou oughtest to prefer and to pursue after that good, which is thine own and thy proper good. For it is not lawful, that anything that is of another and inferior kind and nature, be it what it will, as either popular applause, or honour, or riches, or pleasures; should be suffered to confront and contest as it were, with that which is rational, and operatively good. For all these things, if once though but for a while, they begin to please, they presently prevail, and pervert a man's mind, or turn a man from the right way. Do thou therefore I say absolutely and freely make choice of that which is best, and stick unto it. Now, that they say is best, which is most profitable. If they mean profitable to man as he is a rational man, stand thou to it, and maintain it; but if they mean profitable, as he is a creature, only reject it; and from this thy tenet and conclusion keep off carefully all plausible shows and colours of external appearance, that thou mayest be able to discern things rightly.

VIII. Never esteem of anything as profitable, which shall ever constrain thee either to break thy faith, or to lose thy modesty; to hate any man, to suspect, to curse, to dissemble, to lust after anything, that requireth the secret of walls or veils. But he that preferreth before all things his rational part and spirit, and the sacred mysteries of virtue which issueth from it, he shall never lament and exclaim, never sigh; he shall never want either solitude or company: and which is chiefest of all, he shall live without either desire or fear. And as for life, whether for a long or short time he shall enjoy his soul thus compassed about with a body, he is altogether indifferent. For if even now he were to depart, he is as ready for it, as for any other action, which may be performed with modesty and decency. For all his life long, this is his only care, that his mind may always be occupied in such intentions and objects, as are proper to a rational sociable creature.

IX. In the mind that is once truly disciplined and purged, thou canst not find anything, either foul or impure, or as it were festered: nothing that is either servile, or affected: no partial tie; no malicious averseness; nothing obnoxious; nothing concealed. The life of such an one, death can never surprise as imperfect; as of an actor, that should die before he had ended, or the play itself were at an end, a man might speak.

X. Use thine opinative faculty with all honour and respect, for in her indeed is all: that thy opinion do not beget in thy understanding anything contrary to either nature, or the proper constitution of a rational creature. The end and object of a rational constitution is, to do nothing rashly, to be kindly affected towards men, and in all things willingly to submit unto the gods. Casting therefore all other things aside, keep thyself to these few, and remember withal that no man properly can be said to live more than that which is now present, which is but a moment of time. Whatsoever is besides either is already past, or uncertain. The time therefore that any man doth live, is but a little, and the place where he liveth, is but a very little corner of the earth, and the greatest fame that can remain of a man after his death, even that is but little, and that too, such as it is whilst it is, is by the succession of silly mortal men preserved, who likewise shall shortly die, and even whiles they live know not what in very deed they themselves are: and much less can know one, who long before is dead and gone.

XI. To these ever-present helps and mementoes, let one more be added, ever to make a particular description and delineation as it were of every object that presents itself to thy mind, that thou mayest wholly and throughly contemplate it, in its own proper nature, bare and naked; wholly, and severally; divided into its several parts and quarters: and then by thyself in thy mind, to call both it, and those things of which it doth consist, and in which it shall be resolved, by their own proper true names, and appellations. For there is nothing so effectual to beget true magnanimity, as to be able truly and methodically to examine and consider all things that happen in this life, and so to penetrate into their natures, that at the same time, this also may concur in our apprehensions: what is the true use of it? and what is the true nature of this universe, to which it is useful? how much in regard of the universe may it be esteemed? how much in regard of man, a citizen of the supreme city, of which all other cities in the world are as it were but houses and families?

XII. What is this, that now my fancy is set upon? of what things doth it consist? how long can it last? which of all the virtues is the proper virtue for this present use? as whether meekness, fortitude, truth, faith, sincerity, contentation, or any of the rest? Of everything therefore thou must use thyself to say, This immediately comes from God, this by that fatal connection, and concatenation of things, or (which almost comes to one) by some coincidental casualty. And as for this, it proceeds from my neighbour, my kinsman, my fellow: through his ignorance indeed, because he knows not what is truly natural unto him: but I know it, and therefore carry myself towards him according to the natural law of fellowship; that is kindly, and justly. As for those things that of themselves are altogether indifferent, as in my best judgment I conceive everything to deserve more or less, so I carry myself towards it.

XIII. If thou shalt intend that which is present, following the rule of right and reason carefully, solidly, meekly, and shalt not intermix any other businesses, but shall study this only to preserve thy spirit unpolluted, and pure, and shall cleave unto him without either hope or fear of anything, in all things that thou shalt either do or speak, contenting thyself with heroical truth, thou shalt live happily; and from this, there is no man that can hinder thee.

XIV. As physicians and chirurgeons have always their instruments ready at hand for all sudden cures; so have thou always thy dogmata in a readiness for the knowledge of things, both divine and human: and whatsoever thou dost, even in the smallest things that thou dost, thou must ever remember that mutual relation, and connection that is between these two things divine, and things human. For without relation unto God, thou shalt never speed in any worldly actions; nor on the other side in any divine, without some respect had to things human.

XV. Be not deceived; for thou shalt never live to read thy moral commentaries, nor the acts of the famous Romans and Grecians; nor those excerpta from several books; all which thou hadst provided and laid up for thyself against thine old age. Hasten therefore to an end, and giving over all vain hopes, help thyself in time if thou carest for thyself, as thou oughtest to do.

XVI. To steal, to sow, to buy, to be at rest, to see what is to be done (which is not seen by the eyes, but by another kind of sight:) what these words mean, and how many ways to be understood, they do not understand. The body, the soul, the understanding. As the senses naturally belong to the body, and the desires and affections to the soul, so do the dogmata to the understanding.

XVII. To be capable of fancies and imaginations, is common to man and beast. To be violently drawn and moved by the lusts and desires of the soul, is proper to wild beasts and monsters, such as Phalaris and Nero were. To follow reason for ordinary duties and actions is common to them also, who believe not that there be any gods, and for their advantage would make no conscience to betray their own country; and who when once the doors be shut upon them, dare do anything. If therefore all things else be common to these likewise, it follows, that for a man to like and embrace all things that happen and are destinated unto him, and not to trouble and molest that spirit which is seated in the temple of his own breast, with a multitude of vain fancies and imaginations, but to keep him propitious and to obey him as a god, never either speaking anything contrary to truth, or doing anything contrary to justice, is the only true property of a good man. And such a one, though no man should believe that he liveth as he doth, either sincerely and conscionably, or cheerful and contentedly; yet is he neither with any man at all angry for it, nor diverted by it from the way that leadeth to the end of his life, through which a man must pass pure, ever ready to depart, and willing of himself without any compulsion to fit and accommodate himself to his proper lot and portion.

ΒΙΒΛΙΟ ΤΡΙΤΟ

[Τὰ ἐν Καρνούντῳ]

1. Οὐχὶ τοῦτο μόνον δεῖ λογίζεσθαι, ὅτι καθ᾿ ἑκάστην ἡμέραν ἀπαναλίσκεται ὁ βίος καὶ μέρος ἔλαττον αὐτοῦ καταλείπεται, ἀλλὰ κἀκεῖνο λογιστέον, ὅτι, εἰ ἐπὶ πλέον βιῴη τις, ἐκεῖνό γε ἄδηλον, εἰ ἐξαρκέσει ὁμοία αὖθις ἡ διάνοια πρὸς τὴν σύνεσιν τῶν πραγμάτων καὶ τῆς θεωρίας τῆς συντεινούσης εἰς τὴν ἐμπειρίαν τῶν τε θείων καὶ τῶν ἀνθρωπείων. ἐὰν γὰρ παραληρεῖν ἄρξηται, τὸ μὲν διαπνεῖσθαι καὶ τρέφεσθαι καὶ φαντάζεσθαι καὶ ὁρμᾶν καὶ ὅσα ἄλλα τοιαῦτα, οὐκ ἐνδεήσει· τὸ δὲ ἑαυτῷ χρῆσθαι καὶ τοὺς τοῦ καθήκοντος ἀριθμοὺς ἀκριβοῦν καὶ τὰ προφαινόμενα διαρθροῦν καὶ περὶ αὐτοῦ τοῦ εἰ ἤδη ἐξακτέον αὐτὸν ἐφιστάνειν καὶ ὅσα τοιαῦτα λογισμοῦ συγγεγυμνασμένου πάνυ χρῄζει, προαποσβέννυται. χρὴ οὖν ἐπείγεσθαι οὐ μόνον τῷ ἐγγυτέρω τοῦ θανάτου ἑκάστοτε γίνεσθαι, ἀλλὰ καὶ διὰ τὸ τὴν ἐννόησιν τῶν πραγμάτων καὶ τὴν παρακολούθησιν προαπολήγειν.

2. Χρὴ καὶ τὰ τοιαῦτα παραφυλάσσειν, ὅτι καὶ τὰ ἐπιγινόμενα τοῖς φύσει γινομένοις ἔχει τι εὔχαρι καὶ ἐπαγωγόν. οἷον ἄρτου ὀπτωμένου παρραρήγνυταί τινα μέρη· καὶ ταῦτα οὖν τὰ διέχοντα οὕτως καὶ τρόπον τινὰ παρὰ τὸ ἐπάγγελμα τῆς ἀρτοποιίας ἔχοντα ἐπιπρέπει πως καὶ προθυμίαν πρὸς τὴν τροφὴν ἰδίως ἀνακινεῖ. πάλιν τε τὰ σῦκα, ὁπότε ὡραιότατά ἐστι, κέχηνεν· καὶ ἐν ταῖς δρυπεπέσιν ἐλαίαις αὐτὸ τὸ ἐγγὺς τῇ σήψει ἴδιόν τι κάλλος τῷ καρπῷ προστίθησιν. καὶ οἱ στάχυες δὲ κάτω νεύοντες καὶ τὸ τοῦ λέοντος ἐπισκύνιον καὶ ὁ τῶν συῶν ἐκ τοῦ στόματος ῥέων ἀφρὸς καὶ πολλὰ ἕτερα, κατ᾿ ἰδίαν εἴ τις σκοποίη, πόρρω ὄντα τοῦ εὐειδοῦς ὅμως διὰ τὸ τοῖς φύσει γινομένοις ἐπακολουθεῖν συνεπικοσμεῖ καὶ ψυχαγωγεῖ· ὥστε, εἴ τις ἔχει πάθος καὶ ἔννοιαν βαθυτέραν πρὸς τὰ ἐν τῷ ὅλῳ γινόμενα, σχεδὸν οὐδὲν οὐχὶ δόξει αὐτῷ καὶ τῶν κατ᾿ ἐπακολούθησιν συμβαινόντων ἡδέως πως διασυνίστασθαι. οὗτος δὲ καὶ θηρίων ἀληθῆ χάσματα οὐχ ἧσσον ἡδέως ὄψεται ἢ ὅσα γραφεῖς καὶ πλάσται μιμούμενοι δεικνύουσιν, καὶ γραὸς καὶ γέροντος ἀκμήν τινα καὶ ὥραν .. καὶ τὸ ἐν παισὶν ἐπαφρόδιτον τοῖς ἑαυτοῦ, σώφροσιν ὀφθαλμοῖς ὁρᾶν δυνήσεται· καὶ πολλὰ τοιαῦτα οὐ παντὶ πιθανά, μόνῳ δὲ τῷ πρὸς τὴν φύσιν καὶ τὰ ταύτης ἔργα γνησίως ᾠκειωμένῳ προσπεσεῖται.

3. Ἱπποκράτης πολλὰς νόσους ἰασάμενος αὐτὸς νοσήσας ἀπέθανεν. οἱ Χαλδαῖοι πολλῶν θανάτους προηγόρευσαν, εἶτα καὶ αὐτοὺς τὸ πεπρωμένον κατέλαβεν. Ἀλέξανδρος καὶ Πομπήιος καὶ Γάιος Καῖσαρ, ὅλας πόλεις ἄρδην τοσαυτάκις ἀνελόντες καὶ ἐν παρατάξει πολλὰς μυριάδας ἱππέων καὶ πεζῶν κατακόψαντες, καὶ αὐτοί ποτε ἐξῆλθον τοῦ βίου. Ἡράκλειτος περὶ τῆς τοῦ κόσμου ἐκπυρώσεως τοσαῦτα φυσιολογήσας, ὕδατος τὰ ἐντὸς πληρωθείς, βολβίτῳ κατακεχρισμένος

ἀπέθανεν. Δημόκριτον δὲ οἱ φθεῖρες, Σωκράτην δὲ ἄλλοι φθεῖρες ἀπέκτειναν. τί ταῦτα; ἐνέβης, ἔπλευσας, κατήχθης· ἔκβηθι. εἰ μὲν ἐφ᾽ ἕτερον βίον, οὐδὲν θεῶν κενὸν οὐδὲ ἐκεῖ· εἰ δὲ ἐν ἀναισθησίᾳ, παύσῃ πόνων καὶ ἡδονῶν ἀνεχόμενος καὶ λατρεύων τοσούτῳ χείρονι τῷ ἀγγείῳ ὅσῳ περίεστι τὸ ὑπηρετοῦν· τὸ μὲν γὰρ νοῦς καὶ δαίμων, τὸ δὲ γῆ καὶ λύθρος.

4. Μὴ κατατρίψῃς τὸ ὑπολειπόμενον τοῦ βίου μέρος ἐν ταῖς περὶ ἑτέρων φαντασίαις, ὁπόταν μὴ τὴν ἀναφορὰν ἐπί τι κοινωφελὲς ποιῇ· τί γὰρ ἄλλου ἔργου στέρῃ .., τουτέστι φανταζόμενος τί ὁ δεῖνα πράσσει καὶ τίνος ἕνεκεν καὶ τί λέγει καὶ τί ἐνθυμεῖται καὶ τί τεχνάζεται καὶ ὅσα τοιαῦτα ποιεῖ ἀπορρέμβεσθαι τῆς τοῦ ἰδίου ἡγεμονικοῦ παρατηρήσεως. χρὴ μὲν οὖν καὶ τὸ εἰκῇ καὶ μάτην ἐν τῷ εἰρμῷ τῶν φαντασιῶν περιίστασθαι, πολὺ δὲ μάλιστα τὸ περίεργον καὶ κακόηθες, καὶ ἐθιστέον ἑαυτὸν μόνα φαντάζεσθαι, περὶ ὧν εἴ τις ἄφνω ἐπανέροιτο· τί νῦν διανοῇ; μετὰ παρρησίας παραχρῆμα ἂν ἀποκρίναιο ὅτι τὸ καὶ τό· ὡς ἐξ αὐτῶν εὐθὺς δῆλα εἶναι ὅτι πάντα ἁπλᾶ καὶ εὐμενῆ καὶ ζῴου κοινωνικοῦ καὶ ἀμελοῦντος ἡδονικῶν ἢ καθάπαξ ἀπολαυστικῶν φαντασμάτων ἢ φιλονεικίας τινὸς ἢ βασκανίας καὶ ὑποψίας ἢ ἄλλου τινός ἐφ᾽ ᾧ ἂν ἐρυθριάσειας ἐξηγούμενος, ὅτι ἐν νῷ αὐτὸ εἶχες. ὁ γάρ τοι ἀνὴρ ὁ τοιοῦτος, οὐκ ἔτι ὑπερτιθέμενος τὸ ὡς ἐν ἀρίστοις ἤδη εἶναι, ἱερεύς τίς ἐστι καὶ ὑπουργὸς θεῶν, χρώμενος καὶ τῷ ἔνδον ἱδρυμένῳ αὐτοῦ, ὃ παρέχεται τὸν ἄνθρωπον ἄχραντον ἡδονῶν, ἄτρωτον ὑπὸ παντὸς πόνου, πάσης ὕβρεως ἀνέπαφον, πάσης ἀναίσθητον πονηρίας, ἀθλητὴν ἄθλου τοῦ μεγίστου, τοῦ ὑπὸ μηδενὸς πάθους καταβληθῆναι, δικαιοσύνῃ βεβαμμένον εἰς βάθος, ἀσπαζόμενον μὲν ἐξ ὅλης τῆς ψυχῆς τὰ συμβαίνοντα καὶ ἀπονεμόμενα πάντα, μὴ πολλάκις δὲ μηδὲ χωρὶς μεγάλης καὶ κοινωφελοῦς ἀνάγκης φανταζόμενον τί ποτε ἄλλος λέγει ἢ πράσσει ἢ διανοεῖται. μόνα γὰρ τὰ ἑαυτοῦ πρὸς ἐνέργειαν † ἔχει καὶ τὰ ἑαυτῷ ἐκ τῶν ὅλων συγκλωθόμενα διηνεκῶς ἐννοεῖ κἀκεῖνα μὲν καλὰ παρέχεται, ταῦτα δὲ ἀγαθὰ εἶναι πέπεισται· ἡ γὰρ ἑκάστῳ νεμομένη μοῖρα συνεμφέρεταί τε καὶ συνεμφέρει. μέμνηται δὲ καὶ ὅτι συγγενὲς πᾶν τὸ λογικόν, καὶ ὅτι κήδεσθαι μὲν πάντων ἀνθρώπων κατὰ τὴν τοῦ ἀνθρώπου φύσιν ἐστί, δόξης δὲ οὐχὶ τῆς παρὰ πάντων ἀνθεκτέον, ἀλλὰ τῶν ὁμολογουμένως τῇ φύσει βιούντων μόνων. οἱ δὲ μὴ οὕτως βιοῦντες ὁποῖοί τινες οἴκοι τε καὶ ἔξω τῆς οἰκίας καὶ νύκτωρ καὶ μεθ᾽ ἡμέραν, οἷοι μεθ᾽ οἵων φύρονται, μεμνημένος διατελεῖ. οὐ τοίνυν οὐδὲ τὸν παρὰ τῶν τοιούτων ἔπαινον ἐν λόγῳ τίθεται, οἵγε οὐδὲ αὐτοὶ ἑαυτοῖς ἀρέσκονται.

5. Μήτε ἀκούσιος ἐνέργει μήτε ἀκοινώνητος μήτε ἀνεξέταστος μήτε ἀνθελκόμενος· μήτε κομψείᾳ τὴν διάνοιάν σου καλλωπιζέτω· μήτε πολυρρήμων μήτε πολυπράγμων ἔσο. ἔτι δὲ ὁ ἐν σοὶ θεὸς ἔστω προστάτης ζῴου ἄρρενος καὶ πρεσβύτου καὶ πολιτικοῦ καὶ Ῥωμαίου καὶ ἄρχοντος, ἀνατεταχότος ἑαυτόν, οἷος ἂν εἴη τις περιμένων τὸ ἀνακλητικὸν ἐκ τοῦ βίου εὔλυτος, μήτε ὅρκου δεόμενος μήτε ἀνθρώπου τινὸς μάρτυρος. ἐνέστω δὲ τὸ φαιδρὸν καὶ τὸ ἀπροσδεὲς τῆς

ἔξωθεν ὑπηρεσίας καὶ τὸ ἀπροσδεὲς ἡσυχίας, ἣν ἄλλοι παρέχουσιν. ὀρθὸν οὖν εἶναι χρή, οὐχὶ ὀρθούμενον.

6. Εἰ μὲν κρεῖττον εὑρίσκεις ἐν τῷ ἀνθρωπίνῳ βίῳ δικαιοσύνης, ἀληθείας, σωφροσύνης, ἀνδρείας καὶ καθάπαξ τοῦ ἀρκεῖσθαι ἑαυτῇ τὴν διάνοιάν σου, ἐν οἷς κατὰ τὸν λόγον τὸν ὀρθὸν πράσσοντά σε παρέχεται, καὶ [ἐν] τῇ εἱμαρμένῃ ἐν τοῖς ἀπροαιρέτως ἀπονεμομένοις· εἰ τούτου, φημί, κρεῖττόν τι ὁρᾷς, ἐπ ἐκεῖνο ἐξ ὅλης τῆς ψυχῆς τραπόμενος τοῦ ἀρίστου εὑρισκομένου ἀπόλαυε. εἰ δὲ μηδὲν κρεῖττον φαίνεται αὐτοῦ τοῦ ἐνιδρυμένου ἐν σοὶ δαίμονος, τάς τε ἰδίας ὁρμὰς ὑποτεταχότος ἑαυτῷ καὶ τὰς φαντασίας ἐξετάζοντος καὶ τῶν αἰσθητικῶν πείσεων, ὡς ὁ Σωκράτης ἔλεγεν, ἑαυτὸν ἀφειλκυκότος καὶ τοῖς θεοῖς ὑποτεταχότος ἑαυτὸν καὶ τῶν ἀνθρώπων προκηδομένου· εἰ τούτου πάντα τὰ ἄλλα μικρότερα καὶ εὐτελέστερα εὑρίσκεις, μηδενὶ χώραν δίδου ἑτέρῳ, πρὸς ὃ ῥέψας ἅπαξ καὶ ἀποκλίνας οὐκέτι ἀπερισπάστως τὸ ἀγαθὸν ἐκεῖνο, τὸ ἴδιον καὶ τὸ σόν, προτιμᾶν δυνήσῃ. ἀντικαθῆσθαι γὰρ τῷ λογικῷ καὶ πολιτικῷ ἀγαθῷ οὐ θέμις οὐδ ὁτιοῦν ἑτερογενές, οἷον τὸν παρὰ τῶν πολλῶν ἔπαινον ἢ ἀρχὰς ἢ πλοῦτον ἢ ἀπολαύσεις ἡδονῶν· πάντα ταῦτα, κἂν πρὸς ὀλίγον ἐναρμόζειν δόξῃ, κατεκράτησεν ἄφνω καὶ παρήνεγκεν. σὺ δέ, φημί, ἁπλῶς καὶ ἐλευθέρως ἑλοῦ τὸ κρεῖττον καὶ τούτου ἀντέχου· "κρεῖττον δὲ τὸ συμφέρον." εἰ μὲν τὸ ὡς λογικῷ, τοῦτο τήρει· εἰ δὲ τὸ ὡς ζῴῳ, ἀπόφηναι, καὶ ἀτύφως φύλασσε τὴν κρίσιν· μόνον ὅπως ἀσφαλῶς τὴν ἐξέτασιν ποιήσῃ.

7. Μὴ τιμήσῃς ποτὲ ὡς συμφέρον σεαυτοῦ, ὃ ἀναγκάσει σέ ποτε τὴν πίστιν παραβῆναι, τὴν αἰδῶ ἐγκαταλιπεῖν, μισῆσαί τινα, ὑποπτεῦσαι, καταράσασθαι, ὑποκρίνασθαι, ἐπιθυμῆσαί τινος τοίχων καὶ παραπετασμάτων δεομένου. ὁ γὰρ τὸν ἑαυτοῦ νοῦν καὶ δαίμονα καὶ τὰ ὄργια τῆς τούτου ἀρετῆς προελόμενος τραγῳ δίαν οὐ ποιεῖ, οὐ στενάζει, οὐκ ἐρημίας, οὐ πολυπληθείας δεήσεται· τὸ μέγιστον, ζήσει μήτε διώκων μήτε φεύγων, πότερον δὲ ἐπὶ πλέον διάστημα χρόνου τῷ σώματι περιεχομένῃ τῇ ψυχῇ ἢ ἐπ ἔλασσον χρήσεται, οὐδ ὁτιοῦν αὐτῷ μέλει· κἂν γὰρ ἤδη ἀπαλλάσσεσθαι δέῃ, οὕτως εὔλυτος ἄπεισιν, ὡς ⟨ἂν⟩ ἄλλο τι τῶν αἰδημόνως καὶ κοσμίως ἐνεργεῖσθαι δυναμένων ἐνεργήσειεν, τοῦτο μόνον παρ ὅλον τὸν βίον εὐλαβούμενος, τὸ τὴν διάνοιαν ἔν τινι ἀνοικείῳ νοεροῦ πολιτικοῦ ζῴου τροπῇ γενέσθαι.

8. Οὐδὲν ἂν ἐν τῇ διανοίᾳ τοῦ κεκολασμένου καὶ ἐκκεκαθαρμένου πυῶδες οὐδὲ μὴν μεμωλυσμένον οὐδὲ ὕπουλον εὕροις· οὐδὲ ἀσυντελῆ τὸν βίον αὐτοῦ ἡ πεπρωμένη καταλαμβάνει, ὡς ἄν τις εἴποι τὸν τραγῳδὸν πρὸ τοῦ τελέσαι καὶ διαδραματίσαι ἀπαλλάσσεσθαι· ἔτι δὲ οὐδὲν δοῦλον οὐδὲ κομψὸν οὐδὲ προσδεδεμένον οὐδὲ ἀπεσχισμένον οὐδὲ ὑπεύθυνον οὐδὲ ἐμφωλεῦον.

9. Τὴν ὑποληπτικὴν δύναμιν σέβε. ἐν ταύτῃ τὸ πᾶν, ἵνα ὑπόληψις τῷ ἡγεμονικῷ σου μηκέτι ἐγγένηται ἀνακόλουθος τῇ φύσει καὶ τῇ τοῦ λογικοῦ ζῴου κατασκευῇ· αὕτη δὲ ἐπαγγέλλεται ἀπροπτωσίαν καὶ τὴν πρὸς ἀνθρώπους οἰκείωσιν καὶ τὴν τοῖς θεοῖς ἀκολουθίαν.

10. Πάντα οὖν ῥίψας ταῦτα μόνα τὰ ὀλίγα σύνεχε καὶ ἔτι συμμνημόνευε, ὅτι μόνον ζῇ ἕκαστος τὸ παρὸν τοῦτο, τὸ ἀκαριαῖον· τὰ δὲ ἄλλα ἢ βεβίωται ἢ ἐν ἀδήλῳ. μικρὸν μὲν οὖν ὃ ζῇ ἕκαστος· μικρὸν δὲ τὸ τῆς γῆς γωνίδιον ὅπου ζῇ· μικρὸν δὲ καὶ ἡ μηκίστη ὑστεροφημία καὶ αὕτη δὲ κατὰ διαδοχὴν ἀνθρωπαρίων τάχιστα τεθνηξομένων καὶ οὐκ εἰδότων οὐδὲ ἑαυτούς, οὔτι γε τὸν πρόπαλαι τεθνηκότα.

11. Τοῖς δὲ εἰρημένοις παραστήμασιν ἓν ἔτι προσέστω, τὸ ὅρον ἢ ὑπογραφὴν ἀεὶ ποιεῖσθαι τοῦ ὑποπίπτοντος φανταστοῦ, ὥστε αὐτὸ ὁποῖόν ἐστι κατ οὐσίαν, γυμνόν, ὅλον δι ὅλων διῃρημένως βλέπειν καὶ τὸ ἴδιον ὄνομα αὐτοῦ καὶ τὰ ὀνόματα ἐκείνων, ἐξ ὧν συνεκρίθη καὶ εἰς ἃ ἀναλυθήσεται, λέγειν παρ ἑαυτῷ. οὐδὲν γὰρ οὕτως μεγαλοφροσύνης ποιητικόν, ὡς τὸ ἐλέγχειν ὁδῷ καὶ ἀληθείᾳ ἕκαστον τῶν τῷ βίῳ ὑποπιπτόντων δύνασθαι καὶ τὸ ἀεὶ οὕτως εἰς αὐτὰ ὁρᾶν, ὥστε συνεπιβάλλειν ὁποίῳ τινὶ τῷ κόσμῳ ὁποίαν τινὰ τοῦτο χρείαν παρεχόμενον τίνα μὲν ἔχει ἀξίαν ὡς πρὸς τὸ ὅλον, τίνα δὲ ὡς πρὸς τὸν ἄνθρωπον, πολίτην ὄντα πόλεως τῆς ἀνωτάτης, ἧς αἱ λοιπαὶ πόλεις ὥσπερ οἰκίαι εἰσίν. τί ἐστὶ καὶ ἐκ τίνων συγκέκριται καὶ πόσον χρόνον πέφυκε παραμένειν τοῦτο τὸ τὴν φαντασίαν μοι νῦν ποιοῦν καὶ τίνος ἀρετῆς πρὸς αὐτὸ χρεία, οἷον ἡμερότητος, ἀνδρείας, ἀληθείας, πίστεως, ἀφελείας, αὐταρκείας, τῶν λοιπῶν. διὸ δεῖ ἐφ ἑκάστου λέγειν· τοῦτο μὲν παρὰ θεοῦ ἥκει, τοῦτο δὲ κατὰ τὴν σύλληξιν καὶ τὴν συμμηρυομένην σύγκλωσιν καὶ τὴν τοιαύτην σύντευξίν τε καὶ τύχην, τοῦτο δὲ παρὰ τοῦ συμφύλου καὶ συγγενοῦς καὶ κοινωνοῦ, ἀγνοοῦντος μέντοι ὅ τι αὐτῷ κατὰ φύσιν ἐστίν. ἀλλ ἐγὼ οὐκ ἀγνοῶ· διὰ τοῦτο· χρῶμαι αὐτῷ κατὰ τὸν τῆς κοινωνίας φυσικὸν νόμον εὔνως καὶ δικαίως, ἅμα μέντοι τοῦ κατ ἀξίαν ἐν τοῖς μέσοις συστοχάζομαι.

12. Ἐὰν τὸ παρὸν ἐνεργῇς ἑπόμενος τῷ ὀρθῷ λόγῳ, ἐσπουδασμένως, ἐρρωμένως, εὐμενῶς, καὶ μηδὲν ‹παρίῃς› παρεμπόρευμα, ἀλλὰ τὸν ἑαυτοῦ δαίμονα καθαρὸν ἑστῶτα τηρῇς, ὡς εἰ καὶ ἤδη ἀποδοῦναι δέοι· ἐὰν τοῦτο συνάπτῃς μηδὲν περιμένων μηδὲ φεύγων, ἀλλὰ τῇ παρούσῃ κατὰ φύσιν ἐνεργείᾳ καὶ τῇ ὧν λέγεις καὶ φθέγγῃ ἡρωικῇ ἀληθείᾳ ἀρκούμενος, εὐζωήσεις. ἔστι δὲ οὐδεὶς ὁ τοῦτο κωλῦσαι δυνάμενος.

13. Ὥσπερ οἱ ἰατροὶ ἀεὶ τὰ ὄργανα καὶ σιδήρια πρόχειρα ἔχουσι πρὸς τὰ

αἰφνίδια τῶν θεραπευμάτων, οὕτω τὰ δόγματα σὺ ἕτοιμα ἔχε πρὸς τὸ τὰ θεῖα καὶ ἀνθρώπινα εἰδέναι, καὶ πᾶν καὶ τὸ μικρότατον οὕτω ποιεῖν ὡς τῆς ἀμφοτέρων πρὸς ἄλληλα συνδέσεως μεμνημένον· οὔτε γὰρ ἀνθρώπινόν τι ἄνευ τῆς ἐπὶ τὰ θεῖα συναναφορᾶς εὖ πράξεις οὔτ᾽ ἔμπαλιν. Μηκέτι πλανῶ· οὔτε γὰρ τὰ ὑπομνημάτιά σου μέλλεις ἀνα γινώσκειν οὔτε τὰς τῶν ἀρχαίων Ῥωμαίων καὶ Ἑλλήνων πράξεις καὶ τὰς ἐκ τῶν συγγραμμάτων ἐκλογάς, ἃς εἰς τὸ γῆρας ἑαυτῷ ἀπετίθεσο. σπεῦδε οὖν εἰς τέλος καὶ τὰς κενὰς ἐλπίδας ἀφεὶς σαυτῷ βοήθει, εἴ τί σοι μέλει σεαυτοῦ, ἕως ἔξεστιν.

14. Μηκέτι πλανῶ· οὔτε γὰρ τὰ ὑπομνημάτιά σου μέλλεις ἀνα γινώσκειν οὔτε τὰς τῶν ἀρχαίων Ῥωμαίων καὶ Ἑλλήνων πράξεις καὶ τὰς ἐκ τῶν συγγραμμάτων ἐκλογάς, ἃς εἰς τὸ γῆρας ἑαυτῷ ἀπετίθεσο. Σπεῦδε οὖν εἰς τέλος καὶ τὰς κενὰς ἐλπίδας ἀφεὶς σαυτῷ βοήθει, εἴ τί σοι μέλει σεαυτοῦ, ἕως ἔξεστιν.

15. Οὐκ ἴσασι, πόσα σημαίνει τὸ κλέπτειν, τὸ σπείρειν, τὸ ὠνεῖσθαι, τὸ ἡσυχάζειν, τὸ ὁρᾶν τὰ πρακτέα, ὃ οὐκ ὀφθαλμοῖς γίνεται ἀλλ᾽ ἑτέρᾳ τινὶ ὄψει.

16. Σῶμα, ψυχή, νοῦς· σώματος αἰσθήσεις, ψυχῆς ὁρμαί, νοῦ δόγματα. τὸ μὲν τυποῦσθαι φανταστικῶς καὶ τῶν βοσκημάτων· τὸ δὲ νευροσπαστεῖσθαι ὁρμητικῶς καὶ τῶν θηρίων καὶ τῶν ἀνδρογύνων καὶ Φαλάριδος καὶ Νέρωνος· τὸ δὲ τὸν νοῦν ἡγεμόνα ἔχειν ἐπὶ τὰ φαινόμενα καθήκοντα καὶ τῶν θεοὺς μὴ νομιζόντων καὶ τῶν τὴν πατρίδα ἐγκαταλειπόντων καὶ τῶν ‹ότιοῦν› ποιούντων, ἐπειδὰν κλείσωσι τὰς θύρας. εἰ οὖν τὰ λοιπὰ κοινά ἐστι πρὸς τὰ εἰρημένα, λοιπὸν τὸ ἴδιόν ἐστι τοῦ ἀγαθοῦ φιλεῖν μὲν καὶ ἀσπάζεσθαι τὰ συμβαίνοντα καὶ συγκλωθόμενα αὐτῷ, τὸν δὲ ἔνδον ἐν τῷ στήθει ἱδρυμένον δαίμονα μὴ φύρειν μηδὲ θορυβεῖν ὄχλῳ φαντασιῶν, ἀλλὰ ἵλεων διατηρεῖν, κοσμίως ἑπόμενον θεῷ, μήτε φθεγγόμενόν τι παρὰ τὰ ἀληθῆ μήτε ἐνεργοῦντα παρὰ τὰ δίκαια. εἰ δὲ ἀπιστοῦσιν αὐτῷ πάντες ἄνθρωποι, ὅτι ἁπλῶς καὶ αἰδημόνως καὶ εὐθύμως βιοῖ, οὔτε χαλεπαίνει τινὶ τούτων οὔτε παρατρέπεται τῆς ὁδοῦ τῆς ἀγούσης ἐπὶ τὸ τέλος τοῦ βίου, ἐφ᾽ ὃ δεῖ ἐλθεῖν καθαρόν, ἡσύχιον, εὔλυτον, ἀβιάστως τῇ ἑαυτοῦ μοίρᾳ συνηρμοσμένον.

BOOK FOUR

I. That inward mistress part of man if it be in its own true natural temper, is towards all worldly chances and events ever so disposed and affected, that it will easily turn and apply itself to that which may be, and is within its own power to compass, when that cannot be which at first it intended. For it never doth absolutely addict and apply itself to any one object, but whatsoever it is that it doth now intend and prosecute, it doth prosecute it with exception and reservation; so that whatsoever it is that falls out contrary to its first intentions, even that afterwards it makes its proper object. Even as the fire when it prevails upon those things that are in his way; by which things indeed a little fire would have been quenched, but a great fire doth soon turn to its own nature, and so consume whatsoever comes in his way: yea by those very things it is made greater and greater.

II. Let nothing be done rashly, and at random, but all things according to the most exact and perfect rules of art.

III. They seek for themselves private retiring places, as country villages, the seashore, mountains; yea thou thyself art wont to long much after such places. But all this thou must know proceeds from simplicity in the highest degree. At what time soever thou wilt, it is in thy power to retire into thyself, and to be at rest, and free from all businesses. A man cannot any whither retire better than to his own soul; he especially who is beforehand provided of such things within, which whensoever he doth withdraw himself to look in, may presently afford unto him perfect ease and tranquillity. By tranquillity I understand a decent orderly disposition and carriage, free from all confusion and tumultuousness. Afford then thyself this retiring continually, and thereby refresh and renew thyself. Let these precepts be brief and fundamental, which as soon as thou dost call them to mind, may suffice thee to purge thy soul throughly, and to send thee away well pleased with those things whatsoever they be, which now again after this short withdrawing of thy soul into herself thou dost return unto. For what is it that thou art offended at? Can it be at the wickedness of men, when thou dost call to mind this conclusion, that all reasonable creatures are made one for another? and that it is part of justice to bear with them? and that it is against their wills that they offend? and how many already, who once likewise prosecuted their enmities, suspected, hated, and fiercely contended, are now long ago stretched out, and reduced unto ashes? It is time for thee to make an end. As for those things which among the common chances of the world happen unto thee as thy particular lot and portion, canst thou be displeased with any of them, when thou dost call that our ordinary dilemma to mind, either a providence, or Democritus his atoms; and with it, whatsoever we brought to prove that the whole world is as it were one city? And as for thy body, what canst thou fear, if thou dost consider that thy mind and understanding, when once it hath recollected itself, and knows its own power, hath in this life and breath (whether it run smoothly and gently, or whether harshly and rudely), no interest at all, but is altogether indifferent: and whatsoever else thou hast heard and assented unto concerning either pain or pleasure? But the care of thine honour and reputation will perchance distract thee? How can that be, if thou dost look back, and consider both how quickly all things that are, are forgotten, and what an immense chaos of eternity was before, and will follow after all things: and the vanity of praise, and the inconstancy and variableness of human judgments and opinions, and the narrowness of the place, wherein it is limited and circumscribed? For the whole earth is but as one point; and of it, this inhabited part of it, is but a very little part; and of this part, how many in number, and what manner of men are they, that will commend thee? What remains then, but that thou often put in practice this kind of retiring of thyself, to this little part of thyself; and above all things, keep thyself from distraction, and intend not anything vehemently, but be free and consider all things, as a man whose proper object is Virtue, as a man whose true nature is to be kind and sociable, as a citizen, as a mortal creature. Among other things, which to consider, and look into thou must use to withdraw thyself, let those two be among the most obvious and at hand. One, that the things or objects themselves reach not unto the soul, but stand without still and quiet, and that it is from the opinion only which is within, that all the tumult and all the trouble doth proceed. The next, that all these things, which now thou seest, shall within a very little while be changed, and be no more: and ever call to mind, how many changes and alterations in the world thou thyself hast already been an eyewitness of in thy time. This world is mere change, and this life, opinion.

IV. If to understand and to be reasonable be common unto all men, then is that reason, for which we are termed reasonable, common unto all. If reason is general, then is that reason also, which prescribeth what is to be done and what not, common unto all. If that, then law. If law, then are we fellow-citizens. If so, then are we partners in some one commonweal. If so, then the world is as it were a city. For which other commonweal is it, that all men can be said to be members of? From this common city it is, that understanding, reason, and law is derived unto us, for from whence else? For as that which in me is earthly I have from some common earth; and that which is moist from some other element is imparted; as my breath and life hath its proper fountain; and that likewise which is dry and fiery in me: (for there is nothing which doth not proceed from something; as also there is nothing that can be reduced unto mere nothing:)

54

so also is there some common beginning from whence my understanding hath proceeded.

V. As generation is, so also death, a secret of nature's wisdom: a mixture of elements, resolved into the same elements again, a thing surely which no man ought to be ashamed of: in a series of other fatal events and consequences, which a rational creature is subject unto, not improper or incongruous, nor contrary to the natural and proper constitution of man himself.

VI. Such and such things, from such and such causes, must of necessity proceed. He that would not have such things to happen, is as he that would have the fig-tree grow without any sap or moisture. In sum, remember this, that within a very little while, both thou and he shall both be dead, and after a little while more, not so much as your names and memories shall be remaining.

VII. Let opinion be taken away, and no man will think himself wronged. If no man shall think himself wronged, then is there no more any such thing as wrong. That which makes not man himself the worse, cannot make his life the worse, neither can it hurt him either inwardly or outwardly. It was expedient in nature that it should be so, and therefore necessary.

VIII. Whatsoever doth happen in the world, doth happen justly, and so if thou dost well take heed, thou shalt find it. I say not only in right order by a series of inevitable consequences, but according to justice and as it were by way of equal distribution, according to the true worth of everything. Continue then to take notice of it, as thou hast begun, and whatsoever thou dost, do it not without this proviso, that it be a thing of that nature that a good man (as the word good is properly taken) may do it. This observe carefully in every action.

IX. Conceit no such things, as he that wrongeth thee conceiveth, or would have thee to conceive, but look into the matter itself, and see what it is in very truth.

X. These two rules, thou must have always in a readiness. First, do nothing at all, but what reason proceeding from that regal and supreme part, shall for the good and benefit of men, suggest unto thee. And secondly, if any man that is present shall be able to rectify thee or to turn thee from some erroneous persuasion, that thou be always ready to change thy mind, and this change to proceed, not from any respect of any pleasure or credit thereon depending, but always from some probable apparent ground of justice, or of some public good thereby to be furthered; or from some other such inducement.

XI. Hast thou reason? I have. Why then makest thou not use of it? For if thy reason do her part, what more canst thou require?

XII. As a part hitherto thou hast had a particular subsistence: and now shalt thou vanish away into the common substance of Him, who first begot thee, or rather thou shalt be resumed again into that original rational substance, out of which all others have issued, and are propagated. Many small pieces of frankincense are set upon the same altar, one drops first and is consumed, another after; and it comes all to one.

XIII. Within ten days, if so happen, thou shalt be esteemed a god of them, who now if thou shalt return to the dogmata and to the honouring of reason, will esteem of thee no better than of a mere brute, and of an ape.

XIV. Not as though thou hadst thousands of years to live. Death hangs over thee: whilst yet thou livest, whilst thou mayest, be good.

XV. Now much time and leisure doth he gain, who is not curious to know what his neighbour hath said, or hath done, or hath attempted, but only what he doth himself, that it may be just and holy? or to express it in Agathos' words, Not to look about upon the evil conditions of others, but to run on straight in the line, without any loose and extravagant agitation.

XVI. He who is greedy of credit and reputation after his death, doth not consider, that they themselves by whom he is remembered, shall soon after every one of them be dead; and they likewise that succeed those; until at last all memory, which hitherto by the succession of men admiring and soon after dying hath had its course, be quite extinct. But suppose that both they that shall remember thee, and thy memory with them should be immortal, what is that to thee? I will not say to thee after thou art dead; but even to thee living, what is thy praise? But only for a secret and politic consideration, which we call oikonomian or dispensation. For as for that, that it is the gift of nature, whatsoever is commended in thee, what might be objected from thence, let that now that we are upon another consideration be omitted as unseasonable. That which is fair and goodly, whatsoever it be, and in what respect soever it be, that it is fair and goodly, it is so of itself, and terminates in itself, not admitting praise as a part or member: that therefore which is praised, is not thereby made either better or worse. This I understand even of those things, that are commonly called fair and good, as those which are commended either for the matter itself, or for curious workmanship. As for that which is truly good, what can it stand in need of more than either justice or truth; or more than either kindness and modesty? Which of all those, either becomes good or fair, because commended; or dispraised suffers any damage? Doth the emerald become worse in itself, or more vile if it be not commended? Doth gold, or ivory, or purple? Is there anything that doth though never so common, as a knife, a flower, or a tree?

XVII. If so be that the souls remain after death (say they that will not believe it); how is the air from all eternity able to contain them? How is the earth (say I) ever from that time able to Contain the bodies of them that are buried? For as here the change and resolution of dead bodies into another kind of subsistence (whatsoever it be;) makes place for other dead bodies: so the souls after death transferred into the air, after they have conversed there a while, are either by way of transmutation, or transfusion, or conflagration, received again into that original rational substance, from which all others do proceed: and so give way to those souls, who before coupled and associated unto bodies, now begin to subsist single. This, upon a supposition that the souls after death do for a while subsist single, may be answered. And here, (besides the number of bodies, so buried and contained by the earth), we may further consider the number of several beasts, eaten by us men, and by other creatures. For notwithstanding that such a multitude of them is daily consumed, and as it were buried in the bodies of the eaters, yet is the same place and body able to contain them, by reason of their conversion, partly into blood, partly into air and fire. What in these things is the speculation of truth? to divide things into that which is passive and material; and that which is active and formal.

XVIII. Not to wander out of the way, but upon every motion and desire, to perform that which is just: and ever to be careful to attain to the true natural apprehension of every fancy, that presents itself.

XIX. Whatsoever is expedient unto thee, O World, is expedient unto me; nothing can either be 'unseasonable unto me, or out of date, which unto thee is seasonable. Whatsoever thy seasons bear, shall ever by me be esteemed as happy fruit, and increase. O Nature! from thee are all things, in thee all things subsist, and to thee all tend. Could he say of Athens, Thou lovely city of Cecrops; and shalt not thou say of the world, Thou lovely city of God?

XX. They will say commonly, Meddle not with many things, if thou wilt live cheerfully. Certainly there is nothing better, than for a man to confine himself to necessary actions; to such and so many only, as reason in a creature that knows itself born for society, will command and enjoin. This will not only procure that cheerfulness, which from the goodness, but that also, which from the paucity of actions doth usually proceed. For since it is so, that most of those things, which we either speak or do, are unnecessary; if a man shall cut them off, it must needs follow that he shall thereby gain much leisure, and save much trouble, and there-fore at every action a man must privately by way of admonition suggest unto himself, What? may not this that now I go about, be of the number of unneces-sary actions? Neither must he use himself to cut off actions only, but thoughts and imaginations also, that are unnecessary for so will unnecessary consequent actions the better be prevented and cut off.

XXI. Try also how a good man's life; (of one, who is well pleased with those things whatsoever, which among the common changes and chances of this world fall to his own lot and share; and can live well contented and fully satisfied in the justice of his own proper present action, and in the goodness of his disposition for the future:) will agree with thee. Thou hast had experience of that other kind of life: make now trial of this also. Trouble not thyself any more henceforth, re-duce thyself unto perfect simplicity. Doth any man offend? It is against himself that he doth offend: why should it trouble thee? Hath anything happened unto thee? It is well, whatsoever it be, it is that which of all the common chances of the world from the very beginning in the series of all other things that have, or shall happen, was destinated and appointed unto thee. To comprehend all in a few words, our life is short; we must endeavour to gain the present time with best discretion and justice. Use recreation with sobriety.

XXII. Either this world is a kosmoz or comely piece, because all disposed and governed by certain order: or if it be a mixture, though confused, yet still it is a comely piece. For is it possible that in thee there should be any beauty at all, and that in the whole world there should be nothing but disorder and confusion? and all things in it too, by natural different properties one from another differenced and distinguished; and yet all through diffused, and by natural sympathy, one to another united, as they are?

XXIII. A black or malign disposition, an effeminate disposition; an hard inexo-rable disposition, a wild inhuman disposition, a sheepish disposition, a childish disposition; a blockish, a false, a scurril, a fraudulent, a tyrannical: what then? If he be a stranger in the world, that knows not the things that are in it; why not be a stranger as well, that wonders at the things that are done in it?

XXIV. He is a true fugitive, that flies from reason, by which men are sociable. He blind, who cannot see with the eyes of his understanding. He poor, that stands in need of another, and hath not in himself all things needful for this life. He an aposteme of the world, who by being discontented with those things that happen unto him in the world, doth as it were apostatise, and separate himself from common   nature's rational administration. For the same nature it is that brings this unto thee, whatsoever it be, that first brought thee into the world. He raises sedition in the city, who by irrational actions withdraws his own soul from that one and common soul of all rational creatures.

XXV. There is, who without so much as a coat; and there is, who without so much as a book, doth put philosophy in practice. I am half naked, neither have I bread to eat, and yet I depart not from reason, saith one. But I say; I want the food of good teaching, and instructions, and yet I depart not from reason.

XXVI. What art and profession soever thou hast learned, endeavour to affect it, and comfort thyself in it; and pass the remainder of thy life as one who from his whole heart commits himself and whatsoever belongs unto him, unto the gods: and as for men, carry not thyself either tyrannically or servilely towards any.

XXVII. Consider in my mind, for example's sake, the times of Vespasian: thou shalt see but the same things: some marrying, some bringing up children, some sick, some dying, some fighting, some feasting, some merchandising, some till- ing, some flattering, some boasting, some suspecting, some undermining, some wishing to die, some fretting and murmuring at their present estate, some woo- ing, some hoarding, some seeking after magistracies, and some after kingdoms. And is not that their age quite over, and ended? Again, consider now the times of Trajan. There likewise thou seest the very self-same things, and that age also is now over and ended. In the like manner consider other periods, both of times and of whole nations, and see how many men, after they had with all their might and main intended and prosecuted some one worldly thing or other did soon after drop away, and were resolved into the elements. But especially thou must call to mind them, whom thou thyself in thy lifetime hast known much distracted about vain things, and in the meantime neglecting to do that, and closely and unseparably (as fully satisfied with it) to adhere unto it, which their own proper constitution did require. And here thou must remember, that thy carriage in every business must be according to the worth and due proportion of it, for so shalt thou not easily be tired out and vexed, if thou shalt not dwell upon small matters longer than is fitting.

XXVIII. Those words which once were common and ordinary, are now become obscure and obsolete; and so the names of men once commonly known and famous, are now become in a manner obscure and obsolete names. Camillus, Cieso, Volesius, Leonnatus; not long after, Scipio, Cato, then Augustus, then Adrianus, then Antoninus Pius: all these in a short time will be out of date, and, as things of another world as it were, become fabulous. And this I say of them, who once shined as the wonders of their ages, for as for the rest, no sooner are they expired, than with them all their fame and memory. And what is it then that shall always be remembered? all is vanity. What is it that we must bestow our care and diligence upon? even upon this only: that our minds and wills be just; that our actions be charitable; that our speech be never deceitful, or that our understanding be not subject to error; that our inclination be always set to embrace whatsoever shall happen unto us, as necessary, as usual, as ordinary, as flowing from such a beginning, and such a fountain, from which both thou thyself and all things are. Willingly therefore, and wholly surrender up thyself unto that fatal concatenation, yielding up thyself unto the fates, to be disposed of at their pleasure.

XXIX. Whatsoever is now present, and from day to day hath its existence; all objects of memories, and the minds and memories themselves, incessantly consider, all things that are, have their being by change and alteration. Use thyself therefore often to meditate upon this, that the nature of the universe delights in nothing more, than in altering those things that are, and in making others like unto them. So that we may say, that whatsoever is, is but as it were the seed of that which shall be. For if thou think that that only is seed, which either the earth or the womb receiveth, thou art very simple.

XXX. Thou art now ready to die, and yet hast thou not attained to that perfect simplicity: thou art yet subject to many troubles and perturbations; not yet free from all fear and suspicion of external accidents; nor yet either so meekly disposed towards all men, as thou shouldest; or so affected as one, whose only study and only wisdom is, to be just in all his actions.

XXXI. Behold and observe, what is the state of their rational part; and those that the world doth account wise, see what things they fly and are afraid of; and what things they hunt after.

XXXII. In another man's mind and understanding thy evil Cannot subsist, nor in any proper temper or distemper of the natural constitution of thy body, which is but as it were the coat or cottage of thy soul. Wherein then, but in that part of thee, wherein the conceit, and apprehension of any misery can subsist? Let not that part therefore admit any such conceit, and then all is well. Though thy body which is so near it should either be cut or burnt, or suffer any corruption or putrefaction, yet let that part to which it belongs to judge of these, be still at rest; that is, let her judge this, that whatsoever it is, that equally may happen to a wicked man, and to a good man, is neither good nor evil. For that which happens equally to him that lives according to nature, and to him that doth not, is neither according to nature, nor against it; and by consequent, neither good nor bad.

XXXIII. Ever consider and think upon the world as being but one living substance, and having but one soul, and how all things in the world, are terminated into one sensitive power; and are done by one general motion as it were, and deliberation of that one soul; and how all things that are, concur in the cause of one another's being, and by what manner of connection and concatenation all things happen.

XXXIV. What art thou, that better and divine part excepted, but as Epictetus said well, a wretched soul, appointed to carry a carcass up and down?

XXXV. To suffer change can be no hurt; as no benefit it is, by change to attain to being. The age and time of the world is as it were a flood and swift current, consisting of the things that are brought to pass in the world. For as soon as anything hath appeared, and is passed away, another succeeds, and that also will presently out of sight.

XXXVI. Whatsoever doth happen in the world, is, in the course of nature, as usual and ordinary as a rose in the spring, and fruit in summer. Of the same nature is sickness and death; slander, and lying in wait, and whatsoever else ordinarily doth unto fools use to be occasion either of joy or sorrow. That, whatsoever it is, that comes after, doth always very naturally, and as it were familiarly, follow upon that which was before. For thou must consider the things of the world, not as a loose independent number, consisting merely of necessary events; but as a discreet connection of things orderly and harmoniously disposed. There is then to be seen in the things of the world, not a bare succession, but an admirable correspondence and affinity.

XXXVII. Let that of Heraclitus never be out of thy mind, that the death of earth, is water, and the death of water, is air; and the death of air, is fire; and so on the contrary. Remember him also who was ignorant whither the way did lead, and how that reason being the thing by which all things in the world are administered, and which men are continually and most inwardly conversant with: yet is the thing, which ordinarily they are most in opposition with, and how those things which daily happen among them, cease not daily to be strange unto them, and that we should not either speak, or do anything as men in their sleep, by opinion and bare imagination: for then we think we speak and do, and that we must not be as children, who follow their father's example; for best reason alleging their bare successive tradition from our forefathers we have received it.

XXXVIII. Even as if any of the gods should tell thee, Thou shalt certainly die tomorrow, or next day, thou wouldst not, except thou wert extremely base and pusillanimous, take it for a great benefit, rather to die the next day after, than tomorrow; (for alas, what is the difference!) so, for the same reason, think it no great matter to die rather many years after, than the very next day.

XXXIX. Let it be thy perpetual meditation, how many physicians who once looked so grim, and so theatrically shrunk their brows upon their patients, are dead and gone themselves. How many astrologers, after that in great ostentation they had foretold the death of some others, how many philosophers after so many elaborate tracts and volumes concerning either mortality or immortality; how many brave captains and commanders, after the death and slaughter of so many; how many kings and tyrants, after they had with such horror and insolency abused their power upon men's lives, as though themselves had been immortal; how many, that I may so speak, whole cities both men and towns: Helice, Pompeii, Herculaneum, and others innumerable are dead and gone. Run them over also, whom thou thyself, one after another, hast known in thy time to drop away. Such and such a one took care of such and such a one's burial, and soon after was buried himself. So one, so another: and all things in a short time. For herein lieth all indeed, ever to look upon all worldly things, as things for their continuance, that are but for a day: and for their worth, most vile, and contemptible, as for example, What is man? That which but the other day when he was conceived was vile snivel; and within few days shall be either an embalmed carcass, or mere ashes. Thus must thou according to truth and nature, throughly consider how man's life is but for a very moment of time, and so depart meek and contented: even as if a ripe olive falling should praise the ground that bare her, and give thanks to the tree that begat her.

XL. Thou must be like a promontory of the sea, against which though the waves beat continually, yet it both itself stands, and about it are those swelling waves stilled and quieted.

XLI. Oh, wretched I, to whom this mischance is happened! nay, happy I, to whom this thing being happened, I can continue without grief; neither wounded by that which is present, nor in fear of that which is to come. For as for this, it might have happened unto any man, but any man having such a thing befallen him, could not have continued without grief. Why then should that rather be an unhappiness, than this a happiness? But however, canst thou, O man! term that unhappiness, which is no mischance to the nature of man I Canst thou think that a mischance to the nature of man, which is not contrary to the end and will of his nature? What then hast thou learned is the will of man's nature? Doth that then which hath happened unto thee, hinder thee from being just? or magnanimous? or temperate? or wise? or circumspect? or true? or modest? or free? or from anything else of all those things in the present enjoying and possession whereof the nature of man, (as then enjoying all that is proper unto her,) is fully satisfied? Now to conclude; upon all occasion of sorrow remember henceforth to make use of this dogma, that whatsoever it is that hath happened unto thee, is in very deed no such thing of itself, as a misfortune; but that to bear it generously, is certainly great happiness.

XLII. It is but an ordinary coarse one, yet it is a good effectual remedy against the fear of death, for a man to consider in his mind the examples of such, who greedily and covetously (as it were) did for a long time enjoy their lives. What have they got more, than they whose deaths have been untimely? Are not they themselves dead at the last? as Cadiciant's, Fabius, Julianus Lepidus, or any other who in their lifetime having buried many, were at the last buried themselves. The whole space of any man's life, is but little; and as little as it is, with what troubles, with what manner of dispositions, and in the society of how wretched a body must it be passed! Let it be therefore unto thee altogether as a matter of indifferency. For if thou shalt look backward; behold, what an infinite chaos of time doth present itself unto thee; and as infinite a chaos, if thou shalt look forward. In that which is so infinite, what difference can there be between that which liveth but three days, and that which liveth three ages?

XLIII. Let thy course ever be the most compendious way. The most compendious, is that which is according to nature: that is, in all both words and deeds, ever to follow that which is most sound and perfect. For such a resolution will free a man from all trouble, strife, dissembling, and ostentation.

ΒΙΒΛΙΟ ΤΕΤΑΡΤΟ

1. Τὸ ἔνδον κυριεῦον, ὅταν κατὰ φύσιν ἔχῃ, οὕτως ἔστηκε πρὸς τὰ συμβαίνοντα, ὥστε ἀεὶ πρὸς τὸ δυνατὸν καὶ διδόμενον μετατίθεσθαι ῥᾳδίως. ὕλην γὰρ ἀποτεταγμένην οὐδεμίαν φιλεῖ, ἀλλὰ ὁρμᾷ μὲν πρὸς τὰ ‹προ›ηγούμενα μεθ ὑπεξαιρέσεως, τὸ δὲ ἀντεισαγόμενον ὕλην ἑαυτῷ ποιεῖ, ὥσπερ τὸ πῦρ, ὅταν ἐπικρατῇ τῶν ἐπεμπιπτόντων, ὑφ᾽ ὧν ἂν μικρός τις λύχνος ἐσβέσθη· τὸ δὲ λαμπρὸν πῦρ τάχιστα ἐξῳκείωσεν ἑαυτῷ τὰ ἐπιφορούμενα καὶ κατηνάλωσε καὶ ἐξ αὐτῶν ἐκείνων ἐπὶ μεῖζον ἤρθη.

2. Μηδὲν ἐνέργημα εἰκῇ μηδὲ ἄλλως ἢ κατὰ θεώρημα συμπληρωτικὸν τῆς τέχνης ἐνεργείσθω.

3. Ἀναχωρήσεις αὑτοῖς ζητοῦσιν ἀγροικίας καὶ αἰγιαλοὺς καὶ ὄρη, εἴωθας δὲ καὶ σὺ τὰ τοιαῦτα μάλιστα ποθεῖν. ὅλον δὲ τοῦτο ἰδιωτικώτατόν ἐστιν, ἐξόν, ἧς ἂν ὥρας ἐθελήσῃς, εἰς ἑαυτὸν ἀναχωρεῖν. οὐδαμοῦ γὰρ οὔτε ἡσυχιώτερον οὔτε ἀπραγμονέστερον ἄνθρωπος ἀναχωρεῖ ἢ εἰς τὴν ἑαυτοῦ ψυχήν, μάλισθ ὅστις ἔχει ἔνδον τοιαῦτα, εἰς ἃ ἐγκύψας ἐν πάσῃ εὐμαρείᾳ εὐθὺς γίνεται· τὴν δὲ εὐμάρειαν οὐδὲν ἄλλο λέγω ἢ εὐκοσμίαν. συνεχῶς οὖν δίδου σεαυτῷ ταύτην τὴν ἀναχώρησιν καὶ ἀνανέου σεαυτόν· βραχέα δὲ ἔστω καὶ στοιχειώδη ἃ εὐθὺς ἀπαντήσαντα ἀρκέσει εἰς τὸ πᾶσαν λύπην ἀποκλύσαι καὶ ἀποπέμψαι σε μὴ δυσχεραίνοντα ἐκείνοις ἐφ᾽ ἃ ἐπανέρχῃ. τίνι γὰρ δυσχερανεῖς; τῇ τῶν ἀνθρώπων κακίᾳ; ἀναλογισάμενος τὸ κρῖμα, ὅτι τὰ λογικὰ ζῷα ἀλλήλων ἕνεκεν γέγονε καὶ ὅτι τὸ ἀνέχεσθαι μέρος τῆς δικαιοσύνης καὶ ὅτι ἄκοντες ἁμαρτάνουσι καὶ πόσοι ἤδη διεχθρεύσαντες, ὑποπτεύσαντες, μισήσαντες, διαδορατισθέντες ἐκτέτανται, τετέφρωνται, παῦου ποτέ. ἀλλὰ καὶ τοῖς ἐκ τῶν ὅλων ἀπονεμομένοις δυσχεραίνεις; ἀνανεωσάμενος τὸ διεζευγμένον τό· ἤτοι πρόνοια ἢ ἄτομοι, καὶ ἐξ ὅσων ἀπεδείχθη ὅτι ὁ κόσμος ὡσανεὶ πόλις. ἀλλὰ τὰ σωματικά σου ἅψεται ἔτι; ἐννοήσας ὅτι οὐκ ἐπιμίγνυται λείως ἢ τραχέως κινουμένῳ πνεύματι ἡ διάνοια, ἐπειδὰν ἅπαξ ἑαυτὴν ἀπολάβῃ καὶ γνωρίσῃ τὴν ἰδίαν ἐξουσίαν, καὶ λοιπὸν ὅσα περὶ πόνου καὶ ἡδονῆς ἀκήκοας καὶ συγκατέθου. ἀλλὰ τὸ δοξάριόν σε περισπάσει; ἀπιδὼν εἰς τὸ τάχος τῆς πάντων λήθης καὶ τὸ χάος τοῦ ἐφ᾽ ἑκάτερα ἀπείρου αἰῶνος καὶ τὸ κενὸν τῆς ἀπηχήσεως καὶ τὸ εὐμετάβολον καὶ ἄκριτον τῶν εὐφημεῖν δοκούντων καὶ τὸ στενὸν τοῦ τόπου, ἐν ᾧ περιγράφεται· ὅλη τε γὰρ ἡ γῆ στιγμὴ καὶ ταύτης πόστον γωνίδιον ἡ κατοίκησις αὕτη; καὶ ἐνταῦθα πόσοι καὶ οἷοί τινες οἱ ἐπαινεσόμενοι; λοιπὸν οὖν μέμνησο τῆς ὑποχωρήσεως τῆς εἰς τοῦτο τὸ ἀγρίδιον ἑαυτοῦ καὶ πρὸ παντὸς μὴ σπῶ μηδὲ κατεντείνου, ἀλλὰ ἐλεύθερος ἔσο καὶ ὅρα τὰ πράγματα ὡς ἀνήρ, ὡς ἄνθρωπος, ὡς πολίτης, ὡς θνητὸν ζῷον. ἐν δὲ τοῖς προχειροτάτοις, εἰς ἃ ἐγκύψεις, ταῦτα ἔστω τὰ δύο· ἓν μέν, ὅτι τὰ πράγματα οὐχ ἅπτεται τῆς ψυχῆς, ἀλλ᾽ ἔξω ἕστηκεν ἀτρεμοῦντα,

αἱ δὲ ὀχλήσεις ἐκ μόνης τῆς ἔνδον ὑπολήψεως· ἕτερον δέ, ὅτι πάντα ταῦτα, ὅσα ὁρᾷς, ὅσον οὐδέπω μεταβαλεῖ καὶ οὐκ ἔτι ἔσται· καὶ ὅσων ἤδη μεταβολαῖς αὐτὸς παρατετύχηκας, συνεχῶς διανοοῦ. ὁ κόσμος ἀλλοίωσις, ὁ βίος ὑπόληψις.

4. Εἰ τὸ νοερὸν ἡμῖν κοινόν, καὶ ὁ λόγος, καθ᾿ ὃν λογικοί ἐσμεν, κοινός· εἰ τοῦτο, καὶ ὁ προστακτικὸς τῶν ποιητέων ἢ μὴ λόγος κοινός· εἰ τοῦτο, καὶ ὁ νόμος κοινός· εἰ τοῦτο, πολῖταί ἐσμεν· εἰ τοῦτο, πολιτεύματός τινος μετέχομεν· εἰ τοῦτο, ὁ κόσμος ὡσανεὶ πόλις ἐστί· τίνος γὰρ ἄλλου φήσει τις τὸ τῶν ἀνθρώπων πᾶν γένος κοινοῦ πολιτεύματος μετέχειν; ἐκεῖθεν δέ, ἐκ τῆς κοινῆς ταύτης πόλεως, καὶ αὐτὸ τὸ νοερὸν καὶ λογικὸν καὶ νομικὸν ἡμῖν ἢ πόθεν; ὥσπερ γὰρ τὸ γεῶδές μοι ἀπό τινος γῆς ἀπομεμέρισται καὶ τὸ ὑγρὸν ἀφ᾿ ἑτέρου στοιχείου καὶ τὸ πνευματικὸν ἀπὸ πηγῆς τινος καὶ τὸ θερμὸν καὶ πυρῶδες ἔκ τινος ἰδίας πηγῆς (οὐδὲν γὰρ ἐκ τοῦ μηδενὸς ἔρχεται, ὥσπερ μηδ᾿ εἰς τὸ οὐκ ὂν ἀπέρχεται), οὕτω δὴ καὶ τὸ νοερὸν ἥκει ποθέν.

5. Ὁ θάνατος τοιοῦτον, οἷον γένεσις, φύσεως μυστήριον· σύγκρισις ἐκ τῶν αὐτῶν στοιχείων, εἰς ταὐτὰ ⟨λύσις⟩. ὅλως δὲ οὐκ ἐφ᾿ ᾧ ἄν τις αἰσχυνθείη· οὐ γὰρ παρὰ τὸ ἑξῆς τῷ νοερῷ ζῴῳ οὐδὲ παρὰ τὸν λόγον τῆς κατασκευῆς.

6. Ταῦτα οὕτως ὑπὸ τῶν τοιούτων πέφυκε γίνεσθαι ἐξ ἀνάγκης, ὁ δὲ τοῦτο μὴ θέλων θέλει τὴν συκῆν ὀπὸν μὴ ἔχειν. ὅλως δὲ ἐκείνου μέμνησο, ὅτι ἐντὸς ὀλιγίστου χρόνου καὶ σὺ καὶ οῧτος τεθνήξεσθε, μετὰ βραχὺ δὲ οὐδὲ ὄνομα ὑμῶν ὑπολειφθήσεται.

7. Ἆρον τὴν ὑπόληψιν, ἦρται τὸ βέβλαμμαι· ἆρον τὸ βέβλαμμαι, ἦρται ἡ βλάβη.

8. Ὁ χείρω αὐτὸν ἑαυτοῦ ἄνθρωπον οὐ ποιεῖ, τοῦτο οὐδὲ τὸν βίον αὐτοῦ χείρω ποιεῖ οὐδὲ βλάπτει οὔτε ἔξωθεν οὔτε ἔνδοθεν. Ἠνάγκασται ἡ τοῦ συμφέροντος φύσις τοῦτο ποιεῖν.

9. Ὅτι "πᾶν τὸ συμβαῖνον δικαίως συμβαίνε"· ὃ ἐὰν ἀκριβῶς παραφυλάσσῃς, εὑρήσεις· οὐ λέγω μόνον κατὰ τὸ ἑξῆς, ἀλλ᾿ ὅτι κατὰ τὸ δίκαιον καὶ ὡς ἂν ὑπό τινος ἀπονέμοντος τὸ κατ᾿ ἀξίαν. παραφύλασσε οὖν ὡς ἤρξω, καί, ὅ τι ἂν ποιῇς, σὺν τούτῳ ποίει, σὺν τῷ ἀγαθὸς εἶναι, καθὸ νενόηται ἰδίως ὁ ἀγαθός. τοῦτο ἐπὶ πάσης ἐνεργείας σῷζε.

10. Μὴ τοιαῦτα ὑπολάμβανε, οἷα ὁ ὑβρίζων κρίνει ἢ οἷά σε κρίνειν βούλεται,

ἀλλὰ ἴδε αὐτά, ὁποῖα κατ ἀλήθειάν ἐστιν.

11. Δύο ταύτας ἑτοιμότητας ἔχειν ἀεὶ δεῖ· τὴν μὲν πρὸς τὸ πρᾶξαι μόνον ὅπερ ἂν ὁ τῆς βασιλικῆς καὶ νομοθετικῆς λόγος ὑποβάλλῃ ἐπ ὠφελείᾳ ἀνθρώπων· τὴν δὲ πρὸς τὸ μεταθέσθαι, ἐὰν ἄρα τις παρῇ διορθῶν καὶ μετάγων ἀπό τινος οἰήσεως. τὴν μέντοι μεταγωγὴν ἀεὶ ἀπό τινος πιθανότητος, ὡς δικαίου ἢ κοινωφελοῦς, γίνεσθαι καὶ τὰ προηγμένα τοιαῦτα μόνον εἶναι δεῖ, οὐχ ὅτι ἡδὺ ἢ ἔνδοξον ἐφάνη.

12. "Λόγον ἔχεις;" "ἔχω." "τί οὖν οὐ χρᾷ; τούτου γὰρ τὸ ἑαυτοῦ ποιοῦντος τί ἄλλο θέλεις;"

13. Ἐνυπέστης ὡς μέρος. ἐναφανισθήσῃ τῷ γεννήσαντι· μᾶλλον δὲ ἀναληφθήσῃ εἰς τὸν λόγον αὐτοῦ τὸν σπερματικὸν κατὰ μεταβολήν.

14. Πολλὰ λιβανωτοῦ βωλάρια ἐπὶ τοῦ αὐτοῦ βωμοῦ· τὸ μὲν προκατέπεσεν, τὸ δ ὕστερον, διαφέρει δ οὐδέν.

15. Ἐντὸς δέκα ἡμερῶν θεὸς αὐτοῖς ‹τούτοις› δόξεις οἷς νῦν θηρίον καὶ πίθηκος, ἐὰν ἀνακάμψῃς ἐπὶ τὰ δόγματα καὶ τὸν σεβασμὸν τοῦ λόγου.

16. Μὴ ὡς μύρια μέλλων ἔτη ζῆν. τὸ χρεὼν ἐπήρτηται· ἕως ζῇς, ἕως ἔξεστιν, ἀγαθὸς γενοῦ.

17. Ὅσην εὐσχολίαν κερδαίνει ὁ μὴ βλέπων τί ὁ πλησίον εἶπεν ἢ ἔπραξεν ἢ διενοήθη, ἀλλὰ μόνον τί αὐτὸς ποιεῖ, ἵνα αὐτὸ τοῦτο δίκαιον ᾖ καὶ ὅσιον ᾖ † κατὰ τὸν ἀγαθόν· μὴ μέλαν ἦθος περιβλέπεσθαι, ἀλλ ἐπὶ τῆς γραμμῆς τρέχειν ὀρθόν, μὴ διερριμμένον.

18. Ὁ περὶ τὴν ὑστεροφημίαν ἐπτοημένος οὐ φαντάζεται ὅτι ἕκαστος τῶν μεμνημένων αὐτοῦ τάχιστα καὶ αὐτὸς ἀποθανεῖται· εἶτα πάλιν ὁ ἐκεῖνον διαδεξάμενος, μέχρι καὶ πᾶσα ἡ μνήμη ἀποσβῇ διὰ ἁπτομένων καὶ σβεννυμένων προιοῦσα. ὑπόθου δ, ὅτι καὶ ἀθάνατοι μὲν οἱ μεμνησόμενοι, ἀθάνατος δὲ ἡ μνήμη· τί οὖν τοῦτο πρὸς σέ; καὶ οὐ λέγω, ὅτι οὐδὲν πρὸς τὸν τεθνηκότα, ἀλλὰ πρὸς τὸν ζῶντα τί ὁ ἔπαινος, πλὴν ἄρα δι οἰκονομίαν τινά; παρίης γὰρ νῦν ἀκαίρως τὴν φυσικὴν δόσιν ἄλλου τινὸς ‹οὐκ› ἐχομένην λόγου. Λοιπόν ..

19. Πᾶν τὸ καὶ ὁπωσοῦν καλὸν ἐξ ἑαυτοῦ καλόν ἐστι καὶ ἐφ ἑαυτὸ καταλήγει, οὐκ ἔχον μέρος ἑαυτοῦ τὸν ἔπαινον· οὔτε γοῦν χεῖρον οὔτε κρεῖττον γίνεται τὸ ἐπαινούμενον. τοῦτό φημι καὶ ἐπὶ τῶν κοινότερον καλῶν λεγομένων, οἷον ἐπὶ τῶν ὑλικῶν καὶ ἐπὶ τῶν τεχνικῶν κατασκευασμάτων· τὸ δὲ δὴ ὄντως καλὸν τίνος χρείαν ἔχει; οὐ μᾶλλον ἢ νόμος, οὐ μᾶλλον ἢ ἀλήθεια, οὐ μᾶλλον ἢ εὔνοια ἢ αἰδώς· τί τούτων διὰ τὸ ἐπαινεῖσθαι καλόν ἐστιν ἢ ψεγόμενον φθείρεται; σμαράγδιον γὰρ ἑαυτοῦ χεῖρον γίνεται, ἐὰν μὴ ἐπαινῆται; τί δὲ χρυσός, ἐλέφας, πορφύρα, λύρα, μαχαίριον, ἀνθύλλιον, δενδρύφιον;

20. Εἰ διαμένουσιν αἱ ψυχαί, πῶς αὐτὰς ἐξ ἀιδίου χωρεῖ ὁ ἀήρ; πῶς δὲ ἡ γῆ χωρεῖ τὰ τῶν ἐκ τοσούτου αἰῶνος θαπτομένων σώματα; ὥσπερ γὰρ ἐνθάδε ἡ τούτων ‹μετὰ› ποσήν τινα ἐπιδιαμονὴν μεταβολὴ καὶ διάλυσις χώραν ἄλλοις νεκροῖς ποιεῖ, οὕτως αἱ εἰς τὸν ἀέρα μεθιστάμεναι ψυχαί, ἐπὶ ποσὸν συμμείνασαι, μεταβάλλουσι καὶ χέονται καὶ ἐξάπτονται εἰς τὸν τῶν ὅλων σπερματικὸν λόγον ἀναλαμβανόμεναι καὶ τοῦτον τὸν τρόπον χώραν ταῖς προσσυνοικιζομέναις παρέχουσι. τοῦτο δ ἄν τις ἀποκρίναιτο ἐφ ὑποθέσει τοῦ τὰς ψυχὰς διαμένειν. χρὴ δὲ μὴ μόνον ἐνθυμεῖσθαι τὸ πλῆθος τῶν θαπτομένων οὑτωσὶ σωμάτων, ἀλλὰ καὶ τὸ τῶν ἑκάστης ἡμέρας ἐσθιομένων ζῴων ὑφ ἡμῶν τε καὶ τῶν ἄλλων ζῴων. ὅσος γὰρ ἀριθμὸς καταναλίσκεται καὶ οὑτωσί πως θάπτεται ἐν τοῖς τῶν τρεφομένων σώμασι, καὶ ὅμως δέχεται ἡ χώρα αὐτὰ διὰ τὰς ἐξαιματώσεις, διὰ τὰς εἰς τὸ ἀερῶδες ἢ πυρῶδες ἀλλοιώσεις. Τίς ἐπὶ τούτου ἡ ἱστορία τῆς ἀληθείας; διαίρεσις εἰς τὸ ὑλικὸν καὶ εἰς τὸ αἰτιῶδες.

21. Μὴ ἀπορρέμβεσθαι, ἀλλ ἐπὶ πάσης ὁρμῆς τὸ δίκαιον ἀποδιδόναι καὶ ἐπὶ πάσης φαντασίας σῴζειν τὸ καταληπτικόν.

22. Πᾶν μοι συναρμόζει ὃ σοὶ εὐάρμοστόν ἐστιν, ὦ κόσμε· οὐδέν μοι πρόωρον οὐδὲ ὄψιμον ὃ σοὶ εὔκαιρον. πᾶν μοι καρπὸς ὃ φέρουσιν αἱ σαὶ ὧραι, ὦ φύσις· ἐκ σοῦ πάντα, ἐν σοὶ πάντα, εἰς σὲ πάντα. ἐκεῖνος μέν φησιν· "‹ὦ› πόλι φίλη Κέκροπος"· σὺ δὲ οὐκ ἐρεῖς· "ὦ πόλι φίλη Διός";

23. "Ὀλίγα πρῆσσε, φησίν, εἰ μέλλεις εὐθυμήσειν." μήποτε ἄμεινον τἀναγκαῖα πράσσειν καὶ ὅσα ὁ τοῦ φύσει πολιτικοῦ ζῴου λόγος αἱρεῖ καὶ ὡς αἱρεῖ; τοῦτο γὰρ οὐ μόνον τὴν ἀπὸ τοῦ καλῶς πράσσειν εὐθυμίαν φέρει, ἀλλὰ καὶ τὴν ἀπὸ τοῦ ὀλίγα πράσσειν. τὰ πλεῖστα γὰρ ὧν λέγομεν καὶ πράσσομεν οὐκ ἀναγκαῖα ὄντα ἐάν τις περιέλῃ, εὐσχολώτερος καὶ ἀταρακτότερος ἔσται. ὅθεν δεῖ καὶ παρ ἕκαστα ἑαυτὸν ὑπομιμνήσκειν· μήτι τοῦτο οὐ τῶν ἀναγκαίων; δεῖ δὲ μὴ μόνον πράξεις τὰς μὴ ἀναγκαίας περιαιρεῖν, ἀλλὰ καὶ φαντασίας· οὕτως γὰρ οὐδὲ πράξεις παρέλκουσαι ἐπακολουθήσουσιν.

24. Πείρασον πῶς σοι χωρεῖ καὶ ὁ τοῦ ἀγαθοῦ ἀνθρώπου βίος τοῦ ἀρεσκομένου μὲν τοῖς ἐκ τῶν ὅλων ἀπονεμομένοις, ἀρκουμένου δὲ τῇ ἰδίᾳ πράξει δικαίᾳ καὶ διαθέσει εὐμενεῖ.

25. Ἑώρακας ἐκεῖνα, ἴδε καὶ ταῦτα. σεαυτὸν μὴ τάρασσε· ἅπλωσον σεαυτόν. ἁμαρτάνει τις; ἑαυτῷ ἁμαρτάνει. συμβέβηκέ σοί τι; καλῶς· ἐκ τῶν ὅλων ἀπ ἀρχῆς σοι συγκαθείμαρτο καὶ συνεκλώθετο πᾶν τὸ συμβαῖνον. τὸ δ ὅλον, βραχὺς ὁ βίος· κερδαντέον τὸ παρὸν σὺν εὐλογιστίᾳ καὶ δίκῃ. νῆφε ἀνειμένος.

26. Ἤτοι κόσμος διατεταγμένος ἢ κυκεὼν συμπεφορημένος μέν, ἀλλὰ κόσμος· ἢ ἐν σοὶ μέν τις κόσμος ὑφίστασθαι δύναται, ἐν δὲ τῷ παντὶ ἀκοσμία; καὶ ταῦτα οὕτως πάντων διακεκριμένων καὶ διακεχυμένων καὶ συμπαθῶν.

27. Μέλαν ἦθος, θῆλυ ἦθος, περισκελὲς ἦθος, θηριῶδες, βοσκηματῶδες, παιδαριῶδες, βλακικόν, κίβδηλον, βωμολόχον, καπηλικόν, τυραννικόν.

28. Εἰ ξένος κόσμου ὁ μὴ γνωρίζων τὰ ἐν αὐτῷ ὄντα, οὐχ ἧττον ξένος καὶ ὁ μὴ γνωρίζων τὰ γινόμενα. φυγὰς ὁ φεύγων τὸν πολιτικὸν λόγον· τυφλὸς ὁ καταμύων τῷ νοερῷ ὄμματι· πτωχὸς ὁ ἐνδεὴς ἑτέρου καὶ μὴ πάντα ἔχων παρ ἑαυτοῦ τὰ εἰς τὸν βίον χρήσιμα· ἀπόστημα κόσμου ὁ ἀφιστάμενος καὶ χωρίζων ἑαυτὸν τοῦ τῆς κοινῆς φύσεως λόγου διὰ τοῦ δυσαρεστεῖν τοῖς συμβαίνουσιν· ἐκείνη γὰρ φέρει τοῦτο, ἣ καὶ σὲ ἤνεγκεν· ἀπόσχισμα πόλεως ὁ τὴν ἰδίαν ψυχὴν τῆς τῶν λογικῶν ἀποσχίζων, μιᾶς οὔσης.

29. Ὁ μὲν χωρὶς χιτῶνος φιλοσοφεῖ, ὁ δὲ χωρὶς βιβλίου. ἄλλος οϼτος ἡμίγυμνος· ἄρτους οὐκ ἔχω, φησί, καὶ ἐμμένω τῷ λόγῳ. - ἐγὼ δὲ τροφὰς τὰς ἐκ τῶν μαθημάτων ἔχω καὶ οὐκ ἐμμένω.

30. Τὸ τεχνίον ὃ ἔμαθες φίλει, τούτῳ προσαναπαύου· τὸ δὲ ὑπόλοιπον τοῦ βίου διέξελθε ὡς θεοῖς μὲν ἐπιτετροφὼς τὰ σεαυτοῦ πάντα ἐξ ὅλης τῆς ψυχῆς, ἀνθρώπων δὲ μηδενὸς μήτε τύραννον μήτε δοῦλον σεαυτὸν καθιστάς.

31. Ἐπινόησον λόγου χάριν τοὺς ἐπὶ Οὐεσπασιανοῦ καιρούς, ὄψει τὰ αὐτὰ πάντα· γαμοῦντας, παιδοτροφοῦντας, νοσοῦντας, ἀποθνῄ σκοντας, πολεμοῦντας, ἑορτάζοντας, ἐμπορευομένους, γεωργοῦντας, κολακεύοντας, αὐθαδιζομένους, ὑποπτεύοντας, ἐπιβουλεύοντας, ἀποθανεῖν τινας εὐχομένους, γογγύζοντας ἐπὶ τοῖς παροῦσιν, ἐρῶντας, θησαυρίζοντας, ὑπατείας, βασιλείας ἐπιθυμοῦντας·

71

οὐκοῦν ἐκεῖνος μὲν ὁ τούτων βίος οὐκ ἔτι οὐδαμοῦ. πάλιν ἐπὶ τοὺς καιροὺς τοὺς Τραιανοῦ μετάβηθι· πάλιν τὰ αὐτὰ πάντα· τέθνηκε κἀκεῖνος ὁ βίος. ὁμοίως καὶ τὰς ἄλλας ἐπιγραφὰς χρόνων καὶ ὅλων ἐθνῶν ἐπιθεώρει καὶ βλέπε, πόσοι κατενταθέντες μετὰ μικρὸν ἔπεσον καὶ ἀνελύθησαν εἰς τὰ στοιχεῖα· μάλιστα δὲ ἀναπολητέον ἐκείνους, οὓς αὐτὸς ἔγνως κενὰ σπωμένους, ἀφέντας ποιεῖν τὸ κατὰ τὴν ἰδίαν κατασκευὴν καὶ τούτου ἀπρὶξ ἔχεσθαι καὶ τούτῳ ἀρκεῖσθαι. ἀναγκαῖον δὲ ὧδε τὸ μεμνῆσθαι, ὅτι καὶ ἡ ἐπιστροφὴ καθ ἑκάστην πρᾶξιν ἰδίαν ἀξίαν ἔχει καὶ συμμετρίαν· οὕτως γὰρ οὐκ ἀποδυςπετήσεις, ἐὰν μὴ ἐπὶ πλέον ἢ προσῆκε περὶ τὰ ἐλάσσω καταγίνῃ.

32. Αἱ πάλαι συνήθεις λέξεις γλωσσήματα νῦν· οὕτως οὖν καὶ τὰ ὀνόματα τῶν πάλαι πολυυμνήτων νῦν τρόπον τινὰ γλωσσήματά ἐστιν· Κάμιλλος, Καίσων, Οὐόλεσος, Δεντάτος, κατ ὀλίγον δὲ καὶ Σκιπίων καὶ Κάτων, εἶτα καὶ Αὔγουστος, εἶτα καὶ Ἀδριανὸς καὶ Ἀντωνῖνος· ἐξίτηλα γὰρ πάντα καὶ μυθώδη ταχὺ γίνεται, ταχὺ δὲ καὶ παντελὴς λήθη κατέχωσεν. καὶ ταῦτα λέγω ἐπὶ τῶν θαυμαστῶς πως λαμψάντων· οἱ γὰρ λοιποὶ ἅμα τῷ ἐκπνεῦσαι "ἄιστοι, ἄπυστο". τί δὲ καὶ ἔστιν ὅλως τὸ ἀείμνηστον; ὅλον κενόν. τί οὖν ἐστι περὶ ὃ δεῖ σπουδὴν εἰσφέρεσθαι; ἓν τοῦτο· - διάνοια δικαία καὶ πράξεις κοινωνικαὶ καὶ λόγος, οἷος μήποτε διαψεύσασθαι, καὶ διάθεσις ἀσπαζομένη πᾶν τὸ συμβαῖνον ὡς ἀναγκαῖον, ὡς γνώριμον, ὡς ἀπ ἀρχῆς τοιαύτης καὶ πηγῆς ῥέον.

33. Ἑκὼν σεαυτὸν τῇ Κλωθοῖ συνεπιδίδου παρέχων συννῆσαι οἷστισί ποτε πράγμασι βούλεται.

34. Πᾶν ἐφήμερον, καὶ τὸ μνημονεῦον καὶ τὸ μνημονευόμενον.

35. Θεώρει διηνεκῶς πάντα κατὰ μεταβολὴν γινόμενα καὶ ἐθίζου ἐννοεῖν, ὅτι οὐδὲν οὕτως φιλεῖ ἡ τῶν ὅλων φύσις ὡς τὸ τὰ ὄντα μεταβάλλειν καὶ ποιεῖν νέα ὅμοια. σπέρμα γὰρ τρόπον τινὰ πᾶν τὸ ὂν τοῦ ἐξ αὐτοῦ ἐσομένου, σὺ δὲ μόνα σπέρματα φαντάζῃ τὰ εἰς γῆν ἢ μήτραν καταβαλλόμενα, τοῦτο δὲ λίαν ἰδιωτικόν.

36. Ἤδη τεθνήξῃ καὶ οὔπω οὔτε ἁπλοῦς οὔτε ἀτάραχος οὔτε ἀνύποπτος τοῦ βλαβῆναι ἂν ἔξωθεν οὔτε ἵλεως πρὸς πάντας οὔτε τὸ φρονεῖν ἐν μόνῳ τῷ δικαιοπραγεῖν τιθέμενος.

37. Τὰ ἡγεμονικὰ αὐτῶν διάβλεπε καὶ τοὺς φρονίμους, οἷα μὲν φεύγουσιν, οἷα δὲ διώκουσιν.

38. Ἐν ἀλλοτρίῳ ἡγεμονικῷ κακὸν σὸν οὐχ ὑφίσταται οὐδὲ μὴν ἔν τινι τροπῇ καὶ ἑτεροιώσει τοῦ περιέχοντος. ποῦ οὖν; ὅπου τὸ περὶ κακῶν ὑπολαμβάνον σοί ἐστι. τοῦτο οὖν μὴ ὑπολαμβανέτω καὶ πάντα εὖ ἔχει. κἂν τὸ ἐγγυτάτω αὐτοῦ, τὸ σωμάτιον, τέμνηται, καίηται, διαπυΐσκηται, σήπηται, ὅμως τὸ ὑπολαμβάνον περὶ τούτων μόριον ἡσυχαζέτω· τουτέστι, κρινέτω μήτε κακόν τι εἶναι μήτε ἀγαθόν, ὃ ἐπίσης δύναται κακῷ ἀνδρὶ καὶ ἀγαθῷ συμβαίνειν. ὃ γὰρ ‹καὶ τῷ παρὰ φύσιν› καὶ τῷ κατὰ φύσιν βιοῦντι ἐπίσης συμβαίνει, τοῦτο οὔτε κατὰ φύσιν ἐστὶν οὔτε παρὰ φύσιν.

39. Ὡς ἓν ζῷον τὸν κόσμον, μίαν οὐσίαν καὶ ψυχὴν μίαν ἐπέχον, συνεχῶς ἐπινοεῖν καὶ πῶς εἰς αἴσθησιν μίαν τὴν τούτου πάντα ἀναδίδοται καὶ πῶς ὁρμῇ μιᾷ πάντα πράσσει καὶ πῶς πάντα πάντων τῶν γινομένων συναίτια καὶ οἵα τις ἡ σύννησις καὶ συμμήρυσις.

40. Ψυχάριον εἶ βαστάζον νεκρόν, ὡς Ἐπίκτητος ἔλεγεν.

41. Τοῖς ἐν μεταβολῇ γινομένοις οὐδέν ἐστι κακόν, ὡς οὐδὲ ἀγαθὸν ‹τοῖς› ἐκ μεταβολῆς ὑφισταμένοις.

42. Ποταμός τίς ἐστι τῶν γινομένων καὶ ῥεῦμα βίαιον ὁ αἰών· ἅμα τε γὰρ ὤφθη ἕκαστον, καὶ παρενήνεκται καὶ ἄλλο παραφέρεται, τὸ δὲ ἐνεχθήσεται.

43. Πᾶν τὸ συμβαῖνον οὕτως σύνηθες καὶ γνώριμον ὡς τὸ ῥόδον ἐν τῷ ἔαρι καὶ ὀπώρα ἐν τῷ θέρει· τοιοῦτον γὰρ καὶ νόσος καὶ θάνατος καὶ βλασφημία καὶ ἐπιβουλὴ καὶ ὅσα τοὺς μωροὺς εὐφραίνει ἢ λυπεῖ.

44. Τὰ ἑξῆς ἀεὶ τοῖς προηγησαμένοις οἰκείως ἐπιγίνεται· οὐ γὰρ οἷον καταρίθμησίς τίς ἐστιν ἀπηρτημένων καὶ μόνον τὸ κατηναγκασμένον ἔχουσα, ἀλλὰ συνάφεια εὔλογος· καὶ ὥσπερ συντέτακται συνηρμοσμένως τὰ ὄντα, οὕτως τὰ γινόμενα οὐ διαδοχὴν ψιλήν, ἀλλὰ θαυμαστήν τινα οἰκειότητα ἐμφαίνει.

45. Ἀεὶ τοῦ Ἡρακλειτείου μεμνῆσθαι, ὅτι γῆς θάνατος ὕδωρ γενέσθαι καὶ ὕδατος θάνατος ἀέρα γενέσθαι καὶ ἀέρος πῦρ καὶ ἔμπαλιν. μεμνῆσθαι δὲ καὶ τοῦ ἐπιλανθανομένου, ᾗ ἡ ὁδὸς ἄγει· καὶ ὅτι, ᾧ μάλιστα διηνεκῶς ὁμιλοῦσι, λόγῳ τῷ τὰ ὅλα διοικοῦντι, τούτῳ διαφέρονται· καὶ οἷς καθ᾽ ἡμέραν ἐγκυροῦσι, ταῦτα αὐτοῖς ξένα φαίνεται· καὶ ὅτι οὐ δεῖ ὥσπερ καθεύδοντας ποιεῖν καὶ λέγειν, καὶ γὰρ καὶ τότε δοκοῦμεν ποιεῖν καὶ λέγειν· καὶ ὅτι οὐ δεῖ ‹ὡς› παῖδας τοκεώνων,

73

τουτέστι κατὰ ψιλόν, καθότι παρειλήφαμεν.

46. Ὥσπερ εἴ τίς σοι θεῶν εἶπεν, ὅτι αὔριον τεθνήξῃ ἢ πάντως γε εἰς τρίτην, οὐκέτ ἂν παρὰ μέγα ἐποιοῦ τὸ εἰς τρίτην μᾶλλον ἢ αὔριον, εἴ γε μὴ ἐσχάτως ἀγεννὴς εἶ· (πόσον γάρ ἐστι τὸ μεταξύ;) οὕτως καὶ τὸ εἰς πολλοστὸν ἔτος μᾶλλον ἢ αὔριον μηδὲν μέγα εἶναι νόμιζε.

47. Ἐννοεῖν συνεχῶς πόσοι μὲν ἰατροὶ ἀποτεθνήκασι, πολλάκις τὰς ὀφρῦς ὑπὲρ τῶν ἀρρώστων συσπάσαντες· πόσοι δὲ μαθηματικοί, ἄλλων θανάτους ὥς τι μέγα προειπόντες· πόσοι δὲ φιλόσοφοι, περὶ θανάτου ἢ ἀθανασίας μυρία διατεινάμενοι· πόσοι δὲ ἀριστεῖς, πολλοὺς ἀποκτείναντες· πόσοι δὲ τύραννοι, ἐξουσίᾳ ψυχῶν μετὰ δεινοῦ φρυάγματος ὡς ἀθάνατοι κεχρημένοι· πόσαι δὲ πόλεις ὅλαι, ἵν οὕτως εἴπω, τεθνήκασιν, Ἑλίκη καὶ Πομπήιοι καὶ Ἡρκλᾶνον καὶ ἄλλαι ἀναρίθμητοι. ἔπιθι δὲ καὶ ὅσους οἶδας, ἄλλον ἐπ ἄλλῳ· ὁ μὲν τοῦτον κηδεύσας εἶτα ἐξετάθη, ὁ δὲ ἐκεῖνον, πάντα δὲ ἐν βραχεῖ. τὸ γὰρ ὅλον, κατιδεῖν ἀεὶ τὰ ἀνθρώπινα ὡς ἐφήμερα καὶ εὐτελῆ καὶ ἐχθὲς μὲν μυξάριον, αὔριον δὲ τάριχος ἢ τέφρα. τὸ ἀκαριαῖον οὖν τοῦτο τοῦ χρόνου κατὰ φύσιν διελθεῖν καὶ ἵλεων καταλῦσαι, ὡς ἂν εἰ ἐλαία πέπειρος γενομένη ἔπιπτεν, εὐφημοῦσα τὴν ἐνεγκοῦσαν καὶ χάριν εἰδυῖα τῷ φύσαντι δένδρῳ.

48. Ὅμοιον εἶναι τῇ ἄκρᾳ, ᾗ διηνεκῶς τὰ κύματα προσρήσσεται· ἡ δὲ ἕστηκε καὶ περὶ αὐτὴν κοιμίζεται τὰ φλεγμήναντα τοῦ ὕδατος. "Ἀτυχὴς ἐγώ, ὅτι τοῦτό μοι συνέβη." οὐμενοῦν ἀλλ εὐτυχὴς ἐγώ, ὅτι τούτου μοι συμβεβηκότος ἄλυπος διατελῶ, οὔτε ὑπὸ παρόντος θραυόμενος οὔτε ἐπιὸν φοβούμενος. συμβῆναι μὲν γὰρ τὸ τοιοῦτο παντὶ ἐδύνατο, ἄλυπος δὲ οὐ πᾶς ἐπὶ τούτῳ ἂν διετέλεσε. διὰ τί οὖν ἐκεῖνο μᾶλλον ἀτύχημα ἢ τοῦτο εὐτύχημα; λέγεις δὲ ὅλως ἀτύχημα ἀνθρώπου, ὃ οὐκ ἔστιν ἀπότευγμα τῆς φύσεως τοῦ ἀνθρώπου; ἀπότευγμα δὲ τῆς φύσεως τοῦ ἀνθρώπου εἶναι δοκεῖ σοι, ὃ μὴ παρὰ τὸ βούλημα τῆς φύσεως αὐτοῦ ἐστι; τί οὖν; τὸ βούλημα μεμάθηκας· μήτι οὖν τὸ συμβεβηκὸς τοῦτο κωλύει σε δίκαιον εἶναι, μεγαλόψυχον, σώφρονα, ἔμφρονα, ἀπρόπτωτον, ἀδιάψευστον, αἰδήμονα, ἐλεύθερον, τἆλλα, ὧν συμπαρόντων ἡ φύσις ἡ τοῦ ἀνθρώπου ἀπέχει τὰ ἴδια; μέμνησο λοιπὸν ἐπὶ παντὸς τοῦ εἰς λύπην σε προαγομένου τούτῳ χρῆσθαι τῷ δόγματι· ὅτι οὐχὶ τοῦτο ἀτύχημα, ἀλλὰ τὸ φέρειν αὐτὸ γενναίως εὐτύχημα.

49. Ἰδιωτικὸν μέν, ὅμως δὲ ἀνυστικὸν βοήθημα πρὸς θανάτου καταφρόνησιν ἡ ἀναπόλησις τῶν γλίσχρως ἐνδιατριψάντων τῷ ζῆν. τί οὖν αὐτοῖς πλέον ἢ τοῖς ἀώροις; πάντως πού ποτε κεῖνται, Καιδικιανός, Φάβιος, Ἰουλιανός, Λέπιδος ἢ εἴ τις τοιοῦτος, οἳ πολλοὺς ἐξήνεγκαν, εἶτα ἐξηνέχθησαν· ὅλον, μικρόν ἐστι τὸ διάστημα καὶ τοῦτο δὶ ὅσων καὶ μεθ οἵων ἐξαντλούμενον καὶ ἐν οἵῳ σωματίῳ;

μὴ οὖν ὡς πρᾶγμα ..˙ βλέπε γὰρ ὀπίσω τὸ ἀχανὲς τοῦ αἰῶνος καὶ τὸ πρόσω ἄλλο ἄπειρον. ἐν δὴ τούτῳ τί διαφέρει ὁ τριήμερος τοῦ τριγερηνίου;

50. Ἐπὶ τὴν σύντομον ἀεὶ τρέχε˙ σύντομος δὲ ἡ κατὰ φύσιν. ὥστε κατὰ τὸ ὑγιέστατον πᾶν λέγειν καὶ πράσσειν, ἀπαλλάσσει γὰρ ἡ τοιαύτη πρόθεσις κόπων καὶ στρατείας καὶ πάσης οἰκονομίας καὶ κομψείας.

BOOK FIVE

I. In the morning when thou findest thyself unwilling to rise, consider with thyself presently, it is to go about a man's work that I am stirred up. Am I then yet unwilling to go about that, for which I myself was born and brought forth into this world? Or was I made for this, to lay me down, and make much of myself in a warm bed? 'O but this is pleasing.' And was it then for this that thou wert born, that thou mightest enjoy pleasure? Was it not in very truth for this, that thou mightest always be busy and in action? Seest thou not how all things in the world besides, how every tree md plant, how sparrows and ants, spiders and bees: how all in their kind are intent as it were orderly to perform whatsoever (towards the preservation of this orderly universe) naturally doth become and belong unto thin? And wilt not thou do that, which belongs unto a man to do? Wilt not thou run to do that, which thy nature doth require? 'But thou must have some rest.' Yes, thou must. Nature hath of that also, as well as of eating and drinking, allowed thee a certain stint. But thou guest beyond thy stint, and beyond that which would suffice, and in matter of action, there thou comest short of that which thou mayest. It must needs be therefore, that thou dost not love thyself, for if thou didst, thou wouldst also love thy nature, and that which thy nature doth propose unto herself as her end. Others, as many as take pleasure in their trade and profession, can even pine themselves at their works, and neglect their bodies and their food for it; and doest thou less honour thy nature, than an ordinary mechanic his trade; or a good dancer his art? than a covetous man his silver, and vainglorious man applause? These to whatsoever they take an affection, can be content to want their meat and sleep, to further that every one which he affects: and shall actions tending to the common good of human society, seem more vile unto thee, or worthy of less respect and intention?

II. How easy a thing is it for a man to put off from him all turbulent adventitious imaginations, and presently to be in perfect rest and tranquillity!

III. Think thyself fit and worthy to speak, or to do anything that is according to nature, and let not the reproach, or report of some that may ensue upon it, ever deter thee. If it be right and honest to be spoken or done, undervalue not thyself so much, as to be discouraged from it. As for them, they have their own rational over-ruling part, and their own proper inclination: which thou must not stand and look about to take notice of, but go on straight, whither both thine own particular, and the common nature do lead thee; and the way of both these, is but one.

IV. I continue my course by actions according to nature, until I fall and cease, breathing out my last breath into that air, by which continually breathed in I did live; and falling upon that earth, out of whose gifts and fruits my father gathered his seed, my mother her blood, and my nurse her milk, out of which for so many years I have been provided, both of meat and drink. And lastly, which beareth me that tread upon it, and beareth with me that so many ways do abuse it, or so freely make use of it, so many ways to so many ends.

V. No man can admire thee for thy sharp acute language, such is thy natural disability that way. Be it so: yet there be many other good things, for the want of which thou canst not plead the want or natural ability. Let them be seen in thee, which depend wholly from thee; sincerity, gravity, laboriousness, contempt of pleasures; be not querulous, be Content with little, be kind, be free; avoid all superfluity, all vain prattling; be magnanimous. Doest not thou perceive, how many things there be, which notwithstanding any pretence of natural indisposition and unfitness, thou mightest have performed and exhibited, and yet still thou doest voluntarily continue drooping downwards? Or wilt thou say that it is through defect of thy natural constitution, that thou art constrained to murmur, to be base and wretched to flatter; now to accuse, and now to please, and pacify thy body: to be vainglorious, to be so giddy-headed., and unsettled in thy thoughts? nay (witnesses be the Gods) of all these thou mightest have been rid long ago: only, this thou must have been contented with, to have borne the blame of one that is somewhat slow and dull, wherein thou must so exercise thyself, as one who neither doth much take to heart this his natural defect, nor yet pleaseth himself in it.

VI. Such there be, who when they have done a good turn to any, are ready to set them on the score for it, and to require retaliation. Others there be, who though they stand not upon retaliation, to require any, yet they think with themselves nevertheless, that such a one is their debtor, and they know as their word is what they have done. Others again there be, who when they have done any such thing, do not so much as know what they have done; but are like unto the vine, which beareth her grapes, and when once she hath borne her own proper fruit, is contented and seeks for no further recompense. As a horse after a race, and a hunting dog when he hath hunted, and a bee when she hath made her honey, look not for applause and commendation; so neither doth that man that rightly doth understand his own nature when he hath done a good turn: but from one doth proceed to do another, even as the vine after she hath once borne fruit in her own proper season, is ready for another time. Thou therefore must be one of them, who what they do, barely do it without any further thought, and are in a manner insensible of what they do. 'Nay but,' will some reply perchance, 'this very thing a rational man is bound unto, to understand what it is, that he doeth.' For it is the property, say they, of one that is naturally sociable, to be sensible, that he doth operate sociably: nay, and to desire, that the party him self that is sociably dealt with, should be sensible of it too. I answer, That which thou sayest is true indeed, but the true meaning of that which is said, thou dost not understand. And therefore art thou one of those first, whom I mentioned. For they also are led by a probable appearance of reason. But if thou dost desire to understand truly what it is that is said, fear not that thou shalt therefore give over any sociable action.

VII. The form of the Athenians' prayer did run thus: 'O rain, rain, good Jupiter, upon all the grounds and fields that belong to the Athenians.' Either we should not pray at all, or thus absolutely and freely; and not every one for himself in particular alone.

VIII. As we say commonly, The physician hath prescribed unto this man, riding; unto another, cold baths; unto a third, to go barefoot: so it is alike to say, The nature of the universe hath prescribed unto this man sickness, or blindness, or some loss, or damage or some such thing. For as there, when we say of a physician, that he hath prescribed anything, our meaning is, that he hath appointed this for that, as subordinate and conducing to health: so here, whatsoever doth happen unto any, is ordained unto him as a thing subordinate unto the fates, and therefore do we say of such things, that they do happen, or fall together; as of square stones, when either in walls, or pyramids in a certain position they fit one another, and agree as it were in an harmony, the masons say, that they do (sumbainein) as if thou shouldest say, fall together: so that in the general, though the things be divers that make it, yet the consent or harmony itself is but one. And as the whole world is made up of all the particular bodies of the world, one perfect and complete body, of the same nature that particular bodies; so is the destiny of particular causes and events one general one, of the same nature that particular causes are. What I now say, even they that are mere idiots are not ignorant of: for they say commonly (touto eferen autw) that is, This his destiny hath brought upon him. This therefore is by the fates properly and particularly brought upon this, as that unto this in particular is by the physician prescribed. These therefore let us accept of in like manner, as we do those that are prescribed unto us our physicians. For them also in themselves shall We find to contain many harsh things, but we nevertheless, in hope of health, and recovery, accept of them. Let the fulfilling and accomplishment of those things which the common nature hath determined, be unto thee as thy health. Accept then, and be pleased with whatsoever doth happen, though otherwise harsh and un-pleasing, as tending to that end, to the health and welfare of the universe, and to Jove's happiness and prosperity. For this whatsoever it be, should not have been produced, had it not conduced to the good of the universe. For neither doth any ordinary particular nature bring anything to pass, that is not to whatsoever is within the sphere of its own proper administration and government agreeable and subordinate. For these two considerations then thou must be well pleased with anything that doth happen unto thee. First, because that for thee properly it was brought to pass, and unto thee it was prescribed; and that from the very beginning by the series and connection of the first causes, it hath ever had a reference unto thee. And secondly, because the good success and perfect welfare, and indeed the very continuance of Him, that is the Administrator of the whole, doth in a manner depend on it. For the whole (because whole, therefore entire and perfect) is maimed, and mutilated, if thou shalt cut off anything at all, whereby the coherence, and contiguity as of parts, so of causes, is maintained and preserved. Of which certain it is, that thou doest (as much as lieth in thee) cut off, and in some sort violently take somewhat away, as often as thou art displeased with anything that happeneth.

IX. Be not discontented, be not disheartened, be not out of hope, if often it succeed not so well with thee punctually and precisely to do all things according to the right dogmata, but being once cast off, return unto them again: and as for those many and more frequent occurrences, either of worldly distractions, or human infirmities, which as a man thou canst not but in some measure be subject unto, be not thou discontented with them; but however, love and affect that only which thou dust return unto: a philosopher's life, and proper occupation after the most exact manner. And when thou dust return to thy philosophy, return not unto it as the manner of some is, after play and liberty as it were, to their schoolmasters and pedagogues; but as they that have sore eyes to their sponge and egg: or as another to his cataplasm; or as others to their fomentations: so shalt not thou make it a matter of ostentation at all to obey reason but of ease and comfort. And remember that philosophy requireth nothing of thee, but what thy nature requireth, and wouldest thou thyself desire anything that is not according to nature? for which of these sayest thou; that which is according to nature or against it, is of itself more kind and pleasing? Is it not for that respect especially, that pleasure itself is to so many men's hurt and overthrow, most prevalent, because esteemed commonly most kind, and natural? But consider well whether magnanimity rather, and true liberty, and true simplicity, and equanimity, and holiness; whether these be not most kind and natural? And prudency itself, what more kind and amiable than it, when thou shalt truly consider with thyself, what it is through all the proper objects of thy rational intellectual faculty currently to go on without any fall or stumble? As for the things of the world, their true nature is in a manner so involved with obscurity, that unto many philosophers, and those no mean ones, they seemed altogether incomprehensible, and the Stoics themselves, though they judge them not altogether incomprehensible, yet scarce and not without much difficulty, comprehensible, so that all assent of

ours is fallible, for who is he that is infallible in his conclusions? From the nature of things, pass now unto their subjects and matter: how temporary, how vile are they I such as may be in the power and possession of some abominable loose liver, of some common strumpet, of some notorious oppressor and extortioner. Pass from thence to the dispositions of them that thou doest ordinarily converse with, how hardly do we bear, even with the most loving and amiable! that I may not say, how hard it is for us to bear even with our own selves, in such obscurity, and impurity of things: in such and so continual a flux both of the substances and time; both of the motions themselves, and things moved; what it is that we can fasten upon; either to honour, and respect especially; or seriously, and studiously to seek after; I cannot so much as conceive For indeed they are things contrary.

X. Thou must comfort thyself in the expectation of thy natural dissolution, and in the meantime not grieve at the delay; but rest contented in those two things. First, that nothing shall happen unto thee, which is not according to the nature of the universe. Secondly, that it is in thy power, to do nothing against thine own proper God, and inward spirit. For it is not in any man's power to constrain thee to transgress against him.

XI. What is the use that now at this present I make of my soul? Thus from time to time and upon all occasions thou must put this question to thyself; what is now that part of mine which they call the rational mistress part, employed about? Whose soul do I now properly possess? a child's? or a youth's? a woman's? or a tyrant's? some brute, or some wild beast's soul?

XII. What those things are in themselves, which by the greatest part are esteemed good, thou mayest gather even from this. For if a man shall hear things mentioned as good, which are really good indeed, such as are prudence, temperance, justice, fortitude, after so much heard and conceived, he cannot endure to hear of any more, for the word good is properly spoken of them. But as for those which by the vulgar are esteemed good, if he shall hear them mentioned as good, he doth hearken for more. He is well contented to hear, that what is spoken by the comedian, is but familiarly and popularly spoken, so that even the vulgar apprehend the difference. For why is it else, that this offends not and needs not to be excused, when virtues are styled good: but that which is spoken in commendation of wealth, pleasure, or honour, we entertain it only as merrily and pleasantly spoken? Proceed therefore, and inquire further, whether it may not be that those things also which being mentioned upon the stage were merrily, and with great applause of the multitude, scoffed at with this jest, that they that possessed them had not in all the world of their own, (such was their affluence and plenty) so much as a place where to avoid their excrements. Whether, I say, those ought not also in very deed to be much respected, and esteemed of, as the only things that are truly good.

XIII. All that I consist of, is either form or matter. No corruption can reduce either of these unto nothing: for neither did I of nothing become a subsistent creature. Every part of mine then will by mutation be disposed into a certain part of the whole world, and that in time into another part; and so in infinitum; by which kind of mutation, I also became what I am, and so did they that begot me, and they before them, and so upwards in infinitum. For so we may be allowed to speak, though the age and government of the world, be to some certain periods of time limited, and confined.

XIV. Reason, and rational power, are faculties which content themselves with themselves, and their own proper operations. And as for their first inclination and motion, that they take from themselves. But their progress is right to the end and object, which is in their way, as it were, and lieth just before them: that is, which is feasible and possible, whether it be that which at the first they proposed to themselves, or no. For which reason also such actions are termed katorqwseiz to intimate the directness of the way, by which they are achieved. Nothing must be thought to belong to a man, which doth not belong unto him as he is a man. These, the event of purposes, are not things required in a man. The nature of man doth not profess any such things. The final ends and consummations of actions are nothing at all to a man's nature. The end therefore of a man, or the summum bonum whereby that end is fulfilled, cannot consist in the consummation of actions purposed and intended. Again, concerning these outward worldly things, were it so that any of them did properly belong unto man, then would it not belong unto man, to condemn them and to stand in opposition with them. Neither would he be praiseworthy that can live without them; or he good, (if these were good indeed) who of his own accord doth deprive himself of any of them. But we see contrariwise, that the more a man doth withdraw himself from these wherein external pomp and greatness doth consist, or any other like these; or the better he doth bear with the loss of these, the better he is accounted.

XV. Such as thy thoughts and ordinary cogitations are, such will thy mind be in time. For the soul doth as it were receive its tincture from the fancies, and imaginations. Dye it therefore and thoroughly soak it with the assiduity of these cogitations. As for example. Wheresoever thou mayest live, there it is in thy power to live well and happy. But thou mayest live at the Court, there then also mayest thou live well and happy. Again, that which everything is made for, he is also made unto that, and cannot but naturally incline unto it. That which anything doth naturally incline unto, therein is his end. Wherein the end of everything doth consist, therein also doth his good and benefit consist. Society therefore is the proper good of a rational creature. For that we are made for society, it hath long since been demonstrated. Or can any man make any question of this, that whatsoever is naturally worse and inferior, is ordinarily subordinated to that which is better? and that those things that are best, are made one for another? And those things that have souls, are better than those that have none? and of those that have, those best that have rational souls?

XVI. To desire things impossible is the part of a mad man. But it is a thing impossible, that wicked man should not commit some such things. Neither doth anything happen to any man, which in the ordinary course of nature as natural unto him doth not happen. Again, the same things happen unto others also. And truly, if either he that is ignorant that such a thing hath happened unto him, or he that is ambitious to be commended for his magnanimity, can be patient, and is not grieved: is it not a grievous thing, that either ignorance, or a vain desire to please and to be commended, should be more powerful and effectual than true prudence? As for the things themselves, they touch not the soul, neither can they have any access unto it: neither can they of themselves any ways either affect it, or move it. For she herself alone can affect and move herself, and according as the dogmata and opinions are, which she doth vouchsafe herself; so are those things which, as accessories, have any co-existence with her.

XVII. After one consideration, man is nearest unto us; as we are bound to do them good, and to bear with them. But as he may oppose any of our true proper actions, so man is unto me but as a thing indifferent: even as the sun, or the wind, or some wild beast. By some of these it may be, that some operation or other of mine, may be hindered; however, of my mind and resolution itself, there can be no let or impediment, by reason of that ordinary constant both exception (or reservation wherewith it inclineth) and ready conversion of objects; from that which may not be, to that which may be, which in the prosecution of its inclinations, as occasion serves, it doth observe. For by these the mind doth turn and convert any impediment whatsoever, to be her aim and purpose. So that what before was the impediment, is now the principal object of her working; and that which before was in her way, is now her readiest way.

XVIII. Honour that which is chiefest and most powerful in the world, and that is it, which makes use of all things, and governs all things. So also in thyself; honour that which is chiefest, and most powerful; and is of one kind and nature with that which we now spake of. For it is the very same, which being in thee, turneth all other things to its own use, and by whom also thy life is governed.

XIX. That which doth not hurt the city itself; cannot hurt any citizen. This rule thou must remember to apply and make use of upon every conceit and apprehension of wrong. If the whole city be not hurt by this, neither am I certainly. And if the whole be not, why should I make it my private grievance? consider rather what it is wherein he is overseen that is thought to have done the wrong. Again, often meditate how swiftly all things that subsist, and all things that are done in the world, are carried away, and as it were conveyed out of sight: for both the substance themselves, we see as a flood, are in a continual flux; and all actions in a perpetual change; and the causes themselves, subject to a thousand alterations, neither is there anything almost, that may ever be said to be now settled and constant. Next unto this, and which follows upon it, consider both the infiniteness of the time already past, and the immense vastness of that which is to come, wherein all things are to be resolved and annihilated. Art not thou then a very fool, who for these things, art either puffed up with pride, or distracted with cares, or canst find in thy heart to make such moans as for a thing that would trouble thee for a very long time? Consider the whole universe whereof thou art but a very little part, and the whole age of the world together, whereof but a short and very momentary portion is allotted unto thee, and all the fates and destinies together, of which how much is it that comes to thy part and share! Again: another doth trespass against me. Let him look to that. He is master of his own disposition, and of his own operation. I for my part am in the meantime in possession of as much, as the common nature would have me to possess: and that which mine own nature would have me do, I do.

XX. Let not that chief commanding part of thy soul be ever subject to any variation through any corporal either pain or pleasure, neither suffer it to be mixed with these, but let it both circumscribe itself, and confine those affections to their own proper parts and members. But if at any time they do reflect and rebound upon the mind and understanding (as in an united and compacted body it must needs;) then must thou not go about to resist sense and feeling, it being natural. However let not thy understanding to this natural sense and feeling, which whether

unto our flesh pleasant or painful, is unto us nothing properly, add an opinion of either good or bad and all is well.

XXI. To live with the Gods. He liveth with the Gods, who at all times affords unto them the spectacle of a soul, both contented and well pleased with whatsoever is afforded, or allotted unto her; and performing whatsoever is pleasing to that Spirit, whom (being part of himself) Jove hath appointed to every man as his overseer and governor.

XXII. Be not angry neither with him whose breath, neither with him whose arm holes, are offensive. What can he do? such is his breath naturally, and such are his arm holes; and from such, such an effect, and such a smell must of necessity proceed. 'O, but the man (sayest thou) hath understanding in him, and might of himself know, that he by standing near, cannot choose but offend.' And thou also (God bless thee!) hast understanding. Let thy reasonable faculty, work upon his reasonable faculty; show him his fault, admonish him. If he hearken unto thee, thou hast cured him, and there will be no more occasion of anger.

XXIII. 'Where there shall neither roarer be, nor harlot.' Why so? As thou dost purpose to live, when thou hast retired thyself to some such place, where neither roarer nor harlot is: so mayest thou here. And if they will not suffer thee, then mayest thou leave thy life rather than thy calling, but so as one that doth not think himself anyways wronged. Only as one would say, Here is a smoke; I will out of it. And what a great matter is this! Now till some such thing force me out, I will continue free; neither shall any man hinder me to do what I will, and my will shall ever be by the proper nature of a reasonable and sociable creature, regulated and directed.

XXIV. That rational essence by which the universe is governed, is for community and society; and therefore hath it both made the things that are worse, for the best, and hath allied and knit together those which are best, as it were in an harmony. Seest thou not how it hath sub-ordinated, and co-ordinated? and how it hath distributed unto everything according to its worth? and those which have the pre-eminency and superiority above all, hath it united together, into a mutual consent and agreement.

XXV. How hast thou carried thyself hitherto towards the Gods? towards thy parents? towards thy brethren? towards thy wife? towards thy children? towards thy masters? thy foster-fathers? thy friends? thy domestics? thy servants? Is it so with thee, that hitherto thou hast neither by word or deed wronged any of them?

Remember withal through how many things thou hast already passed, and how many thou hast been able to endure; so that now the legend of thy life is full, and thy charge is accomplished. Again, how many truly good things have certainly by thee been discerned? how many pleasures, how many pains hast thou passed over with contempt? how many things eternally glorious hast thou despised? towards how many perverse unreasonable men hast thou carried thyself kindly, and discreetly?

XXVI. Why should imprudent unlearned souls trouble that which is both learned, and prudent? And which is that that is so? she that understandeth the beginning and the end, and hath the true knowledge of that rational essence, that passeth through all things subsisting, and through all ages being ever the same, disposing and dispensing as it were this universe by certain periods of time.

XXVII. Within a very little while, thou wilt be either ashes, or a sceletum; and a name perchance; and perchance, not so much as a name. And what is that but an empty sound, and a rebounding echo? Those things which in this life are dearest unto us, and of most account, they are in themselves but vain, putrid, contemptible. The most weighty and serious, if rightly esteemed, but as puppies, biting one another: or untoward children, now laughing and then crying. As for faith, and modesty, and justice, and truth, they long since, as one of the poets hath it, have abandoned this spacious earth, and retired themselves unto heaven. What is it then that doth keep thee here, if things sensible be so mutable and unsettled? and the senses so obscure, and so fallible? and our souls nothing but an exhalation of blood? and to be in credit among such, be but vanity? What is it that thou dost stay for? an extinction, or a translation; either of them with a propitious and contented mind. But still that time come, what will content thee? what else, but to worship and praise the Gods; and to do good unto men. To bear with them, and to forbear to do them any wrong. And for all external things belonging either to this thy wretched body, or life, to remember that they are neither thine, nor in thy power.

XXVIII. Thou mayest always speed, if thou wilt but make choice of the right way; if in the course both of thine opinions and actions, thou wilt observe a true method. These two things be common to the souls, as of God, so of men, and of every reasonable creature, first that in their own proper work they cannot be hindered by anything: and secondly, that their happiness doth consist in a disposition to, and in the practice of righteousness; and that in these their desire is terminated.

XXIX. If this neither be my wicked act, nor an act anyways depending from any wickedness of mine, and that by it the public is not hurt; what doth it concern me? And wherein can the public be hurt? For thou must not altogether be carried by conceit and common opinion: as for help thou must afford that unto them after thy best ability, and as occasion shall require, though they sustain damage, but in these middle or worldly things; but however do not thou conceive that they are truly hurt thereby: for that is not right. But as that old foster-father in the comedy, being now to take his leave doth with a great deal of ceremony, require his foster-child's rhombus, or rattle-top, remembering nevertheless that it is but a rhombus; so here also do thou likewise. For indeed what is all this pleading and public bawling for at the courts? O man, hast thou forgotten what those things are! yea but they are things that others much care for, and highly esteem of. Wilt thou therefore be a fool too? Once I was; let that suffice.

XXX. Let death surprise rue when it will, and where it will, I may be a happy man, nevertheless. For he is a happy man, who in his lifetime dealeth unto himself a happy lot and portion. A happy lot and portion is, good inclinations of the soul, good desires, good actions.

ΒΙΒΛΙΟ ΠΕΜΠΤΟ

Meditations

1. Ὄρθρου, ὅταν δυσόκνως ἐξεγείρῃ, πρόχειρον ἔστω ὅτι ἐπὶ ἀνθρώπου ἔργον ἐγείρομαι· ἔτι οὖν δυσκολαίνω, εἰ πορεύομαι ἐπὶ τὸ ποιεῖν ὧν ἕνεκεν γέγονα καὶ ὧν χάριν προῆγμαι εἰς τὸν κόσμον; ἢ ἐπὶ τοῦτο κατεσκεύασμαι, ἵνα κατακείμενος ἐν στρωματίοις ἐμαυτὸν θάλπω; "ἀλλὰ τοῦτο ἥδιον." πρὸς τὸ ἥδεσθαι οὖν γέγονας, ὅλως δὲ πρὸς πεῖσιν, οὐ πρὸς ἐνέργειαν; οὐ βλέπεις τὰ φυτάρια, τὰ στρουθάρια, τοὺς μύρμηκας, τοὺς ἀράχνας, τὰς μελίσσας τὸ ἴδιον ποιούσας, τὸ καθ αὑτὰς συγκοσμούσας κόσμον; ἔπειτα σὺ οὐ θέλεις τὰ ἀνθρωπικὰ ποιεῖν· οὐ τρέχεις ἐπὶ τὸ κατὰ τὴν σὴν φύσιν· "ἀλλὰ δεῖ καὶ ἀναπαύεσθαι." δεῖ φημὶ κἀγώ· ἔδωκε μέντοι καὶ τούτου μέτρα ἡ φύσις, ἔδωκε μέντοι καὶ τοῦ ἐσθίειν καὶ πίνειν, καὶ ὅμως σὺ ὑπὲρ τὰ μέτρα, ὑπὲρ τὰ ἀρκοῦντα προχωρεῖς, ἐν δὲ ταῖς πράξεσιν οὐκ ἔτι, ἀλλ ἐντὸς τοῦ δυνατοῦ. οὐ γὰρ φιλεῖς ἑαυτόν, ἐπεί τοι καὶ τὴν φύσιν ἄν σου καὶ τὸ βούλημα ταύτης ἐφίλεις. ἄλλοι δὲ τὰς τέχνας ἑαυτῶν φιλοῦντες συγκατατήκονται τοῖς κατ αὐτὰς ἔργοις ἄλουτοι καὶ ἄσιτοι· σὺ τὴν φύσιν τὴν σαυτοῦ ἔλασσον τιμᾷς ἢ ὁ τορευτὴς τὴν τορευτικὴν ἢ ὁ ὀρχηστὴς τὴν ὀρχηστικὴν ἢ ὁ φιλάργυρος τὸ ἀργύριον ἢ ὁ κενόδοξος τὸ δοξάριον. καὶ οῦτοι, ὅταν προσπαθῶσιν, οὔτε φαγεῖν οὔτε κοιμηθῆναι θέλουσι μᾶλλον ἢ ταῦτα συναύξειν, πρὸς ἃ διαφέρονται· σοὶ δὲ αἱ κοινωνικαὶ πράξεις εὐτελέστεραι φαίνονται καὶ ἥσσονος σπουδῆς ἄξιαι.

2. Ὡς εὔκολον ἀπώσασθαι καὶ ἀπαλεῖψαι πᾶσαν φαντασίαν [τὴν] ὀχληρὰν ἢ ἀνοίκειον καὶ εὐθὺς ἐν πάσῃ γαλήνῃ εἶναι.

3. Ἄξιον ἑαυτὸν κρῖνε παντὸς λόγου καὶ ἔργου τοῦ κατὰ φύσιν καὶ μή σε παρειπάτω ἢ ἐπακολουθοῦσά τινων μέμψις ἢ λόγος, ἀλλά, εἰ καλὸν πεπρᾶχθαι ἢ εἰρῆσθαι, μὴ σεαυτὸν ἀπαξίου. ἐκεῖνοι μὲν γὰρ ἴδιον ἡγεμονικὸν ἔχουσι καὶ ἰδίᾳ ὁρμῇ χρῶνται· ἃ σὺ μὴ περιβλέπου, ἀλλ εὐθεῖαν πέραινε ἀκολουθῶν τῇ φύσει τῇ ἰδίᾳ καὶ τῇ κοινῇ, μία δὲ ἀμφοτέρων τούτων ἡ ὁδός.

4. Πορεύομαι διὰ τῶν κατὰ φύσιν, μέχρι πεσὼν ἀναπαύσωμαι ἐναποπνεύσας μὲν τούτῳ, ἐξ οῦ καθ ἡμέραν ἀναπνέω, πεσὼν δὲ ἐπὶ τοῦτο, ἐξ οῦ καὶ τὸ σπερμάτιον ὁ πατήρ μου συνέλεξε καὶ τὸ αἱμάτιον ἡ μήτηρ καὶ τὸ γαλάκτιον ἡ τροφός· ἐξ οῦ καθ ἡμέραν τοσούτοις ἔτεσι βόσκομαι καὶ ἀρδεύομαι· ὃ φέρει με πατοῦντα καὶ εἰς τοσαῦτα ἀποχρώμενον ἑαυτῷ.

5. Δριμύτητά σου οὐκ ἔχουσι θαυμάσαι· ἔστω, ἀλλὰ ἕτερα πολλά, ἐφ ὧν οὐκ ἔχεις εἰπεῖν· οὐ γὰρ πέφυκα. ἐκεῖνα οὖν παρέχου, ἅπερ ὅλα ἐστὶν ἐπὶ σοί, τὸ ἀκίβδηλον, τὸ σεμνόν, τὸ φερέπονον, τὸ ἀφιλήδονον, τὸ ἀμεμψίμοιρον, τὸ ὀλιγοδεές, τὸ

93

εὐμενές, τὸ ἐλεύθερον, τὸ ἀπέρισσον, τὸ ἀφλύαρον, τὸ μεγαλεῖον. οὐκ αἰσθάνῃ
πόσα ἤδη παρέχεσθαι δυνάμενος, ἐφ᾽ ὧν οὐδεμία ἀφυΐας καὶ ἀνεπιτηδειότητος
πρόφασις, ὅμως ἔτι κάτω μένεις ἑκών; ἢ καὶ γογγύζειν καὶ γλισχρεύεσθαι καὶ
κολακεύειν καὶ τὸ σωμάτιον καταιτιᾶσθαι καὶ ἀρεσκεύεσθαι καὶ περπερεύεσθαι
καὶ τοσαῦτα ῥιπτάζεσθαι τῇ ψυχῇ διὰ τὸ ἀφυῶς κατεσκευάσθαι ἀναγκάζῃ; οὐ
μὰ τοὺς θεούς, ἀλλὰ τούτων μὲν πάλαι ἀπηλλάχθαι ἐδύνασο, μόνον δέ, εἰ ἄρα,
ὡς βραδύτερος καὶ δυσπαρακολουθητότερος καταγινώσκεσθαι. καὶ τοῦτο δὲ
ἀσκητέον μὴ παρενθυμουμένῳ μηδὲ ἐμφιληδοῦντι τῇ νωθείᾳ.

6. Ὁ μέν τίς ἐστιν, ὅταν τι δεξιὸν περί τινα πράξῃ, πρόχειρος καὶ λογίσασθαι
αὐτῷ τὴν χάριν. ὁ δὲ πρὸς μὲν τοῦτο οὐ πρόχειρος, ἀλλὰ μέντοι παρ᾽ ἑαυτῷ ὡς
περὶ χρεώστου διανοεῖται καὶ οἶδεν ὃ πεποίηκεν. ὁ δέ τις τρόπον τινὰ οὐδὲ οἶδεν
ὃ πεποίηκεν, ἀλλὰ ὅμοιός ἐστιν ἀμπέλῳ βότρυν ἐνεγκούσῃ καὶ μηδὲν ἄλλο
προσεπιζητούσῃ μετὰ τὸ ἅπαξ τὸν ἴδιον καρπὸν ἐνηνοχέναι. ἵππος δραμών, κύων
ἰχνεύσας, μέλισσα μέλι ποιήσασα, ἄνθρωπος δ᾽ εὖ ποιήσας οὐκ ἐπίσταται, ἀλλὰ
μεταβαίνει ἐφ᾽ ἕτερον, ὡς ἄμπελος ἐπὶ τὸ πάλιν ἐν τῇ ὥρᾳ τὸν βότρυν ἐνεγκεῖν.
ἐν τούτοις οὖν δεῖ εἶναι τοῖς τρόπον τινὰ ἀπαρακολουθήτως αὐτὸ ποιοῦσι.
"ναί· ἀλλ᾽ αὐτὸ τοῦτο δεῖ παρακολουθεῖν· ἴδιον γάρ," φησί, "τοῦ κοινωνικοῦ τὸ
αἰσθάνεσθαι ὅτι κοινωνικῶς ἐνεργεῖ, καὶ νὴ Δία βούλεσθαι καὶ τὸν κοινωνὸν
αἰσθέσθαι." "ἀληθὲς μέν ἐστιν ὃ λέγεις, τὸ δὲ νῦν λεγόμενον παρεκδέχῃ· διὰ
τοῦτο ἔσῃ εἷς ἐκείνων ὧν πρότερον ἐπεμνήσθην· καὶ γὰρ ἐκεῖνοι λογικῇ τινι
πιθανότητι παράγονται. ἐὰν δὲ θελήσῃς συνεῖναι τί ποτέ ἐστι τὸ λεγόμενον, μὴ
φοβοῦ, μὴ παρὰ τοῦτο παραλίπῃς τι ἔργον κοινωνικόν."

7. Εὐχὴ Ἀθηναίων· ῥσον, ῥσον, ὦ φίλε Ζεῦ, κατὰ τῆς ἀρούρας τῆς Ἀθηναίων
καὶ τῶν πεδίων. ἤτοι οὐ δεῖ εὔχεσθαι ἢ οὕτως ἁπλῶς καὶ ἐλευθέρως.

8. Ὁποῖόν τί ἐστι τὸ λεγόμενον, ὅτι· συνέταξεν ὁ Ἀσκληπιὸς τούτῳ ἱππασίαν
ἢ ψυχρολουσίαν ἢ ἀνυποδησίαν, τοιοῦτόν ἐστι καὶ τό· συνέταξε τούτῳ ἡ τῶν
ὅλων φύσις νόσον ἢ πήρωσιν ἢ ἀποβολὴν ἢ ἄλλο τι τῶν τοιούτων. καὶ γὰρ
ἐκεῖ τὸ συνέταξε τοιοῦτόν τι σημαίνει· ἔταξε τούτῳ τοῦτο ὡς κατάλληλον εἰς
ὑγίειαν, καὶ ἐνταῦθα τὸ συμβαῖνον ἑκάστῳ τέτακταί πως αὐτῷ ⟨ὡς⟩ κατάλληλον
εἰς τὴν εἱμαρμένην. οὕτως γὰρ καὶ συμβαίνειν αὐτὰ ἡμῖν λέγομεν ὡς καὶ τοὺς
τετραγώνους λίθους ἐν τοῖς τείχεσιν ἢ ἐν ταῖς πυραμίσι συμβαίνειν οἱ τεχνῖται
λέγουσι, συναρμόζοντας ἀλλήλοις τῇ ποιᾷ συνθέσει. ὅλως γὰρ ἁρμονία ἐστὶ μία
καὶ ὥσπερ ἐκ πάντων τῶν σωμάτων ὁ κόσμος τοιοῦτον σῶμα συμπληροῦται,
οὕτως ἐκ πάντων τῶν αἰτίων ἡ εἱμαρμένη τοιαύτη αἰτία συμπληροῦται. νοοῦσι
δὲ ὃ λέγω καὶ οἱ τέλεον ἰδιῶται· φασὶ γάρ· "τοῦτο ἔφερεν αὐτ". οὐκοῦν τοῦτο
τούτῳ ἐφέρετο καὶ τοῦτο τούτῳ συνετάττετο· δεχώμεθα οὖν αὐτὰ ὡς ἐκεῖνα
⟨ἃ⟩ ὁ Ἀσκληπιὸς συντάττει. πολλὰ γοῦν καὶ ἐν ἐκείνοις ἐστὶ τραχέα, ἀλλὰ

ἀσπαζόμεθα τῇ ἐλπίδι τῆς ὑγιείας. τοιοῦτόν τί σοι δοκείτω ἄνυσις καὶ συντέλεια τῶν τῇ κοινῇ φύσει δοκούντων, οἷον ἡ σὴ ὑγίεια, καὶ οὕτως ἀσπάζου πᾶν τὸ γινόμενον, κἂν ἀπηνέστερον δοκῇ, διὰ τὸ ἐκεῖσε ἄγειν, ἐπὶ τὴν τοῦ κόσμου ὑγίειαν καὶ τὴν τοῦ Διὸς εὐοδίαν καὶ εὐπραγίαν. οὐ γὰρ ἂν τοῦτό τινι ἔφερεν, εἰ μὴ τῷ ὅλῳ συνέφερεν· οὐδὲ γὰρ ἡ τυχοῦσα φύσις φέρει τι, ὃ μὴ τῷ διοικουμένῳ ὑπ αὐτῆς κατάλληλόν ἐστιν. οὐκοῦν κατὰ δύο λόγους στέργειν χρὴ τὸ συμβαῖνόν σοι· καθ ἕνα μέν, ὅτι σοὶ ἐγίνετο καὶ σοὶ συνετάττετο καὶ πρὸς σέ πως εἶχεν, ἄνωθεν ἐκ τῶν πρεσβυτάτων αἰτίων συγκλωθόμενον· καθ ἕτερον δέ, ὅτι τῷ τὸ ὅλον διοικοῦντι τῆς εὐοδίας καὶ τῆς συντελείας καὶ νὴ Δία τῆς συμμονῆς αὐτῆς καὶ τὸ ἰδίᾳ εἰς ἕκαστον ἧκον αἴτιόν ἐστι. πηροῦται γὰρ τὸ ὁλόκληρον, ἐὰν καὶ ὁτιοῦν διακόψῃ ς τῆς συναφείας καὶ συνεχείας ὥσπερ τῶν μορίων, οὕτω δὴ καὶ τῶν αἰτίων· διακόπτεις δέ, ὅσον ἐπὶ σοί, ὅταν δυσαρεστῇς, καὶ τρόπον τινὰ ἀναιρεῖς.

9. Μὴ σικχαίνειν μηδὲ ἀπαυδᾶν μηδὲ ἀποδυσπετεῖν, εἰ μὴ καταπυκνοῦταί σοι τὸ ἀπὸ δογμάτων ὀρθῶν ἕκαστα πράσσειν, ἀλλὰ ἐκκρουσθέντα πάλιν ἐπανιέναι καὶ ἀσμενίζειν, εἰ ‹σοὶ› τὰ πλείω ἀνθρωπικώτερα, καὶ φιλεῖν τοῦτο, ἐφ ὃ ἐπανέρχῃ, καὶ μὴ ὡς πρὸς παιδαγωγὸν τὴν φιλοσοφίαν ἐπανιέναι, ἀλλ ὡς οἱ ὀφθαλμιῶντες πρὸς τὸ σπογγάριον καὶ τὸ ᾠόν, ὡς ἄλλος πρὸς κατάπλασμα, ὡς πρὸς καταιόνησιν. οὕτως γὰρ οὐδὲν ἐπιδείξῃ τὸ πειθαρχεῖν τῷ λόγῳ, ἀλλὰ προσαναπαύσῃ αὐτῷ. μέμνησο δὲ ὅτι φιλοσοφία μόνα, ἃ θέλει ἡ φύσις σου, θέλει· σὺ δὲ ἄλλο ἤθελες οὐ κατὰ φύσιν. τί γὰρ τούτων προσηνέστερον; ἡ γὰρ ἡδονὴ οὐχὶ διὰ τοῦτο σφάλλει; ἀλλὰ θέασαι, εἰ προσηνέστερον μεγαλοψυχία, ἐλευθερία, ἁπλότης, εὐγνωμοσύνη, ὁσιότης. αὐτῆς γὰρ φρονήσεως τί προσηνέστερον, ὅταν τὸ ἄπταιστον καὶ εὔρουν ἐν πᾶσι τῆς παρακολουθητικῆς καὶ ἐπιστημονικῆς δυνάμεως ἐνθυμηθῇς;

10. Τὰ μὲν πράγματα ἐν τοιαύτῃ τρόπον τινὰ ἐγκαλύψει ἐστίν, ὥστε φιλοσόφοις οὐκ ὀλίγοις οὐδὲ τοῖς τυχοῦσιν ἔδοξε παντάπασιν ἀκατάληπτα εἶναι, πλὴν αὐτοῖς γε τοῖς Στωικοῖς δυσκατάληπτα δοκεῖ· καὶ πᾶσα ἡ ἡμετέρα συγκατάθεσις μεταπτώτη· ποῦ γὰρ ὁ ἀμετάπτωτος; μέτιθι τοίνυν ἐπ αὐτὰ τὰ ὑποκείμενα ὡς ὀλιγοχρόνια καὶ εὐτελῆ καὶ δυνάμενα ἐν κτήσει κιναίδου ἢ πόρνης ἢ λῃστοῦ εἶναι. μετὰ τοῦτο ἔπιθι ἐπὶ τὰ τῶν συμβιούντων ἤθη, ὧν μόλις ἐστὶ καὶ τοῦ χαριεστάτου ἀνασχέσθαι, ἵνα μὴ λέγω, ὅτι καὶ ἑαυτόν τις μόγις ὑπομένει. ἐν τοιούτῳ οὖν ζόφῳ καὶ ῥύπῳ καὶ τοσαύτῃ ῥύσει τῆς τε οὐσίας καὶ τοῦ χρόνου καὶ τῆς κινήσεως καὶ τῶν κινουμένων τί ποτέ ἐστι τὸ ἐκτιμηθῆναι ἢ τὸ ὅλως σπουδασθῆναι δυνάμενον, οὐδ ἐπινοῶ. τοὐναντίον γὰρ δεῖ παραμυθούμενον ἑαυτὸν περιμένειν τὴν φυσικὴν λύσιν καὶ μὴ ἀσχάλλειν τῇ διατριβῇ, ἀλλὰ τούτοις μόνοις προσαναπαύεσθαι· ἑνὶ μὲν τῷ, ὅτι οὐδὲν συμβήσεταί μοι ὃ οὐχὶ κατὰ τὴν τῶν ὅλων φύσιν ἐστίν· ἑτέρῳ δέ, ὅτι ἔξεστί μοι μηδὲν πράσσειν παρὰ τὸν ἐμὸν θεὸν καὶ δαίμονα· οὐδεὶς γὰρ ὁ ἀναγκάσων τοῦτον παραβῆναι.

11. Πρὸς τί ποτε ἄρα νῦν χρῶμαι τῇ ἐμαυτοῦ ψυχῇ; παρ᾽ ἕκαστα τοῦτο ἐπανερωτᾶν ἑαυτὸν καὶ ἐξετάζειν τί μοί ἐστι νῦν ἐν τούτῳ τῷ μορίῳ, ὃ δὴ ἡγεμονικὸν καλοῦσι, καὶ τίνος ἄρα νῦν ἔχω ψυχήν; μήτι παιδίου; μήτι μειρακίου; μήτι γυναικαρίου; μήτι τυράννου; μήτι κτήνους; μήτι θηρίου;

12. Ὁποῖά τινά ἐστι τὰ τοῖς πολλοῖς δοκοῦντα ἀγαθά, κἂν ἐντεῦθεν λάβοις. εἰ γάρ τις ἐπινοήσειεν ὑπάρχοντά τινα ὡς ἀληθῶς ἀγαθά, οἷον φρόνησιν, σωφροσύνην, δικαιοσύνην, ἀνδρείαν, οὐκ ἂν ταῦτα προεπινοήσας ἔτι ἀκοῦσαι δυνηθείη τό· "ὑπὸ τῶν ἀγαθῶν", ‹οὐ› γὰρ ἐφαρμόσει. τὰ δέ γε τοῖς πολλοῖς φαινόμενα ἀγαθὰ προεπινοήσας τις ἐξακούσεται καὶ ῥᾳδίως δέξεται ὡς οἰκείως ἐπιλεγόμενον τὸ ὑπὸ τοῦ κωμικοῦ εἰρημένον. οὕτως καὶ οἱ πολλοὶ φαντάζονται τὴν διαφοράν· οὐ γὰρ ἂν τοῦτο μὲν [οὐ] προσέκοπτε καὶ ἀπηξιοῦτο, τὸ δὲ ἐπὶ τοῦ πλούτου καὶ τῶν πρὸς τρυφὴν ἢ δόξαν εὐκληρημάτων παρεδεχόμεθα ὡς ἱκνουμένως καὶ ἀστείως εἰρημένον. πρόιθι οὖν καὶ ἐρώτα, εἰ τιμητέον καὶ ἀγαθὰ ὑποληπτέον τὰ τοιαῦτα, ὧν προεπινοηθέντων οἰκείως ἂν ἐπιφέροιτο τὸ τὸν κεκτημένον αὐτὰ ὑπὸ τῆς εὐπορίας "οὐκ ἔχειν ὅποι χέσ".

13. Ἐξ αἰτιώδους καὶ ὑλικοῦ συνέστηκα, οὐδέτερον δὲ τούτων εἰς τὸ μὴ ὂν φθαρήσεται, ὥσπερ οὐδὲ ἐκ τοῦ μὴ ὄντος ὑπέστη. οὐκοῦν κατατάχθήσεται πᾶν μέρος ἐμὸν κατὰ μεταβολὴν εἰς μέρος τι τοῦ κόσμου καὶ πάλιν ἐκεῖνο εἰς ἕτερον μέρος τι τοῦ κόσμου μεταβαλεῖ καὶ ἤδη εἰς ἄπειρον. κατὰ τοιαύτην δὲ μεταβολὴν κἀγὼ ὑπέστην καὶ οἱ ἐμὲ γεννήσαντες καὶ ἐπανιόντι εἰς ἄλλο ἄπειρον. οὐδὲν γὰρ κωλύει οὕτως φάναι, κἂν κατὰ περιόδους πεπερασμένας ὁ κόσμος διοικῆται.

14. Ὁ λόγος καὶ ἡ λογικὴ τέχνη δυνάμεις εἰσὶν ἑαυταῖς ἀρκούμεναι καὶ τοῖς καθ αὑτὰς ἔργοις. ὁρμῶνται μὲν οὖν ἀπὸ τῆς οἰκείας ἀρχῆς, ὁδεύουσι δὲ εἰς τὸ προκείμενον τέλος, καθὸ κατορθώσεις αἱ τοιαῦται πράξεις ὀνομάζονται τὴν ὀρθότητα τῆς ὁδοῦ σημαίνουσαι.

15. Οὐδὲν τούτων τηρητέον ἀνθρώπῳ, ἃ ἀνθρώπῳ, καθὸ ἄνθρωπός ἐστιν, οὐκ ἐπιβάλλει. οὐκ ἔστιν ἀπαιτήματα ἀνθρώπου οὐδὲ ἐπαγγέλλεται αὐτὰ ἡ τοῦ ἀνθρώπου φύσις οὐδὲ τελειότητές εἰσι τῆς τοῦ ἀνθρώπου φύσεως. οὐ τοίνυν οὐδὲ τὸ τέλος ἐν αὐτοῖς ἐστι τῷ ἀνθρώπῳ κείμενον οὐδέ γε τὸ συμπληρωτικὸν τοῦ τέλους, τὸ ἀγαθόν. ἔτι, εἴ τι τούτων ἦν ἐπιβάλλον τῷ ἀνθρώπῳ, οὐκ ἂν τὸ ὑπερφρονεῖν αὐτῶν καὶ κατεξανίστασθαι ἐπιβάλλον ἦν οὐδὲ ἐπαινετὸς ἦν ὁ ἀπροσδεῆ τούτων ἑαυτὸν παρεχόμενος, οὐδ᾽ ἂν ὁ ἐλαττωτικὸς ἑαυτοῦ ἔν τινι τούτων ἀγαθὸς ἦν, εἴπερ ταῦτα ἀγαθὰ ἦν. νῦν δ, ὅσῳπερ πλείω τις ἀφαιρῶν ἑαυτοῦ τούτων ἢ τοιούτων ἑτέρων ἢ καὶ ἀφαιρούμενός τι τούτων ἀνέχεται,

τοσῷδε μᾶλλον ἀγαθός ἐστιν.

16. Οἷα ἂν πολλάκις φαντασθῇς, τοιαύτη σοι ἔσται ἡ διάνοια· βάπτεται γὰρ ὑπὸ τῶν φαντασιῶν ἡ ψυχή. βάπτε οὖν αὐτὴν τῇ συνεχείᾳ τῶν τοιούτων φαντασιῶν· οἷον, ὅτι ὅπου ζῆν ἐστιν, ἐκεῖ καὶ εὖ ζῆν· ἐν αὐλῇ δὲ ζῆν ἐστιν· ἔστιν ἄρα καὶ εὖ ζῆν ἐν αὐλῇ. καὶ πάλιν, ὅτι οῦπερ ἕνεκεν ἕκαστον κατεσκεύασται, ‹πρὸς τοῦτο κατεσκεύασται·› πρὸς ὃ δὲ κατεσκεύασται, πρὸς τοῦτο φέρεται· πρὸς ὃ φέρεται δέ, ἐν τούτῳ τὸ τέλος αὐτοῦ· ὅπου δὲ τὸ τέλος, ἐκεῖ καὶ τὸ συμφέρον καὶ τὸ ἀγαθὸν ἑκάστου· τὸ ἄρα ἀγαθὸν τοῦ λογικοῦ ζῴου κοινωνία. ὅτι γὰρ πρὸς κοινωνίαν γεγόναμεν, πάλαι δέδεικται· ἢ οὐκ ἦν ἐναργὲς ὅτι τὰ χείρω τῶν κρειττόνων ἕνεκεν, τὰ δὲ κρείττω ἀλλήλων; κρείττω δὲ τῶν μὲν ἀψύχων τὰ ἔμψυχα, τῶν δὲ ἐμψύχων τὰ λογικά.

17. Τὸ τὰ ἀδύνατα διώκειν μανικόν· ἀδύνατον δὲ τὸ τοὺς φαύλους μὴ τοιαῦτά τινα ποιεῖν.

18. Οὐδὲν οὐδενὶ συμβαίνει ὃ οὐχὶ ἐκεῖνο πέφυκε φέρειν. ἄλλῳ τὰ αὐτὰ συμβαίνει καὶ ἤτοι ἀγνοῶν ὅτι συμβέβηκεν, ἢ ἐπιδεικνύμενος μεγαλοφροσύνην, εὐσταθεῖ καὶ ἀκάκωτος μένει. ‹οὐ› δεινὸν οὖν ἄγνοιαν καὶ ἀρέσκειαν ἰσχυροτέρας εἶναι φρονήσεως ..;

19. Τὰ πράγματα αὐτὰ οὐδ᾽ ὁπωστιοῦν ψυχῆς ἅπτεται οὐδὲ ἔχει εἴσοδον πρὸς ψυχὴν οὐδὲ τρέψαι οὐδὲ κινῆσαι ψυχὴν δύναται, τρέπει δὲ καὶ κινεῖ αὐτὴ ἑαυτὴν μόνη καὶ οἵων ἂν κριμάτων καταξιώσῃ ἑαυτήν, τοιαῦτα ἑαυτῇ ποιεῖ τὰ προσυφεστῶτα.

20. Καθ᾽ ἕτερον μὲν λόγον ἡμῖν ἐστιν οἰκειότατον ἄνθρωπος, καθ᾽ ὅσον εὖ ποιητέον αὐτοὺς καὶ ἀνεκτέον· καθ᾽ ὅσον δὲ ἐνίστανταί τινες εἰς τὰ οἰκεῖα ἔργα, ἕν τι τῶν ἀδιαφόρων μοι γίνεται ὁ ἄνθρωπος οὐχ ἧσσον ἢ ἥλιος ἢ ἄνεμος ἢ θηρίον. ὑπὸ τούτων δὲ ἐνέργεια μέν τις ἐμποδισθείη ἄν, ὁρμῆς δὲ καὶ διαθέσεως οὐ γίνεται ἐμπόδια διὰ τὴν ὑπεξαίρεσιν καὶ τὴν περιτροπήν. περιτρέπει γὰρ καὶ μεθίστησι πᾶν τὸ τῆς ἐνεργείας κώλυμα ἡ διάνοια εἰς τὸ προηγούμενον καὶ πρὸ ἔργου γίνεται τὸ τοῦ ἔργου τούτου ἐφεκτικὸν καὶ πρὸ ὁδοῦ τὸ τῆς ὁδοῦ ταύτης ἐνστατικόν.

21. Τῶν ἐν τῷ κόσμῳ τὸ κράτιστον τίμα· ἔστι δὲ τοῦτο τὸ πᾶσι χρώμενον καὶ πάντα διέπον. ὁμοίως δὲ καὶ τῶν ἐν σοὶ τὸ κράτιστον τίμα· ἔστι δὲ τοῦτο τὸ ἐκείνῳ ὁμογενές. καὶ γὰρ ἐπὶ σοῦ τὸ τοῖς ἄλλοις χρώμενον τοῦτό ἐστι, καὶ ὁ σὸς

βίος ὑπὸ τούτου διοικεῖται.

22. Ὃ τῇ πόλει οὐκ ἔστι βλαβερόν, οὐδὲ τὸν πολίτην βλάπτει. ἐπὶ πάσης τῆς τοῦ βεβλάφθαι φαντασίας τοῦτον ἔπαγε τὸν κανόνα· εἰ ἡ πόλις ὑπὸ τούτου μὴ βλάπτεται, οὐδὲ ἐγὼ βέβλαμμαι· εἰ δὲ ἡ πόλις βλάπτεται, οὐκ ὀργιστέον, ‹ἀλλὰ δεικτέον› τῷ βλάπτοντι τὴν πόλιν τί τὸ παρορώμενον.

23. Πολλάκις ἐνθυμοῦ τὸ τάχος τῆς παραφορᾶς καὶ ὑπεξαγωγῆς τῶν ὄντων τε καὶ γινομένων. ἥ τε γὰρ οὐσία οἷον ποταμὸς ἐνδιηνεκεῖ ῥύσει καὶ αἱ ἐνέργειαι ἐν συνεχέσι μεταβολαῖς καὶ τὰ αἴτια ἐν μυρίαις τροπαῖς καὶ σχεδὸν οὐδὲν ἑστὼς καὶ τὸ πάρεγγυς· τὸ δὲ ἄπειρον τοῦ τε παρῳχηκότος καὶ μέλλοντος ἀχανές, ᾧ πάντα ἐναφανίζεται. πῶς οὖν οὐ μωρὸς ὁ ἐν τούτοις φυσώμενος ἢ σπώμενος ἢ σχετλιάζων ὡς ἔν τινι χρονίῳ καὶ ἐπὶ μακρὸν ἐνοχλήσαντι;

24. Μέμνησο τῆς συμπάσης οὐσίας, ἧς ὀλίγιστον μετέχεις, καὶ τοῦ σύμπαντος αἰῶνος, οῥ βραχὺ καὶ ἀκαριαῖόν σοι διάστημα ἀφώρισται, καὶ τῆς εἱμαρμένης, ἧς πόστον εἶ μέρος;

25. Ἄλλος ἁμαρτάνει. τί εἰς ἐμέ; ὄψεται· ἰδίαν ἔχει διάθεσιν, ἰδίαν ἐνέργειαν. ἐγὼ νῦν ἔχω, ὅ με θέλει νῦν ἔχειν ἡ κοινὴ φύσις, καὶ πράσσω, ὅ με νῦν πράσσειν θέλει ἡ ἐμὴ φύσις.

26. Τὸ ἡγεμονικὸν καὶ κυριεῦον τῆς ψυχῆς σου μέρος ἄτρεπτον ἔστω ὑπὸ τῆς ἐν τῇ σαρκὶ λείας ἢ τραχείας κινήσεως καὶ μὴ συγκιρνάσθω, ἀλλὰ περιγραφέτω αὐτὸ καὶ περιοριζέτω τὰς πείσεις ἐκείνας ἐν τοῖς μορίοις. ὅταν δὲ ἀναδιδῶνται κατὰ τὴν ἑτέραν συμπάθειαν εἰς τὴν διάνοιαν ὡς ἐν σώματι ἡνωμένῳ, τότε πρὸς μὲν τὴν αἴσθησιν φυσικὴν οὖσαν οὐ πειρατέον ἀντιβαίνειν, τὴν δὲ ὑπόληψιν τὴν ὡς περὶ ἀγαθοῦ ἢ κακοῦ μὴ προστιθέτω τὸ ἡγεμονικὸν ἐξ ἑαυτοῦ.

27. "Συζῆν θεοῖς." συζῇ δὲ θεοῖς ὁ συνεχῶς δεικνὺς αὐτοῖς τὴν ἑαυτοῦ ψυχὴν ἀρεσκομένην μὲν τοῖς ἀπονεμομένοις, ποιοῦσαν δὲ ὅσα βούλεται ὁ δαίμων, ὃν ἑκάστῳ προστάτην καὶ ἡγεμόνα ὁ Ζεὺς ἔδωκεν, ἀπόσπασμα ἑαυτοῦ. οῥτος δέ ἐστιν ὁ ἑκάστου νοῦς καὶ λόγος.

28. Τῷ γράσωνι μήτι ὀργίζῃ, μήτι τῷ ὀζοστόμῳ ὀργίζῃ; τί σοι ποιήσει; τοιοῦτον στόμα ἔχει, τοιαύτας μάλας ἔχει, ἀνάγκη τοιαύτην ἀποφορὰν ἀπὸ τοιούτων γίνεσθαι. "ἀλλ' ὁ ἄνθρωπος λόγον ἔχει," φησί, "καὶ δύναται συννοεῖν ἐφιστάνων

τί πλημμελεῖ." εὖ σοι γένοιτο· τοιγαροῦν καὶ σὺ λόγον ἔχεις, κίνησον λογικῇ διαθέσει λογικὴν διάθεσιν, δεῖξον, ὑπόμνησον· εἰ γὰρ ἐπαΐει, θεραπεύσεις καὶ οὐ χρεία ὀργῆς. Οὔτε τραγῳδὸς οὔτε πόρνη.

29. Ὡς ἐξελθὼν ζῆν διανοῇ, οὕτως ἐνταῦθα ζῆν ἔξεστιν· ἐὰν δὲ μὴ ἐπιτρέπωσι, τότε καὶ τοῦ ζῆν ἔξιθι, οὕτως μέντοι ὡς μηδὲν κακὸν πάσχων. καπνὸς καὶ ἀπέρχομαι· τί αὐτὸ πρᾶγμα δοκεῖς; μέχρι δέ με τοιοῦτον οὐδὲν ἐξάγει, μένω ἐλεύθερος καὶ οὐδείς με κωλύσει ποιεῖν ἃ θέλω· θέλω δὲ ‹ἃ› κατὰ φύσιν τοῦ λογικοῦ καὶ κοινωνικοῦ ζῴου.

30. Ὁ τοῦ ὅλου νοῦς κοινωνικός. πεποίηκε γοῦν τὰ χείρω τῶν κρειττόνων ἕνεκεν καὶ τὰ κρείττω ἀλλήλοις συνήρμοσεν. ὁρᾷς πῶς ὑπέταξε, συνέταξε, καὶ τὸ κατ᾽ ἀξίαν ἀπένειμεν ἑκάστοις καὶ τὰ κρατιστεύοντα εἰς ὁμόνοιαν ἀλλήλων συνήγαγεν.

31. Πῶς προσενήνεξαι μέχρι νῦν θεοῖς, γονεῦσιν, ἀδελφῷ, γυναικί, τέκνοις, διδασκάλοις, τροφεῦσι, φίλοις, οἰκείοις, οἰκέταις· εἰ πρὸς πάντας σοι μέχρι νῦν ἐστι τό· μήτε τινὰ ῥέξαι ἐξαίσιον μήτε εἰπεῖν. ἀναμιμνήσκου δὲ καὶ δι᾽ οἵων διελήλυθας καὶ οἷα ἤρκεσας ὑπομεῖναι καὶ ὅτι πλήρης ἤδη σοι ἡ ἱστορία τοῦ βίου καὶ τελεία ἡ λειτουργία καὶ πόσα ὦπται καλὰ καὶ πόσων μὲν ἡδονῶν καὶ πόνων ὑπερεῖδες, πόσα δὲ ἔνδοξα παρεῖδες, εἰς ὅσους δὲ ἀγνώμονας εὐγνώμων ἐγένου.

32. Διὰ τί συγχέουσιν ἄτεχνοι καὶ ἀμαθεῖς ψυχαὶ ἔντεχνον καὶ ἐπιστήμονα; τίς οὖν ψυχὴ ἔντεχνος καὶ ἐπιστήμων; ἡ εἰδυῖα ἀρχὴν καὶ τέλος καὶ τὸν δι᾽ ὅλης τῆς οὐσίας διήκοντα λόγον καὶ διὰ παντὸς τοῦ αἰῶνος κατὰ περιόδους τεταγμένας οἰκονομοῦντα τὸ πᾶν.

33. Ὅσον οὐδέπω σποδὸς ἢ σκελετὸς καὶ ἤτοι ὄνομα ἢ οὐδὲ ὄνομα, τὸ δὲ ὄνομα ψόφος καὶ ἀπήχημα. τὰ δὲ ἐν τῷ βίῳ πολυτίμητα κενὰ καὶ σαπρὰ καὶ μικρά· καὶ κυνίδια διαδακνόμενα καὶ παιδία φιλόνεικα, γελῶντα εἶτα εὐθὺς κλαίοντα. Πίστις δὲ καὶ Αἰδὼς καὶ Δίκη καὶ Ἀλήθεια πρὸς Ὄλυμπον ἀπὸ χθονὸς εὐρυοδείης. τί οὖν ἔτι τὸ ἐνταῦθα κατέχον, εἴ γε τὰ μὲν αἰσθητὰ εὐμετάβλητα καὶ οὐχ ἑστῶτα, τὰ δὲ αἰσθητήρια ἀμυδρὰ καὶ εὐπαρατύπωτα, αὐτὸ δὲ τὸ ψυχάριον ἀναθυμίασις ἀφ᾽ αἵματος, τὸ δὲ εὐδοκιμεῖν παρὰ τοιούτοις κενόν; τί οὖν; περιμένειν ἵλεων τὴν εἴτε σβέσιν εἴτε μετάστασιν· ἕως δὲ ἐκείνης ὁ καιρὸς ἐφίσταται, τί ἀρκεῖ; τί δὲ ἄλλο ἢ θεοὺς μὲν σέβειν καὶ εὐφημεῖν, ἀνθρώπους δὲ εὖ ποιεῖν καὶ ἀνέχεσθαι αὐτῶν καὶ ἀπέχεσθαι· ὅσα δὲ ἐντὸς ὅρων τοῦ κρεαδίου καὶ τοῦ πνευματίου, ταῦτα μεμνῆσθαι μήτε σὰ ὄντα μήτε ἐπὶ σοί;

34. Δύνασαι ἀεὶ εὐροεῖν, εἴ γε καὶ εὐοδεῖν, εἴ γε καὶ ὁδῷ ὑπολαμβάνειν καὶ πράσσειν. δύο ταῦτα κοινὰ τῇ τε τοῦ θεοῦ καὶ τῇ τοῦ ἀνθρώπου καὶ παντὸς λογικοῦ ζῴου ψυχῇ· τὸ μὴ ἐμποδίζεσθαι ὑπ ἄλλου καὶ τὸ ἐν τῇ δικαϊκῇ διαθέσει καὶ πράξει ἔχειν τὸ ἀγαθὸν καὶ ἐνταῦθα τὴν ὄρεξιν ἀπολήγειν.

35. Εἰ μήτε κακία ἐστὶ τοῦτο ἐμὴ μήτε ἐνέργεια κατὰ κακίαν ἐμὴν μήτε τὸ κοινὸν βλάπτεται, τί ὑπὲρ αὐτοῦ διαφέρομαι; τίς δὲ βλάβη τοῦ κοινοῦ;

36. Μὴ ὁλοσχερῶς τῇ φαντασίᾳ συναρπάζεσθαι, ἀλλὰ βοηθεῖν μὲν κατὰ δύναμιν καὶ κατ ἀξίαν, κἂν εἰς τὰ μέσα ἐλαττῶνται, μὴ μέντοι βλάβην αὐτὸ φαντάζεσθαι· κακὸν γὰρ ἔθος. ἀλλ ὡςό γέρων ἀπελθὼν τὸν τοῦ θρεπτοῦ ῥόμβον ἀπήτει, μεμνημένος ὅτι ῥόμβος, οὕτως οὖν καὶ ‹σὺ› ὧδε. ἐπεί τοι γίνῃ κλαίων ἐπὶ τῶν ἐμβόλων· ἄνθρωπε, ἐπελάθου τί ταῦτα ἦν; "ναί· ἀλλὰ τούτοις περισπούδαστα." διὰ τοῦτ οὖν καὶ σὺ μωρὸς γένῃ;

37. "Ἐγενόμην ποτέ, ὁπουδήποτε καταληφθείς, εὔμοιρος ἄνθρωπος." τὸ δὲ εὔμοιρος, ἀγαθὴν μοῖραν σεαυτῷ ἀπονείμας· ἀγαθὴ δὲ μοῖρα· ἀγαθαὶ τροπαὶ ψυχῆς, ἀγαθαὶ ὁρμαί, ἀγαθαὶ πράξεις.

BOOK SIX

I. The matter itself, of which the universe doth consist, is of itself very tractable and pliable. That rational essence that doth govern it, hath in itself no cause to do evil. It hath no evil in itself; neither can it do anything that is evil: neither can anything be hurt by it. And all things are done and determined according to its will and prescript.

II. Be it all one unto thee, whether half frozen or well warm; whether only slumbering, or after a full sleep; whether discommended or commended thou do thy duty: or whether dying or doing somewhat else; for that also 'to die,' must among the rest be reckoned as one of the duties and actions of our lives.

III. Look in, let not either the proper quality, or the true worth of anything pass thee, before thou hast fully apprehended it.

IV. All substances come soon to their change, and either they shall be resolved by way of exhalation (if so be that all things shall be reunited into one substance), or as others maintain, they shall be scattered and dispersed. As for that Rational Essence by which all things are governed, as it best understandeth itself, both its own disposition, and what it doth, and what matter it hath to do with and accordingly doth all things; so we that do not, no wonder, if we wonder at many things, the reasons whereof we cannot comprehend.

V. The best kind of revenge is, not to become like unto them.

VI. Let this be thy only joy, and thy only comfort, from one sociable kind action without intermission to pass unto another, God being ever in thy mind.

VII. The rational commanding part, as it alone can stir up and turn itself; so it maketh both itself to be, and everything that happeneth, to appear unto itself, as it will itself.

VIII. According to the nature of the universe all things particular are determined, not according to any other nature, either about compassing and containing; or within, dispersed and contained; or without, depending. Either this universe is a mere confused mass, and an intricate context of things, which shall in time be scattered and dispersed again: or it is an union consisting of order, and administered by Providence. If the first, why should I desire to continue any longer in this fortuit confusion and commixtion? or why should I take care for anything else, but that as soon as may be I may be earth again? And why should I trouble myself any more whilst I seek to please the Gods? Whatsoever I do, dispersion is my end, and will come upon me whether I will or no. But if the latter be, then am not I religious in vain; then will I be quiet and patient, and put my trust in Him, who is the Governor of all.

IX. Whensoever by some present hard occurrences thou art constrained to be in some sort troubled and vexed, return unto thyself as soon as may be, and be not out of tune longer than thou must needs. For so shalt thou be the better able to keep thy part another time, and to maintain the harmony, if thou dost use thyself to this continually; once out, presently to have recourse unto it, and to begin again.

X. If it were that thou hadst at one time both a stepmother, and a natural mother living, thou wouldst honour and respect her also; nevertheless to thine own natural mother would thy refuge, and recourse be continually. So let the court and thy philosophy be unto thee. Have recourse unto it often, and comfort thyself in her, by whom it is that those other things are made tolerable unto thee, and thou also in those things not intolerable unto others.

XI. How marvellous useful it is for a man to represent unto himself meats, and all such things that are for the mouth, under a right apprehension and imagination! as for example: This is the carcass of a fish; this of a bird; and this of a hog. And again more generally; This phalernum, this excellent highly commended wine, is but the bare juice of an ordinary grape. This purple robe, but sheep's hairs, dyed with the blood of a shellfish. So for coitus, it is but the attrition of an ordinary base entrail, and the excretion of a little vile snivel, with a certain kind of convulsion: according to Hippocrates his opinion. How excellent useful are these lively fancies and representations of things, thus penetrating and passing through the objects, to make their true nature known and apparent! This must thou use all thy life long, and upon all occasions: and then especially, when matters are apprehended as of great worth and respect, thy art and care must be to uncover them, and to behold their vileness, and to take away from them all those serious circumstances and expressions, under which they made so grave a show. For outward pomp and appearance is a great juggler; and then especially art thou most in danger to be beguiled by it, when (to a man's thinking) thou most seemest to be employed about matters of moment.

XII. See what Crates pronounceth concerning Xenocrates himself.

XIII. Those things which the common sort of people do admire, are most of them such things as are very general, and may be comprehended under things merely natural, or naturally affected and qualified: as stones, wood, figs, vines, olives. Those that be admired by them that are more moderate and restrained, are comprehended under things animated: as flocks and herds. Those that are yet more gentle and curious, their admiration is commonly confined to reasonable creatures only; not in general as they are reasonable, but as they are capable of art, or of some craft and subtile invention: or perchance barely to reasonable creatures; as they that delight in the possession of many slaves. But he that honours a reasonable soul in general, as it is reasonable and naturally sociable, doth little regard anything else: and above all things is careful to preserve his own, in the continual habit and exercise both of reason and sociableness: and thereby doth cooperate with him, of whose nature he doth also participate; God.

XIV. Some things hasten to be, and others to be no more. And even whatsoever now is, some part thereof hath already perished. Perpetual fluxes and alterations renew the world, as the perpetual course of time doth make the age of the world (of itself infinite) to appear always fresh and new. In such a flux and course of all things, what of these things that hasten so fast away should any man regard, since among all there is not any that a man may fasten and fix upon? as if a man would settle his affection upon some ordinary sparrow living by him, who is no sooner seen, than out of sight. For we must not think otherwise of our lives, than as a mere exhalation of blood, or of an ordinary respiration of air. For what in our common apprehension is, to breathe in the air and to breathe it out again, which we do daily: so much is it and no more, at once to breathe out all thy respirative faculty into that common air from whence but lately (as being but from yesterday, and today), thou didst first breathe it in, and with it, life.

XV. Not vegetative spiration, it is not surely (which plants have) that in this life should be so dear unto us; nor sensitive respiration, the proper life of beasts, both tame and wild; nor this our imaginative faculty; nor that we are subject to be led and carried up and down by the strength of our sensual appetites; or that we can gather, and live together; or that we can feed: for that in effect is no better, than that we can void the excrements of our food. What is it then that should be dear unto us? to hear a clattering noise? if not that, then neither to be applauded by the tongues of men. For the praises of many tongues, is in effect no better than the clattering of so many tongues. If then neither applause, what is there remaining that should be dear unto thee? This I think: that in all thy motions and actions thou be moved, and restrained according to thine own true natural constitution and Construction only. And to this even ordinary arts and professions do lead us. For it is that which every art doth aim at, that whatsoever it is, that is by art effected and prepared, may be fit for that work that it is prepared for. This is the end that he that dresseth the vine, and he that takes upon him either to tame colts, or to train up dogs, doth aim at. What else doth the education of children, and all learned professions tend unto? Certainly then it is that, which should be dear unto us also. If in this particular it go well with thee, care not for the obtaining of other things. But is it so, that thou canst not but respect other things also? Then canst not thou truly be free? then canst thou not have selfcontent: then wilt thou ever be subject to passions. For it is not possible, but that thou must be envious, and jealous, and suspicious of them whom thou knowest can bereave thee of such things; and again, a secret underminer of them, whom thou seest in present possession of that which is dear unto thee. To be short, he must of necessity be full of confusion within himself, and often accuse the Gods, whosoever stands in need of these things. But if thou shalt honour and respect thy mind only, that will make thee acceptable towards thyself, towards thy friends very tractable; and conformable and concordant with the Gods; that is, accepting with praises whatsoever they shall think good to appoint and allot unto thee.

XVI. Under, above, and about, are the motions of the elements; but the motion of virtue, is none of those motions, but is somewhat more excellent and divine. Whose way (to speed and prosper in it) must be through a way, that is not easily comprehended.

XVII. Who can choose but wonder at them? They will not speak well of them that are at the same time with them, and live with them; yet they themselves are very ambitious, that they that shall follow, whom they have never seen, nor shall ever see, should speak well of them. As if a man should grieve that he hath not been commended by them, that lived before him.

XVIII. Do not ever conceive anything impossible to man, which by thee cannot, or not without much difficulty be effected; but whatsoever in general thou canst Conceive possible and proper unto any man, think that very possible unto thee also.

XIX. Suppose that at the palestra somebody hath all to torn thee with his nails, and hath broken thy head. Well, thou art wounded. Yet thou dost not exclaim;

thou art not offended with him. Thou dost not suspect him for it afterwards, as one that watcheth to do thee a mischief. Yea even then, though thou dost thy best to save thyself from him, yet not from him as an enemy. It is not by way of any suspicious indignation, but by way of gentle and friendly declination. Keep the same mind and disposition in other parts of thy life also. For many things there be, which we must conceit and apprehend, as though we had had to do with an antagonist at the palestra. For as I said, it is very possible for us to avoid and decline, though we neither suspect, nor hate.

XX. If anybody shall reprove me, and shall make it apparent unto me, that in any either opinion or action of mine I do err, I will most gladly retract. For it is the truth that I seek after, by which I am sure that never any man was hurt; and as sure, that he is hurt that continueth in any error, or ignorance whatsoever.

XXI. I for my part will do what belongs unto me; as for other things, whether things unsensible or things irrational; or if rational, yet deceived and ignorant of the true way, they shall not trouble or distract me. For as for those creatures which are not endued with reason and all other things and matters of the world whatsoever I freely, and generously, as one endued with reason, of things that have none, make use of them. And as for men, towards them as naturally partakers of the same reason, my care is to carry myself sociably. But whatsoever it is that thou art about, remember to call upon the Gods. And as for the time how long thou shalt live to do these things, let it be altogether indifferent unto thee, for even three such hours are sufficient.

XXII. Alexander of Macedon, and he that dressed his mules, when once dead both came to one. For either they were both resumed into those original rational essences from whence all things in the world are propagated; or both after one fashion were scattered into atoms.

XXIII Consider how many different things, whether they concern our bodies, or our souls, in a moment of time come to pass in every one of us, and so thou wilt not wonder if many more things or rather all things that are done, can at one time subsist, and coexist in that both one and general, which we call the world.

XXIV. if any should put this question unto thee, how this word Antoninus is written, wouldst thou not presently fix thine intention upon it, and utter out in order every letter of it? And if any shall begin to gainsay thee, and quarrel with thee about it; wilt thou quarrel with him again, or rather go on meekly as thou hast begun, until thou hast numbered out every letter? Here then likewise remember, that every duty that belongs unto a man doth consist of some certain letters or numbers as it were, to which without any noise or tumult keeping thyself thou must orderly proceed to thy proposed end, forbearing to quarrel with him that would quarrel and fall out with thee.

XXV. Is it not a cruel thing to forbid men to affect those things, which they conceive to agree best with their own natures, and to tend most to their own proper good and behoof? But thou after a sort deniest them this liberty, as often as thou art angry with them for their sins. For surely they are led unto those sins whatsoever they be, as to their proper good and commodity. But it is not so (thou wilt object perchance). Thou therefore teach them better, and make it appear unto them: but be not thou angry with them.

XXVI. Death is a cessation from the impression of the senses, the tyranny of the passions, the errors of the mind, and the servitude of the body.

XXVII. If in this kind of life thy body be able to hold out, it is a shame that thy soul should faint first, and give over, take heed, lest of a philosopher thou become a mere Caesar in time, and receive a new tincture from the court. For it may happen if thou dost not take heed. Keep thyself therefore, truly simple, good, sincere, grave, free from all ostentation, a lover of that which is just, religious, kind, tender-hearted, strong and vigorous to undergo anything that becomes thee. Endeavour to continue such, as philosophy (hadst thou wholly and constantly applied thyself unto it) would have made, and secured thee. Worship the Gods, procure the welfare of men, this life is short. Charitable actions, and a holy disposition, is the only fruit of this earthly life.

XXVIII. Do all things as becometh the disciple of Antoninus Pius. Remember his resolute constancy in things that were done by him according to reason, his equability in all things, his sanctity; the cheerfulness of his countenance, his sweetness, and how free he was from all vainglory; how careful to come to the true and exact knowledge of matters in hand, and how he would by no means give over till he did fully, and plainly understand the whole state of the business; and how patiently, and without any contestation he would bear with them, that did unjustly condemn him: how he would never be over-hasty in anything, nor give ear to slanders and false accusations, but examine and observe with best diligence the several actions and dispositions of men. Again, how he was no backbiter, nor easily frightened, nor suspicious, and in his language free from all affectation and curiosity: and how easily he would content himself with few things, as lodging, bedding, clothing, and ordinary nourishment, and attendance. How able to endure labour, how patient; able through his spare diet to continue from morning to evening without any necessity of withdrawing before his accustomed hours to the necessities of nature: his uniformity and constancy in matter of friendship. How he would bear with them that with all boldness and liberty opposed his opinions; and even rejoice if any man could better advise him: and lastly, how religious he was without superstition. All these things of him remember, that whensoever thy last hour shall come upon thee, it may find thee, as it did him, ready for it in the possession of a good conscience.

XXIX. Stir up thy mind, and recall thy wits again from thy natural dreams, and visions, and when thou art perfectly awoken, and canst perceive that they were but dreams that troubled thee, as one newly awakened out of another kind of sleep look upon these worldly things with the same mind as thou didst upon those, that thou sawest in thy sleep.

XXX. I consist of body and soul. Unto my body all things are indifferent, for of itself it cannot affect one thing more than another with apprehension of any difference; as for my mind, all things which are not within the verge of her own operation, are indifferent unto her, and for her own operations, those altogether depend of her; neither does she busy herself about any, but those that are present; for as for future and past operations, those also are now at this present indifferent unto her.

XXXI. As long as the foot doth that which belongeth unto it to do, and the hand that which belongs unto it, their labour, whatsoever it be, is not unnatural. So a man as long as he doth that which is proper unto a man, his labour cannot be against nature; and if it be not against nature, then neither is it hurtful unto him. But if it were so that happiness did consist in pleasure: how came notorious robbers, impure abominable livers, parricides, and tyrants, in so large a measure to have their part of pleasures?

XXXII. Dost thou not see, how even those that profess mechanic arts, though in some respect they be no better than mere idiots, yet they stick close to the course of their trade, neither can they find in their heart to decline from it: and is it not a grievous thing that an architect, or a physician shall respect the course and mysteries of their profession, more than a man the proper course and condition of his own nature, reason, which is common to him and to the Gods?

XXXIII. Asia, Europe; what are they, but as corners of the whole world; of which the whole sea, is but as one drop; and the great Mount Athos, but as a clod, as all present time is but as one point of eternity. All, petty things; all things that are soon altered, soon perished. And all things come from one beginning; either all severally and particularly deliberated and resolved upon, by the general ruler and governor of all; or all by necessary consequence. So that the dreadful hiatus of a gaping lion, and all poison, and all hurtful things, are but (as the thorn and the mire) the necessary consequences of goodly fair things. Think not of these therefore, as things contrary to those which thou dost much honour, and respect; but consider in thy mind the true fountain of all.

XXXIV He that seeth the things that are now, hath Seen all that either was ever, or ever shall be, for all things are of one kind; and all like one unto another. Meditate often upon the connection of all things in the world; and upon the mutual relation that they have one unto another. For all things are after a sort folded and involved one within another, and by these means all agree well together. For one thing is consequent unto another, by local motion, by natural conspiration and agreement, and by substantial union, or, reduction of all substances into one.

XXXV. Fit and accommodate thyself to that estate and to those occurrences, which by the destinies have been annexed unto thee; and love those men whom thy fate it is to live with; but love them truly. An instrument, a tool, an utensil, whatsoever it be, if it be fit for the purpose it was made for, it is as it should be though he perchance that made and fitted it, be out of sight and gone. But in things natural, that power which hath framed and fitted them, is and abideth within them still: for which reason she ought also the more to be respected, and we are the more obliged (if we may live and pass our time according to her purpose and intention) to think that all is well with us, and according to our own minds. After this manner also, and in this respect it is, that he that is all in all doth enjoy his happiness.

XXXVI. What things soever are not within the proper power and jurisdiction of thine own will either to compass or avoid, if thou shalt propose unto thyself any of those things as either good, or evil; it must needs be that according as thou shalt either fall into that which thou dost think evil, or miss of that which thou dost think good, so wilt thou be ready both to complain of the Gods, and to hate those men, who either shall be so indeed, or shall by thee be suspected as the cause either of thy missing of the one, or falling into the other. And indeed we must needs commit many evils, if we incline to any of these things, more or less, with an opinion of any difference. But if we mind and fancy those things only, as good and bad, which wholly depend of our own wills, there is no more occasion why we should either murmur against the Gods, or be at enmity with any man.

XXXVII. We all work to one effect, some willingly, and with a rational apprehension of what we do: others without any such knowledge. As I think Heraclitus in a place speaketh of them that sleep, that even they do work in their kind, and do confer to the general operations of the world. One man therefore doth cooperate after one sort, and another after another sort; but even he that doth murmur, and to his power doth resist and hinder; even he as much as any doth cooperate. For of such also did the world stand in need. Now do thou consider among which of these thou wilt rank thyself. For as for him who is the Administrator of all, he will make good use of thee whether thou wilt or no, and make thee (as a part and member of the whole) so to cooperate with him, that whatsoever thou doest, shall turn to the furtherance of his own counsels, and resolutions. But be not thou for shame such a part of the whole, as that vile and ridiculous verse (which Chrysippus in a place doth mention) is a part of the comedy.

XXXVIII. Doth either the sun take upon him to do that which belongs to the rain? or his son Aesculapius that, which unto the earth doth properly belong? How is it with every one of the stars in particular? Though they all differ one from another, and have their several charges and functions by themselves, do they not all nevertheless concur and cooperate to one end?

XXXIX. If so be that the Gods have deliberated in particular of those things that should happen unto me, I must stand to their deliberation, as discrete and wise. For that a God should be an imprudent God, is a thing hard even to conceive: and why should they resolve to do me hurt? for what profit either unto them or the universe (which they specially take care for) could arise from it? But if so be that they have not deliberated of me in particular, certainly they have of the whole in general, and those things which in consequence and coherence of this general deliberation happen unto me in particular, I am bound to embrace and accept of. But if so be that they have not deliberated at all (which indeed is very irreligious for any man to believe: for then let us neither sacrifice, nor pray, nor respect our oaths, neither let us any more use any of those things, which we persuaded of the presence and secret conversation of the Gods among us, daily use and practise:) but, I say, if so be that they have not indeed either in general, or particular deliberated of any of those things, that happen unto us in this world;

yet God be thanked, that of those things that concern myself, it is lawful for me to deliberate myself, and all my deliberation is but concerning that which may be to me most profitable. Now that unto every one is most profitable, which is according to his own constitution and nature. And my nature is, to be rational in all my actions and as a good, and natural member of a city and commonwealth, towards my fellow members ever to be sociably and kindly disposed and affected. My city and country as I am Antoninus, is Rome; as a man, the whole world. Those things therefore that are expedient and profitable to those cities, are the only things that are good and expedient for me.

XL. Whatsoever in any kind doth happen to any one, is expedient to the whole. And thus much to content us might suffice, that it is expedient for the whole in general. But yet this also shalt thou generally perceive, if thou dost diligently take heed, that whatsoever doth happen to any one man or men…. And now I am content that the word expedient, should more generally be understood of those things which we otherwise call middle things, or things indifferent; as health, wealth, and the like.

XLI. As the ordinary shows of the theatre and of other such places, when thou art presented with them, affect thee; as the same things still seen, and in the same fashion, make the sight ingrateful and tedious; so must all the things that we see all our life long affect us. For all things, above and below, are still the same, and from the same causes. When then will there be an end?

XLII. Let the several deaths of men of all sorts, and of all sorts of professions, and of all sort of nations, be a perpetual object of thy thoughts,… so that thou mayst even come down to Philistio, Phoebus, and Origanion. Pass now to other generations. Thither shall we after many changes, where so many brave orators are; where so many grave philosophers; Heraclitus, Pythagoras, Socrates. Where so many heroes of the old times; and then so many brave captains of the latter times; and so many kings. After all these, where Eudoxus, Hipparchus, Archimedes; where so many other sharp, generous, industrious, subtile, peremptory dispositions; and among others, even they, that have been the greatest scoffers and deriders of the frailty and brevity of this our human life; as Menippus, and others, as many as there have been such as he. Of all these consider, that they long since are all dead, and gone. And what do they suffer by it! Nay they that have not so much as a name remaining, what are they the worse for it? One thing there is, and that only, which is worth our while in this world, and ought by us much to be esteemed; and that is, according to truth and righteousness, meekly and lovingly to converse with false, and unrighteous men.

XLIII. When thou wilt comfort and cheer thyself, call to mind the several gifts and virtues of them, whom thou dost daily converse with; as for example, the industry of the one; the modesty of another; the liberality of a third; of another some other thing. For nothing can so much rejoice thee, as the resemblances and parallels of several virtues, visible and eminent in the dispositions of those who live with thee; especially when, all at once, as near as may be, they represent themselves unto thee. And therefore thou must have them always in a readiness.

XLIV. Dost thou grieve that thou dost weigh but so many pounds, and not three hundred rather? Just as much reason hast thou to grieve that thou must live but so many years, and not longer. For as for bulk and substance thou dost content thyself with that proportion of it that is allotted unto thee, so shouldst thou for time.

XLV. Let us do our best endeavours to persuade them; but however, if reason and justice lead thee to it, do it, though they be never so much against it. But if any shall by force withstand thee, and hinder thee in it, convert thy virtuous inclination from one object unto another, from justice to contented equanimity, and cheerful patience: so that what in the one is thy hindrance, thou mayst make use of it for the exercise of another virtue: and remember that it was with due exception, and reservation, that thou didst at first incline and desire. For thou didst not set thy mind upon things impossible. Upon what then? that all thy desires might ever be moderated with this due kind of reservation. And this thou hast, and mayst always obtain, whether the thing desired be in thy power or no. And what do I care for more, if that for which I was born and brought forth into the world (to rule all my desires with reason and discretion) may be?

XLVI. The ambitious supposeth another man's act, praise and applause, to be his own happiness; the voluptuous his own sense and feeling; but he that is wise, his own action.

XLVII. It is in thy power absolutely to exclude all manner of conceit and opinion, as concerning this matter; and by the same means, to exclude all grief and sorrow from thy soul. For as for the things and objects themselves, they of themselves have no such power, whereby to beget and force upon us any opinion at all.

XLVIII. Use thyself when any man speaks unto thee, so to hearken unto him, as that in the interim thou give not way to any other thoughts; that so thou mayst (as far as is possible) seem fixed and fastened to his very soul, whosoever he be that speaks unto thee.

XLIX. That which is not good for the beehive, cannot be good for the bee.

L. Will either passengers, or patients, find fault and complain, either the one if they be well carried, or the others if well cured? Do they take care for any more than this; the one, that their shipmaster may bring them safe to land, and the other, that their physician may effect their recovery?

LI. How many of them who came into the world at the same time when I did, are already gone out of it?

LII. To them that are sick of the jaundice, honey seems bitter; and to them that are bitten by a mad dog, the water terrible; and to children, a little ball seems a fine thing. And why then should I be angry? or do I think that error and false opinion is less powerful to make men transgress, than either choler, being immoderate and excessive, to cause the jaundice; or poison, to cause rage?

LIII. No man can hinder thee to live as thy nature doth require. Nothing can happen unto thee, but what the common good of nature doth require.

LIV. What manner of men they be whom they seek to please, and what to get, and by what actions: how soon time will cover and bury all things, and how many it hath already buried!

ΒΙΒΛΙΟ ΕΚΤΟ

1. Ἡ τῶν ὅλων οὐσία εὐπειθὴς καὶ εὐτρεπής, ὁ δὲ ταύτην διοικῶν λόγος οὐδεμίαν ἐν ἑαυτῷ αἰτίαν ἔχει τοῦ κακοποιεῖν, κακίαν γὰρ οὐκ ἔχει· οὐδέ τι κακῶς ποιεῖ οὐδὲ βλάπτεταί τι ὑπ ἐκείνου. πάντα δὲ κατ ἐκεῖνον γίνεται καὶ περαίνεται.

2. Μὴ διαφέρου πότερον ῥιγῶν ἢ θαλπόμενος τὸ πρέπον ποιεῖς, καὶ πότερον νυστάζων ἢ ἱκανῶς ὕπνου ἔχων, καὶ πότερον κακῶς ἀκούων ἢ εὐφημούμενος, καὶ πότερον ἀποθνήσκων ἢ πράττων τι ἀλλοῖον· μία γὰρ τῶν βιωτικῶν πράξεων καὶ αὕτη ἐστί, καθ ἣν ἀποθνήσκομεν· ἀρκεῖ οὖν καὶ ἐπὶ ταύτης τὸ παρὸν εὖ θέσθαι.

3. Ἔσω βλέπε· μηδενὸς πράγματος μήτε ἡ ἰδία ποιότης μήτε ἡ ἀξία παρατρεχέτω σε.

4. Πάντα τὰ ὑποκείμενα τάχιστα μεταβαλεῖ καὶ ἤτοι ἐκθυμιαθήσεται, εἴπερ ἥνωται ἡ οὐσία, ἢ σκεδασθήσεται.

5. Ὁ διοικῶν λόγος οἶδε πῶς διακείμενος καὶ τί ποιεῖ καὶ ἐπὶ τίνος ὕλης.

6. Ἄριστος τρόπος τοῦ ἀμύνεσθαι τὸ μὴ ἐξομοιοῦσθαι.

7. Ἑνὶ τέρπου καὶ προσαναπαύου, τῷ ἀπὸ πράξεως κοινωνικῆς μεταβαίνειν ἐπὶ πρᾶξιν κοινωνικὴν σὺν μνήμῃ θεοῦ.

8. Τὸ ἡγεμονικόν ἐστι τὸ ἑαυτὸ ἐγεῖρον καὶ τρέπον καὶ ποιοῦν μὲν ἑαυτὸ οἷον ἂν καὶ θέλῃ, ποιοῦν δὲ ἑαυτῷ φαίνεσθαι πᾶν τὸ συμβαῖνον οἷον αὐτὸ θέλει.

9. Κατὰ τὴν τῶν ὅλων φύσιν ἕκαστα περαίνεται· οὐ γὰρ κατ ἄλλην γέ τινα φύσιν ἤτοι ἔξωθεν περιέχουσαν ἢ ἐμπεριεχομένην ἔνδον ἢ ἔξω ἀπηρτημένην.

10. Ἤτοι κυκεὼν καὶ ἀντεμπλοκὴ καὶ σκεδασμὸς ἢ ἕνωσις καὶ τάξις καὶ πρόνοια. εἰ μὲν οὖν τὰ πρότερα, τί καὶ ἐπιθυμῶ εἰκαίῳ συγκρίματι καὶ φυρμῷ

τοιούτῳ ἐνδιατρίβειν; τί δέ μοι καὶ μέλει ἄλλου τινὸς ἢ τοῦ ὅπως ποτὲ "αἶα γίνεσθα"; τί δὲ καὶ ταράσσομαι; ἥξει γὰρ ἐπ ἐμὲ ὁ σκεδασμός, ὅ τι ἂν ποιῶ. εἰ δὲ θάτερά ἐστι, σέβω καὶ εὐσταθῶ καὶ θαρρῶ τῷ διοικοῦντι.

11. Ὅταν ἀναγκασθῇς ὑπὸ τῶν περιεστηκότων οἱονεὶ διαταραχθῆναι, ταχέως ἐπάνιθι εἰς ἑαυτὸν καὶ μὴ ὑπὲρ τὰ ἀναγκαῖα ἐξίστασο τοῦ ῥυθμοῦ· ἔσῃ γὰρ ἐγκρατέστερος τῆς ἁρμονίας τῷ συνεχῶς εἰς αὐτὴν ἐπανέρχεσθαι.

12. Εἰ μητρυιάν τε ἅμα εἶχες καὶ μητέρα, ἐκείνην τ ἂν ἐθεράπευες καὶ ὅμως ἡ ἐπάνοδός σοι πρὸς τὴν μητέρα συνεχὴς ἐγίνετο. τοῦτό σοι νῦν ἐστιν ἡ αὐλὴ καὶ ἡ φιλοσοφία· ὧδε πολλάκις ἐπάνιθι καὶ προσαναπαύου ταύτῃ, δι ἣν καὶ τὰ ἐκεῖ σοι ἀνεκτὰ φαίνεται καὶ σὺ ἐν αὐτοῖς ἀνεκτός.

13. Οἷον δὴ τὸ φαντασίαν λαμβάνειν ἐπὶ τῶν ὄψων καὶ τῶν τοιούτων ἐδωδίμων, ὅτι νεκρὸς οᾗτος ἰχθύος, οᾗτος δὲ νεκρὸς ὄρνιθος ἢ χοίρου· καὶ πάλιν, ὅτι ὁ Φάλερνος χυλάριόν ἐστι σταφυλίου καὶ ἡ περιπόρφυρος τριχία προβατίου αἵματίῳ κόγχης δεδευμένα· καὶ ἐπὶ τῶν κατὰ τὴν συνουσίαν ἐντερίου παράτριψις καὶ μετά τινος σπασμοῦ μυξαρίου ἔκκρισις· οἶαι δὴ αᾗταί εἰσιν αἱ φαντασίαι καθικνούμεναι αὐτῶν τῶν πραγμάτων καὶ διεξιοῦσαι δι αὐτῶν, ὥστε ὁρᾶν οἷά τινά ποτ ἐστιν. οὕτως δεῖ παρ ὅλον τὸν βίον ποιεῖν καὶ ὅπου λίαν ἀξιόπιστα τὰ πράγματα φαντάζεται, ἀπογυμνοῦν αὐτὰ καὶ τὴν εὐτέλειαν αὐτῶν καθορᾶν καὶ τὴν ἱστορίαν ἐφ ᾗ σεμνύνεται περιαιρεῖν. δεινὸς γὰρ ὁ τῦφος παραλογιστὴς καὶ ὅτε δοκεῖς μάλιστα περὶ τὰ σπουδαῖα καταγίνεσθαι, τότε μάλιστα καταγοητεύῃ. ὅρα γοῦν ὁ Κράτης τί περὶ αὐτοῦ τοῦ Ξενοκράτους λέγει.

14. Τὰ πλεῖστα, ὧν ἡ πληθὺς θαυμάζει, εἰς γενικώτατα ἀνάγεται τὰ ὑπὸ ἕξεως ἢ φύσεως συνεχόμενα, λίθους, ξύλα, συκᾶς, ἀμπέλους, ἐλαίας· τὰ δὲ ὑπὸ τῶν ὀλίγῳ μετριωτέρων εἰς τὰ ὑπὸ ψυχῆς, οἷον ποίμνας, ἀγέλας ἢ κατὰ ψιλὸν τὸ πλῆθος ἀνδραπόδων κεκτῆσθαι. τὰ δὲ ὑπὸ τῶν ἔτι χαριεστέρων εἰς τὰ ὑπὸ λογικῆς ψυχῆς, οὐ μέντοι καθὸ λογική, ἀλλὰ καθὸ τεχνικὴ ἢ ἄλλως πως ἐντρεχής. ὁ δὲ ψυχὴν λογικὴν καὶ πολιτικὴν τιμῶν οὐδὲν ἔτι τῶν ἄλλων ἐπιστρέφεται, πρὸ ἁπάντων δὲ τὴν ἑαυτοῦ ψυχὴν λογικῶς καὶ κοινωνικῶς ἔχουσαν καὶ κινουμένην διασῴζει καὶ τῷ ὁμογενεῖ εἰς τοῦτο συνεργεῖ.

15. Τὰ μὲν σπεύδει γίνεσθαι, τὰ δὲ σπεύδει γεγονέναι, καὶ τοῦ γινομένου δὲ ἤδη τι ἀπέσβη· ῥύσεις καὶ ἀλλοιώσεις ἀνανεοῦσι τὸν κόσμον διηνεκῶς, ὥσπερ τὸν ἄπειρον αἰῶνα ἡ τοῦ χρόνου ἀδιάλειπτος φορὰ νέον ἀεὶ παρέχεται. ἐν δὴ τούτῳ τῷ ποταμῷ, ἐφ ᾧ στῆναι οὐκ ἔξεστιν, τί ἄν τις τούτων τῶν παραθεόντων ἐκτιμήσειεν; ὥσπερ εἴ τίς τι τῶν παραπετομένων στρουθαρίων φιλεῖν ἄρχοιτο,

τὸ δ ἤδη ἐξ ὀφθαλμῶν ἀπελήλυθεν. τοιοῦτον δή τι καὶ αὐτὴ ἡ ζωὴ ἑκάστου, οἷον ἡ ἀφ αἵματος ἀναθυμίασις καὶ ἡ ἐκ τοῦ ἀέρος ἀνάπνευσις· ὁποῖον γάρ ἐστι τὸ ἅπαξ ἑλκύσαι τὸν ἀέρα καὶ ἀποδοῦναι, ὅπερ παρ ἕκαστον ποιοῦμεν, τοιοῦτόν ἐστι καὶ τὸ τὴν πᾶσαν ἀναπνευστικὴν δύναμιν, ἣν χθὲς καὶ πρῴ ἣν ἀποτεχθεὶς ἐκτήσω, ἀποδοῦναι ἐκεῖ ὅθεν τὸ πρῶτον ἔσπασας.

16. Οὔτε τὸ διαπνεῖσθαι ὡς τὰ φυτὰ τίμιον οὔτε τὸ ἀναπνεῖν ὡς τὰ βοσκήματα καὶ τὰ θηρία οὔτε τὸ τυποῦσθαι κατὰ φαντασίαν οὔτε τὸ νευροσπαστεῖσθαι καθ ὁρμὴν οὔτε τὸ συναγελάζεσθαι οὔτε τὸ τρέφεσθαι· τοῦτο γὰρ ὅμοιον τῷ ἀποκρίνειν τὰ περιττώματα τῆς τροφῆς. τί οὖν τίμιον; τὸ κροτεῖσθαι; οὐχί. οὐκοῦν οὐδὲ τὸ ὑπὸ γλωσσῶν κροτεῖσθαι· αἱ γὰρ παρὰ τῶν πολλῶν εὐφημίαι κρότος γλωσσῶν. ἀφῆκας οὖν καὶ τὸ δοξάριον· τί καταλείπεται τίμιον; δοκῶ μὲν τὸ κατὰ τὴν ἰδίαν κατασκευὴν κινεῖσθαι καὶ ἴσχεσθαι, ἐφ ὃ καὶ αἱ ἐπιμέλειαι ἄγουσι καὶ αἱ τέχναι· (ἥ τε γὰρ τέχνη πᾶσα τούτου στοχάζεται, ἵνα τὸ κατασκευασθὲν ἐπιτηδείως ἔχῃ πρὸς τὸ ἔργον πρὸς ὃ κατεσκεύασται· ὅ τε φυτουργὸς ‹καὶ› ὁ ἐπιμελούμενος τῆς ἀμπέλου, καὶ ὁ πωλοδάμνης καὶ ὁ τοῦ κυνὸς ἐπιμελούμενος τοῦτο ζητεῖ.) αἱ δὲ παιδαγωγίαι, αἱ δὲ διδασκαλίαι ἐπὶ τί σπεύδουσιν; ὧδε οὖν τὸ τίμιον· καὶ τοῦτο μὲν ἂν εὖ ἔχῃ, οὐδὲν τῶν ἄλλων περιποιήσεις ἑαυτῷ. οὐ παύσῃ καὶ ἄλλα πολλὰ τιμῶν; οὔτ οὖν ἐλεύθερος ἔσῃ οὔτε αὐτάρκης οὔτε ἀπαθής· ἀνάγκη γὰρ φθονεῖν, ζηλοτυπεῖν, ὑφορᾶσθαι τοὺς ἀφελέσθαι ἐκεῖνα δυναμένους, ἐπιβουλεύειν τοῖς ἔχουσι τὸ τιμώμενον ὑπὸ σοῦ· ὅλως πεφύρθαι ἀνάγκη τὸν ἐκείνων τινὸς ἐνδεῆ, προσέτι δὲ πολλὰ καὶ τοῖς θεοῖς μέμφεσθαι. ἡ δὲ τῆς ἰδίας διανοίας αἰδὼς καὶ τιμὴ σεαυτῷ τε ἀρεστόν σε ποιήσει καὶ τοῖς κοινωνοῖς εὐάρμοστον καὶ τοῖς θεοῖς σύμφωνον, τουτέστιν ἐπαινοῦντα ὅσα ἐκεῖνοι διανέμουσι καὶ διατετάχασιν.

17. Ἄνω, κάτω, κύκλῳ ‹αἱ› φοραὶ τῶν στοιχείων, ἡ δὲ τῆς ἀρετῆς κίνησις ἐν οὐδεμιᾷ τούτων, ἀλλὰ θειότερόν τι καὶ ὁδῷ δυσεπινοήτῳ προιοῦσα εὐοδεῖ.

18. Οἷόν ἐστιν ὃ ποιοῦσι. τοὺς μὲν ἐπὶ τοῦ αὐτοῦ χρόνου καὶ μεθ ἑαυτῶν ζῶντας ἀνθρώπους εὐφημεῖν οὐ θέλουσιν, αὐτοὶ δὲ ὑπὸ τῶν μεταγενεστέρων εὐφημηθῆναι, οὓς οὔτε εἶδόν ποτε οὔτε ὄψονται, περὶ πολλοῦ ποιοῦνται. τοῦτο δὲ ἐγγύς ἐστι τῷ λυπηθῆναι ἄν, ὅτι οὐχὶ καὶ οἱ προγενέστεροι περὶ σοῦ λόγους εὐφήμους ἐποιοῦντο.

19. Μή, εἴ τι αὐτῷ σοὶ δυσκαταπόνητον, τοῦτο ἀνθρώπῳ ἀδύνατον ὑπολαμβάνειν, ἀλλ εἴ τι ἀνθρώπῳ δυνατὸν καὶ οἰκεῖον, τοῦτο καὶ σεαυτῷ ἐφικτὸν νομίζειν.

20. Ἐν τοῖς γυμνασίοις καὶ ὄνυξι κατέδρυψέ τις καὶ τῇ κεφαλῇ ἐρραγεὶς πληγὴν ἐποίησεν, ἀλλ οὔτε ἐπισημαινόμεθα οὔτε προσκόπτομεν οὔτε ὑφορώμεθα ὕστερον ὡς ἐπίβουλον· καίτοι φυλαττόμεθα, οὐ μέντοι ὡς ἐχθρὸν οὐδὲ μεθ ὑποψίας, ἀλλ ἐκκλίσεως εὐμενοῦς. τοιοῦτόν τι γινέσθω καὶ ἐν τοῖς λοιποῖς μέρεσι τοῦ βίου· πολλὰ παρενθυμώμεθα τῶν οἷον προσγυμναζομένων. ἔξεστι γάρ, ὡς ἔφην, ἐκκλίνειν καὶ μήτε ὑποπτεύειν μήτε ἀπέχθεσθαι.

21. Εἴ τίς με ἐλέγξαι καὶ παραστῆσαί μοι, ὅτι οὐκ ὀρθῶς ὑπολαμβάνω ἢ πράσσω, δύναται, χαίρων μεταθήσομαι· ζητῶ γὰρ τὴν ἀλήθειαν, ὑφ ἧς οὐδεὶς πώποτε ἐβλάβη, βλάπτεται δὲ ὁ ἐπιμένων ἐπὶ τῆς ἑαυτοῦ ἀπάτης καὶ ἀγνοίας.

22. Ἐγὼ τὸ ἐμαυτοῦ καθῆκον ποιῶ, τὰ ἄλλα με οὐ περισπᾷ· ἤτοι γὰρ ἄψυχα ἢ ἄλογα ἢ πεπλανημένα καὶ τὴν ὁδὸν ἀγνοοῦντα.

23. Τοῖς μὲν ἀλόγοις ζῴοις καὶ καθόλου πράγμασι καὶ ὑποκειμένοις, ὡς λόγον ἔχων λόγον μὴ ἔχουσι, χρῶ μεγαλοφρόνως καὶ ἐλευθέρως· τοῖς δὲ ἀνθρώποις, ὡς λόγον ἔχουσι, χρῶ κοινωνικῶς· ἐφ ἅπασι δὲ θεοὺς ἐπικαλοῦ. καὶ μὴ διαφέρου πρὸς τὸ πόσῳ χρόνῳ ταῦτα πράξεις· ἀρκοῦσι γὰρ καὶ τρεῖς ὧραι τοιαῦται.

24. Ἀλέξανδρος ὁ Μακεδὼν καὶ ὁ ὀρεωκόμος αὐτοῦ ἀποθανόντες εἰς ταὐτὸ κατέστησαν· ἤτοι γὰρ ‹ἀν›ελήφθησαν εἰς τοὺς αὐτοὺς τοῦ κόσμου σπερματικοὺς λόγους ἢ διεσκεδάσθησαν ὁμοίως εἰς τὰς ἀτόμους.

25. Ἐνθυμήθητι πόσα κατὰ τὸν αὐτὸν ἀκαριαῖον χρόνον ἐν ἑκάστῳ ἡμῶν ἅμα γίνεται σωματικὰ ὁμοῦ καὶ ψυχικά, καὶ οὕτως οὐ θαυμάσεις εἰ πολὺ πλείω, μᾶλλον δὲ πάντα τὰ γινόμενα ἐν τῷ ἑνί τε καὶ σύμπαντι, ὃ δὴ κόσμον ὀνομάζομεν, ἅμα ἐνυφίσταται.

26. Ἐάν τίς σοι προβάλῃ πῶς γράφεται τὸ Ἀντωνίνου ὄνομα, μήτι κατεντεινόμενος προοίσῃ ἕκαστον τῶν στοιχείων; τί οὖν ἐὰν ὀργίζωνται, μήτι ἀντοργιῇ; μήτι οὐκ ἐξαριθμήσῃ πράως προϊὼν ἕκαστον τῶν γραμμάτων; οὕτως οὖν καὶ ἐνθάδε μέμνησο ὅτι πᾶν καθῆκον ἐξ ἀριθμῶν τινῶν συμπληροῦται. τούτους δεῖ τηροῦντα καὶ μὴ θορυβούμενον μηδὲ τοῖς δυσχεραίνουσιν ἀντιδυσχεραίνοντα περαίνειν ὁδῷ τὸ προκείμενον.

27. Πῶς ὠμόν ἐστι μὴ ἐπιτρέπειν τοῖς ἀνθρώποις ὁρμᾶν ἐπὶ τὰ φαινόμενα αὐτοῖς οἰκεῖα καὶ συμφέροντα. καίτοι τρόπον τινὰ οὐ συγχωρεῖς αὐτοῖς τοῦτο

ποιεῖν, ὅταν ἀγανακτῇς, ὅτι ἁμαρτάνουσι· φέρονται γὰρ πάντως ὡς ἐπὶ οἰκεῖα καὶ συμφέροντα αὐτοῖς. "ἀλλ οὐκ ἔχει οὕτως." οὐκοῦν δίδασκε καὶ δείκνυε μὴ ἀγανακτῶν.

28. Θάνατος ἀνάπαυλα αἰσθητικῆς ἀντιτυπίας καὶ ὁρμητικῆς νευροσπαστίας καὶ διανοητικῆς διεξόδου καὶ τῆς πρὸς τὴν σάρκα λειτουργίας.

29. Αἰσχρόν ἐστιν, ἐν ᾧ βίῳ τὸ σῶμά σοι μὴ ἀπαυδᾷ, ἐν τούτῳ τὴν ψυχὴν προαπαυδᾶν.

30. Ὅρα μὴ ἀποκαισαρωθῇς, μὴ βαφῇς· γίνεται γάρ. τήρησον οὖν σεαυτὸν ἁπλοῦν, ἀγαθόν, ἀκέραιον, σεμνόν, ἄκομψον, τοῦ δικαίου φίλον, θεοσεβῆ, εὐμενῆ, φιλόστοργον, ἐρρωμένον πρὸς τὰ πρέποντα ἔργα. ἀγώνισαι, ἵνα τοιοῦτος συμμείνῃς, οἷόν σε ἠθέλησε ποιῆσαι φιλοσοφία. αἰδοῦ θεούς, σῷζε ἀνθρώπους. βραχὺς ὁ βίος· εἷς καρπὸς τῆς ἐπιγείου ζωῆς, διάθεσις ὁσία καὶ πράξεις κοινωνικαί. πάντα ὡς Ἀντωνίνου μαθητής· τὸ ὑπὲρ τῶν κατὰ λόγον πρασσομένων εὔτονον ἐκείνου καὶ τὸ ὁμαλὲς πανταχοῦ καὶ τὸ ὅσιον καὶ τὸ εὔδιον τοῦ προσώπου καὶ τὸ μειλίχιον καὶ τὸ ἀκενόδοξον καὶ τὸ περὶ τὴν κατάληψιν τῶν πραγμάτων φιλότιμον· καὶ ὡς ἐκεῖνος οὐκ ἄν τι ὅλως παρῆκε, μὴ πρότερον εὖ μάλα κατιδὼν καὶ σαφῶς νοήσας· καὶ ὡς ἔφερεν ἐκεῖνος τοὺς ἀδίκως αὐτῷ μεμφομένους μὴ ἀντιμεμφόμενος· καὶ ὡς ἐπ οὐδὲν ἔσπευδεν· καὶ ὡς διαβολὰς οὐκ ἐδέχετο· καὶ ὡς ἀκριβὴς ἦν ἐξεταστὴς ἠθῶν καὶ πράξεων καὶ οὐκ ὀνειδιστής, οὐ ψοφοδεής, οὐχ ὑπόπτης, οὐ σοφιστής· καὶ ὡς ὀλίγοις ἀρκούμενος, οἷον οἰκήσει, στρωμνῇ, ἐσθῆτι, τροφῇ, ὑπηρεσίᾳ· καὶ ὡς φιλόπονος καὶ μακρόθυμος· καὶ οἷος μέν‹ειν› ἐν τῷ ‹αὐτῷ› μέχρι ἑσπέρας διὰ τὴν λιτὴν δίαιταν μηδὲ τοῦ ἀποκρίνειν τὰ περιττώματα παρὰ τὴν συνήθη ὥραν χρῄζων· καὶ τὸ βέβαιον καὶ ὅμοιον ἐν ταῖς φιλίαις αὐτοῦ· καὶ τὸ ἀνέχεσθαι ‹τῶν› ἀντιβαινόντων παρρησιαστικῶς ταῖς γνώμαις αὐτοῦ καὶ χαίρειν εἴ τίς ‹τι› δεικνύοι κρεῖττον· καὶ ὡς θεοσεβὴς χωρὶς δεισιδαιμονίας· ἵν οὕτως εὐσυνειδήτω σοι ἐπιστῇ ἡ τελευταία ὥρα ὡς ἐκείνῳ.

31. Ἀνάνηψε καὶ ἀνακαλοῦ σεαυτὸν καὶ ἐξυπνισθεὶς πάλιν καὶ ἐννοήσας ὅτι ὄνειροί σοι ἠνώχλουν, πάλιν ἐγρηγορὼς βλέπε ταῦτα, ὡς ἐκεῖνα ἔβλεπες.

32. Ἐκ σωματίου εἰμὶ καὶ ψυχῆς. τῷ μὲν οὖν σωματίῳ πάντα ἀδιάφορα· οὐδὲ γὰρ δύναται διαφέρεσθαι. τῇ δὲ διανοίᾳ ἀδιάφορα ὅσα μή ἐστιν αὐτῆς ἐνεργήματα· ὅσα δέ γε αὐτῆς ἐστιν ἐνεργήματα, ταῦτα πάντα ἐπ αὐτῇ ἐστιν. καὶ τούτων μέντοι περὶ μόνον τὸ παρὸν πραγματεύεται· τὰ γὰρ μέλλοντα καὶ παρῳχηκότα ἐνεργήματα αὐτῆς καὶ αὐτὰ ἤδη ἀδιάφορα.

121

33. Οὐκ ἔστιν ὁ πόνος τῇ χειρὶ οὐδὲ τῷ ποδὶ παρὰ φύσιν, μέχρις ἂν ποιῇ ὁ ποὺς τὰ τοῦ ποδὸς καὶ ἡ χεὶρ τὰ τῆς χειρός. οὕτως οὖν οὐδὲ ἀνθρώπῳ ὡς ἀνθρώπῳ παρὰ φύσιν ἐστὶν ὁ πόνος, μέχρις ἂν ποιῇ τὰ τοῦ ἀνθρώπου· εἰ δὲ παρὰ φύσιν αὐτῷ οὐκ ἔστιν, οὐδὲ κακόν ἐστιν αὐτῷ.

34. Ἡλίκας ἡδονὰς ἥσθησαν λησταί, κίναιδοι, πατραλοῖαι, τύραννοι.

35. Οὐχ ὁρᾷς πῶς οἱ βάναυσοι τεχνῖται ἁρμόζονται μὲν μέχρι τινὸς πρὸς τοὺς ἰδιώτας, οὐδὲν ἧσσον μέντοι ἀντέχονται τοῦ λόγου τῆς τέχνης καὶ τούτου ἀποστῆναι οὐχ ὑπομένουσιν; οὐ δεινὸν εἰ ὁ ἀρχιτέκτων καὶ ὁ ἰατρὸς μᾶλλον αἰδέσονται τὸν τῆς ἰδίας τέχνης λόγον ἢ ὁ ἄνθρωπος τὸν ἑαυτοῦ, ὃς αὐτῷ κοινός ἐστι πρὸς τοὺς θεούς;

36. Ἡ Ἀσία, ἡ Εὐρώπη γωνίαι τοῦ κόσμου· πᾶν πέλαγος σταγὼν τοῦ κόσμου· Ἄθως βωλάριον τοῦ κόσμου· πᾶν τὸ ἐνεστὼς τοῦ χρόνου στιγμὴ τοῦ αἰῶνος. πάντα μικρά, εὔτρεπτα, ἐναφανιζόμενα. Πάντα ἐκεῖθεν ἔρχεται, ἀπ᾽ ἐκείνου τοῦ κοινοῦ ἡγεμονικοῦ ὁρμήσαντα ἢ κατ᾽ ἐπακολούθησιν. καὶ τὸ χάσμα οὖν τοῦ λέοντος καὶ τὸ δηλητήριον καὶ πᾶσα κακουργία, ὡς ἄκανθα, ὡς βόρβορος, ἐκείνων ἐπιγεννήματα τῶν σεμνῶν καὶ καλῶν. μὴ οὖν αὐτὰ ἀλλότρια τούτου οὗ σέβεις φαντάζου, ἀλλὰ τὴν πάντων πηγὴν ἐπιλογίζου.

37. Ὁ τὰ νῦν ἰδὼν πάντα ἑώρακεν, ὅσα τε ἐξ ἀϊδίου ἐγένετο καὶ ὅσα εἰς τὸ ἄπειρον ἔσται· πάντα γὰρ ὁμογενῆ καὶ ὁμοειδῆ.

38. Πολλάκις ἐνθυμοῦ τὴν ἐπισύνδεσιν πάντων τῶν ἐν τῷ κόσμῳ καὶ σχέσιν πρὸς ἄλληλα. τρόπον γάρ τινα πάντα ἀλλήλοις ἐπιπέπλεκται καὶ πάντα κατὰ τοῦτο φίλα ἀλλήλοις ἐστί· καὶ γὰρ ἄλλῳ ‹ἄλλο› ἑξῆς ἐστι ταῦτα διὰ τὴν τονικὴν κίνησιν καὶ σύμπνοιαν καὶ τὴν ἕνωσιν τῆς οὐσίας.

39. Οἷς συγκεκλήρωσαι πράγμασι, τούτοις συνάρμοζε σεαυτόν, καὶ οἷς συνείληχας ἀνθρώποις, τούτους φίλει, ἀλλ᾽ ἀληθινῶς.

40. Ὄργανον, ἐργαλεῖον, σκεῦος πᾶν εἰς πρὸς ὃ κατεσκεύασται ποιεῖ, εὖ ἔχει· καίτοι ἐκεῖ ὁ κατασκευάσας ἐκποδών. ἐπὶ δὲ τῶν ὑπὸ φύσεως συνεχομένων ἔνδον ἐστὶ καὶ παραμένει ἡ κατασκευάσασα δύναμις· καθὸ καὶ μᾶλλον αἰδεῖσθαι αὐτὴν δεῖ καὶ νομίζειν, ἐὰν κατὰ τὸ βούλημα ταύτης ἔχῃς καὶ διεξάγῃς, ἔχειν σοι πάντα κατὰ νοῦν. ἔχει δὲ οὕτως καὶ τῷ παντὶ κατὰ νοῦν τὰ ἑαυτοῦ.

122

41. Ὅ τι ἂν τῶν ἀπροαιρέτων ὑποστήσῃ σαυτῷ ἀγαθὸν ἢ κακόν, ἀνάγκη κατὰ τὴν περίπτωσιν τοῦ τοιούτου κακοῦ ἢ τὴν ἀπότευξιν τοῦ τοιούτου ἀγαθοῦ μέμψασθαί σε θεοῖς καὶ ἀνθρώπους δὲ μισῆσαι τοὺς αἰτίους ὄντας ἢ ὑποπτευομένους ἔσεσθαι τῆς ἀποτεύξεως ἢ τῆς περιπτώσεως· καὶ ἀδικοῦμεν δὴ πολλὰ διὰ τὴν πρὸς ταῦτα διαφοράν. ἐὰν δὲ μόνα τὰ ἐφ᾽ ἡμῖν ἀγαθὰ καὶ κακὰ κρίνωμεν, οὐδεμία αἰτία καταλείπεται οὔτε θεῷ ἐγκαλέσαι οὔτε πρὸς ἄνθρωπον στῆναι στάσιν πολεμίου.

42. Πάντες εἰς ἓν ἀποτέλεσμα συνεργοῦμεν, οἱ μὲν εἰδότως καὶ παρακολουθητικῶς, οἱ δὲ ἀνεπιστάτως, ὥσπερ καὶ τοὺς καθεύδοντας, οἶμαι, ὁ Ἡράκλειτος ἐργάτας εἶναι λέγει καὶ συνεργοὺς τῶν ἐν τῷ κόσμῳ γινομένων. ἄλλος δὲ κατ᾽ ἄλλο συνεργεῖ, ἐκ περιουσίας δὲ καὶ ὁ μεμφόμενος καὶ ὁ ἀντιβαίνειν πειρώμενος καὶ ἀναιρεῖν τὰ γινόμενα· καὶ γὰρ τοῦ τοιούτου ἔχρῃζεν ὁ κόσμος. λοιπὸν οὖν σύνες εἰς τίνας ἑαυτὸν κατατάσσεις· ἐκεῖνος μὲν γὰρ πάντως σοι καλῶς χρήσεται ὁ τὰ ὅλα διοικῶν καὶ παραδέξεταί σε εἰς μέρος τι τῶν συνεργῶν καὶ συνεργητικῶν, ἀλλὰ σὺ μὴ τοιοῦτο μέρος γένῃ, οἷος ὁ εὐτελὴς καὶ γελοῖος στίχος ἐν τῷ δράματι, οὗ Χρύσιππος μέμνηται.

43. Μήτι ὁ Ἥλιος τὰ τοῦ Ὑετίου ἀξιοῖ ποιεῖν; μήτι ὁ Ἀσκληπιὸς τὰ τῆς Καρποφόρου; τί δὲ τῶν ἄστρων ἕκαστον; οὐχὶ διάφορα μέν, συνεργὰ δὲ πρὸς ταὐτόν;

44. Εἰ μὲν οὖν ἐβουλεύσαντο περὶ ἐμοῦ καὶ τῶν ἐμοὶ συμβῆναι ὀφειλόντων οἱ θεοί, καλῶς ἐβουλεύσαντο· ἄβουλον γὰρ θεὸν οὐδὲ ἐπινοῆσαι ῥάδιον, κακοποιῆσαι δέ με διὰ τίνα αἰτίαν ἔμελλον ὁρμᾶν; τί γὰρ αὐτοῖς ἢ τῷ κοινῷ, οὗ μάλιστα προνοοῦνται, ἐκ τούτου περιεγένετο; εἰ δὲ μὴ ἐβουλεύσαντο κατ᾽ ἰδίαν περὶ ἐμοῦ, περί γε τῶν κοινῶν πάντως ἐβουλεύσαντο, οἷς κατ᾽ ἐπακολούθησιν καὶ ταῦτα συμβαίνοντα ἀσπάζεσθαι καὶ στέργειν ὀφείλω. εἰ δ᾽ ἄρα περὶ μηδενὸς βουλεύονται (πιστεύειν μὲν οὐχ ὅσιον ἢ μηδὲ θύωμεν μηδὲ εὐχώμεθα μηδὲ ὀμνύωμεν μηδὲ τὰ ἄλλα πράσσωμεν ἃ παρ᾽ ἕκαστα ὡς πρὸς παρόντας καὶ συμβιοῦντας τοὺς θεοὺς πράσσομεν), εἰ δ᾽ ἄρα περὶ μηδενὸς τῶν καθ᾽ ἡμᾶς βουλεύονται, ἐμοὶ μὲν ἔξεστι περὶ ἐμαυτοῦ βουλεύεσθαι, ἐμοὶ δέ ἐστι σκέψις περὶ τοῦ συμφέροντος. συμφέρει δὲ ἑκάστῳ τὸ κατὰ τὴν ἑαυτοῦ κατασκευὴν καὶ φύσιν, ἡ δὲ ἐμὴ φύσις λογικὴ καὶ πολιτική. Πόλις καὶ πατρὶς ὡς μὲν Ἀντωνίνῳ μοι ἡ Ῥώμη, ὡς δὲ ἀνθρώπῳ ὁ κόσμος. τὰ ταῖς πόλεσιν οὖν ταύταις ὠφέλιμα μόνα ἐστί μοι ἀγαθά.

45. Ὅσα ἑκάστῳ συμβαίνει, ταῦτα τῷ ὅλῳ συμφέρει· ἤρκει τοῦτο. ἀλλ᾽ ἔτι ἐκεῖνο ὡς ἐπίπαν ὄψει παραφυλάξας, ὅσα ἀνθρώπῳ, καὶ ἑτέροις ἀνθρώποις.

κοινότερον δὲ νῦν τὸ συμφέρον ἐπὶ τῶν μέσων λαμβανέσθω.

46. Ὥσπερ προσίσταταί σοι τὰ ἐν τῷ ἀμφιθεάτρῳ καὶ τοῖς τοιούτοις χωρίοις ὡς ἀεὶ τὰ αὐτὰ ὁρώμενα, καὶ τὸ ὁμοειδὲς προσκορῆ τὴν θέαν ποιεῖ, τοῦτο καὶ ἐπὶ ὅλου τοῦ βίου πάσχεις· πάντα γὰρ ἄνω κάτω τὰ αὐτὰ καὶ ἐκ τῶν αὐτῶν. μέχρι τίνος οὖν;

47. Ἐννόει συνεχῶς παντοίους ἀνθρώπους καὶ παντοίων μὲν ἐπιτηδευμάτων, παντοδαπῶν δὲ ἐθνῶν τεθνεῶτας, ὥστε κατιέναι τοῦτο μέχρι Φιλιστίωνος καὶ Φοίβου καὶ Ὀριγανίωνος. μέτιθι νῦν ἐπὶ τὰ ἄλλα φῦλα· ἐκεῖ δὴ μεταβαλεῖν ἡμᾶς δεῖ ὅπου τοσοῦτοι μὲν δεινοὶ ῥήτορες, τοσοῦτοι δὲ σεμνοὶ φιλόσοφοι, Ἡράκλειτος, Πυθαγόρας, Σωκράτης, τοσοῦτοι δὲ ἥρωες πρότερον, τοσοῦτοι δὲ ὕστερον στρατηγοί, τύραννοι· ἐπὶ τούτοις δὲ Εὔδοξος, Ἵππαρχος, Ἀρχιμήδης, ἄλλαι φύσεις ὀξεῖαι, μεγαλόφρονες, φιλόπονοι, πανοῦργοι, αὐθάδεις, αὐτῆς τῆς ἐπικήρου καὶ ἐφημέρου τῶν ἀνθρώπων ζωῆς χλευασταί, οἷον Μένιππος καὶ ὅσοι τοιοῦτοι. περὶ πάντων τούτων ἐννόει ὅτι πάλαι κεῖνται· τί οὖν τοῦτο δεινὸν αὐτοῖς; τί δαὶ τοῖς μηδ᾽ ὀνομαζομένοις ὅλως; ἓν ὧδε πολλοῦ ἄξιον, τὸ μετ᾽ ἀληθείας καὶ δικαιοσύνης εὐμενῆ τοῖς ψεύσταις καὶ ἀδίκοις διαβιοῦν.

48. Ὅταν εὐφρᾶναι σεαυτὸν θέλῃς, ἐνθυμοῦ τὰ προτερήματα τῶν συμβιούντων· οἷον τοῦ μὲν τὸ δραστήριον, τοῦ δὲ τὸ αἰδῆμον, τοῦ δὲ τὸ εὐμετάδοτον, ἄλλου δὲ ἄλλο τι. οὐδὲν γὰρ οὕτως εὐφραίνει ὡς τὰ ὁμοιώματα τῶν ἀρετῶν ἐμφαινόμενα τοῖς ἤθεσι τῶν συζώντων καὶ ἀθρόα ὡς οἷόν τε συμπίπτοντα. διὸ καὶ πρόχειρα αὐτὰ ἑκτέον.

49. Μήτι δυσχεραίνεις ὅτι τοσῶνδέ τινων λιτρῶν εἶ καὶ οὐ τριακοσίων; οὕτω δὴ καὶ ὅτι μέχρι τοσῶνδε ἐτῶν βιωτέον σοι καὶ οὐ μέχρι πλείονος; ὥσπερ γὰρ τῆς οὐσίας ὅσον ἀφώρισταί σοι στέργεις, οὕτως καὶ ἐπὶ τοῦ χρόνου.

50. Πειρῶ μὲν πείθειν αὐτούς, πρᾶττε δὲ καὶ ‹αὐ›τῶν ἀκόντων, ὅταν τῆς δικαιοσύνης ὁ λόγος οὕτως ἄγῃ. ἐὰν μέντοι βίᾳ τις προσχρώμενος ἐνίστηται, μετάβαινε ἐπὶ τὸ εὐάρεστον καὶ ἄλυπον καὶ συγχρῶ εἰς ἄλλην ἀρετὴν τῇ κωλύσει, καὶ μέμνησο ὅτι μεθ᾽ ὑπεξαιρέσεως ὥρμας καὶ ὅτι τῶν ἀδυνάτων οὐκ ὠρέγου. τίνος οὖν; τῆς τοιᾶσδέ τινος ὁρμῆς. τούτου δὲ τυγχάνεις· ἐφ᾽ οἷς προήχθημεν, ταῦτα γίνεται.

51. Ὁ μὲν φιλόδοξος ἀλλοτρίαν ἐνέργειαν ἴδιον ἀγαθὸν ὑπολαμβάνει, ὁ δὲ φιλήδονος ἰδίαν πεῖσιν, ὁ δὲ νοῦν ἔχων ἰδίαν πρᾶξιν.

52. Ἔξεστι περὶ τούτου μηδὲν ὑπολαμβάνειν καὶ μὴ ὀχλεῖσθαι τῇ ψυχῇ· αὐτὰ γὰρ τὰ πράγματα οὐκ ἔχει φύσιν ποιητικὴν τῶν ἡμετέρων κρίσεων.

53. Ἔθισον σεαυτὸν πρὸς τῷ ὑφ᾽ ἑτέρου λεγομένῳ γίνεσθαι ἀπαρενθυμήτως καὶ ὡς οἷόν τε ἐν τῇ ψυχῇ τοῦ λέγοντος γίνου. Τὸ τῷ σμήνει μὴ συμφέρον οὐδὲ τῇ μελίσσῃ συμφέρει.

54. Εἰ κυβερνῶντα οἱ ναῦται ἢ ἰατρεύοντα οἱ κάμνοντες κακῶς ἔλεγον, ἄλλῳ τινὶ ἂν προσεῖχον; ἢ πῶς ⟨ἂν⟩ αὐτὸς ἐνεργοίη τὸ τοῖς ἐμπλέουσι σωτήριον ἢ τὸ τοῖς θεραπευομένοις ὑγιεινόν;

55. Πόσοι, μεθ᾽ ὧν εἰσῆλθον εἰς τὸν κόσμον, ἤδη ἀπεληλύθασιν.

56. Ἰκτεριῶσι τὸ μέλι πικρὸν φαίνεται καὶ λυσσοδήκτοις τὸ ὕδωρ φοβερὸν καὶ παιδίοις τὸ σφαιρίον καλόν. τί οὖν ὀργίζομαι; ἢ δοκεῖ σοι ἔλασσον ἰσχύειν τὸ διεψευσμένον ἢ τὸ χόλιον τῷ ἰκτεριῶντι καὶ ὁ ἰὸς τῷ λυσσοδήκτῳ;

57. Κατὰ τὸν λόγον τῆς σῆς φύσεως βιοῦν σε οὐδεὶς κωλύσει· παρὰ τὸν λόγον τῆς κοινῆς φύσεως οὐδέν σοι συμβήσεται.

58. Οἷοί εἰσιν οἷς θέλουσιν ἀρέσκειν, καὶ δι᾽ οἷα περιγινόμενοι καὶ δι᾽ οἵων ἐνεργειῶν. ὡς ταχέως ὁ αἰὼν πάντα καλύψει καὶ ὅσα ἐκάλυψεν ἤδη.

BOOK SEVEN

I. What is wickedness? It is that which many time and often thou hast already seen and known in the world. And so oft as anything doth happen that might otherwise trouble thee, let this memento presently come to thy mind, that it is that which thou hast already often Seen and known. Generally, above and below, thou shalt find but the same things. The very same things whereof ancient stories, middle age stories, and fresh stories are full whereof towns are full, and houses full. There is nothing that is new. All things that are, are both usual and of little continuance.

II. What fear is there that thy dogmata, or philosophical resolutions and conclusions, should become dead in thee, and lose their proper power and efficacy to make thee live happy, as long as those proper and correlative fancies, and representations of things on which they mutually depend (which continually to stir up and revive is in thy power,) are still kept fresh and alive? It is in my power concerning this thing that is happened, what soever it be, to conceit that which is right and true. If it be, why then am I troubled? Those things that are without my understanding, are nothing to it at all: and that is it only, which doth properly concern me. Be always in this mind, and thou wilt be right.

III. That which most men would think themselves most happy for, and would prefer before all things, if the Gods would grant it unto them after their deaths, thou mayst whilst thou livest grant unto thyself; to live again. See the things of the world again, as thou hast already seen them. For what is it else to live again? Public shows and solemnities with much pomp and vanity, stage plays, flocks and herds; conflicts and contentions: a bone thrown to a company of hungry curs; a bait for greedy fishes; the painfulness, and continual burden-bearing of wretched ants, the running to and fro of terrified mice: little puppets drawn up and down with wires and nerves: these be the objects of the world among all these thou must stand steadfast, meekly affected, and free from all manner of indignation; with this right ratiocination and apprehension; that as the worth is of those things which a man doth affect, so is in very deed every man's worth more or less.

IV. Word after word, every one by itself, must the things that are spoken be conceived and understood; and so the things that are done, purpose after purpose, every one by itself likewise. And as in matter of purposes and actions, we must presently see what is the proper use and relation of every one; so of words must we be as ready, to consider of every one what is the true meaning, and signification of it according to truth and nature, however it be taken in common use.

V. Is my reason, and understanding sufficient for this, or no? If it be sufficient, without any private applause, or public ostentation as of an instrument, which by nature I am provided of, I will make use of it for the work in hand, as of an instrument, which by nature I am provided of. if it be not, and that otherwise it belong not unto me particularly as a private duty, I will either give it over, and leave it to some other that can better effect it: or I will endeavour it; but with the help of some other, who with the joint help of my reason, is able to bring somewhat to pass, that will now be seasonable and useful for the common good. For whatsoever I do either by myself, or with some other, the only thing that I must intend, is, that it be good and expedient for the public. For as for praise, consider how many who once were much commended, are now already quite forgotten, yea they that commended them, how even they themselves are long since dead and gone. Be not therefore ashamed, whensoever thou must use the help of others. For whatsoever it be that lieth upon thee to effect, thou must propose it unto thyself, as the scaling of walls is unto a soldier. And what if thou through either lameness or some other impediment art not able to reach unto the top of the battlements alone, which with the help of another thou mayst; wilt thou therefore give it over, or go about it with less courage and alacrity, because thou canst not effect it all alone?

VI. Let not things future trouble thee. For if necessity so require that they come to pass, thou shalt (whensoever that is) be provided for them with the same reason, by which whatsoever is now present, is made both tolerable and acceptable unto thee. All things are linked and knitted together, and the knot is sacred, neither is there anything in the world, that is not kind and natural in regard of any other thing, or, that hath not some kind of reference and natural correspondence with whatsoever is in the world besides. For all things are ranked together, and by that decency of its due place and order that each particular doth observe, they all concur together to the making of one and the same ["Kosmos" ed] or world: as if you said, a comely piece, or an orderly composition. For all things throughout, there is but one and the same order; and through all things, one and the same God, the same substance and the same law. There is one common reason, and one common truth, that belongs unto all reasonable creatures, for neither is there save one perfection of all creatures that are of the same kind, and partakers of the same reason.

VII. Whatsoever is material, doth soon vanish away into the common substance of the whole; and whatsoever is formal, or, whatsoever doth animate that which is material, is soon resumed into the common reason of the whole; and the fame and memory of anything, is soon swallowed up by the general age and duration of the whole.

VIII. To a reasonable creature, the same action is both according to nature, and according to reason.

IX. Straight of itself, not made straight.

X. As several members in one body united, so are reasonable creatures in a body divided and dispersed, all made and prepared for one common operation. And this thou shalt apprehend the better, if thou shalt use thyself often to say to thyself, I am meloz, or a member of the mass and body of reasonable substances. But if thou shalt say I am meroz, or a part, thou dost not yet love men from thy heart. The joy that thou takest in the exercise of bounty, is not yet grounded upon a due ratiocination and right apprehension of the nature of things. Thou dost exercise it as yet upon this ground barely, as a thing convenient and fitting; not, as doing good to thyself, when thou dost good unto others.

XI. Of things that are external, happen what will to that which can suffer by external accidents. Those things that suffer let them complain themselves, if they will; as for me, as long as I conceive no such thing, that that which is happened is evil, I have no hurt; and it is in my power not to conceive any such thing.

XII. Whatsoever any man either doth or saith, thou must be good; not for any man's sake, but for thine own nature's sake; as if either gold, or the emerald, or purple, should ever be saying to themselves, Whatsoever any man either doth or saith, I must still be an emerald, and I must keep my colour.

XIII. This may ever be my comfort and security: my understanding, that ruleth over all, will not of itself bring trouble and vexation upon itself. This I say; it will not put itself in any fear, it will not lead itself into any concupiscence. If it be in the power of any other to compel it to fear, or to grieve, it is free for him to use his power. But sure if itself do not of itself, through some false opinion or supposition incline itself to any such disposition; there is no fear. For as for the body, why should I make the grief of my body, to be the grief of my mind? If that itself can either fear or complain, let it. But as for the soul, which indeed, can only be truly sensible of either fear or grief; to which only it belongs according to its different imaginations and opinions, to admit of either of these, or of their contraries; thou mayst look to that thyself, that it suffer nothing. Induce her not to any such opinion or persuasion. The understanding is of itself sufficient unto itself, and needs not (if itself doth not bring itself to need) any other thing besides itself, and by consequent as it needs nothing, so neither can it be troubled or hindered by anything, if itself doth not trouble and hinder itself.

XIV. What is love, or happiness: but a good spirit? What then dost thou do here, O opinion? By the Gods I adjure thee, that thou get thee gone, as thou earnest: for I need thee not. Thou earnest indeed unto me according to thy ancient wonted manner. It is that, that all men have ever been subject unto. That thou camest therefore I am not angry with thee, only begone, now that I have found thee what thou art.

XV. Is any man so foolish as to fear change, to which all things that once were not owe their being? And what is it, that is more pleasing and more familiar to the nature of the universe? How couldst thou thyself use thy ordinary hot baths, should not the wood that heateth them first be changed? How couldst thou receive any nourishment from those things that thou hast eaten, if they should not be changed? Can anything else almost (that is useful and profitable) be brought to pass without change? How then dost not thou perceive, that for thee also, by death, to come to change, is a thing of the very same nature, and as necessary for the nature of the universe?

XVI. Through the substance of the universe, as through a torrent pass all particular bodies, being all of the same nature, and all joint workers with the universe itself as in one of our bodies so many members among themselves. How many such as Chrysippus, how many such as Socrates, how many such as Epictetus, hath the age of the world long since swallowed up and devoured? Let this, be it either men or businesses, that thou hast occasion to think of, to the end that thy thoughts be not distracted and thy mind too earnestly set upon anything, upon every such occasion presently come to thy mind. Of all my thoughts and cares, one only thing shall be the object, that I myself do nothing which to the proper constitution of man, (either in regard of the thing itself, or in regard of the manner, or of the time of doing,) is contrary. The time when thou shalt have forgotten all things, is at hand. And that time also is at hand, when thou thyself shalt be forgotten by all. Whilst thou art, apply thyself to that especially which unto man as he is a mart, is most proper and agreeable, and that is, for a man even to love them that transgress against him. This shall be, if at the same time that any such thing doth happen, thou call to mind, that they are thy kinsmen; that it is through ignorance and against their wills that they sin; and that within a very short while after, both thou and he shall be no more. But above all things, that he hath not done thee any hurt; for that by him thy mind and understanding is not made worse or more vile than it was before.

XVII. The nature of the universe, of the common substance of all things as it were of so much wax hath now perchance formed a horse; and then, destroying that figure, hath new tempered and fashioned the matter of it into the form and substance of a tree: then that again into the form and substance of a man: and then that again into some other. Now every one of these doth subsist but for a very little while. As for dissolution, if it be no grievous thing to the chest or trunk, to be joined together; why should it be more grievous to be put asunder?

XVIII. An angry countenance is much against nature, and it is oftentimes the proper countenance of them that are at the point of death. But were it so, that all anger and passion were so thoroughly quenched in thee, that it were altogether impossible to kindle it any more, yet herein must not thou rest satisfied, but further endeavour by good consequence of true ratiocination, perfectly to conceive and understand, that all anger and passion is against reason. For if thou shalt not be sensible of thine innocence; if that also shall be gone from thee, the comfort of a good conscience, that thou doest all things according to reason: what shouldest thou live any longer for? All things that now thou seest, are but for a moment. That nature, by which all things in the world are administered, will soon bring change and alteration upon them, and then of their substances make other things like unto them: and then soon after others again of the matter and substance of these: that so by these means, the world may still appear fresh and new.

XIX. Whensoever any man doth trespass against other, presently consider with thyself what it was that he did suppose to be good, what to be evil, when he did trespass. For this when thou knowest, thou wilt pity him thou wilt have no occasion either to wonder, or to be angry. For either thou thyself dust yet live in that error and ignorance, as that thou dust suppose either that very thing that he doth, or some other like worldly thing, to be good; and so thou art bound to pardon him if he have done that which thou in the like case wouldst have done thyself. Or if so be that thou dost not any more suppose the same things to be good or evil, that he doth; how canst thou but be gentle unto him that is in an error?

XX. Fancy not to thyself things future, as though they were present but of those that are present, take some aside, that thou takest most benefit of, and consider of them particularly, how wonderfully thou wouldst want them, if they were not present. But take heed withal, lest that whilst thou dust settle thy contentment in things present, thou grow in time so to overprize them, as that the want of them (whensoever it shall so fall out) should be a trouble and a vexation unto thee. Wind up thyself into thyself. Such is the nature of thy reasonable commanding part, as that if it exercise justice, and have by that means tranquillity within itself, it doth rest fully satisfied with itself without any other thing.

XXI. Wipe off all opinion stay the force and violence of unreasonable lusts and affections: circumscribe the present time examine whatsoever it be that is happened, either to thyself or to another: divide all present objects, either in that which is formal or material think of the last hour. That which thy neighbour hath committed, where the guilt of it lieth, there let it rest. Examine in order whatsoever is spoken. Let thy mind penetrate both into the effects, and into the causes. Rejoice thyself with true simplicity, and modesty; and that all middle things between virtue and vice are indifferent unto thee. Finally, love mankind; obey God.

XXII. All things (saith he) are by certain order and appointment. And what if the elements only. It will suffice to remember, that all things in general are by certain order and appointment: or if it be but few. And as concerning death, that either dispersion, or the atoms, or annihilation, or extinction, or translation will ensue. And as concerning pain, that that which is intolerable is soon ended by death; and that which holds long must needs be tolerable; and that the mind in the meantime (which is all in all) may by way of interclusion, or interception, by stopping all manner of commerce and sympathy with the body, still retain its own tranquillity. Thy understanding is not made worse by it. As for those parts that suffer, let them, if they can, declare their grief themselves. As for praise and commendation, view their mind and understanding, what estate they are in; what kind of things they fly, and what things they seek after: and that as in the seaside, whatsoever was before to be seen, is by the continual succession of new heaps of sand cast up one upon another, soon hid and covered; so in this life, all former things by those which immediately succeed.

XXIII. Out of Plato. 'He then whose mind is endowed with true magnanimity, who hath accustomed himself to the contemplation both of all times, and of all things in general; can this mortal life (thinkest thou) seem any great matter unto him? It is not possible, answered he. Then neither will such a one account death a grievous thing? By no means.'

XXIV. Out of Antisthenes. 'It is a princely thing to do well, and to be ill-spoken of. It is a shameful thing that the face should be subject unto the mind, to be put into what shape it will, and to be dressed by it as it will; and that the mind should not bestow so much care upon herself, as to fashion herself, and to dress herself as best becometh her.'

XXV. Out of several poets and comics. 'It will but little avail thee, to turn thine anger and indignation upon the things themselves that have fallen across unto thee. For as for them, they are not sensible of it, &c. Thou shalt but make thyself a laughing-stock; both unto the Gods and men, &c. Our life is reaped like a ripe ear of corn; one is yet standing and another is down, &c. But if so be that I and my children be neglected by the gods, there is some reason even for that, &c. As long as right and equity is of my side, &c. Not to lament with them, not to tremble, &c.'

XXVI. Out of Plato. 'My answer, full of justice and equity, should be this: Thy speech is not right, O man! if thou supposest that he that is of any worth at all, should apprehend either life or death, as a matter of great hazard and danger; and should not make this rather his only care, to examine his own actions, whether just or unjust: whether actions of a good, or of a wicked man, &c. For thus in very truth stands the case, O ye men of Athens. What place or station soever a man either hath chosen to himself, judging it best for himself; or is by lawful authority put and settled in, therein do I think (all appearance of danger notwithstanding) that he should continue, as one who feareth neither death, nor anything else, so much as he feareth to commit anything that is vicious and shameful, &c. But, O noble sir, consider I pray, whether true generosity and true happiness, do not consist in somewhat else rather, than in the preservation either of our, or other men's lives. For it is not the part of a man that is a man indeed, to desire to live long or to make much of his life whilst he liveth: but rather (he that is such) will in these things wholly refer himself unto the Gods, and believing that which every woman can tell him, that no man can escape death; the only thing that he takes thought and care for is this, that what time he liveth, he may live as well and as virtuously as he can possibly, &c. To look about, and with the eyes to follow the course of the stars and planets as though thou wouldst run with them; and to mind perpetually the several changes of the elements one into another. For such fancies and imaginations, help much to purge away the dross and filth of this our earthly life,' &c. That also is a fine passage of Plato's, where he speaketh of worldly things in these words: 'Thou must also as from some higher place look down, as it were, upon the things of this world, as flocks, armies, husbandmen's labours, marriages, divorces, generations, deaths: the tumults of courts and places of judicatures; desert places; the several nations of barbarians, public festivals, mournings, fairs, markets.' How all things upon earth are pellmell; and how miraculously things contrary one to another, concur to the beauty and perfection of this universe.

XXVII. To look back upon things of former ages, as upon the manifold changes and conversions of several monarchies and commonwealths. We may also foresee things future, for they shall all be of the same kind; neither is it possible that they should leave the tune, or break the concert that is now begun, as it were, by these things that are now done and brought to pass in the world. It comes all to one therefore, whether a man be a spectator of the things of this life but forty years, or whether he see them ten thousand years together: for what shall he see more? 'And as for those parts that came from the earth, they shall return unto the earth again; and those that came from heaven, they also shall return unto those heavenly places.' Whether it be a mere dissolution and unbinding of the manifold intricacies and entanglements of the confused atoms; or some such dispersion of the simple and incorruptible elements... 'With meats and drinks and divers charms, they seek to divert the channel, that they might not die. Yet must we needs endure that blast of wind that cometh from above, though we toil and labour never so much.'

XXVIII. He hath a stronger body, and is a better wrestler than I. What then? Is he more bountiful? is he more modest? Doth he bear all adverse chances with more equanimity: or with his neighbour's offences with more meekness and gentleness than I?

XXIX. Where the matter may be effected agreeably to that reason, which both unto the Gods and men is common, there can be no just cause of grief or sorrow. For where the fruit and benefit of an action well begun and prosecuted according to the proper constitution of man may be reaped and obtained, or is sure and certain, it is against reason that any damage should there be suspected. In all places, and at all times, it is in thy power religiously to embrace whatsoever by God's appointment is happened unto thee, and justly to converse with those men, whom thou hast to do with, and accurately to examine every fancy that presents itself, that nothing may slip and steal in, before thou hast rightly apprehended the true nature of it.

XXX. Look not about upon other men's minds and understandings; but look right on forwards whither nature, both that of the universe, in those things that happen unto thee; and thine in particular, in those things that are done by thee:

doth lead, and direct thee. Now every one is bound to do that, which is consequent and agreeable to that end which by his true natural constitution he was ordained unto. As for all other things, they are ordained for the use of reasonable creatures: as in all things we see that that which is worse and inferior, is made for that which is better. Reasonable creatures, they are ordained one for another. That therefore which is chief in every man's constitution, is, that he intend the common good. The second is, that he yield not to any lusts and motions of the flesh. For it is the part and privilege of the reasonable and intellective faculty, that she can so bound herself, as that neither the sensitive, nor the appetitive faculties, may not anyways prevail upon her. For both these are brutish. And therefore over both she challengeth mastery, and cannot anyways endure, if in her right temper, to be subject unto either. And this indeed most justly. For by nature she was ordained to command all in the body. The third thing proper to man by his constitution, is, to avoid all rashness and precipitancy; and not to be subject to error. To these things then, let the mind apply herself and go straight on, without any distraction about other things, and she hath her end, and by consequent her happiness.

XXXI. As one who had lived, and were now to die by right, whatsoever is yet remaining, bestow that wholly as a gracious overplus upon a virtuous life. Love and affect that only, whatsoever it be that happeneth, and is by the fates appointed unto thee. For what can be more reasonable? And as anything doth happen unto thee by way of cross, or calamity, call to mind presently and set before thine eyes, the examples of some other men, to whom the self-same thing did once happen likewise. Well, what did they? They grieved; they wondered; they complained. And where are they now? All dead and gone. Wilt thou also be like one of them? Or rather leaving to men of the world (whose life both in regard of themselves, and them that they converse with, is nothing but mere mutability; or men of as fickle minds, as fickle bodies; ever changing and soon changed themselves) let it be thine only care and study, how to make a right use of all such accidents. For there is good use to be made of them, and they will prove fit matter for thee to work upon, if it shall be both thy care and thy desire, that whatsoever thou doest, thou thyself mayst like and approve thyself for it. And both these, see, that thou remember well, according as the diversity of the matter of the action that thou art about shall require. Look within; within is the fountain of all good. Such a fountain, where springing waters can never fail, so thou dig still deeper and deeper.

XXXII. Thou must use thyself also to keep thy body fixed and steady; free from all loose fluctuant either motion, or posture. And as upon thy face and looks, thy mind hath easily power over them to keep them to that which is grave and decent; so let it challenge the same power over the whole body also. But so observe all things in this kind, as that it be without any manner of affectation.

XXXIII. The art of true living in this world is more like a wrestler's, than a dancer's practice. For in this they both agree, to teach a man whatsoever falls upon him, that he may be ready for it, and that nothing may cast him down.

XXXIV. Thou must continually ponder and consider with thyself, what manner of men they be, and for their minds and understandings what is their present estate, whose good word and testimony thou dost desire. For then neither wilt thou see cause to complain of them that offend against their wills; or find any want of their applause, if once thou dost but penetrate into the true force and ground both of their opinions, and of their desires. 'No soul (saith he) is willingly bereft of the truth,' and by consequent, neither of justice, or temperance, or kindness, and mildness; nor of anything that is of the same kind. It is most needful that thou shouldst always remember this. For so shalt thou be far more gentle and moderate towards all men.

XXXV. What pain soever thou art in, let this presently come to thy mind, that it is not a thing whereof thou needest to be ashamed, neither is it a thing whereby thy understanding, that hath the government of all, can be made worse. For neither in regard of the substance of it, nor in regard of the end of it (which is, to intend the common good) can it alter and corrupt it. This also of Epicurus mayst thou in most pains find some help of, that it is 'neither intolerable, nor eternal;' so thou keep thyself to the true bounds and limits of reason and give not way to opinion. This also thou must consider, that many things there be, which oftentimes unsensibly trouble and vex thee, as not armed against them with patience, because they go not ordinarily under the name of pains, which in very deed are of the same nature as pain; as to slumber unquietly, to suffer heat, to want appetite: when therefore any of these things make thee discontented, check thyself with these words: Now hath pain given thee the foil; thy courage hath failed thee.

XXXVI. Take heed lest at any time thou stand so affected, though towards unnatural evil men, as ordinary men are commonly one towards another.

XXXVII. How know we whether Socrates were so eminent indeed, and of so extraordinary a disposition? For that he died more gloriously, that he disputed with the Sophists more subtilty; that he watched in the frost more assiduously; that being commanded to fetch innocent Salaminius, he refused to do it more generously; all this will not serve. Nor that he walked in the streets, with much gravity and majesty, as was objected unto him by his adversaries: which nevertheless a man may well doubt of, whether it were so or no, or, which above all the rest, if so be that it were true, a man would well consider of, whether commendable, or discommendable. The thing therefore that we must inquire into, is this; what manner of soul Socrates had: whether his disposition was such; as that all that he stood upon, and sought after in this world, was barely this, that he might ever carry himself justly towards men, and holily towards the Gods. Neither vexing himself to no purpose at the wickedness of others, nor yet ever condescending to any man's evil fact, or evil intentions, through either fear, or engagement of friendship. Whether of those things that happened unto him by God's appointment, he neither did wonder at any when it did happen, or thought it intolerable in the trial of it. And lastly, whether he never did suffer his mind to sympathise with the senses, and affections of the body. For we must not think that Nature hath so mixed and tempered it with the body, as that she hath not power to circumscribe herself, and by herself to intend her own ends and occasions.

XXXVIII. For it is a thing very possible, that a man should be a very divine man, and yet be altogether unknown. This thou must ever be mindful of, as of this also, that a man's true happiness doth consist in very few things. And that although thou dost despair, that thou shalt ever be a good either logician, or naturalist, yet thou art never the further off by it from being either liberal, or modest, or charitable, or obedient unto God.

XXXIX. Free from all compulsion in all cheerfulness and alacrity thou mayst run out thy time, though men should exclaim against thee never so much, and the wild beasts should pull in sunder the poor members of thy pampered mass of flesh. For what in either of these or the like cases should hinder the mind to retain her own rest and tranquillity, consisting both in the right judgment of those things that happen unto her, and in the ready use of all present matters and occasions? So that her judgment may say, to that which is befallen her by way of cross: this thou art in very deed, and according to thy true nature: notwithstanding that in the judgment of opinion thou dust appear otherwise: and her discretion to the present object; thou art that, which I sought for. For whatsoever it be, that is now present, shall ever be embraced by me as a fit and seasonable object, both for my reasonable faculty, and for my sociable, or charitable inclination to work upon. And that which is principal in this matter, is that it may be referred either unto the praise of God, or to the good of men. For either unto God or man, whatsoever it is that doth happen in the world hath in   the ordinary course of nature its proper reference; neither is there anything, that in regard of nature is either new, or reluctant and intractable, but all things both usual and easy.

XL. Then hath a man attained to the estate of perfection in his life and con- versation, when he so spends every day, as if it were his last day: never hot and vehement in his affections, nor yet so cold and stupid as one that had no sense; and free from all manner of dissimulation.

XLI. Can the Gods, who are immortal, for the continuance of so many ages bear without indignation with such and so many sinners, as have ever been, yea not only so, but also take such care for them, that they want nothing; and dust thou so grievously take on, as one that could bear with them no longer; thou that art but for a moment of time? yea thou that art one of those sinners thyself? A very ridiculous thing it is, that any man should dispense with vice and wickedness in himself, which is in his power to restrain; and should go about to suppress it in others, which is altogether impossible.

XLII. What object soever, our reasonable and sociable faculty doth meet with, that affords nothing either for the satisfaction of reason, or for the practice of charity, she worthily doth think unworthy of herself.

XLIII. When thou hast done well, and another is benefited by thy action, must thou like a very fool look for a third thing besides, as that it may appear unto oth- ers also that thou hast done well, or that thou mayest in time, receive one good turn for another? No man useth to be weary of that which is beneficial unto him. But every action according to nature, is beneficial. Be not weary then of doing that which is beneficial unto thee, whilst it is so unto others.

XLIV. The nature of the universe did once certainly before it was created, what- soever it hath done since, deliberate and so resolve upon the creation of the world. Now since that time, whatsoever it is, that is and happens in the world, is either but a consequent of that one and first deliberation: or if so be that this ruling rational part of the world, takes any thought and care of things particular, they are surely his reasonable and principal creatures, that are the proper object of his particular care and providence. This often thought upon, will much con- duce to thy tranquillity.

ΒΙΒΛΙΟ ΕΒΔΟΜΟ

1. Τί ἐστι κακία; τοῦτ ἔστιν ὃ πολλάκις εἶδες. καὶ ἐπὶ παντὸςδὲ τοῦ συμβαίνοντος πρόχειρον ἔχε ὅτι τοῦτό ἐστιν ὃ πολλάκιςεἶδες. ὅλως ἄνω κάτω τὰ αὐτὰ εὑρήσεις, ὧν μεσταὶ αἱ ἱστορίαιαὶ παλαιαί, αἱ μέσαι, αἱ ὑπόγυιοι· ὧν νῦν μεσταὶ αἱ πόλεις καὶοἰκίαι. οὐδὲν καινόν· πάντα καὶ συνήθη καὶ ὀλιγοχρόνια.

2. Ζῇ τὰ δόγματα· πῶς γὰρ ἄλλως δύναται νεκρωθῆναι, ἐὰν μὴαἱ κατάλληλοι αὐτοῖς φαντασίαι σβεσθῶσιν, ἃς διηνεκῶςἀναζωπυρεῖν ἐπὶ σοί ἐστιν; δύναμαι περὶ τούτου ὃ δεῖὑπολαμβάνειν· εἰ δύναμαι, τί ταράσσομαι; τὰ ἔξω τῆς ἐμῆςδιανοίας οὐδὲν ὅλως πρὸς τὴν ἐμὴν διάνοιαν. τοῦτο μάθε καὶὀρθὸς εἶ. ἀναβιῶναί σοι ἔξεστιν· ἴδε πάλιν τὰ πράγματα, ὡςἑώρας· ἐν τούτῳ γὰρ τὸ ἀναβιῶναι.

3. Πομπῆς κενοσπουδία, ἐπὶ σκηνῆς δράματα, ποίμνια, ἀγέλαι,διαδορατισμοί, κυνιδίοις ὀστάριον ἐρριμμένον, ψωμίον εἰς τὰςτῶν ἰχθύων δεξαμενάς, μυρμήκων ταλαιπωρίαι καὶ ἀχθοφορίαι,μυιδίων ἐπτοημένων διαδρομαί, σιγιλλάρια νευροσπαστούμενα.χρὴ οὖν ἐν τούτοις εὐμενῶς μὲν καὶ μὴ καταφρυαττόμενονἑστάναι, παρακολουθεῖν μέντοι, ὅτι τοσούτου ἄξιος ἕκαστόςἐστιν, ὅσου ἄξιά ἐστι ταῦτα περὶ ἃ ἐσπούδακεν.

4. Δεῖ κατὰ λέξιν παρακολουθεῖν τοῖς λεγομένοις καὶ καθεκάστην ὁρμὴν τοῖς γινομένοις, καὶ ἐπὶ μὲν τοῦ ἑτέρου εὐθὺςὁρᾶν ἐπὶ τίνα σκοπὸν ἡ ἀναφορά, ἐπὶ δὲ τοῦ ἑτέρου παραφυλάσσειντί τὸ σημαινόμενον.

5. Πότερον ἐξαρκεῖ ἡ διάνοιά μου πρὸς τοῦτο ἢ οὔ; εἰ μὲν ἐξαρκεῖ,χρῶμαι αὐτῇ πρὸς τὸ ἔργον ὡς ὀργάνῳ παρὰ τῆς τῶν ὅλων φύσεωςδοθέντι. εἰ δὲ μὴ ἐξαρκεῖ, ἤτοι παραχωρῶ τοῦ ἔργου τῷ δυναμένῳκρεῖττον ἐπιτελέσαι, ἐὰν ἄλλως τοῦτό μοι καθήκῃ, ἢ πράσσω ὡςδύναμαι, προσπαραλαβὼν τὸν δυνάμενον κατὰ πρόσχρησιν τοῦἐμοῦ ἡγεμονικοῦ ποιῆσαι τὸ εἰς τὴν κοινωνίαν νῦν καίριον καὶχρήσιμον. ὅ τι γὰρ ἂν δι᾽ ἐμαυτοῦ ἢ σὺν ἄλλῳ ποιῶ, ὧδε μόνονχρὴ συντείνειν, εἰς τὸ κοινῇ χρήσιμον καὶ εὐάρμοστον.

6. Ὅσοι μὲν πολυύμνητοι γενόμενοι ἤδη λήθῃ παραδέδονται,ὅσοι δὲ τούτους ὑμνήσαντες πάλαι ἐκποδών.

7. Μὴ αἰσχύνου βοηθούμενος· πρόκειται γάρ σοι ἐνεργεῖν τὸἐπιβάλλον ὡς στρατιώτη ἐν τειχομαχίᾳ. τί οὖν, ἐὰν σὺ μὲνχωλαίνων ἐπὶ τὴν ἔπαλξιν ἀναβῆναι μόνος μὴ δύνῃ, σὺν ἄλλῳδὲ δυνατὸν ᾖ τοῦτο;

8. Τὰ μέλλοντα μὴ ταρασσέτω· ἥξεις γὰρ ἐπ αὐτά, ἐὰν δεήσῃ,φέρων τὸν αὐτὸν λόγον ᾧ νῦν πρὸς τὰ παρόντα χρᾷ.

9. Πάντα ἀλλήλοις ἐπιπέπλεκται καὶ ἡ σύνδεσις ἱερά, καὶ σχεδόντι οὐδὲν ἀλλότριον ἄλλο ἄλλῳ· συγκατατέτακται γὰρ καὶσυγκοσμεῖ τὸν αὐτὸν κόσμον. κόσμος τε γὰρ εἷς ἐξ ἁπάντων καὶθεὸς εἷς δὶ ἁπάντων καὶ οὐσία μία καὶ νόμος εἷς, λόγος κοινὸςπάντων τῶν νοερῶν ζῴων, καὶ ἀλήθεια μία, εἴγε καὶ τελειότηςμία τῶν ὁμογενῶν καὶ τοῦ αὐτοῦ λόγου μετεχόντων ζῴων.

10. Πᾶν τὸ ἔνυλον ἐναφανίζεται τάχιστα τῇ τῶν ὅλων οὐσίᾳ καὶπᾶν αἴτιον εἰς τὸν τῶν ὅλων λόγον τάχιστα ἀναλαμβάνεται καὶπαντὸς μνήμη τάχιστα ἐγκαταχώννυται τῷ αἰῶνι.

11. Τῷ λογικῷ ζῴῳ ἡ αὐτὴ πρᾶξις κατὰ φύσιν ἐστὶ καὶ κατὰ λόγον.

12. Ὀρθός, ἢ ὀρθούμενος.

13. Οἷόν ἐστιν ἐν ἡνωμένοις τὰ μέλη τοῦ σώματος, τοῦτον ἔχειτὸν λόγον ἐν διεστῶσι τὰ λογικά, πρὸς μίαν τινὰ συνεργίανκατεσκευασμένα. μᾶλλον δέ σοι ἡ τούτου νόησις προσπεσεῖται,ἐὰν πρὸς ἑαυτὸν πολλάκις λέγῃς, ὅτι μέλος εἰμὶ τοῦ ἐκ τῶν λογικῶνσυστήματος. ἐὰν δὲ διὰ τοῦ ῥῶ στοιχείου μέρος εἶναι ἑαυτὸνλέγῃς, οὔπω ἀπὸ καρδίας φιλεῖς τοὺς ἀνθρώπους· οὔπω σεκαταληκτικῶς εὐφραίνει τὸ εὐεργετεῖν· ἔτι ὡς πρέπον αὐτὸ ψιλὸνποιεῖς, οὔπω ὡς ἑαυτὸν εὖ ποιῶν.

14. Ὃ θέλει, ἔξωθεν προσπιπτέτω τοῖς παθεῖν ἐκ τῆς προσπτώσεωςταύτης δυναμένοις. ἐκεῖνα γάρ, ἐὰν θελήσῃ, μέμψεται τὰ παθόντα,ἐγὼ δέ, ἐὰν μὴ ὑπολάβω ὅτι κακὸν τὸ συμβεβηκός, οὔπωβέβλαμμαι· ἔξεστι δέ μοι μὴ ὑπολαβεῖν.

15. Ὅ τι ἄν τις ποιῇ ἢ λέγῃ, ἐμὲ δεῖ ἀγαθὸν εἶναι, ὡς ἂν εἰ ὁχρυσὸς ἢ ὁ σμάραγδος ἢ ἡ πορφύρα τοῦτο ἀεὶ ἔλεγεν· ὅ τι ἄν τιςποιῇ ἢ λέγῃ, ἐμὲ δεῖ σμάραγδον εἶναι

καὶ τὸ ἐμαυτοῦ χρῶμαἔχειν.

16. Τὸ ἡγεμονικὸν αὐτὸ ἑαυτῷ οὐκ ἐνοχλεῖ, οἷον λέγω, οὐ φοβεῖἑαυτὸ .. εἰς ἐπιθυμίαν. εἰ δέ τις ἄλλος αὐτὸ φοβῆσαι ἢ λυπῆσαιδύναται, ποιείτω· αὐτὸ γὰρ ἑαυτὸ ὑποληπτικῶς οὐ τρέψει εἰςτοιαύτας τροπάς. τὸ σωμάτιον μὴ πάθῃ τι, αὐτὸ μεριμνάτω, εἰδύναται· καὶ λεγέτω, εἴ τι πάσχει, τὸ [δὲ] ψυχάριον τὸ φοβούμενον,τὸ λυπούμενον· τὸ ‹δὲ› περὶ τούτων ὅλως ὑπολαμβάνον οὐδὲν μὴπάθῃ· οὐ γὰρ ἄξει αὐτὸ εἰς κρίσιν τοιαύτην. ἀπροσδεές ἐστινὅσον ἐφ ἑαυτῷ τὸ ἡγεμονικόν, ἐὰν μὴ ἑαυτῷ ἔνδειαν ποιῇ· κατὰταὐτὰ δὲ καὶ ἀτάραχον καὶ ἀνεμπόδιστον, ἐὰν μὴ ἑαυτὸ ταράσσῃκαὶ ἐμποδίζῃ.

17. Εὐδαιμονία ἐστὶ δαίμων ἀγαθὸς ἢ ‹δαιμόνιον› ἀγαθόν. τί οὖνὧδε ποιεῖς, ὦ φαντασία; ἀπέρχου, τοὺς θεούς σοι, ὡς ἦλθες· οὐγὰρ χρῄζω σου. ἐλήλυθας δὲ κατὰ τὸ ἀρχαῖον ἔθος. οὐκὀργίζομαί σοι· μόνον ἄπιθι.

18. Φοβεῖταί τις μεταβολήν; τί γὰρ δύναται χωρὶς μεταβολῆςγενέσθαι; τί δὲ φίλτερον ἢ οἰκειότερον τῇ τῶν ὅλων φύσει; σὺ δὲαὐτὸς λούσασθαι δύνασαι, ἐὰν μὴ τὰ ξύλα μεταβάλῃ; τραφῆναιδὲ δύνασαι, ἐὰν μὴ τὰ ἐδώδιμα μεταβάλῃ; ἄλλο δέ τι τῶν χρησίμωνδύναται συντελεσθῆναι χωρὶς μεταβολῆς; οὐχ ὁρᾷς οὖν ὅτι καὶαὐτὸ τὸ σὲ μεταβαλεῖν ὅμοιόν ἐστι καὶ ὁμοίως ἀναγκαῖον τῇτῶν ὅλων φύσει;

19. Διὰ τῆς τῶν ὅλων οὐσίας ὡς διὰ χειμάρρου διεκπορεύεταιπάντα τὰ σώματα, τῷ ὅλῳ συμφυῆ καὶ συνεργὰ ὡς τὰ ἡμέτεραμέλη ἀλλήλοις. πόσους ἤδη ὁ αἰὼν Χρυσίππους, πόσους Σωκράτεις,πόσους Ἐπικτήτους καταπέπωκεν. τὸ δ αὐτὸ καὶ ἐπὶπαντὸς οὑτινοσοῦν σοι ἀνθρώπου τε καὶ πράγματος προσπιπτέτω.

20. Ἐμὲ ἓν μόνον περισπᾷ, μή τι αὐτὸς ποιήσω, ὃ ἡ κατασκευὴτοῦ ἀνθρώπου οὐ θέλει ἢ ὡς οὐ θέλει ἢ ὃ νῦν οὐ θέλει.

21. Ἐγγὺς μὲν ἡ σὴ περὶ πάντων λήθη, ἐγγὺς δὲ ἡ πάντων περὶ σοῦλήθη.

22. Ἴδιον ἀνθρώπου φιλεῖν καὶ τοὺς πταίοντας. τοῦτο δὲ γίνεται,ἐὰν συμπροσπίπτῃ σοι, ὅτι καὶ συγγενεῖς καὶ δὶ ἄγνοιαν καὶἄκοντες ἁμαρτάνουσι καὶ ὡς μετ ὀλίγον ἀμφότεροι τεθνήξεσθε,καὶ πρὸ πάντων, ὅτι οὐκ ἔβλαψέ σε· οὐ γὰρ τὸ ἡγεμονικόν σουχεῖρον ἐποίησεν ἢ πρόσθεν ἦν.

145

23. Ἡ τῶν ὅλων φύσις ἐκ τῆς ὅλης οὐσίας ὡς κηροῦ νῦν μὲνίππάριον ἔπλασε, συγχέασα δὲ τοῦτο εἰς δενδρύφιον συνεχρήσατοτῇ ὕλῃ αὐτοῦ· εἶτα εἰς ἀνθρωπάριον· εἶτα εἰς ἄλλο τι· ἕκαστονδὲ τούτων πρὸς ὀλίγιστον ὑπέστη. δεινὸν δὲ οὐδὲν τὸ διαλυθῆναιτῷ κιβωτίῳ, ὥσπερ οὐδὲ τὸ συμπαγῆναι.

24. Τὸ ἐπίκοτον τοῦ προσώπου λίαν παρὰ φύσιν, ὅταν ‹δὲ› †πολλάκις ᾖ, ἐναποθνήσκει ‹τὸ› πρόσχημα ἢ τὸ τελευταῖονἀπεσβέσθη, ὥστε ὅλως ἐξαφθῆναι μὴ δύνασθαι .. αὐτῷ γε τούτῳπαρακολουθεῖν πειρῶ, ὅτι παρὰ τὸν λόγον. εἰ γὰρ καὶ ἡσυναίσθησις τοῦ ἁμαρτάνειν οἰχήσεται, τίς ἔτι τοῦ ζῆν αἰτία;

25. Πάντα ὅσα ὁρᾷς ὅσον οὔπω μεταβαλεῖ ἡ τὰ ὅλα διοικοῦσαφύσις καὶ ἄλλα ἐκ τῆς οὐσίας αὐτῶν ποιήσει καὶ πάλιν ἄλλα ἐκτῆς ἐκείνων οὐσίας, ἵνα ἀεὶ νεαρὸς ᾖ ὁ κόσμος.

26. Ὅταν τις ἁμάρτῃ τι εἰς σέ, εὐθὺς ἐνθυμοῦ τί ἀγαθὸν ἢ κακὸνὑπολαβὼν ἥμαρτεν. τοῦτο γὰρ ἰδὼν ἐλεήσεις αὐτὸν καὶ οὔτεθαυμάσεις οὔτε ὀργισθήσῃ. ἤτοι γὰρ καὶ αὐτὸς τὸ αὐτὸ ἐκείνῳἀγαθὸν ἔτι ὑπολαμβάνεις ἢ ἄλλο ὁμοειδές· δεῖ οὖν συγγινώσκειν.εἰ δὲ μηκέτι ὑπολαμβάνεις τὰ τοιαῦτα ἀγαθὰ καὶ κακά, ῥᾷονεὐμενὴς ἔσῃ τῷ παρορῶντι.

27. Μὴ τὰ ἀπόντα ἐννοεῖν ὡς ἤδη ὄντα, ἀλλὰ τῶν παρόντων τάδεξιώτατα ἐκλογίζεσθαι καὶ τούτων χάριν ὑπομιμνήσκεσθαι πῶςἂν ἐπεζητεῖτο, εἰ μὴ παρῆν. ἅμα μέντοι φυλάσσου, μὴ διὰ τοῦοὕτως ἀσμενίζειν αὐτοῖς ἐθίσῃς ἐκτιμᾶν αὐτά, ὥστε, ἐάν ποτεμὴ παρῇ, ταραχθήσεσθαι.

28. Εἰς ἑαυτὸν συνειλοῦ· φύσιν ἔχει τὸ λογικὸν ἡγεμονικὸν ἑαυτῷἀρκεῖσθαι δικαιοπραγοῦντι καὶ παρ᾽ αὐτὸ τοῦτο γαλήνην ἔχοντι.

29. Ἐξάλειψον τὴν φαντασίαν. στῆσον τὴν νευροσπαστίαν.περίγραψον τὸ ἐνεστὼς τοῦ χρόνου. γνώρισον τὸ συμβαῖνον ἢσοὶ ἢ ἄλλῳ. δίελε καὶ μέρισον τὸ ὑποκείμενον εἰς τὸ αἰτιῶδεςκαὶ ὑλικόν. ἐννόησον τὴν ἐσχάτην ὥραν. τὸ ἐκείνῳ ἁμαρτηθὲνἐκεῖ κατάλιπε ὅπου ἡ ἁμαρτία ὑπέστη.

30. Συμπαρεκτείνειν τὴν νόησιν τοῖς λεγομένοις. εἰσδύεσθαι τὸννοῦν εἰς τὰ γινόμενα καὶ ‹τὸν› ποιοῦντα.

31. Φαίδρυνον σεαυτὸν ἁπλότητι καὶ αἰδοῖ καὶ τῇ πρὸς τὸ ἀνάμεσον ἀρετῆς καὶ κακίας ἀδιαφορίᾳ. φίλησον τὸ ἀνθρώπινονγένος. ἀκολούθησον θεῷ. ἐκεῖνος μέν φησιν ὅτι "πάντα νομιστί,ἐτεῇ δὲ μόνα τὰ στοιχεῖ", ἀρκεῖ δὲ μεμνῆσθαι ὅτι τὰ πάντανομιστὶ ἔχει· ἤδη λίαν ὀλίγα.

32. Περὶ θανάτου· ἢ σκεδασμός, εἰ ἄτομοι· εἰ δ ἕνωσις, ἤτοι σβέσιςἢ μετάστασις.

33. Περὶ πόνου· τὸ μὲν ἀφόρητον ἐξάγει, τὸ δὲ χρονίζον φορητόν· καὶ ἡ διάνοια τὴν ἑαυτῆς γαλήνην κατὰ ἀπόληψιν διατηρεῖ καὶοὐ χεῖρον τὸ ἡγεμονικὸν γέγονε, τὰ δὲ κακούμενα μέρη ὑπὸ τοῦπόνου, εἴ τι δύναται, περὶ αὐτοῦ ἀποφηνάσθω.

34. Περὶ δόξης· ἴδε τὰς διανοίας αὐτῶν, οἷαι καὶ οἷα μὲν φεύγουσι,οἷα δὲ διώκουσι. καὶ ὅτι, ὡς αἱ θῖνες ἄλλαι ἐπ ἄλλαιςἐπιφορούμεναι κρύπτουσι τὰς προτέρας, οὕτως ἐν τῷ βίῳ τὰπρότερα ὑπὸ τῶν ἐπενεχθέντων τάχιστα ἐκαλύφθη.

35. "Ὧι οὖν ὑπάρχει διάνοια μεγαλοπρεπὴς καὶ θεωρία παντὸςμὲν χρόνου, πάσης δὲ οὐσίας, ἆρα οἴει τούτῳ μέγα τι δοκεῖνεἶναι τὸν ἀνθρώπινον βίον; ἀδύνατον, ἦ δ ὅς. οὐκοῦν καὶθάνατον οὐ δεινόν τι ἡγήσεται ὁ τοιοῦτος; ἥκιστά γε."

36. "Βασιλικὸν εὖ μὲν πράττειν, κακῶς δὲ ἀκούειν."

37. Αἰσχρόν ἐστι τὸ μὲν πρόσωπον ὑπήκοον εἶναι καὶ σχηματίζεσθαικαὶ κατακοσμεῖσθαι, ὡς κελεύει ἡ διάνοια, αὐτὴν δ ὑφ̓ἑαυτῆς μὴ σχηματίζεσθαι καὶ κατακοσμεῖσθαι.

38. Τοῖς πράγμασιν γὰρ οὐχὶ θυμοῦσθαι χρεών· μέλει γὰρ αὐτοῖςοὐδέν.

39. Ἀθανάτοις τε θεοῖσι καὶ ἡμῖν χάρματα δοίης.

40. Βίον θερίζειν ὥστε κάρπιμον στάχυν καὶ τὸν μὲν εἶναι, τὸν δὲμή.

41. Εἰ δ ἡμελήθην ἐκ θεῶν καὶ παῖδ ἐμώ, ἔχει λόγον καὶ τοῦτο.

42. Τὸ γὰρ εὖ μετ ἐμοῦ καὶ τὸ δίκαιον.

43. Μὴ συνεπιθρηνεῖν, μη‹δὲ› ‹συ›σφύζειν ‹χρεών.›

44. "Ἐγὼ δὲ τούτῳ δίκαιον ἂν λόγον ἀντείποιμι, ὅτι οὐ καλῶςλέγεις, ὦ ἄνθρωπε, εἰ οἴει δεῖν κίνδυνον ὑπολογίζεσθαι τοῦ ζῆνἢ τεθνάναι ἄνδρα, ὅτου τι καὶ σμικρὸν ὄφελός ‹ἐστιν›, ἀλλ οὐκἐκεῖνο μόνον σκοπεῖν, ὅταν πράττῃ, πότερον δίκαια ἢ ἄδικαπράττει καὶ ἀνδρὸς ἀγαθοῦ ‹ἔργα› ἢ κακοῦ."

45. "Οὕτω γὰρ ἔχει, ὦ ἄνδρες Ἀθηναῖοι, τῇ ἀληθείᾳ· οῬ ἄν τιςαὑτὸν τάξῃ ἡγησάμενος βέλτιστον εἶναι ἢ ὑπ ἄρχοντος ταχθῇ,ἐνταῦθα ‹δεῖ›, ὡς ἐμοὶ δοκεῖ[ν], μένοντα κινδυνεύειν, μηδὲνὑπολογιζόμενον μήτε θάνατον μήτε ἄλλο μηδὲν πρὸ τοῦ αἰσχροῦ."

46. "Ἀλλ, ὦ μακάριε, ὅρα μὴ ἄλλο τι τὸ γενναῖον καὶ τὸ ἀγαθὸν‹ἦ› ἢ τὸ σῴζειν τε καὶ σῴζεσθαι· μὴ γὰρ τοῦτο μέν, τὸ ζῆνὁποσονδὴ χρόνον, τόν γε ὡς ἀληθῶς ἄνδρα ἐατέον ἐστὶ καὶ οὐφιλοψυχητέον, ἀλλ ἐπιτρέψαντα περὶ τούτων τῷ θεῷ καὶπιστεύσαντα ταῖς γυναιξίν, ὅτι τὴν εἱμαρμένην οὐδ ἂν εἷς ἐκφύγοι,τὸ ἐπὶ τούτῳ σκεπτέον τίνα ἂν τρόπον τοῦτον ὃν μέλλει χρόνονβιῶναι ὡς ἄριστα βιῴη."

47. Περισκοπεῖν ἄστρων δρόμους ὥσπερ συμπεριθέοντα καὶ τὰςτῶν στοιχείων εἰς ἄλληλα μεταβολὰς συνεχῶς ἐννοεῖν· ἀποκαθαίρουσιγὰρ αἱ τούτων φαντασίαι τὸν ῥύπον τοῦ χαμαὶ βίου.

48. Καὶ δὴ περὶ ἀνθρώπων τοὺς λόγους ποιούμενον ἐπισκοπεῖν[δεῖ] καὶ τὰ ἐπίγεια ὥσπερ ποθὲν ἄνωθεν κάτω· ἀγέλας,στρατεύματα, γεώργια, γάμους, διαλύσεις, γενέσεις, θανάτους,δικαστηρίων θόρυβον, ἐρήμους χώρας, βαρβάρων ἔθνη ποικίλα,ἑορτάς, θρήνους, ἀγοράς, τὸ παμμιγὲς καὶ τὸ ἐκ τῶν ἐναντίωνσυγκοσμούμενον.

49. Τὰ προγεγονότα ἀναθεωρεῖν, τὰς τοσαύτας τῶν ἡγεμονιῶνμεταβολάς. ἔξεστι καὶ τὰ ἐσόμενα προεφορᾶν· ὁμοειδῆ γὰρπάντως ἔσται καὶ οὐχ οἷόν τε ἐκβῆναι τοῦ ῥυθμοῦ τῶν νῦνγινομένων· ὅθεν καὶ ἴσον τὸ τεσσαράκοντα ἔτεσιν ἱστορῆσαιτὸν ἀνθρώπινον βίον τῷ ἐπὶ ἔτη μύρια· τί γὰρ πλέον ὄψει;

50. Καὶ τὰ μὲν ἐκ γαίας φύντ εἰς γαῖαν, τὰ δ ἀπ αἰθερίου βλαστόνταγονῆς εἰς αἰθέριον πάλιν ἦλθε πόλον.

51. Η τοῦτο· διάλυσις τῶν ἐν ταῖς ἀτόμοις ἀντεμπλοκῶν καὶτοιοῦτός τις σκορπισμὸς τῶν ἀπαθῶν στοιχείων.

52. Καὶ σίτοισι καὶ ποτοῖσι καὶ μαγεύμασι παρεκτρέποντες ὀχετὸνὥστε μὴ θανεῖν. θεόθεν δὲ πνέοντ οὖρον ἀνάγκη τλῆναι καμάτοιςἀνοδύρτοις.

53. "Καββαλικώτερος", ἀλλ οὐχὶ κοινωνικώτερος οὐδὲ αἰδημονέστεροςοὐδὲ εὐτακτότερος ἐπὶ τοῖς συμβαίνουσιν οὐδὲ εὐμενέστεροςπρὸς τὰ τῶν πλησίον παροράματα.

54. Ὅπου ἔργον ἐπιτελεῖσθαι δύναται κατὰ τὸν κοινὸν θεοῖς καὶἀνθρώποις λόγον, ἐκεῖ οὐδὲν δεινόν· ὅπου γὰρ ὠφελείας τυχεῖνἔξεστι διὰ τῆς εὐοδούσης καὶ κατὰ τὴν κατασκευὴν προιούσηςἐνεργείας, ἐκεῖ οὐδεμίαν βλάβην ὑφορατέον.

55. Πανταχοῦ καὶ διηνεκῶς ἐπὶ σοί ἐστι καὶ τῇ παρούσῃ συμβάσειθεοσεβῶς εὐαρεστεῖν καὶ τοῖς παροῦσιν ἀνθρώποις κατὰ δικαιοσύνηνπροσφέρεσθαι καὶ τῇ ‹παρ›ούσῃ φαντασίᾳ ἐμφιλοτεχνεῖν,ἵνα μή τι ἀκατάληπτον παρεισρυῇ.

56. Μὴ περιβλέπου ἀλλότρια ἡγεμονικά, ἀλλ ἐκεῖ βλέπε κατ εὐθὺἐπὶ τί σε ἡ φύσις ὁδηγεῖ, ἥ τε τοῦ ὅλου διὰ τῶν συμβαινόντωνσοι καὶ ἡ σὴ διὰ τῶν πρακτέων ὑπὸ σοῦ· πρακτέον δὲ ἑκάστῳ τὸἐξῆς τῇ κατασκευῇ· κατεσκεύασται δὲ τὰ μὲν λοιπὰ τῶν λογικῶνἕνεκεν, ὥσπερ καὶ ἐπὶ παντὸς ἄλλου τὰ χείρω τῶν κρειττόνωνἕνεκεν, τὰ δὲ λογικὰ ἀλλήλων ἕνεκεν. τὸ μὲν οὖν προηγούμενονἐν τῇ τοῦ ἀνθρώπου κατασκευῇ τὸ κοινωνικόν ἐστι, δεύτερον δὲτὸ ἀνένδοτον πρὸς τὰς σωματικὰς πείσεις· λογικῆς γὰρ καὶ νοερᾶςκινήσεως ἴδιον περιορίζειν ἑαυτὴν καὶ μήποτε ἡττᾶσθαι μήτεαἰσθητικῆς μήτε ὁρμητικῆς κινήσεως· ζῳώδεις γὰρ ἑκάτεραι, ἥδὲ νοερὰ ἐθέλει πρωτιστεύειν καὶ μὴ κατακρατεῖσθαι ὑπ ἐκείνων. δικαίως γε· πέφυκε γὰρ χρηστικὴ πᾶσιν ἐκείνοις. τρίτον ἐν τῇλογικῇ κατασκευῇ τὸ ἀπρόπτωτον καὶ ἀνεξαπάτητον. τούτωνοὖν ἐχόμενον τὸ ἡγεμονικὸν εὐθεῖαν περαινέτω καὶ ἔχει τὰἑαυτοῦ.

57. Ὡς ἀποτεθνηκότα ἤδη καὶ μέχρι νῦν ‹μὴ› βεβιωκότα, τὸ λοιπὸνἐκ τοῦ περιόντος ζῆσαι κατὰ τὴν φύσιν.

58. Μόνως φιλεῖν τὸ ἑαυτῷ συμβαῖνον καὶ συγκλωθόμενον· τί γὰράρμοδιώτερον;

59. Ἐφ ἑκάστου συμβάματος ἐκείνους πρὸ ὀμμάτων ἔχειν, οἷς τὰαὐτὰ συνέβαινεν, ἔπειτα ἤχθοντο, ἐξενίζοντο, ἐμέμφοντο· νῦνοῦν ἐκεῖνοι ποῦ; οὐδαμοῦ. τί οὖν; καὶ σὺ θέλεις ὁμοίως; οὐχὶ δὲτὰς μὲν ἀλλοτρίας τροπὰς καταλιπεῖν τοῖς τρέπουσι καὶ τρεπομένοις,αὐτὸς δὲ περὶ τὸ πῶς χρῆσθαι αὐτοῖς ὅλος γίνεσθαι; χρήσηγὰρ καλῶς καὶ ὕλη σοι ἔσται· μόνον πρόσεχε, καὶ θέλε σεαυτῷκαλὸς εἶναι ἐπὶ παντός, οϸ πράσσεις, καὶ μέμνησο ἀμφοτέρων,ὅτι καὶ διάφορον ‹ὃ πράσσεις καὶ ἀδιάφορον› ἐφ οϸ ἡ πρᾶξις.

60. Ἔνδον σκάπτε, ἔνδον ἡ πηγὴ τοῦ ἀγαθοῦ καὶ ἀεὶ ἀναβλύεινδυναμένη, ἐὰν ἀεὶ σκάπτῃς.

61. Δεῖ καὶ τὸ σῶμα πεπηγέναι καὶ μὴ διερρῖφθαι μήτε ἐν κινήσειμήτε ἐν σχέσει. οἷον γάρ τι ἐπὶ τοῦ προσώπου παρέχεται ἡ διάνοιασυνετὸν αὐτὸ καὶ εὔσχημον συντηροῦσα, τοιοῦτο καὶ ἐπὶ ὅλουτοῦ σώματος ἀπαιτητέον. πάντα δὲ ταῦτα σὺν τῷ ἀνεπιτηδεύτῳφυλακτέα.

62. Ἡ βιωτικὴ τῇ παλαιστικῇ ὁμοιοτέρα ἤπερ τῇ ὀρχηστικῇ κατὰτὸ πρὸς τὰ ἐμπίπτοντα καὶ οὐ προεγνωσμένα ἕτοιμος καὶ ἀπτῶςἑστάναι.

63. Συνεχῶς ἐφιστάναι, τίνες εἰσὶν οϸτοι, ὑφ ὧν μαρτυρεῖσθαιθέλεις, καὶ τίνα ἡγεμονικὰ ἔχουσιν· οὔτε γὰρ μέμψῃ τοῖς ἀκουσίωςπταίουσιν οὔτε ἐπιμαρτυρήσεως δεήσῃ, ἐμβλέπων εἰς τὰς πηγὰςτῆς ὑπολήψεως καὶ ὁρμῆς αὐτῶν.

64. "Πᾶσα ψυχή, φησίν, ἄκουσα στέρεται ἀληθείας·" οὕτως οὖνκαὶ δικαιοσύνης καὶ σωφροσύνης καὶ εὐμενείας καὶ παντὸς τοῦτοιούτου. ἀναγκαιότατον δὲ τὸ διηνεκῶς τούτου μεμνῆσθαι· ἔσῃ γὰρ πρὸς πάντας πραότερος.

65. Ἐπὶ μὲν παντὸς πόνου πρόχειρον ἔστω ὅτι οὐκ αἰσχρὸν οὐδετὴν διάνοιαν τὴν κυβερνῶσαν χείρω ποιεῖ· οὔτε γὰρ καθὸ λογικήἐστιν οὔτε καθὸ κοινωνικὴ διαφθείρει αὐτήν. ἐπὶ μέντοι τῶνπλείστων πόνων καὶ τὸ τοῦ Ἐπικούρου σοι βοηθείτω, ὅτι οὔτεἀφόρητον οὔτε αἰώνιον, ἐὰν τῶν ὅρων μνημονεύῃς καὶ μὴπροσδοξάζῃς. κἀκείνου δὲ μέμνησο, ὅτι πολλὰ πόνῳ τὰ αὐτὰὄντα λανθάνει, δυσχεραινόμενα· οἷον τὸ νυστάζειν καὶ τὸκαυματίζεσθαι καὶ τὸ ἀνορεκτεῖν· ὅταν οὖν τινι τούτωνδυσαρεστῇς, λέγε σεαυτῷ, ὅτι πόνῳ ἐνδίδως.

66. Ὅρα μήποτε τοιοῦτον πάθῃς πρὸς τοὺς ἀπανθρώπους, οἷονοί ‹ἀπ›άνθρωποι πρὸς τοὺς ἀνθρώπους.

67. Πόθεν ἴσμεν, εἰ μὴ Τηλαύγης Σωκράτους τὴν διάθεσιν κρείττωνῆν; οὐ γὰρ ἀρκεῖ, εἰ Σωκράτης ἐνδοξότερον ἀπέθανε καὶἐντρεχέστερον τοῖς σοφισταῖς διελέγετο καὶ καρτερικώτερον ἐντῷ πάγῳ διενυκτέρευε καὶ τὸν Σαλαμίνιον κελευσθεὶς ἄγεινγεννικώτερον ἔδοξεν ἀντιβῆναι καὶ "ἐν ταῖς ὁδοῖς ἐβρενθύετ",περὶ οῦ καὶ μάλιστ ἄν τις ἐπιστήσειεν, εἴπερ ἀληθὲς ἦν· ἀλλἐκεῖνο δεῖ σκοπεῖν, ποίαν τινὰ τὴν ψυχὴν εἶχε Σωκράτης καὶ εἰἐδύνατο ἀρκεῖσθαι τῷ δίκαιος εἶναι τὰ πρὸς ἀνθρώπους καὶ ὅσιοςτὰ πρὸς θεούς, μήτε εἰκῇ πρὸς τὴν κακίαν ἀγανακτῶν μήτε μὴνδουλεύων τινὸς ἀγνοίᾳ, μήτε τῶν ἀπονεμομένων ἐκ τοῦ ὅλου ὡςξένον τι δεχόμενος ἢ ὡς ἀφόρητον ὑπομένων, μήτε τοῖς τοῦσαρκιδίου πάθεσιν ἐμπαρέχων συμπαθῆ τὸν νοῦν.

68. Ἡ φύσις οὐχ οὕτως συνεκέρασέ ‹σε› τῷ συγκρίματι, ὡς μὴἐφεῖσθαι περιορίζειν ἑαυτὸν καὶ τὰ ἑαυτοῦ ὑφ ἑαυτῷ ποιεῖσθαι.τούτου μέμνησο ἀεὶ καὶ ἔτι ἐκείνου, ὅτι ἐν ὀλιγίστοις κεῖται τὸεὐδαιμόνως βιῶσαι· καὶ μή, ὅτι ἀπήλπισας διαλεκτικὸς καὶφυσικὸς ἔσεσθαι, διὰ τοῦτο ἀπογνῷς καὶ ἐλεύθερος καὶ αἰδήμωνκαὶ κοινωνικὸς καὶ εὐπειθὴς θεῷ. λίαν γὰρ ἐνδέχεται θεῖον ἄνδραγενέσθαι καὶ ὑπὸ μηδενὸς γνωρισθῆναι.

69. Ἀβιάστως διαζῆσαι ἐν πλείστῃ θυμηδίᾳ, κἂν πάντες καταβοῶσινἄτινα βούλονται, κἂν τὰ θηρία διασπᾷ τὰ μελύδρια τοῦπεριτεθραμμένου τούτου φυράματος. τί γὰρ κωλύει ἐν πᾶσιτούτοις τὴν διάνοιαν σῴζειν ἑαυτὴν ἐν γαλήνῃ καὶ κρίσει [τῇ]περὶ τῶν περιεστηκότων ἀληθεῖ καὶ χρήσει τῶν ὑποβεβλημένωνέτοίμῃ, ὥστε τὴν μὲν κρίσιν λέγειν τῷ προσπίπτοντι· "τοῦτοὑπάρχεις κατ οὐσίαν, κἂν κατὰ δόξαν ἀλλοῖον φαίνῃ·" τὴν δὲχρῆσιν λέγειν τῷ ὑποπίπτοντι· "σὲ ἐζήτουν· ἀεὶ γάρ μοι τὸ παρὸνὕλη ἀρετῆς λογικῆς καὶ πολιτικῆς καὶ τὸ σύνολον τέχνης ἀνθρώπουἢ θεοῦ·" πᾶν γὰρ τὸ συμβαῖνον θεῷ ἢ ἀνθρώπῳἐξοικειοῦται καὶ οὔτε καινὸν οὔτε δυσμεταχείριστον, ἀλλὰγνώριμον καὶ εὐεργές.

70. Τοῦτο ἔχει ἡ τελειότης τοῦ ἤθους, τὸ πᾶσαν ἡμέραν ὡςτελευταίαν διεξάγειν καὶ μήτε σφύζειν μήτε ναρκᾶν μήτεὑποκρίνεσθαι.

71. Οἱ θεοί, ἀθάνατοι ὄντες, οὐ δυσχεραίνουσιν ὅτι ἐν τοσούτῳαἰῶνι δεήσει αὐτοὺς πάντως ἀεὶ τοιούτων ὄντων καὶ τοσούτωνφαύλων ἀνέχεσθαι· προσέτι δὲ καὶ κήδονται αὐτῶν παντοίως.σὺ δέ, ὅσον οὐδέπω λήγειν μέλλων, ἀπαυδᾷς, καὶ ταῦτα εἷς ὢντῶν φαύλων;

72. Γελοῖόν ἐστι τὴν μὲν ἰδίαν κακίαν μὴ φεύγειν, ὃ καὶ δυνατόνἐστι, τὴν δὲ τῶν ἄλλων φεύγειν, ὅπερ ἀδύνατον.

73. Ὃ ἂν ἡ λογικὴ καὶ πολιτικὴ δύναμις εὑρίσκῃ μήτε νοερὸνμήτε κοινωνικόν, εὐλόγως καταδεέστερον ἑαυτῆς κρίνει.

74. Ὅταν σὺ εὖ πεποιηκὼς ᾖς καὶ ἄλλος εὖ πεπονθώς, τί ἔτι ζητεῖςτρίτον παρὰ ταῦτα, ὥσπερ οἱ μωροί, τὸ καὶ δόξαι εὖ πεποιηκέναιἢ τὸ ἀμοιβῆς τυχεῖν;

75. Οὐδεὶς κάμνει ὠφελούμενος, ὠφέλεια δὲ πρᾶξις κατὰ φύσιν· μὴ οὖν κάμνε ὠφελούμενος, ἐν ᾧ ὠφελεῖς.

76. Ἡ τοῦ ὅλου φύσις ἐπὶ τὴν κοσμοποιίαν ὥρμησε· νῦν δὲ ἤτοιπᾶν τὸ γινόμενον κατ᾽ ἐπακολούθησιν γίνεται ἢ ἀλόγιστα καὶ τὰκυριώτατά ἐστιν ἐφ᾽ ἃ ποιεῖται ἰδίαν ὁρμὴν τὸ τοῦ κόσμουἡγεμονικόν. εἰς πολλά σε γαληνότερον ποιήσει τοῦτομνημονευόμενον.

152

BOOK EIGHT

I. This also, among other things, may serve to keep thee from vainglory; if thou shalt consider, that thou art now altogether incapable of the commendation of one, who all his life long, or from his youth at least, hath lived a philosopher's life. For both unto others, and to thyself especially, it is well known, that thou hast done many things contrary to that perfection of life. Thou hast therefore been confounded in thy course, and henceforth it will be hard for thee to recover the title and credit of a philosopher. And to it also is thy calling and profession repugnant. If therefore thou dost truly understand, what it is that is of moment indeed; as for thy fame and credit, take no thought or care for that: let it suffice thee if all the rest of thy life, be it more or less, thou shalt live as thy nature requireth, or according to the true and natural end of thy making. Take pains therefore to know what it is that thy nature requireth, and let nothing else distract thee. Thou hast already had sufficient experience, that of those many things that hitherto thou hast erred and wandered about, thou couldst not find happiness in any of them. Not in syllogisms, and logical subtilties, not in wealth, not in honour and reputation, not in pleasure. In none of all these. Wherein then is it to be found? In the practice of those things, which the nature of man, as he is a man, doth require. How then shall he do those things? if his dogmata, or moral tenets and opinions (from which all motions and actions do proceed), be right and true. Which be those dogmata? Those that concern that which is good or evil, as that there is nothing truly good and beneficial unto man, but that which makes him just, temperate, courageous, liberal; and that there is nothing truly evil and hurtful unto man, but that which causeth the contrary effects.

II. Upon every action that thou art about, put this question to thyself; How will this when it is done agree with me? Shall I have no occasion to repent of it? Yet a very little while and I am dead and gone; and all things are at end. What then do I care for more than this, that my present action whatsoever it be, may be the proper action of one that is reasonable; whose end is, the common good; who in all things is ruled and governed by the same law of right and reason, by which God Himself is.

III. Alexander, Caius, Pompeius; what are these to Diogenes, Heraclitus, and Socrates? These penetrated into the true nature of things; into all causes, and all subjects: and upon these did they exercise their power and authority. But as for those, as the extent of their error was, so far did their slavery extend.

IV. What they have done, they will still do, although thou shouldst hang thyself. First; let it not trouble thee. For all things both good and evil: come to pass according to the nature and general condition of the universe, and within a very little while, all things will be at an end; no man will be remembered: as now of Africanus (for example) and Augustus it is already come to pass. Then secondly; fix thy mind upon the thing itself; look into it, and remembering thyself, that thou art bound nevertheless to be a good man, and what it is that thy nature requireth of thee as thou art a man, be not diverted from what thou art about, and speak that which seemeth unto thee most just: only speak it kindly, modestly, and without hypocrisy.

V. That which the nature of the universe doth busy herself about, is; that which is here, to transfer it thither, to change it, and thence again to take it away, and to carry it to another place. So that thou needest not fear any new thing. For all things are usual and ordinary; and all things are disposed by equality.

VI. Every particular nature hath content, when in its own proper course it speeds. A reasonable nature doth then speed, when first in matter of fancies and imaginations, it gives no consent to that which is either false uncertain. Secondly, when in all its motions and resolutions it takes its level at the common good only, and that it desireth nothing, and flieth from nothing, bet what is in its own power to compass or avoid. And lastly, when it willingly and gladly embraceth, whatsoever is dealt and appointed unto it by the common nature. For it is part of it; even as the nature of any one leaf, is part of the common nature of all plants and trees. But that the nature of a leaf, is part of a nature both unreasonable and unsensible, and which in its proper end may be hindered; or, which is servile and slavish: whereas the nature of man is part of a common nature which cannot be hindered, and which is both reasonable and just. From whence also it is, that accord ing to the worth of everything, she doth make such equal distribution of all things, as of duration, substance form, operation, and of events and accidents. But herein consider not whether thou shalt find this equality in everything absolutely and by itself; but whether in all the particulars of some one thing taken together, and compared with all the particulars of some other thing, and them together likewise.

VII. Thou hast no time nor opportunity to read. What then? Hast thou not time and opportunity to exercise thyself, not to wrong thyself; to strive against all carnal pleasures and pains, and to aet the upper hand of them; to contemn honour and vainglory; and not only, not to be angry with them, whom towards thee thou doest find unsensible and unthankful; but also to have a care of them still, and of their welfare?

VIII. Forbear henceforth to complain of the trouble of a courtly life, either in public before others, or in private by thyself.

IX. Repentance is an inward and self-reprehension for the neglect or omission of somewhat that was profitable. Now whatsoever is good, is also profitable, and it is the part of an honest virtuous man to set by it, and to make reckoning of it accordingly. But never did any honest virtuous man repent of the neglect or omission of any carnal pleasure: no carnal pleasure then is either good or profitable.

X. This, what is it in itself, and by itself, according to its proper constitution? What is the substance of it? What is the matter, or proper use? What is the form or efficient cause? What is it for in this world, and how long will it abide? Thus must thou examine all things, that present themselves unto thee.

XI. When thou art hard to be stirred up and awaked out of thy sleep, admonish thyself and call to mind, that, to perform actions tending to the common good is that which thine own proper constitution, and that which the nature of man do require. But to sleep, is common to unreasonable creatures also. And what more proper and natural, yea what more kind and pleasing, than that which is according to nature?

XII. As every fancy and imagination presents itself unto thee, consider (if it be possible) the true nature, and the proper qualities of it, and reason with thyself about it.

XIII. At thy first encounter with any one, say presently to thyself: This man, what are his opinions concerning that which is good or evil? as concerning pain, pleasure, and the causes of both; concerning honour, and dishonour, concerning life and death? thus and thus. Now if it be no wonder that a man should have such and such opinions, how can it be a wonder that he should do such and such things? I will remember then, that he cannot but do as he doth, holding those opinions that he doth. Remember, that as it is a shame for any man to wonder that a fig tree should bear figs, so also to wonder that the world should bear anything, whatsoever it is which in the ordinary course of nature it may bear. To a physician also and to a pilot it is a shame either for the one to wonder, that such and such a one should have an ague; or for the other, that the winds should prove Contrary.

XIV. Remember, that to change thy mind upon occasion, and to follow him that is able to rectify thee, is equally ingenuous, as to find out at the first, what is right and just, without help. For of thee nothing is required, ti, is beyond the extent of thine own deliberation and jun. merit, and of thine own understanding.

XV. If it were thine act and in thine own power, wouldest thou do it? If it were not, whom dost tin accuse? the atoms, or the Gods? For to do either, the part of a mad man. Thou must therefore blame nobody, but if it be in thy power, redress what is amiss; if it be not, to what end is it to complain? For nothing should be done but to some certain end.

XVI. Whatsoever dieth and falleth, however and wheresoever it die and fall, it cannot fall out of the world, here it have its abode and change, here also shall it have its dissolution into its proper elements. The same are the world's elements, and the elements of which thou dost consist. And they when they are changed, they murmur not; why shouldest thou?

XVII. Whatsoever is, was made for something: as a horse, a vine. Why wonderest thou? The sun itself will say of itself, I was made for something; and so hath every god its proper function. What then were then made for? to disport and delight thyself? See how even common sense and reason cannot brook it.

XVIII. Nature hath its end as well in the end and final consummation of anything that is, as in the begin-nine and continuation of it.

XIX. As one that tosseth up a ball. And what is a ball the better, if the motion of it be upwards; or the worse if it be downwards; or if it chance to fall upon the ground? So for the bubble; if it continue, what it the better? and if it dissolve, what is it the worse And so is it of a candle too. And so must thou reason with thyself, both in matter of fame, and in matter of death. For as for the body itself, (the subject of death) wouldest thou know the vileness of it? Turn it about that thou mayest behold it the worst sides upwards as well, as in its more ordinary pleasant shape; how doth it look, when it is old and withered? when sick and pained? when in the act of lust, and fornication? And as for fame. This life is short. Both he that praiseth, and he that is praised; he that remembers, and he that is remembered, will soon be dust and ashes. Besides, it is but in one corner of this part of the world that thou art praised; and yet in this corner, thou hast not the joint praises of all men; no nor scarce of any one constantly. And yet the whole earth itself, what is it but as one point, in regard of the whole world?

XX. That which must be the subject of thy consideration, is either the matter itself, or the dogma, or the operation, or the true sense and signification.

XXI. Most justly have these things happened unto thee: why dost not thou amend? O but thou hadst rather become good tomorrow, than to be so today.

XXII. Shall I do it? I will; so the end of my action be to do good unto men. Doth anything by way of cross or adversity happen unto me? I accept it, with reference unto the Gods, and their providence; the fountain of all things, from which whatsoever comes to pass, doth hang and depend.

XXIII. By one action judge of the rest: this bathing which usually takes up so much of our time, what is it? Oil, sweat, filth; or the sordes of the body: an excrementitious viscosity, the excrements of oil and other ointments used about the body, and mixed with the sordes of the body: all base and loathsome. And such almost is every part of our life; and every worldly object.

XXIV. Lucilla buried Verus; then was Lucilla herself buried by others. So Secunda Maximus, then Secunda herself. So Epitynchanus, Diotimus; then Epitynchanus himself. So Antoninus Pius, Faustina his wife; then Antoninus himself. This is the course of the world. First Celer, Adrianus; then Adrianus himself. And those austere ones; those that foretold other men's deaths; those that were so proud and stately, where are they now? Those austere ones I mean, such as were Charax, and Demetrius the Platonic, and Eudaemon, and others like unto those. They were all but for one day; all dead and gone long since. Some of them no sooner dead, than forgotten. Others soon turned into fables. Of others, even that which was fabulous, is now long since forgotten. This thereafter thou must remember, that whatsoever thou art compounded of, shall soon be dispersed, and that thy life and breath, or thy soul, shall either be no more or shall ranslated (sp.), and appointed to some certain place and station.

XXV. The true joy of a man, is to do that which properly belongs unto a man. That which is most proper unto a man, is, first, to be kindly affected towards them that are of the same kind and nature as he is himself to contemn all sensual motions and appetites, to discern rightly all plausible fancies and imaginations, to contemplate the nature of the universe; both it, and things that are done in it. In which kind of contemplation three several relations are to be observed The first, to the apparent secondary cause. The Second to the first original cause, God, from whom originally proceeds whatsoever doth happen in the world. The third and last, to them that we live and converse with: what use may be made of it, to their use and benefit.

XXVI. If pain be an evil, either it is in regard of the body; (and that cannot be, because the body of itself is altogether insensible:) or in regard of the soul But it is in the power of the soul, to preserve her own peace and tranquillity, and not to suppose that pain is evil. For all judgment and deliberation; all prosecution, or aversation is from within, whither the sense of evil (except it be let in by opinion) cannot penetrate.

XXVII. Wipe off all idle fancies, and say unto thyself incessantly; Now if I will, it is in my power to keep out of this my soul all wickedness, all lust, and concupiscences, all trouble and confusion. But on the contrary to behold and consider all things according to their true nature, and to carry myself towards everything according to its true worth. Remember then this thy power that nature hath given thee.

XXVIII. Whether thou speak in the Senate or whether thou speak to any particular, let thy speech In always grave and modest. But thou must not openly and vulgarly observe that sound and exact form of speaking, concerning that which is truly good and truly civil; the vanity of the world, and of worldly men: which otherwise truth and reason doth prescribe.

XXIX. Augustus his court; his wife, his daughter, his nephews, his sons-in-law his sister, Agrippa, his kinsmen, his domestics, his friends; Areus, Maecenas, his slayers of beasts for sacrifice and divination: there thou hast the death of a whole court together. Proceed now on to the rest that have been since that of Augustus. Hath death dwelt with them otherwise, though so many and so stately whilst they lived, than it doth use to deal with any one particular man? Consider now the death of a whole kindred and family, as of that of the Pompeys, as that also that useth to be written upon some monuments, HE WAS THE LAST OF HIS

OWN KINDRED. O what care did his predecessors take, that they might leave a successor, yet behold at last one or other must of necessity be THE LAST. Here again therefore consider the death of a whole kindred.

XXX. Contract thy whole life to the measure and proportion of one single action. And if in every particular action thou dost perform what is fitting to the utmost of thy power, let it suffice thee. And who can hinder thee, but that thou mayest perform what is fitting? But there may be some outward let and impediment. Not any, that can hinder thee, but that whatsoever thou dost, thou may do it, justly, temperately, and with the praise of God. Yea, but there may be somewhat, whereby some operation or other of thine may be hindered. And then, with that very thing that doth hinder, thou mayest he well pleased, and so by this gentle and equanimious conversion of thy mind unto that which may be, instead of that which at first thou didst intend, in the room of that former action there succeedeth another, which agrees as well with this contraction of thy life, that we now speak of.

XXXI. Receive temporal blessings without ostentation, when they are sent and thou shalt be able to part with them with all readiness and facility when they are taken from thee again.

XXXII. If ever thou sawest either a hand, or a foot, or a head lying by itself, in some place or other, as cut off from the rest of the body, such must thou conceive him to make himself, as much as in him lieth, that either is offended with anything that is happened, (whatsoever it be) and as it were divides himself from it: or that commits anything against the natural law of mutual correspondence, and society among men: or, he that, commits any act of uncharitableness. Whosoever thou art, thou art such, thou art cast forth I know not whither out of the general unity, which is according to nature. Thou went born indeed a part, but now thou hast cut thyself off. However, herein is matter of joy and exultation, that thou mayst be united again. God hath not granted it unto any other part, that once separated and cut off, it might be reunited, and come together again. But, behold, that GOODNESS how great and immense it is! which hath so much esteemed MAN. As at first he was so made, that he needed not, except he would himself, have divided himself from the whole; so once divided and cut off, IT hath so provided and ordered it, that if he would himself, he might return, and grow together again, and be admitted into its former rank and place of a part, as he was before.

XXXIII. As almost all her other faculties and properties the nature of the universe hath imparted unto every reasonable creature, so this in particular we have received from her, that as whatsoever doth oppose itself unto her, and doth withstand her in her purposes and intentions, she doth, though against its will and intention, bring it about to herself, to serve herself of it in the execution of her own destinated ends; and so by this though not intended co-operation of it with herself makes it part of herself whether it will or no. So may every reasonable creature, what crosses and impediments soever it meets with in the course of this mortal life, it may use them as fit and proper objects, to the furtherance of whatsoever it intended and absolutely proposed unto itself as its natural end and happiness.

XXXIV. Let not the general representation unto thyself of the wretchedness of this our mortal life, trouble thee. Let not thy mind wander up and down, and heap together in her thoughts the many troubles and grievous calamities which thou art as subject unto as any other. But as everything in particular doth happen, put this question unto thyself, and say: What is it that in this present matter, seems unto thee so intolerable? For thou wilt be ashamed to confess it. Then upon this presently call to mind, that neither that which is future, nor that which is past can hurt thee; but that only which is present. (And that also is much lessened, if thou dost lightly circumscribe it:) and then check thy mind if for so little a while, (a mere instant), it cannot hold out with patience.

XXXV. What? are either Panthea or Pergamus abiding to this day by their masters' tombs? or either Chabrias or Diotimus by that of Adrianus? O foolery! For what if they did, would their masters be sensible of It? or if sensible, would they be glad of it? or if glad, were these immortal? Was not it appointed unto them also (both men and women,) to become old in time, and then to die? And these once dead, what would become of these former? And when all is done, what is all this for, but for a mere bag of blood and corruption?

XXXVI. If thou beest quick-sighted, be so in matter of judgment, and best discretion, saith he.

XXXVII. In the whole constitution of man, I see not any virtue contrary to justice, whereby it may be resisted and opposed. But one whereby pleasure and voluptuousness may be resisted and opposed, I see: continence.

XXXVIII. If thou canst but withdraw conceit and opinion concerning that which may seem hurtful and offensive, thou thyself art as safe, as safe may be. Thou thyself? and who is that? Thy reason. 'Yea, but I am not reason.' Well, be it so. However, let not thy reason or understanding admit of grief, and if there be anything in thee that is grieved, let that, (whatsoever it be,) conceive its own grief, if it can.

XXXIX. That which is a hindrance of the senses, is an evil to the sensitive nature. That which is a hindrance of the appetitive and prosecutive faculty, is an evil to the sensitive nature. As of the sensitive, so of the vegetative constitution, what-soever is a hindrance unto it, is also in that respect an evil unto the same. And so likewise, whatsoever is a hindrance unto the mind and understanding, must needs be the proper evil of the reasonable nature. Now apply all those things unto thyself. Do either pain or pleasure seize on thee? Let the senses look to that. Hast thou met with Some obstacle or other in thy purpose and intention? If thou didst propose without due reservation and exception now hath thy reasonable part received a blow indeed But if in general thou didst propose unto thyself what soever might be, thou art not thereby either hurt, nor properly hindered. For in those things that properly belong unto the mind, she cannot be hindered by any man. It is not fire, nor iron; nor the power of a tyrant nor the power of a slandering tongue; nor anything else that can penetrate into her.

XL. If once round and solid, there is no fear that ever it will change.

XLI. Why should I grieve myself; who never did willingly grieve any other! One thing rejoices one and another thing another. As for me, this is my joy, if my understanding be right and sound, as neither averse from any man, nor refus-ing any of those things which as a man I am subject unto; if I can look upon all things in the world meekly and kindly; accept all things and carry myself towards everything according to to true worth of the thing itself.

XLII. This time that is now present, bestow thou upon thyself. They that rather hunt for fame after death, do not consider, that those men that shall be hereafter, will be even such, as these whom now they can so hardly bear with. And besides they also will be mortal men. But to consider the thing in itself, if so many with so many voices, shall make such and such a sound, or shall have such and such an opinion concerning thee, what is it to thee?

XLIII. Take me and throw me where thou wilt: I am indifferent. For there also I shall have that spirit which is within me propitious; that is well pleased and fully contented both in that constant disposition, and with those particular actions, which to its own proper constitution are suitable and agreeable.

XLIV. Is this then a thing of that worth, that for it my soul should suffer, and become worse than it was? as either basely dejected, or disordinately affected, or confounded within itself, or terrified? What can there be, that thou shouldest so much esteem?

XLV. Nothing can happen unto thee, which is not incidental unto thee, as thou art a man. As nothing can happen either to an ox, a vine, or to a stone, which is not incidental unto them; unto every one in his own kind. If therefore nothing can happen unto anything, which is not both usual and natural; why art thou displeased? Sure the common nature of all would not bring anything upon any, that were intolerable. If therefore it be a thing external that causes thy grief, know, that it is not that properly that doth cause it, but thine own conceit and opinion concerning the thing: which thou mayest rid thyself of, when thou wilt. But if it be somewhat that is amiss in thine own disposition, that doth grieve thee, mayest thou not rectify thy moral tenets and opinions. But if it grieve thee, that thou doest not perform that which seemeth unto thee right and just, why doest not thou choose rather to perform it than to grieve? But somewhat that is stronger than thyself doth hinder thee. Let it not grieve thee then, if it be not thy fault that the thing is not performed. 'Yea but it is a thing of that nature, as that thy life is not worth the while, except it may be performed.' If it be so, upon condition that thou be kindly and lovingly disposed towards all men, thou mayest be gone. For even then, as much as at any time, art thou in a very good estate of performance, when thou doest die in charity with those, that are an obstacle unto thy performance.

XLVI. Remember that thy mind is of that nature as that it becometh altogether unconquerable, when once recollected in herself, she seeks no other content than this, that she cannot be forced: yea though it so fall out, that it be even against reason itself, that it cloth bandy. How much less when by the help of reason she is able to judge of things with discretion? And therefore let thy chief fort and place of defence be, a mind free from passions. A stronger place, (whereunto to make his refuge, and so to become impregnable) and better fortified than this, hath no man. He that seeth not this is unlearned. He that seeth it, and betaketh not himself to this place of refuge, is unhappy.

164

XLVII. Keep thyself to the first bare and naked apprehensions of things, as they present themselves unto thee, and add not unto them. It is reported unto thee, that such a one speaketh ill of thee. Well; that he speaketh ill of thee, so much is reported. But that thou art hurt thereby, is not reported: that is the addition of opinion, which thou must exclude. I see that my child is sick. That he is sick, I see, but that he is in danger of his life also, I see it not. Thus thou must use to keep thyself to the first motions and apprehensions of things, as they present themselves outwardly; and add not unto them from within thyself through mere conceit and opinion. Or rather add unto them: hut as one that understandeth the true nature of all things that happen in the world.

XLVIII. Is the cucumber bitter? set it away. Brambles are in the way? avoid them. Let this suffice. Add not presently speaking unto thyself, What serve these things for in the world? For, this, one that is acquainted with the mysteries of nature, will laugh at thee for it; as a carpenter would or a shoemaker, if meeting in either of their shops with some shavings, or small remnants of their work, thou shouldest blame them for it. And yet those men, it is not for want of a place where to throw them that they keep them in their shops for a while: but the nature of the universe hath no such out-place; but herein doth consist the wonder of her art and skill, that she having once circumscribed herself within some certain bounds and limits, whatsoever is within her that seems either corrupted, or old, or unprofitable, she can change it into herself, and of these very things can make new things; so that she needeth not to seek elsewhere out of herself either for a new supply of matter and substance, or for a place where to throw out whatsoever is irrecoverably putrid and corrupt. Thus she, as for place, so for matter and art, is herself sufficient unto herself.

XLIX. Not to be slack and negligent; or loose, and wanton in thy actions; nor contentious, and troublesome in thy conversation; nor to rove and wander in thy fancies and imaginations. Not basely to contract thy soul; nor boisterously to sally out with it, or furiously to launch out as it were, nor ever to want employment.

L. 'They kill me, they cut my flesh; they persecute my person with curses.' What then? May not thy mind for all this continue pure, prudent, temperate, just? As a fountain of sweet and clear water, though she be cursed by some stander by, yet do her springs nevertheless still run as sweet and clear as before; yea though either dirt or dung be thrown in, yet is it no sooner thrown, than dispersed, and she cleared. She cannot be dyed or infected by it. What then must I do, that I may have within myself an overflowing fountain, and not a well? Beget thyself by continual pains and endeavours to true liberty with charity, and true simplicity and modesty.

LI. He that knoweth not what the world is, knoweth not where he himself is. And he that knoweth not what the world was made for, cannot possibly know either what are the qualities, or what is the nature of the world. Now he that in either of these is to seek, for what he himself was made is ignorant also. What then dost thou think of that man, who proposeth unto himself, as a matter of great moment, the noise and applause of men, who both where they are, and what they are themselves, are altogether ignorant? Dost thou desire to be commended of that man, who thrice in one hour perchance, doth himself curse himself? Dost thou desire to please him, who pleaseth not himself? or dost thou think that he pleaseth himself, who doth use to repent himself almost of everything that he doth?

LII. Not only now henceforth to have a common breath, or to hold correspondency of breath, with that air, that compasseth us about; but to have a common mind, or to hold correspondency of mind also with that rational substance, which compasseth all things. For, that also is of itself, and of its own nature (if a man can but draw it in as he should) everywhere diffused; and passeth through all things, no less than the air doth, if a man can but suck it in.

LIII. Wickedness in general doth not hurt the world. Particular wickedness doth not hurt any other: only unto him it is hurtful, whosoever he be that offends, unto whom in great favour and mercy it is granted, that whensoever he himself shall but first desire it, he may be presently delivered of it. Unto my free will my neighbour's free will, whoever he be, (as his life, or his bode), is altogether indifferent. For though we are all made one for another, yet have our minds and understandings each of them their own proper and limited jurisdiction. For else another man's wickedness might be my evil which God would not have, that it might not be in another man's power to make me unhappy: which nothing now can do but mine own wickedness.

LIV. The sun seemeth to be shed abroad. And indeed it is diffused but not effused. For that diffusion of it is a [-r~Jo-tc] or an exten- sion. For therefore are the beams of it called [~i-~m'~] from the word [~KTEIVEO-Oa,,] to be stretched out and extended. Now what a sunbeam is, thou mayest know if thou observe the light of the sun, when through some narrow hole it pierceth into some room that is dark. For it is always in a direct line. And as by any solid body, that it meets with in the way that is not penetrable by air, it is divided and abrupted, and yet neither slides off, or falls down, but stayeth there nevertheless: such must the diffusion in the mind be; not an effusion, but an extension. What obstacles and impediments soever she meeteth within her way, she must not violently, and by way of an impetuous onset light upon them; neither must she fall down; but she must stand, and give light unto that which doth admit of it. For as for that which doth not, it is its own fault and loss, if it bereave itself of her light.

LV. He that feareth death, either feareth that he shall have no sense at all, or that his senses will not be the same. Whereas, he should rather comfort himself, that either no sense at all, and so no sense of evil; or if any sense, then another life, and so no death properly.

LVI. All men are made one for another: either then teach them better, or bear with them.

LVII. The motion of the mind is not as the motion of a dart. For the mind when it is wary and cautelous, and by way of diligent circumspection turneth herself many ways, may then as well be said to go straight on to the object, as when it useth no such circumspection.

LVIII. To pierce and penetrate into the estate of every one's understanding that thou hast to do with: as also to make the estate of thine own open, and penetrable to any other.

ΒΙΒΛΙΟ ΟΓΔΟΟ

1. Καὶ τοῦτο πρὸς τὸ ἀκενόδοξον φέρει, ὅτι οὐκέτι δύνασαι τὸνβίον ὅλον ἢ τόν γε ἀπὸ νεότητος φιλόσοφον βεβιωκέναι, ἀλλὰπολλοῖς τε ἄλλοις καὶ αὐτὸς ἑαυτῷ δῆλος γέγονας πόρρωφιλοσοφίας ὤν. πέφυρσαι οὖν, ὥστε τὴν μὲν δόξαν τὴν τοῦφιλοσόφου κτήσασθαι οὐκέτι σοι ῥᾴδιον· ἀνταγωνίζεται δὲ καὶἡ ὑπόθεσις. εἴπερ οὖν ἀληθῶς ἑώρακας ποῦ κεῖται τὸ πρᾶγμα,τὸ μὲν τί δόξεις ἄφες, ἀρκέσθητι δέ, εἰ κἂν τὸ λοιπὸν τοῦ βίουὅσον δήποτε, ‹ᾗ› ἡ [σὴ] φύσις σου θέλει, βιώσῃ. κατανόησονοὖν τί θέλει, καὶ ἄλλο μηδέν σε περισπάτω· πεπείρασαι γὰρ περὶπόσα πλανηθεὶς οὐδαμοῦ εῢρες τὸ εὖ ζῆν, οὐκ ἐν συλλογισμοῖς,οὐκ ἐν πλούτῳ, οὐκ ἐν δόξῃ, οὐκ ἐν ἀπολαύσει, οὐδαμοῦ. ποῦοὖν ἐστιν; ἐν τῷ ποιεῖν ἃ ἐπιζητεῖ ἡ τοῦ ἀνθρώπου φύσις. πῶςοὖν ταῦτα ποιήσει; ἐὰν δόγματα ἔχῃ ἀφ᾽ ὧν αἱ ὁρμαὶ καὶ αἱπράξεις. τίνα δόγματα; τὰ περὶ ἀγαθῶν καὶ κακῶν, ὡς οὐδενὸςμὲν ἀγαθοῦ ὄντος ἀνθρώπῳ ὃ οὐχὶ ποιεῖ δίκαιον, σώφρονα,ἀνδρεῖον, ἐλεύθερον, οὐδενὸς δὲ κακοῦ ὃ οὐχὶ ποιεῖ τἀναντίατοῖς εἰρημένοις.

2. Καθ᾽ ἑκάστην πρᾶξιν ἐρώτα σεαυτόν· πῶς μοι αὕτη ἔχει; μὴμετανοήσω ἐπ᾽ αὐτῇ; μικρὸν καὶ τέθνηκα καὶ πάντ᾽ ἐκ μέσου· τίπλέον ἐπιζητῶ, εἰ τὸ παρὸν ἔργον ζῴου νοεροῦ καὶ κοινωνικοῦκαὶ ἰσονόμου θεῷ;

3. Ἀλέξανδρος [δὲ] καὶ Γάιος καὶ Πομπήιος τί πρὸς Διογένη καὶἩράκλειτον καὶ Σωκράτην; οἱ μὲν γὰρ εἶδον τὰ πράγματα καὶτὰς αἰτίας καὶ τὰς ὕλας, καὶ τὰ ἡγεμονικὰ ἦν αὐτῶν αὐτά‹ρκη›,ἐκεί‹νων› δὲ ὅσων πρόνοια καὶ δουλεία πόσων.

4. Ὅτι οὐδὲν ἧττον τὰ αὐτὰ ποιήσουσι, κἂν σὺ διαρραγῇς.

5. Τὸ πρῶτον μὴ ταράσσου· πάντα γὰρ κατὰ τὴν τοῦ ὅλου φύσιν,καὶ ὀλίγου χρόνου οὐδεὶς οὐδαμοῦ ἔσῃ, ὥσπερ οὐδὲ Ἀδριανὸςοὐδὲ Αὔγουστος. ἔπειτα ἀτενίσας εἰς τὸ πρᾶγμα ἴδε αὐτὸ καὶσυμμνημονεύσας ὅτι ἀγαθόν σε ἄνθρωπον εἶναι δεῖ καὶ τί τοῦἀνθρώπου ἡ φύσις ἀπαιτεῖ, πρᾶξον τοῦτο ἀμεταστρεπτὶ καὶεἰπέ, ὡς δικαιότατον φαίνεταί σοι· μόνον εὐμενῶς καὶ αἰδημόνωςκαὶ ἀνυποκρίτως.

6. Ἡ τῶν ὅλων φύσις τοῦτο ἔργον ἔχει, τὰ ὧδε ὄντα ἐκεῖμετατιθέναι, μεταβάλλειν, αἴρειν ἔνθεν καὶ ἐκεῖ φέρειν. πάντατροπαί· ἀλλὰ ἴσαι καὶ αἱ ἀπονεμήσεις. πάντα συνήθη· οὐχ ὥστεφοβηθῆναι, μή τι καινόν.

7. Ἀρκεῖται πᾶσα φύσις ἑαυτῇ εὐοδούσῃ, φύσις δὲ λογικὴ εὐοδεῖἐν μὲν φαντασίαις μήτε ψευδεῖ μήτε ἀδήλῳ συγκατατιθεμένη,τὰς ὁρμὰς δὲ ἐπὶ τὰ κοινωνικὰ ἔργα μόνα ἀπευθύνουσα, τὰςὀρέξεις δὲ καὶ τὰς ἐκκλίσεις τῶν ἐφ ἡμῖν μόνων περιποιουμένη,τὸ δὲ ὑπὸ τῆς κοινῆς φύσεως ἀπονεμόμενον πᾶν ἀσπαζομένη μέρος γὰρ αὐτῆς ἐστιν ὡς ἡ τοῦ φύλλου φύσις τῆς τοῦ φυτοῦφύσεως πλὴν ὅτι ἐκεῖ μὲν ἡ τοῦ φύλλου φύσις μέρος ἐστὶ φύσεωςκαὶ ἀναισθήτου καὶ ἀλόγου καὶ ἐμποδίζεσθαι δυναμένης, ἡ δὲτοῦ ἀνθρώπου φύσις μέρος ἐστὶν ἀνεμποδίστου φύσεως καὶνοερᾶς καὶ δικαίας, εἴγε ἴσους καὶ κατ ἀξίαν τοὺς μερισμοὺςχρόνων, οὐσίας, αἰτίου, ἐνεργείας, συμβάσεως ἑκάστοις ποιεῖται.σκόπει δέ, μὴ εἰ τὸ ‹ἓν› πρὸς τὸ ἓν ἴσον εὑρήσεις ἐπὶ παντός,ἀλλὰ εἰ συλλήβδην τὰ πάντα τοῦδε πρὸς ἀθρόα τὰ τοῦ ἑτέρου.

8. Ἀναγινώσκειν οὐκ ἔξεστιν. ἀλλὰ ὕβριν ἀνείργειν ἔξεστιν· ἀλλὰἡδονῶν καὶ πόνων καθυπερτερεῖν ἔξεστιν· ἀλλὰ τοῦ δοξαρίουὑπεράνω εἶναι ἔξεστιν· ἀλλὰ ἀναισθήτοις καὶ ἀχαρίστοις μὴθυμοῦσθαι, προσέτι κήδεσθαι αὐτῶν ἔξεστιν.

9. Μηκέτι σου μηδεὶς ἀκούσῃ καταμεμφομένου τὸν ἐν αὐλῇ βίονμηδὲ σὺ σεαυτοῦ.

10. Ἡ μετάνοιά ἐστιν ἐπίληψίς τις ἑαυτοῦ ὡς χρήσιμόν τι παρεικότος·τὸ δὲ ἀγαθὸν χρήσιμόν τι δεῖ εἶναι καὶ ἐπιμελητέον αὐτοῦτῷ καλῷ καὶ ἀγαθῷ ἀνδρί· οὐδεὶς δ ἂν καλὸς καὶ ἀγαθὸς ἀνὴρμετανοήσειεν ἐπὶ τῷ ἡδονήν τινα παρεικέναι· οὔτε ἄρα χρήσιμονοὔτε ἀγαθὸν ἡδονή.

11. Τοῦτο τί ἐστιν αὐτὸ καθ αὑτὸ τῇ ἰδίᾳ κατασκευῇ, τί μὲν τὸοὐσιῶδες αὐτοῦ καὶ ὑλικόν, τί δὲ τὸ αἰτιῶδες, τί δὲ ποιεῖ ἐν τῷκόσμῳ, πόσον δὲ χρόνον ὑφίσταται;

12. Ὅταν ἐξ ὕπνου δυσχερῶς ἐγείρῃ, ἀναμιμνήσκου ὅτι κατὰ τὴνκατασκευήν σου ἐστὶ καὶ κατὰ τὴν ἀνθρωπικὴν φύσιν τὸ πράξειςκοινωνικὰς ἀποδιδόναι, τὸ δὲ καθεύδειν κοινὸν καὶ τῶν ἀλόγωνζῴων· ὃ δὲ κατὰ φύσιν ἑκάστῳ, τοῦτο οἰκειότερον καὶπροσφυέστερον καὶ δὴ καὶ προσηνέστερον.

13. Διηνεκῶς καὶ ἐπὶ πάσης, εἰ οἷόν τε, φαντασίας φυσιολογεῖν,παθολογεῖν, διαλεκτικεύεσθαι.

14. Ὧι ἂν ἐντυγχάνῃς, εὐθὺς ἑαυτῷ πρόλεγε· οῦτος τίνα δόγματαἔχει περὶ ἀγαθῶν καὶ κακῶν; εἰ γὰρ περὶ ἡδονῆς καὶ πόνου καὶτῶν ποιητικῶν ἑκατέρου καὶ περὶ δόξης, ἀδοξίας, θανάτου, ζωῆς,τοιάδε τινὰ δόγματα ἔχει, οὐδὲν θαυμαστὸν ἢ ξένον μοι δόξει,ἐὰν τάδε τινὰ ποιῇ, καὶ μεμνήσομαι ὅτι ἀναγκάζεται οὕτως

ποιεῖν.

15. Μέμνησο ὅτι, ὥσπερ αἰσχρόν ἐστι ξενίζεσθαι, εἰ ἡ συκῆ σῦκαφέρει, οὕτως, εἰ ὁ κόσμος τάδε τινὰ φέρει ὧν ἐστι φορός· καὶἰατρῷ δὲ καὶ κυβερνήτῃ αἰσχρὸν ξενίζεσθαι, εἰ πεπύρεχεν οῬτοςῇ εἰ ἀντίπνοια γέγονεν.

16. Μέμνησο ὅτι καὶ τὸ μετατίθεσθαι καὶ ἕπεσθαι τῷ διορθοῦντιὅμοίως ἐλεύθερόν ἐστι· σὴ γὰρ ἐνέργεια, κατὰ τὴν σὴν ὁρμὴνκαὶ κρίσιν καὶ δὴ καὶ κατὰ νοῦν τὸν σὸν περαινομένη.

17. Εἰ μὲν ἐπὶ σοί, τί αὐτὸ ποιεῖς; εἰ δὲ ἐπ ἄλλῳ, τίνι μέμφῃ; ταῖςἀτόμοις ἢ τοῖς θεοῖς; ἀμφότερα μανιώδη. οὐδενὶ μεμπτέον. εἰμὲν γὰρ δύνασαι, διόρθωσον· εἰ δὲ τοῦτο μὴ δύνασαι, τό γε πρᾶγμααὐτό· εἰ δὲ μηδὲ τοῦτο, πρὸς τί ἔτι σοι φέρει τὸ μέμψασθαι; εἰκῆγὰρ οὐδὲν ποιητέον.

18. Ἔξω τοῦ κόσμου τὸ ἀποθανὸν οὐ πίπτει. εἰ ὧδε μένει καὶμεταβάλλει, ὧδε καὶ διαλύεται εἰς τὰ ‹ἀ›ίδια, ἃ στοιχεῖά ἐστιτοῦ κόσμου καὶ σά. καὶ αὐτὰ δὲ μεταβάλλει καὶ οὐ γογγύζει.

19. Ἕκαστον πρός τι γέγονεν, ἵππος, ἄμπελος. τί θαυμάζεις; καὶ ὁἭλιος ἐρεῖ· πρός τι ἔργον γέγονα, καὶ οἱ λοιποὶ θεοί. σὺ οὖνπρὸς τί; τὸ ἥδεσθαι; ἴδε εἰ ἀνέχεται ἡ ἔννοια.

20. Ἡ φύσις ἐστόχασται ἑκάστου οὐδέν τι ἔλασσον τῆς ἀπολήξεωςἢ τῆς ἀρχῆς τε καὶ διεξαγωγῆς, ὡς ὁ ἀναβάλλων τὴν σφαῖραν· τίοὖν ἀγαθὸν τῷ σφαιρίῳ ἀναφερομένῳ ἢ κακὸν καταφερομένῳ ἢκαὶ πεπτωκότι; τί δὲ ἀγαθὸν τῇ πομφόλυγι συνεστώσῃ ἢ κακὸνδιαλυθείσῃ; τὰ ὅμοια δὲ καὶ ἐπὶ λύχνου.

21. Ἔκστρεψον καὶ θέασαι οἷόν ἐστι, γηράσαν δὲ οἷον γίνεται,νοσῆσαν δέ, † πορνεῦσαν. Βραχύβιον καὶ ὁ ἐπαινῶν καὶ ὁἐπαινούμενος καὶ ὁ μνημονεύων καὶ ὁ μνημονευόμενος. προσέτιδὲ καὶ ἐν γωνίᾳ τούτου τοῦ κλίματος καὶ οὐδὲ ἐνταῦθα πάντεςσυμφωνοῦσι καὶ οὐδὲ αὐτός τις ἑαυτῷ· καὶ ὅλη δὲ ἡ γῆ στιγμή.

22. Πρόσεχε τῷ ὑποκειμένῳ ἢ τῇ ἐνεργείᾳ ἢ τῷ δόγματι ἢ τῷσημαινομένῳ. Δικαίως ταῦτα πάσχεις· μᾶλλον δὴ θέλεις ἀγαθὸςαὔριον γενέσθαι ἢ σήμερον εἶναι.

23. Πράσσω τι; πράσσω ἐπ ἀνθρώπων εὐποιίαν ἀναφέρων.συμβαίνει τί μοι; δέχομαι ἐπὶ τοὺς θεοὺς ἀναφέρων καὶ τὴνπάντων πηγήν, ἀφ ἧς πάντα τὰ γινόμενα συμμηρύεται.

24. Ὁποῖόν σοι φαίνεται τὸ λούεσθαι, - ἔλαιον, ἱδρώς, ῥύπος,ὕδωρ γλοιῶδες, πάντα σικχαντά, - τοιοῦτον πᾶν μέρος τοῦ βίουκαὶ πᾶν ὑποκείμενον.

25. Λούκιλλα Οὐῆρον, εἶτα Λούκιλλα· Σέκουνδα Μάξιμον, εἶταΣέκουνδα· Ἐπιτύγχανος Διότιμον, εἶτα Ἐπιτύγχανος· ΦαυστῖνανἈντωνῖνος, εἶτα Ἀντωνῖνος. τοιαῦτα πάντα· Κέλερ Ἀδριανόν,εἶτα Κέλερ. οἱ δὲ δριμεῖς ἐκεῖνοι ἢ προγνωστικοὶ ἢ τετυφωμένοιποῦ; οἷον, δριμεῖς μὲν Χάραξ καὶ Δημήτριος [ὁ Πλατωνικὸς] καὶΕὐδαίμων καὶ εἴ τις τοιοῦτος. πάντα ἐφήμερα, τεθνηκότα πάλαι· ἔνιοι μὲν οὐδὲ ἐπ ὀλίγον μνημονευθέντες, οἱ δὲ εἰς μύθουςμεταβαλόντες, οἱ δὲ ἤδη καὶ ἐκ μύθων ἐξίτηλοι. τούτων οὖνμεμνῆσθαι, ὅτι δεήσει ἤτοι σκεδασθῆναι τὸ συγκριμάτιόν σου ἢσβεσθῆναι τὸ πνευμάτιον ἢ μεταστῆναι καὶ ἀλλαχοῦ καταταχθῆναι.

26. Εὐφροσύνη ἀνθρώπου ποιεῖν τὰ ἴδια ἀνθρώπου, ἴδιον δὲἀνθρώπου εὔνοια πρὸς τὸ ὁμόφυλον, ὑπερόρασις τῶν αἰσθητικῶνκινήσεων, διάκρισις τῶν πιθανῶν φαντασιῶν, ἐπιθεώρησις τῆςτῶν ὅλων φύσεως καὶ τῶν κατ αὐτὴν γινομένων.

27. Τρεῖς σχέσεις· ἡ μὲν πρὸς [τὸ αἴτιον] τὸ περικείμενον, ἡ δὲπρὸς τὴν θείαν αἰτίαν, ἀφ ἧς συμβαίνει πᾶσι πάντα, ἡ δὲ πρὸςτοὺς συμβιοῦντας.

28. Ὁ πόνος ἤτοι τῷ σώματι κακόν· οὐκοῦν ἀποφαινέσθω· ἢ τῇψυχῇ· ἀλλ ἔξεστιν αὐτῇ τὴν ἰδίαν αἰθρίαν καὶ γαλήνην διαφυλάσσεινκαὶ μὴ ὑπολαμβάνειν ὅτι κακόν. πᾶσα γὰρ κρίσις καὶὁρμὴ καὶ ὄρεξις καὶ ἔκκλισις ἔνδον καὶ οὐδὲν κακὸν ὧδε ἀναβαίνει.

29. Ἐξάλειφε τὰς φαντασίας συνεχῶς ἑαυτῷ λέγων· νῦν ἐπ ἐμοίἐστιν ἵνα ἐν ταύτῃ τῇ ψυχῇ μηδεμία πονηρία ἢ μηδὲ ἐπιθυμίαμηδὲ ὅλως ταραχή τις, ἀλλὰ βλέπων πάντα ὁποῖά ἐστι χρῶμαιἑκάστῳ κατ ἀξίαν. μέμνησο ταύτης τῆς ἐξουσίας κατὰ φύσιν.

30. Λαλεῖν καὶ ἐν συγκλήτῳ καὶ πρὸς πάνθ ὁντινοῦν κοσμίως, μὴπεριτράνως· ὑγιεῖ λόγῳ χρῆσθαι.

174

31. Αὐλὴ Αὐγούστου, γυνή, θυγάτηρ, ἔγγονοι, πρόγονοι, ἀδελφή, Ἀγρίππας, συγγενεῖς, οἰκεῖοι, φίλοι, Ἄρειος, Μαικήνας, ἰατροί, θύται· ὅλης αὐλῆς θάνατος. εἶτα ἔπιθι τὰς ἄλλας .. μὴ καθενὸς ἀνθρώπου θάνατον, οἷον Πομπηίων. κἀκεῖνο δὲ τὸ ἐπιγραφόμενον τοῖς μνήμασιν· ἔσχατος τοῦ ἰδίου γένους. ἐπιλογίζεσθαι πόσα ἐσπάσθησαν οἱ πρὸ αὐτῶν, ἵνα διάδοχόν τινα καταλίπωσιν, εἶτα ἀνάγκη ἔσχατόν τινα γενέσθαι· πάλιν ὧδε ὅλου γένους θάνατον.

32. Συντιθέναι δεῖ τὸν βίον κατὰ μίαν πρᾶξιν καὶ εἰ ἑκάστη τὸ ἑαυτῆς ἀπέχει ὡς οἷόν τε, ἀρκεῖσθαι· ἵνα δὲ τὸ ἑαυτῆς ἀπέχῃ, οὐδὲ εἷς σε κωλῦσαι δύναται· "ἀλλ᾽ ‹ἐν›στήσεταί τι ἔξωθεν·" οὐδὲν εἴς γε τὸ δικαίως καὶ σωφρόνως καὶ εὐλογίστως· "ἄλλο δέ τι ἴσως ἐνεργητικὸν κωλυθήσεται·" ἀλλὰ τῇ πρὸς αὐτὸ τὸ κώλυμα εὐαρεστήσει καὶ τῇ ἐπὶ τὸ διδόμενον εὐγνώμονι μεταβάσει εὐθὺς ἄλλη πρᾶξις ἀντικαθίσταται ἐναρμόσουσα εἰς τὴν σύνθεσιν, περὶ ἧς ὁ λόγος.

33. Ἀτύφως μὲν λαβεῖν, εὐλύτως δὲ ἀφεῖναι.

34. Εἴ ποτε εἶδες χεῖρα ἀποκεκομμένην ἢ πόδα ἢ κεφαλὴν ἀποτετμημένην, χωρίς πού ποτε ἀπὸ τοῦ λοιποῦ σώματος κειμένην· τοιοῦτον ἑαυτὸν ποιεῖ, ὅσον ἐφ᾽ ἑαυτῷ, ὁ μὴ θέλων τὸ συμβαῖνον καὶ ἀποσχίζων ἑαυτὸν ἢ ὁ ἀκοινώνητόν τι πράσσων. ἀπέρριψαί πού ποτε ἀπὸ τῆς κατὰ φύσιν ἑνώσεως· ἐπεφύκεις γὰρ μέρος· νῦν δὲ σεαυτὸν ἀπέκοψας. ἀλλ᾽ ὧδε κομψὸν ἐκεῖνο, ὅτι ἔξεστί σοι πάλιν ἑνῶσαι σεαυτόν. τοῦτο ἄλλῳ μέρει οὐδενὶ θεὸς ἐπέτρεψεν, χωρισθέντι καὶ διακοπέντι πάλιν συνελθεῖν, ἀλλὰ σκέψαι τὴν χρηστότητα ᾗ τετίμηκε τὸν ἄνθρωπον· καὶ γὰρ ἵνα τὴν ἀρχὴν μὴ ἀπορραγῇ ἀπὸ τοῦ ὅλου ἐπ᾽ αὐτῷ ἐποίησε, καὶ ἀπορραγέντι πάλιν ἐπανελθεῖν καὶ συμφῦναι καὶ τὴν τοῦ μέρους τάξιν ἀπολαβεῖν [ἐποίησεν].

35. Ὥσπερ τὰς ἄλλας δυνάμεις ἑκάστῳ τῶν λογικῶν † σχεδὸν ὅσον ἡ τῶν ὅλων φύσις, οὕτως καὶ ταύτην παρ᾽ αὐτῆς εἰλήφαμεν. ὃν τρόπον γὰρ ἐκείνη πᾶν τὸ ἐνιστάμενον καὶ ἀντιβαῖνον ἐπιπεριτρέπει καὶ κατατάσσει εἰς τὴν εἱμαρμένην καὶ μέρος ἑαυτῆς ποιεῖ, οὕτως καὶ τὸ λογικὸν ζῷον δύναται πᾶν κώλυμα ὕλην ἑαυτοῦ ποιεῖν καὶ χρῆσθαι αὐτῷ, ἐφ᾽ οἷον ἂν καὶ ὥρμησεν.

36. Μή σε συγχείτω ἡ τοῦ ὅλου βίου φαντασία, μὴ συμπερινόει ἐπίπονα οἷα καὶ ὅσα πιθανὸν ἐπιγεγενῆσθαι ‹καὶ ἐπιγενήσεσθαι›· ἀλλὰ καθ᾽ ἕκαστον τῶν παρόντων ἐπερώτα σεαυτόν· τί τοῦ ἔργου τὸ ἀφόρητον καὶ ἀνύποιστον; αἰσχυνθήσῃ γὰρ ὁμολογῆσαι. ἔπειτα ἀναμίμνησκε σεαυτὸν ὅτι οὔτε τὸ μέλλον οὔτε τὸ παρῳχηκὸς βαρεῖ σε, ἀλλ᾽ ἀεὶ τὸ παρόν, τοῦτο δὲ κατασμικρύνεται, ἐὰν αὐτὸ μόνον περιορίσῃς καὶ ἀπελέγχῃς τὴν διάνοιαν, εἰ πρὸς τοῦτο ψιλὸν ἀντέχειν

μὴ δύναται.

37. Μήτι νῦν παρακάθηται τῇ [τοῦ] Οὐήρου σορῷ Πάνθεια ἢΠέργαμος; τί δέ, τῇ Ἀδριανοῦ Χαβρίας ἢ Διότιμος; γελοῖον. τίδέ, εἰ παρεκάθηντο, ἔμελλον αἰσθάνεσθαι; τί δέ, εἰ ᾐσθάνοντο,ἔμελλον ἥδεσθαι; τί δέ, εἰ ἥδοντο, ἔμελλον οῬτοι ἀθάνατοι εἶναι;οὐχὶ καὶ τούτους πρῶτον μὲν γραίας καὶ γέροντας γενέσθαι οὕτωςεἵμαρτο, εἶτα ἀποθανεῖν; τί οὖν ὕστερον ἔμελλον ἐκεῖνοι ποιεῖντούτων ἀποθανόντων; γράσος πᾶν τοῦτο καὶ λύθρον ἐν θυλάκῳ.

38. Εἰ δύνασαι ὀξὺ βλέπειν, βλέπε κρίνων ‹κρίμασι›, φησί, σοφωτάτοις.

39. Δικαιοσύνης κατεξαναστατικὴν ἀρετὴν οὐχ ὁρῶ ἐν τῇ τοῦλογικοῦ ζῴου κατασκευῇ, ἡδονῆς δὲ ὁρῶ τὴν ἐγκράτειαν.

40. Ἐὰν ἀφέλῃς τὴν σὴν ὑπόληψιν περὶ τοῦ λυπεῖν σε δοκοῦντος,αὐτὸς ἐν τῷ ἀσφαλεστάτῳ ἕστηκας. "τίς αὐτός;" ὁ λόγος. "ἀλλοὐκ εἰμὶ λόγος." ἔστω. οὐκοῦν ὁ μὲν λόγος αὐτὸς ἑαυτὸν μὴλυπείτω, εἰ δέ τι ἄλλο σοι κακῶς ἔχει, ὑπολαβέτω αὐτὸ περὶ αὑτοῦ.

41. Ἐμποδισμὸς αἰσθήσεως κακὸν ζωτικῆς φύσεως. ἐμποδισμὸςὁρμῆς ὁμοίως κακὸν ζωτικῆς φύσεως. ἔστι δέ τι ἄλλο ὁμοίωςἐμποδιστικὸν καὶ κακὸν τῆς φυτικῆς κατασκευῆς. οὕτως τοίνυνἐμποδισμὸς νοῦ κακὸν νοερᾶς φύσεως. πάντα δὴ ταῦτα ἐπὶσεαυτὸν μετάφερε. πόνος, ἡδονὴ ἅπτεταί σου; ὄψεται ἡ αἴσθησις.ὁρμήσαντι ἔνστημα ἐγένετο; εἰ μὲν ἀνυπεξαιρέτως ὥρμας, ἤδηὡς λογικοῦ κακόν, εἰ δὲ τὸ κοινὸν λαμβάνεις, οὔπω βέβλαψαιοὐδὲ ἐμπεπόδισαι. τὰ μέντοι τοῦ νοῦ ἴδια οὐδεὶς ἄλλος εἴωθενἐμποδίζειν· τούτου γὰρ οὐ πῦρ, οὐ σίδηρος, οὐ τύραννος, οὐβλασφημία, οὐχ ὁτιοῦν ἅπτεται, ὅταν γένηται "σφαῖρος κυκλοτερὴςμονί".

42. Οὐκ εἰμὶ ἄξιος ἐμαυτὸν λυπεῖν· οὐδὲ γὰρ ἄλλον πώποτε ἑκὼνἐλύπησα.

43. Εὐφραίνει ἄλλον ἄλλο· ἐμὲ δέ, ἐὰν ὑγιὲς ἔχω τὸ ἡγεμονικόν,μὴ ἀποστρεφόμενον μήτε ἄνθρωπόν τινα μήτε ‹τι› τῶν ἀνθρώποιςσυμβαινόντων, ἀλλὰ πᾶν εὐμενέσιν ὀφθαλμοῖς ὁρῶν τε καὶδεχόμενον καὶ χρώμενον ἑκάστῳ κατ᾽ ἀξίαν.

44. Τοῦτον ἰδοὺ τὸν χρόνον σεαυτῷ χάρισαι. οἱ τὴν ὑστεροφημίανμᾶλλον διώκοντες οὐ λογίζονται ὅτι ἄλλοι τοιοῦτοι μέλλουσινἐκεῖνοι εἶναι, οἷοί εἰσιν οῬτοι οὓς βαροῦνται· κἀκεῖνοι δὲ θνητοί.τί δὲ ὅλως πρὸς σέ, ἂν ἐκεῖνοι φωναῖς τοιαύταις ἀπηχῶσιν ἢὑπόληψιν τοιαύτην περὶ σοῦ ἔχωσιν;

45. Ἆρόν με καὶ βάλε, ὅπου θέλεις. ἐκεῖ γὰρ ἕξω τὸν ἐμὸν δαίμοναἵλεως, τουτέστιν ἀρκούμενον, εἰ ἔχοι καὶ ἐνεργοίη κατὰ τὸ ἑξῆςτῇ ἰδίᾳ κατασκευῇ. Ἆρα τοῦτο ἄξιον, ἵνα δι᾽ αὐτὸ κακῶς μοιἔχῃ ἡ ψυχὴ καὶ χείρων ἑαυτῆς ᾖ, ταπεινουμένη, ὀρεγομένη,συνδουμένη, πτυρομένη; καὶ τί εὑρήσεις τούτου ἄξιον;

46. Ἀνθρώπῳ οὐδενὶ συμβαίνειν τι δύναται ὃ οὐκ ἔστινἀνθρωπικὸν σύμπτωμα, οὐδὲ βοῒ ὃ οὐκ ἔστι βοϊκόν, οὐδὲ ἀμπέλῳ ὃ οὐκ ἔστιν ἀμπελικόν, οὐδὲ λίθῳ ὃ οὐκ ἔστι λίθου ἴδιον. εἰ οὖνἑκάστῳ συμβαίνει ὃ καὶ εἴωθε καὶ πέφυκε, τί ἂν δυσχεραίνοις;οὐ γὰρ ἀφόρητόν σοι ἔφερεν ἡ κοινὴ φύσις.

47. Εἰ μὲν διά τι τῶν ἐκτὸς λυπῇ, οὐκ ἐκεῖνό σοι ἐνοχλεῖ, ἀλλὰ τὸσὸν περὶ αὐτοῦ κρῖμα, τοῦτο δὲ ἤδη ἐξαλεῖψαι ἐπὶ σοί ἐστιν. εἰδὲ λυπεῖ σέ τι τῶν ἐν τῇ σῇ διαθέσει, τίς ὁ κωλύων διορθῶσαι τόδόγμα; ὁμοίως δὲ καὶ εἰ λυπῇ ὅτι οὐχὶ τόδε τι ἐνεργεῖς ὑγιές σοιφαινόμενον, τί οὐχὶ μᾶλλον ἐνεργεῖς ἢ λυπῇ; "ἀλλὰ ἰσχυρότερόντι ἐνίσταται." μὴ οὖν λυποῦ· οὐ γὰρ παρὰ σὲ ἡ αἰτία τοῦ μὴἐνεργεῖσθαι. "ἀλλὰ οὐκ ἄξιον ζῆν μὴ ἐνεργουμένου τούτου."ἄπιθι οὖν ἐκ τοῦ ζῆν εὐμενής, ᾗ καὶ ὁ ἐνεργῶν ἀποθνῄσκει, ἅμαἵλεως τοῖς ἐνισταμένοις.

48. Μέμνησο ὅτι ἀκαταμάχητον γίνεται τὸ ἡγεμονικόν, ὅταν εἰςἑαυτὸ συστραφὲν ἀρκεσθῇ ἑαυτῷ, μὴ ποιοῦν τι ὃ μὴ θέλει, κἂνἀλόγως παρατάξηται. τί οὖν, ὅταν καὶ μετὰ λόγου καὶ περιεσκεμμένως κρίνῃ περί τινος; διὰ τοῦτο ἀκρόπολίς ἐστιν ἡ ἐλευθεραπαθῶν διάνοια· οὐδὲν γὰρ ὀχυρώτερον ἔχει ἄνθρωπος, ἐφ᾽ ὃκαταφυγὼν ἀνάλωτος λοιπὸν ἂν εἴη. ὁ μὲν οὖν μὴ ἑωρακὼςτοῦτο ἀμαθής, ὁ δὲ ἑωρακὼς καὶ μὴ καταφεύγων ἀτυχής.

49. Μηδὲν πλέον ἑαυτῷ λέγε ὧν αἱ προηγούμεναι φαντασίαιἀναγγέλλουσιν. ἤγγελται ὅτι ὁ δεῖνά σε κακῶς λέγει. ἤγγελταιτοῦτο· τὸ δέ, ὅτι βέβλαψαι, οὐκ ἤγγελται. βλέπω ὅτι νοσεῖ τὸπαιδίον. βλέπω· ὅτι δὲ κινδυνεύει, οὐ βλέπω. οὕτως οὖν μένεἀεὶ ἐπὶ τῶν πρώτων φαντασιῶν καὶ μηδὲν αὐτὸς ἔνδοθεν ἐπίλεγεκαὶ οὐδέν σοι γίνεται· μᾶλλον δὲ ἐπίλεγε ὡς γνωρίζων ἕκαστατῶν ἐν τῷ κόσμῳ συμβαινόντων.

50. Σίκυος πικρός; ἄφες. βάτοι ἐν τῇ ὁδῷ; ἔκκλινον. ἀρκεῖ, μὴπροσεπείπῃς· τί δὲ καὶ ἐγένετο ταῦτα ἐν τῷ κόσμῳ; ἐπεὶ καταγελασθήσῃὑπὸ ἀνθρώπου φυσιολόγου, ὡς ἂν καὶ ὑπὸ τέκτονοςκαὶ σκυτέως γελασθείης καταγινώσκων ὅτι ἐν τῷ ἐργαστηρίῳξέσματα καὶ περιτμήματα τῶν κατασκευαζομένων ὁρᾷς. καίτοιἐκεῖνοί γε ἔχουσι ποῦ αὐτὰ ῥίψωσιν, ἡ δὲ τῶν ὅλων φύσις ἔξωοὐδὲν ἔχει, ἀλλὰ τὸ θαυμαστὸν τῆς τέχνης ταύτης ἐστὶν ὅτιπεριορίσασα ἑαυτὴν πᾶν τὸ ἔνδον διαφθείρεσθαι καὶ γηράσκεινκαὶ ἄχρηστον εἶναι δοκοῦν εἰς ἑαυτὴν μεταβάλλει, καὶ ὅτι πάλινἄλλα νεαρὰ ἐκ τούτων αὐτῶν ποιεῖ, ἵνα μήτε οὐσίας ἔξωθεν χρήζῃ μήτε ὅπου ἐκβάλῃ τὰ σαπρότερα προσδέηται. ἀρκεῖται οὖνκαὶ χώρᾳ τῇ ἑαυτῆς καὶ ὕλῃ τῇ ἑαυτῆς καὶ τέχνῃ τῇ ἰδίᾳ.

51. Μήτε ἐν ταῖς πράξεσιν ἐπισύρειν μήτε ἐν ταῖς ὁμιλίαις φύρεινμήτε ἐν ταῖς φαντασίαις ἀλᾶσθαι μήτε τῇ ψυχῇ καθάπαξσυνέλκεσθαι ἢ ἐκθόρνυσθαι μήτε ἐν τῷ βίῳ ἀσχολεῖσθαι."Κτείνουσι, κρεανομοῦσι, κατάραις ἐλαύνουσι." τί ταῦτα πρὸςτὸ τὴν διάνοιαν μένειν καθαράν, φρενήρη, σώφρονα, δικαίαν;οἷον εἴ τις παραστὰς πηγῇ διαυγεῖ καὶ γλυκείᾳ βλασφημοίη αὐτήν,ἡ δὲ οὐ παύεται πότιμον ἀναβλύουσα· κἂν πηλὸν ἐμβάλῃ, κἂνκοπρίαν, τάχιστα διασκεδάσει αὐτὰ καὶ ἐκκλύσει καὶ οὐδαμῶςβαφήσεται. πῶς οὖν πηγὴν ἀέναον ἕξεις [καὶ] μὴ φρέαρ; ἂνφυλάσσῃς σεαυτὸν πάσης ὥρας εἰς ἐλευθερίαν μετὰ τοῦ εὐμενῶςκαὶ ἁπλῶς καὶ αἰδημόνως.

52. Ὁ μὲν μὴ εἰδὼς ὅτι ἔστι κόσμος, οὐκ οἶδεν ὅπου ἐστίν. ὁ δὲ μὴεἰδὼς πρὸς ὅ τι πέφυκεν ‹κόσμος›, οὐκ οἶδεν ὅστις ἐστὶν οὐδὲ τίἐστι κόσμος. ὁ δὲ ἕν τι τούτων ἀπολιπὼν οὐδ᾽ ἂν πρὸς ὅ τι αὐτὸςπέφυκεν εἴποι. τίς οὖν φαίνεταί σοι ὁ τὸν τῶν κροτούντων ἔπαινονφεύγων ἢ διώκων, οἳ οὔθ᾽ ὅπου εἰσὶν οὔτε οἵτινές εἰσι γινώσκουσιν;

53. Ἐπαινεῖσθαιθέλειςὑπὸἀνθρώπουτρὶςτῆςὥραςἑαυτῷκαταρωμένου;ἀρέσκειν θέλεις ἀνθρώπῳ ὃς οὐκ ἀρέσκει ἑαυτῷ;ἀρέσκει ἑαυτῷ ὁ μετανοῶν ἐφ᾽ ἅπασι σχεδὸν οἷς πράσσει;

54. Μηκέτι μόνον συμπνεῖν τῷ περιέχοντι ἀέρι, ἀλλ᾽ ἤδη καὶσυμφρονεῖν τῷ περιέχοντι πάντα νοερῷ. οὐ γὰρ ἧττον ἡ νοερὰδύναμις πάντη κέχυται καὶ διαπεφοίτηκε τῷ σπάσαι βουλομένῷἤπερ ἡ ἀερώδης τῷ ἀναπνεῦσαι δυναμένῳ.

55. Γενικῶς μὲν ἡ κακία οὐδὲν βλάπτει τὸν κόσμον, ἡ δὲ κατὰμέρος οὐδὲν βλάπτει τὸν ἕτερον, μόνῳ δὲ βλαβερά ἐστι τούτῳ ᾧἐπιτέτραπται καὶ ἀπηλλάχθαι αὐτῆς, ὁπόταν πρῶτον αὐτὸςθελήσῃ.

56. Τῷ ἐμῷ προαιρετικῷ τὸ τοῦ πλησίον προαιρετικὸν ἐπίσης ἀδιάφορόν ἐστιν, ὡς καὶ τὸ πνευμάτιον αὐτοῦ καὶ τὸ σαρκίδιον. καὶ γὰρ εἰ ὅτι μάλιστα ἀλλήλων ἕνεκεν γεγόναμεν, ὅμως τὰ ἡγεμονικὰ ἡμῶν ἕκαστον τὴν ἰδίαν κυρίαν ἔχει· ἐπεί τοι ἔμελλεν ἡ τοῦ πλησίον κακία ἐμοῦ κακὸν εἶναι, ὅπερ οὐκ ἔδοξε τῷ θεῷ, ἵνα μὴ ἐπ ἄλλῳ ᾖ τὸ ἐμὲ ἀτυχεῖν.

57. Ὁ ἥλιος κατακεχύσθαι δοκεῖ καὶ πάντῃ γε κέχυται, οὐ μὴν ἐκκέχυται. ἡ γὰρ χύσις αὕτη τάσις ἐστίν· ἀκτῖνες γοῦν αἱ αὐγαὶ αὐτοῦ ἀπὸ τοῦ ἐκτείνεσθαι λέγονται. ὁποῖον δέ τι ἐστὶν ἀκτίς, ἴδοις ἄν, εἰ διά τινος στενοῦ εἰς ἐσκιασμένον οἶκον τὸ ἀφ ἡλίου φῶς εἰσδυόμενον θεάσαιο· τείνεται γὰρ κατ εὐθὺ καὶ ὥσπερ διερείδεται πρὸς τὸ στερέμνιον ὅ τι ἂν ἀπαντήσῃ διεῖργον τὸν ἐπέκεινα ἀέρα, ἐνταῦθα δὲ ἔστη καὶ οὐ κατώλισθεν οὐδὲ ἔπεσεν. τοιαύτην οὖν τὴν χύσιν καὶ διάχυσιν τῆς διανοίας εἶναι χρή, μηδαμῶς ἔκχυσιν, ἀλλὰ τάσιν, καὶ πρὸς τὰ ἀπαντῶντα κωλύματα μὴ βίαιον μηδὲ ῥαγδαίαν τὴν ἐπέρεισιν ποιεῖσθαι μηδὲ μὴν καταπίπτειν, ἀλλὰ ἵστασθαι καὶ ἐπιλάμπειν τὸ δεχόμενον· αὐτὸ γὰρ ἑαυτὸ στερήσει τῆς αὐγῆς τὸ μὴ παραπέμπον αὐτήν.

58. Ὁ τὸν θάνατον φοβούμενος ἤτοι ἀναισθησίαν φοβεῖται ἢ αἴσθησιν ἑτεροίαν. ἀλλ εἴτε οὐκέτι αἴσθησιν ⟨ἕξεις⟩ οὐδὲ κακοῦ τινος αἰσθήσῃ· εἴτε ἀλλοιοτέραν αἴσθησιν κτήσῃ, ἀλλοῖον ζῷον ἔσῃ καὶ τοῦ ζῆν οὐ παύσῃ.

59. Οἱ ἄνθρωποι γεγόνασιν ἀλλήλων ἕνεκεν· ἢ δίδασκε οὖν ἢ φέρε.

60. Ἄλλως βέλος, ἄλλως νοῦς φέρεται. ὁ μέντοι νοῦς καὶ ὅταν εὐλαβῆται καὶ ὅταν περὶ τὴν σκέψιν στρέφηται, φέρεται κατευθὺ οὐδὲν ἧττον καὶ ἐπὶ τὸ προκείμενον.

61. Εἰσιέναι εἰς τὸ ἡγεμονικὸν ἑκάστου, παρέχειν δὲ καὶ ἑτέρῳ παντὶ εἰσιέναι εἰς τὸ ἑαυτοῦ ἡγεμονικόν.

BOOK NINE

I. He that is unjust, is also impious. For the nature of the universe, having made all reasonable creatures one for another, to the end that they should do one another good; more or less according to the several persons and occasions but in nowise hurt one another: it is manifest that he that doth transgress against this her will, is guilty of impiety towards the most ancient and venerable of all the deities. For the nature of the universe, is the nature the common parent of all, and therefore piously to be observed of all things that are, and that which now is, to whatsoever first was, and gave it its being, hath relation of blood and kindred. She is also called truth and is the first cause of all truths. He therefore that willingly and wittingly doth lie, is impious in that he doth receive, and so commit injustice: but he that against his will, in that he disagreeth from the nature of the universe, and in that striving with the nature of the world he doth in his particular, violate the general order of the world. For he doth no better than strive and war against it, who contrary to his own nature applieth himself to that which is contrary to truth. For nature had before furnished him with instincts and opportunities sufficient for the attainment of it; which he having hitherto neglected, is not now able to discern that which is false from that which is true. He also that pursues after pleasures, as that which is truly good and flies from pains, as that which is truly evil: is impious. For such a one must of necessity oftentimes accuse that common nature, as distributing many things both unto the evil, and unto the good, not according to the deserts of either: as unto the bad often times pleasures, and the causes of pleasures; so unto the good, pains, and the occasions of pains. Again, he that feareth pains and crosses in this world, feareth some of those things which some time or other must needs happen in the world. And that we have already showed to be impious. And he that pursueth after pleasures, will not spare, to compass his desires, to do that which is unjust, and that is manifestly impious. Now those things which unto nature are equally indifferent (for she had not created both, both pain and pleasure, if both had not been unto her equally indifferent): they that will live according to nature, must in those things (as being of the same mind and disposition that she is) be as equally indifferent. Whosoever therefore in either matter of pleasure and pain; death and life; honour and dishonour, (which things nature in the administration of the world, indifferently doth make use of), is not as indifferent, it is apparent that he is impious. When I say that common nature doth indifferently make use of them, my meaning is, that they happen indifferently in the ordinary course of things, which by a necessary consequence, whether as principal or accessory, come to pass in the world, according to that first and ancient deliberation of Providence, by which she from some certain beginning, did resolve upon the creation of such a world, conceiving then in her womb

183

as it were some certain rational generative seeds and faculties of things future, whether subjects, changes, successions; both such and such, and just so many.

II. It were indeed more happy and comfortable, for a man to depart out of this world, having lived all his life long clear from all falsehood, dissimulation, voluptuousness, and pride. But if this cannot be, yet it is some comfort for a man joyfully to depart as weary, and out of love with those; rather than to desire to live, and to continue long in those wicked courses. Hath not yet experience taught thee to fly from the plague? For a far greater plague is the corruption of the mind, than any certain change and distemper of the common air can be. This is a plague of creatures, as they are living creatures; but that of men as they are men or reasonable.

III. Thou must not in matter of death carry thyself scornfully, but as one that is well pleased with it, as being one of those things that nature hath appointed. For what thou dost conceive of these, of a boy to become a young man, to wax old, to grow, to ripen, to get teeth, or a beard, or grey hairs to beget, to bear, or to be delivered; or what other action soever it be, that is natural unto man according to the several seasons of his life; such a thing is it also to be dissolved. It is therefore the part of a wise man, in matter of death, not in any wise to carry himself either violently, or proudly but patiently to wait for it, as one of nature's operations: that with the same mind as now thou dost expect when that which yet is but an embryo in thy wife's belly shall come forth, thou mayst expect also when thy soul shall fall off from that outward coat or skin: wherein as a child in the belly it lieth involved and shut up. But thou desirest a more popular, and though not so direct and philosophical, yet a very powerful and penetrative recipe against the fear of death, nothing can make they more willing to part with thy life, than if thou shalt consider, both what the subjects themselves are that thou shalt part with, and what manner of disposition thou shalt no more have to do with. True it is, that, offended with them thou must not be by no means, but take care of them, and meekly bear with them However, this thou mayst remember, that whensoever it happens that thou depart, it shall not be from men that held the same opinions that thou dost. For that indeed, (if it were so) is the only thing that might make thee averse from death, and willing to continue here, if it were thy hap to live with men that had obtained the same belief that thou hast. But now, what a toil it is for thee to live with men of different opinions, thou seest: so that thou hast rather occasion to say, Hasten, I thee pray, O Death; lest I also in time forget myself.

IV. He that sinneth, sinneth unto himself. He that is unjust, hurts himself, in that he makes himself worse than he was before. Not he only that committeth, but he also that omitteth something, is oftentimes unjust.

V. If my present apprehension of the object be right, and my present action charitable, and this, towards whatsoever doth proceed from God, be my present disposition, to be well pleased with it, it sufficeth.

VI. To wipe away fancy, to use deliberation, to quench concupiscence, to keep the mind free to herself.

VII. Of all unreasonable creatures, there is but one unreasonable soul; and of all that are reasonable, but one reasonable soul, divided betwixt them all. As of all earthly things there is but one earth, and but one light that we see by; and but one air that we breathe in, as many as either breathe or see. Now whatsoever partakes of some common thing, naturally affects and inclines unto that whereof it is part, being of one kind and nature with it. Whatsoever is earthly, presseth downwards to the common earth. Whatsoever is liquid, would flow together. And whatsoever is airy, would be together likewise. So that without some obstacle, and some kind of violence, they cannot well be kept asunder. Whatsoever is fiery, doth not only by reason of the elementary fire tend upwards; but here also is so ready to join, and to burn together, that whatsoever doth want sufficient moisture to make resistance, is easily set on fire. Whatsoever therefore is partaker of that reasonable common nature, naturally doth as much and more long after his own kind. For by how much in its own nature it excels all other things, by so much more is it desirous to be joined and united unto that, which is of its own nature. As for unreasonable creatures then, they had not long been, but presently begun among them swarms, and flocks, and broods of young ones, and a kind of mutual love and affection. For though but unreasonable, yet a kind of soul these had, and therefore was that natural desire of union more strong and intense in them, as in creatures of a more excellent nature, than either in plants, or stones, or trees. But among reasonable creatures, begun commonwealths, friendships, families, public meetings, and even in their wars, conventions, and truces. Now among them that were yet of a more excellent nature, as the stars and planets, though by their nature far distant one from another, yet even among them began some mutual correspondency and unity. So proper is it to excellency in a high degree to affect unity, as that even in things so far distant, it could operate unto a mutual sympathy. But now behold, what is now come to pass. Those creatures that are reasonable, are now the only creatures that have forgotten their natural affection and inclination of one towards another. Among them alone of all other things that are of one kind, there is not to be found a general disposition to flow together. But though they fly from nature, yet are they stopt in their course, and apprehended. Do they what they can, nature doth prevail. And so shalt thou confess, if thou dost observe it. For sooner mayst thou find a thing earthly, where no earthly thing is, than find a man that naturally can live by himself alone.

VIII. Man, God, the world, every one in their kind, bear some fruits. All things have their proper time to bear. Though by custom, the word itself is in a manner become proper unto the vine, and the like, yet is it so nevertheless, as we have said. As for reason, that beareth both common fruit for the use of others; and peculiar, which itself doth enjoy. Reason is of a diffusive nature, what itself is in itself, it begets in others, and so doth multiply.

IX. Either teach them better if it be in thy power; or if it be not, remember that for this use, to bear with them patiently, was mildness and goodness granted unto thee. The Gods themselves are good unto such; yea and in some things, (as in matter of health, of wealth, of honour,) are content often to further their endeavours: so good and gracious are they. And mightest thou not be so too? or, tell me, what doth hinder thee?

X. Labour not as one to whom it is appointed to be wretched, nor as one that either would be pitied, or admired; but let this be thine only care and desire; so always and in all things to prosecute or to forbear, as the law of charity, or mutual society doth require.

XI. This day I did come out of all my trouble. Nay I have cast out all my trouble; it should rather be for that which troubled thee, whatsoever it was, was not without anywhere that thou shouldest come out of it, but within in thine own opinions, from whence it must be cast out, before thou canst truly and constantly be at ease.

XII. All those things, for matter of experience are usual and ordinary; for their continuance but for a day; and for their matter, most base and filthy. As they were in the days of those whom we have buried, so are they now also, and no otherwise.

XIII. The things themselves that affect us, they stand without doors, neither knowing anything themselves nor able to utter anything unto others concerning themselves. What then is it, that passeth verdict on them? The understanding.

XIV. As virtue and wickedness consist not in passion, but in action; so neither doth the true good or evil of a reasonable charitable man consist in passion, but in operation and action.

XV. To the stone that is cast up, when it comes down it is no hurt unto it; as neither benefit, when it doth ascend.

XVI. Sift their minds and understandings, and behold what men they be, whom thou dost stand in fear of what they shall judge of thee, what they themselves judge of themselves.

XVII. All things that are in the world, are always in the estate of alteration. Thou also art in a perpetual change, yea and under corruption too, in some part: and so is the whole world.

XVIII. it is not thine, but another man's sin. Why should it trouble thee? Let him look to it, whose sin it is.

XIX. Of an operation and of a purpose there is an ending, or of an action and of a purpose we say commonly, that it is at an end: from opinion also there is an absolute cessation, which is as it were the death of it. In all this there is no hurt. Apply this now to a man's age, as first, a child; then a youth, then a young man, then an old man; every change from one age to another is a kind of death And all this while here no matter of grief yet. Pass now unto that life first, that which thou livedst under thy grandfather, then under thy mother, then under thy father. And thus when through the whole course of thy life hitherto thou hast found and observed many alterations, many changes, many kinds of endings and cessations, put this question to thyself What matter of grief or sorrow dost thou find in any of these? Or what doest thou suffer through any of these? If in none of these, then neither in the ending and consummation of thy whole life, which is also but a cessation and change.

XX. As occasion shall require, either to thine own understanding, or to that of the universe, or to his, whom thou hast now to do with, let thy refuge be with all speed. To thine own, that it resolve upon nothing against justice. To that of the universe, that thou mayest remember, part of whom thou art. Of his, that thou mayest consider whether in the estate of ignorance, or of knowledge. And then also must thou call to mind, that he is thy kinsman.

XXI. As thou thyself, whoever thou art, were made for the perfection and consummation, being a member of it, of a common society; so must every action of thine tend to the perfection and consummation of a life that is truly sociable. What action soever of thine therefore that either immediately or afar off, hath not reference to the common good, that is an exorbitant and disorderly action; yea it is seditious; as one among the people who from such and such a consent and unity, should factiously divide and separate himself.

XXII. Children's anger, mere babels; wretched souls bearing up dead bodies, that they may not have their fall so soon: even as it is in that common dirge song.

XXIII. Go to the quality of the cause from which the effect doth proceed. Behold it by itself bare and naked, separated from all that is material. Then consider the utmost bounds of time that that cause, thus and thus qualified, can subsist and abide.

XXIV. Infinite are the troubles and miseries, that thou hast already been put to, by reason of this only, because that for all happiness it did not suffice thee, or, that thou didst not account it sufficient happiness, that thy understanding did operate according to its natural constitution.

XXV. When any shall either impeach thee with false accusations, or hatefully reproach thee, or shall use any such carriage towards thee, get thee presently to their minds and understandings, and look in them, and behold what manner of men they be. Thou shalt see, that there is no such occasion why it should trouble thee, what such as they are think of thee. Yet must thou love them still, for by nature they are thy friends. And the Gods themselves, in those things that they seek from them as matters of great moment, are well content, all manner of ways, as by dreams and oracles, to help them as well as others.

XXVI. Up and down, from one age to another, go the ordinary things of the world; being still the same. And either of everything in particular before it come to pass, the mind of the universe doth consider with itself and deliberate: and if so, then submit for shame unto the determination of such an excellent understanding: or once for all it did resolve upon all things in general; and since that whatsoever happens, happens by a necessary consequence, and all things indivisibly in a manner and inseparably hold one of another. In sum, either there is a God, and then all is well; or if all things go by chance and fortune, yet mayest thou use thine own providence in those things that concern thee properly; and then art thou well.

XXVII. Within a while the earth shall cover us all, and then she herself shall have her change. And then the course will be, from one period of eternity unto another, and so a perpetual eternity. Now can any man that shall consider with himself in his mind the several rollings or successions of so many changes and alterations, and the swiftness of all these rulings; can he otherwise but contemn in his heart and despise all worldly things? The cause of the universe is as it were a strong torrent, it carrieth all away.

XXVIII. And these your professed politicians, the only true practical philosophers of the world, (as they think of themselves) so full of affected gravity, or such professed lovers of virtue and honesty, what wretches be they in very deed; how vile and contemptible in themselves? O man! what ado doest thou keep? Do what thy nature doth now require. Resolve upon it, if thou mayest: and take no thought, whether anybody shall know it or no. Yea, but sayest thou, I must not expect a Plato's commonwealth. If they profit though never so little, I must be content; and think much even of that little progress. Doth then any of them forsake their former false opinions that I should think they profit? For without a change of opinions, alas! what is all that ostentation, but mere wretchedness of slavish minds, that groan privately, and yet would make a show of obedience to reason, and truth? Go too now and tell me of Alexander and Philippus, and Demetrius Phalereus. Whether they understood what the common nature requireth, and could rule themselves or no, they know best themselves. But if they kept a life, and swaggered; I (God be thanked) am not bound to imitate them. The effect of true philosophy is, unaffected simplicity and modesty. Persuade me not to ostentation and vainglory.

XXIX. From some high place as it were to look down, and to behold here flocks, and there sacrifices, without number; and all kind of navigation; some in a rough and stormy sea, and some in a calm: the general differences, or different estates of things, some, that are now first upon being; the several and mutual relations of those things that are together; and some other things that are at their last. Their lives also, who were long ago, and theirs who shall be hereafter, and the present estate and life of those many nations of barbarians that are now in the world, thou must likewise consider in thy mind. And how many there be, who never so much as heard of thy name, how many that will soon forget it; how many who but even now did commend thee, within a very little while perchance will speak ill of thee. So that neither fame, nor honour, nor anything else that this world doth afford, is worth the while. The sum then of all; whatsoever doth happen unto thee, whereof God is the cause, to accept it contentedly: whatsoever thou doest, whereof thou thyself art the cause, to do it justly: which will be, if both in thy resolution and in thy action thou have no further end, than to do good unto others, as being that, which by thy natural constitution, as a man, thou art bound unto.

XXX. Many of those things that trouble and straiten thee, it is in thy power to cut off, as wholly depending from mere conceit and opinion; and then thou shalt have room enough.

XXXI. To comprehend the whole world together in thy mind, and the whole course of this present age to represent it unto thyself, and to fix thy thoughts upon the sudden change of every particular object. How short the time is from the generation of anything, unto the dissolution of the same; but how immense and infinite both that which was before the generation, and that which after the generation of it shall be. All things that thou seest, will soon be perished, and they that see their corruptions, will soon vanish away themselves. He that dieth a hundred years old, and he that dieth young, shall come all to one.

XXXII. What are their minds and understandings; and what the things that they apply themselves unto: what do they love, and what do they hate for? Fancy to thyself the estate of their souls openly to be seen. When they think they hurt them shrewdly, whom they speak ill of; and when they think they do them a very good turn, whom they commend and extol: O how full are they then of conceit, and opinion!

XXXIII. Loss and corruption, is in very deed nothing else but change and alteration; and that is it, which the nature of the universe doth most delight in, by which, and according to which, whatsoever is done, is well done. For that was the estate of worldly things from the beginning, and so shall it ever be. Or wouldest thou rather say, that all things in the world have gone ill from the beginning for so many ages, and shall ever go ill? And then among so many deities, could no divine power be found all this while, that could rectify the things of the world? Or is the world, to incessant woes and miseries, for ever condemned?

XXXIV. How base and putrid, every common matter is! Water, dust, and from the mixture of these bones, and all that loathsome stuff that our bodies do consist of: so subject to be infected, and corrupted. And again those other things that are so much prized and admired, as marble stones, what are they, but as it were the kernels of the earth? gold and silver, what are they, but as the more gross faeces of the earth? Thy most royal apparel, for matter, it is but as it were the hair of a silly sheep, and for colour, the very blood of a shellfish; of this nature are all other things. Thy life itself, is some such thing too; a mere exhalation of blood: and it also, apt to be changed into some other common thing.

XXXV. Will this querulousness, this murmuring, this complaining and dissembling never be at an end? What then is it, that troubleth thee? Doth any new thing happen unto thee? What doest thou so wonder at? At the cause, or the matter? Behold either by itself, is either of that weight and moment indeed? And besides these, there is not anything. But thy duty towards the Gods also, it is time thou shouldst acquit thyself of it with more goodness and simplicity.

XXXVI. It is all one to see these things for a hundred of years together or but for three years.

XXXVII. If he have sinned, his is the harm, not mine. But perchance he hath not.

XXXVIII. Either all things by the providence of reason happen unto every particular, as a part of one general body; and then it is against reason that a part should complain of anything that happens for the good of the whole; or if, according to Epicurus, atoms be the cause of all things and that life be nothing else but an accidentary confusion of things, and death nothing else, but a mere dispersion and so of all other things: what doest thou trouble thyself for?

XXXIX. Sayest thou unto that rational part, Thou art dead; corruption hath taken hold on thee? Doth it then also void excrements? Doth it like either oxen, or sheep, graze or feed; that it also should be mortal, as well as the body?

XL. Either the Gods can do nothing for us at all, or they can still and allay all the distractions and distempers of thy mind. If they can do nothing, why doest thou pray? If they can, why wouldst not thou rather pray, that they will grant unto thee, that thou mayst neither fear, nor lust after any of those worldly things which cause these distractions and distempers of it? Why not rather, that thou mayst not at either their absence or presence, be grieved and discontented: than either that thou mayst obtain them, or that thou mayst avoid them? For certainly it must needs be, that if the Gods can help us in anything, they may in this kind also. But thou wilt say perchance, 'In those things the Gods have given me my liberty: and it is in mine own power to do what I will.' But if thou mayst use this liberty, rather to set thy mind at true liberty, than wilfully with baseness and servility of mind to affect those things, which either to compass or to avoid is not in thy power, wert not thou better? And as for the Gods, who hath told thee, that they may not help us up even in those things that they have put in our own power? whether it be so or no, thou shalt soon perceive, if thou wilt but try thyself and pray. One prayeth that he may compass his desire, to lie with such or such a one, pray thou that thou mayst not lust to lie with her. Another how he may be rid of such a one; pray thou that thou mayst so patiently bear with him, as that thou have no such need to be rid of him. Another, that he may not lose his child. Pray thou that thou mayst not fear to lose him. To this end and purpose, let all thy prayer be, and see what will be the event.

XLI. 'In my sickness' (saith Epicurus of himself:) 'my discourses were not concerning the nature of my disease, neither was that, to them that came to visit me, the subject of my talk; but in the consideration and contemplation of that, which was of especial weight and moment, was all my time bestowed and spent, and among others in this very thing, how my mind, by a natural and unavoidable sympathy partaking in some sort with the present indisposition of my body, might nevertheless keep herself free from trouble, and in present possession of her own proper happiness. Neither did I leave the ordering of my body to the physicians altogether to do with me what they would, as though I expected any great matter from them, or as though I thought it   a matter of such great consequence, by their means to recover my health: for my present estate, methought, liked me very well, and gave me good content.' Whether therefore in sickness (if thou chance to sicken) or in what other kind of extremity soever, endeavour thou also to be in thy mind so affected, as he doth report of himself: not to depart from thy philosophy for anything that can befall thee, nor to give ear to the discourses of silly people, and mere naturalists.

XLII. It is common to all trades and professions to mind and intend that only, which now they are about, and the instrument whereby they work.

XLIII. When at any time thou art offended with any one's impudency, put presently this question to thyself: 'What? Is it then possible, that there should not be any impudent men in the world! Certainly it is not possible.' Desire not then that which is impossible. For this one, (thou must think) whosoever he be, is one of those impudent ones, that the world cannot be without. So of the subtile and crafty, so of the perfidious, so of every one that offendeth, must thou ever be ready to reason with thyself. For whilst in general thou dost thus reason with thyself, that the kind of them must needs be in the world, thou wilt be the better able to use meekness towards every particular. This also thou shalt find of very good use, upon every such occasion, presently to consider with thyself, what proper virtue nature hath furnished man with, against such a vice, or to encounter with a disposition vicious in this kind. As for example, against the unthankful, it hath given goodness and meekness, as an antidote, and so against another vicious in another kind some other peculiar faculty. And generally, is it not in thy power to instruct him better, that is in an error? For whosoever sinneth, doth in that decline from his purposed end, and is certainly deceived, And again, what art thou the worse for his sin? For thou shalt not find that any one of these, against whom thou art incensed, hath in very deed done anything whereby thy mind (the only true subject of thy hurt and evil) can be made worse than it was. And what a matter of either grief or wonder is this, if he that is unlearned, do the deeds of one that is unlearned? Should not thou rather blame thyself, who, when upon very good grounds of reason, thou mightst have thought it very probable, that such a thing would by such a one be committed, didst not only not foresee it, but moreover dost wonder at it, that such a thing should be. But then especially, when thou dost find fault with either an unthankful, or a false man, must thou reflect upon thyself. For without all question, thou thyself art much in fault, if either of one that were of such a disposition, thou didst expect that he should be true unto thee: or when unto any thou didst a good turn, thou didst not there bound thy thoughts, as one that had obtained his end; nor didst not think that from the action itself thou hadst received a full reward of the good that thou hadst done. For what wouldst thou have more? Unto him that is a man, thou hast done a good turn: doth not that suffice thee? What thy nature required, that hast thou done. Must thou be rewarded for it? As if either the eye for that it seeth, or the feet that they go, should require satisfaction. For as these being by nature appointed for such an use, can challenge no more, than that they may work according to their natural constitution: so man being born to do good unto others whensoever he doth a real good unto any by helping them out of error;

or though but in middle things, as in matter of wealth, life, preferment, and the like, doth help to further their desires he doth that for which he was made, and therefore can require no more.

ΒΙΒΛΙΟ ΕΝΑΤΟ

1. Ὁ ἀδικῶν ἀσεβεῖ· τῆς γὰρ τῶν ὅλων φύσεως κατεσκευακυίαςτὰ λογικὰ ζῷα ἕνεκεν ἀλλήλων, ὥστε ὠφελεῖν μὲν ἄλληλα κατάξίαν βλάπτειν δὲ μηδαμῶς, ὁ τὸ βούλημα ταύτης παραβαίνωνἀσεβεῖ δηλονότι εἰς τὴν πρεσβυτάτην τῶν θεῶν. ἡ γὰρ τῶν ὅλωνφύσις ὄντων ἐστὶ φύσις· τὰ δέ γε ὄντα πρὸς τὰ ὑπάρχοντα πάνταοἰκείως ἔχει. ἔτι δὲ καὶ ὁ ψευδόμενος [δὲ] ἀσεβεῖ περὶ τὴν αὐτὴνθεόν· καὶ Ἀλήθεια αὕτη ὀνομάζεται καὶ τῶν ἀληθῶν ἀπάντωνπρώτη αἰτία ἐστιν. ὁ μὲν οὖν ἑκὼν ψευδόμενος ἀσεβεῖ, καθόσονἐξαπατῶν ἀδικεῖ· ὁ δὲ ἄκων, καθόσον διαφωνεῖ τῇ τῶν ὅλωνφύσει καὶ καθόσον ἀκοσμεῖ μαχόμενος τῇ τοῦ κόσμου φύσει· μάχεται γὰρ ὁ ἐπὶ τἀναντία τοῖς ἀληθέσι φερόμενος παρ᾽ ἑαυτόν· ἀφορμὰς γὰρ προειλήφει παρὰ τῆς φύσεως, ὧν ἀμελήσας οὐχοῖός τέ ἐστι νῦν διακρίνειν τὰ ψευδῆ ἀπὸ τῶν ἀληθῶν. καὶ μὴνκαὶ ὁ τὰς ἡδονὰς ὡς ἀγαθὰ διώκων, τοὺς δὲ πόνους ὡς κακὰφεύγων ἀσεβεῖ· ἀνάγκη γὰρ τὸν τοιοῦτον μέμφεσθαιπολλάκιςτῇ κοινῇ φύσει ὡς παρ᾽ ἀξίαν τι ἀπονεμούσῃ τοῖς φαύλοις καὶτοῖς σπουδαίοις, διὰ τὸ πολλάκις τοὺς μὲν φαύλους ἐν ἡδοναῖςεἶναι καὶ τὰ ποιητικὰ τούτων κτᾶσθαι, τοὺς δὲ σπουδαίους πόνῳκαὶ τοῖς ποιητικοῖς τούτου περιπίπτειν. ἔτι δὲ ὁ φοβούμενος τοὺςπόνους φοβηθήσεταί ποτε καὶ τῶν ἐσομένων τι ἐν τῷ κόσμῳ,τοῦτο δὲ ἤδη ἀσεβές· ὅ τε διώκων τὰς ἡδονὰς οὐκ ἀφέξεται τοῦἀδικεῖν, τοῦτο δὲ ἐναργῶς ἀσεβές· χρὴ δὲ πρὸς ἃ ἡ κοινὴ φύσιςἐπίσης ἔχει (οὐ γὰρ ἀμφότερα ἂν ἐποίει, εἰ μὴ πρὸς ἀμφότεραἐπίσης εἶχε), πρὸς ταῦτα καὶ τοὺς τῇ φύσει βουλομένους ἕπεσθαι,ὁμογνώμονας ὄντας, ἐπίσης διακεῖσθαι· ὅστις οὖν πρὸς πόνονκαὶ ἡδονὴν ἢ θάνατον καὶ ζωὴν ἢ δόξαν καὶ ἀδοξίαν, οἷς ἐπίσηςἡ τῶν ὅλων φύσις χρῆται, αὐτὸς οὐκ ἐπίσης ἔχει, δῆλον ὡς ἀσεβεῖ.λέγω δὲ τὸ χρῆσθαι τούτοις ἐπίσης τὴν κοινὴν φύσιν ἀντὶ τοῦκατὰ τὸ ἐξῆς συμβαίνειν ἐπίσης τοῖς γινομένοις καὶ ἐπιγινομένοιςὁρμῇ τινι ἀρχαίᾳ τῆς προνοίας, καθ᾽ ἣν ἀπό τινος ἀρχῆς ὥρμησενἐπὶ τήνδε τὴν διακόσμησιν, συλλαβοῦσά τινας λόγους τῶνἐσομένων καὶ δυνάμεις γονίμους ἀφορίσασα ὑποστάσεών τε καὶμεταβολῶν καὶ διαδοχῶν τοιούτων.

2. Χαριεστέρου μὲν ἦν ἀνδρός, ἄγευστον ψευδολογίας καὶ πάσηςὑποκρίσεως καὶ τρυφῆς καὶ τύφου γενόμενον, ἐξ ἀνθρώπωνἀπελθεῖν. τὸ δ᾽ οὖν κορεσθέντα γε τούτων ἀποπνεῦσαι δεύτεροςπλοῦς. ἢ προήρησαι προσκαθῆσθαι τῇ κακίᾳ καὶ οὔπω σε οὐδὲἡ πεῖρα πείθει φεύγειν ἐκ τοῦ λοιμοῦ; λοιμὸς γὰρ διαφθορὰδιανοίας πολλῷ γε μᾶλλον ἤπερ ἡ τοῦ περικεχυμένου τούτουπνεύματος τοιάδε τις δυσκρασία καὶ τροπή· αὕτη μὲν γὰρ ζῴωνλοιμός, καθὸ ζῷά ἐστιν, ἐκείνη δὲ ἀνθρώπων, καθὸ ἄνθρωποίεἰσιν.

3. Μὴ καταφρόνει θανάτου, ἀλλὰ εὐαρέστει αὐτῷ, ὡς καὶ τούτουἑνὸς ὄντος ὧν ἡ φύσις ἐθέλει. οἷον γάρ ἐστι τὸ νεᾶσαι καὶ τὸγηρᾶσαι, καὶ τὸ αὐξῆσαι

καὶ τὸ ἀκμάσαι, καὶ ὀδόντας καὶ γένειονκαὶ πολιὰς ἐνεγκεῖν, καὶ σπεῖραι καὶ κυοφορῆσαι καὶ ἀποκυῆσαι,καὶ τὰ ἄλλα φυσικὰ ἐνεργήματα ὅσα αἱ τοῦ βίου ὧραι φέρουσι,τοιοῦτο καὶ αὐτὸ τὸ διαλυθῆναι. τοῦτο μὲν οὖν κατὰ ἄνθρωπόνἐστι λελογισμένον, μὴ ὁλοσχερῶς μηδὲ ὠστικῶς μηδὲ ὑπερηφάνωςπρὸς τὸν θάνατον ἔχειν ἀλλὰ περιμένειν ὡς μίαν τῶν φυσικῶνἐνεργειῶν, καὶ ὡς νῦν περιμένεις πότε ἔμβρυον ἐκ τῆς γαστρὸςτῆς γυναικός σου ἐξέλθῃ, οὕτως ἐκδέχεσθαι τὴν ὥραν ἐν ᾗ τὸψυχάριόν σου τοῦ ἐλύτρου τούτου ἐκπεσεῖται. εἰ δὲ καὶ ἰδιωτικὸνπαράπηγμα ἀψικάρδιον θέλεις, μάλιστά σε εὔκολον πρὸς τὸνθάνατον ποιήσει ἡ ἐπίστασις ἡ ἐπὶ τὰ ὑποκείμενα, ὧν μέλλειςἀφίστασθαι, καὶ μεθ᾽ οἵων ἠθῶν οὐκέτι ἔσται ἡ ‹ψυχή σου›συμπεφυρμένη. προσκόπτεσθαι μὲν γὰρ αὐτοῖς ἥκιστα δεῖ, ἀλλὰκαὶ κήδεσθαι καὶ πράως φέρειν, μεμνῆσθαι μέντοι ὅτι οὐκ ἀπ᾽ἀνθρώπων ὁμοδογματούντων σοι ἡ ἀπαλλαγὴ ἔσται. τοῦτο γὰρμόνον, εἴπερ ἄρα, ἀνθεῖλκεν ἂν καὶ κατεῖχεν ἐν τῷ ζῆν, εἰ συζῆνἐφεῖτο τοῖς τὰ αὐτὰ δόγματα περιπεποιημένοις· νῦν δ᾽ ὁρᾷς ὅσοςό κόπος ἐν τῇ διαφωνίᾳ τῆς συμβιώσεως, ὥστε εἰπεῖν· θᾶττονἔλθοις, ὦ θάνατε, μή που καὶ αὐτὸς ἐπιλάθωμαι ἐμαυτοῦ.

4. Ὁ ἁμαρτάνων ἑαυτῷ ἁμαρτάνει· ὁ ἀδικῶν ἑαυτὸν ἀδικεῖ,ἑαυτὸν κακὸν ποιῶν.

5. Ἀδικεῖ πολλάκις ὁ μὴ ποιῶν τι, οὐ μόνον ὁ ποιῶν τι.

6. Ἀρκεῖ ἡ παροῦσα ὑπόληψις καταληπτικὴ καὶ ἡ παροῦσαπρᾶξις κοινωνικὴ καὶ ἡ παροῦσα διάθεσις εὐαρεστικὴ πρὸς πᾶντὸ παρὰ τὴν ἐκτὸς αἰτίαν συμβαῖνον.

7. Ἐξαλεῖψαι φαντασίαν· στῆσαι ὁρμήν· σβέσαι ὄρεξιν· ἐφ᾽ ἑαυτῷἔχειν τὸ ἡγεμονικόν.

8. Εἰς μὲν τὰ ἄλογα ζῷα μία ψυχὴ διήρηται, εἰς δὲ τὰ λογικὰ μίανοερὰ ψυχὴ μεμέρισται, ὥσπερ καὶ μία γῆ ἐστιν ἁπάντων τῶνγεωδῶν καὶ ἑνὶ φωτὶ ὁρῶμεν καὶ ἕνα ἀέρα ἀναπνέομεν, ὅσαὁρατικὰ καὶ ἔμψυχα πάντα.

9. ‹Πάντα› ὅσα κοινοῦ τινος μετέχει πρὸς τὸ ὁμογενὲς σπεύδει.τὸ γεῶδες πᾶν ῥέπει ἐπὶ τὴν γῆν· τὸ ὑγρὸν πᾶν σύρρουν· τὸ ἀερῶδεςὁμοίως, ὥστε χρῄζειν τῶν διειργόντων καὶ βίᾳ· τὸ πῦρ ἀνωφερὲςμὲν διὰ τὸ στοιχειῶδες πῦρ, παντὶ δὲ πυρὶ ἐνταῦθα πρὸς τὸσυνεξάπτεσθαιἕτοιμον οὕτως, ὥστε καὶ πᾶν τὸ ὑλικὸν τὸὀλίγῳξηρότερον εὐέξαπτον εἶναι διὰ τὸ ἔλαττον ἐγκεκρᾶσθαι αὐτῷ τὸκωλυτικὸν πρὸς ἔξαψιν. καὶ τοίνυν πᾶν τὸ κοινῆς νοερᾶς φύσεωςμέτοχον πρὸς τὸ συγγενὲς ὁμοίως σπεύδει ἢ καὶ μᾶλλον· ὅσῳ γάρἐστι κρεῖττον παρὰ τὰ ἄλλα, τοσούτῳ καὶ πρὸς τὸ συγκιρνᾶσθαιτῷ οἰκείῳ καὶ συγχεῖσθαι ἑτοιμότερον. εὐθὺς γοῦν ἐπὶ μὲν τῶνἀλόγων εὑρέθη σμήνη καὶ ἀγέλαι καὶ νεοσσοτροφίαι καὶ οἷονἔρωτες·

ψυχαὶ γὰρ ἤδη ἦσαν ἐνταῦθα καὶ τὸ συναγωγὸν ἐν τῷκρείττονι ἐπιτεινόμενον εὑρίσκετο, οἷον οὔτε ἐπὶ φυτῶν ἦν οὔτεἐπὶ λίθων ἢ ξύλων. ἐπὶ δὲ τῶν λογικῶν ζῴων πολιτεῖαι καὶ φιλίαικαὶ οἶκοι καὶ σύλλογοι καὶ ἐν πολέμοις συνθῆκαι καὶ ἀνοχαί.ἐπὶ δὲ τῶν ἔτι κρειττόνων καὶ διεστηκότων τρόπον τινὰ ἕνωσιςὑπέστη οἷα ἐπὶ τῶν ἄστρων· οὕτως ἡ ἐπὶ τὸ κρεῖττον ἐπανάβασιςσυμπάθειαν καὶ ἐν διεστῶσιν ἐργάσασθαι ἐδύνατο. ὅρα οὖν τὸνῦν γινόμενον· μόνα γὰρ τὰ νοερὰ νῦν ἐπιλέλησται τῆς πρὸςἄλληλα σπουδῆς καὶ συννεύσεως καὶ τὸ σύρρουν ὧδε μόνον οὐβλέπεται. ἀλλ ὅμως καίτοι φεύγοντες περικαταλαμβάνονται·κρατεῖ γὰρ ἡ φύσις. ὄψει δὲ ὃ λέγω παραφυλάσσων· θᾶσσονγοῦν εὕροι τις ἂν γεῶδές τι μηδενὸς γεώδους προσαπτόμενον ἤπερἄνθρωπον ἀνθρώπου ἀπεσχισμένον.

10. Φέρει καρπὸν καὶ ἄνθρωπος καὶ θεὸς καὶ ὁ κόσμος· ἐν ταῖςοἰκείαις ὥραις ἕκαστα φέρει. εἰ δὲ ἡ συνήθεια κυρίως τέτριφενἐπὶ ἀμπέλου καὶ τῶν ὁμοίων, οὐδὲν τοῦτο. ὁ λόγος δὲ καὶ κοινὸνκαὶ ἴδιον καρπὸν ἔχει καὶ γίνεται ἐξ αὐτοῦ τοιαῦθ ἕτερα, ὁποῖόντι αὐτός ἐστιν ὁ λόγος.

11. Εἰ μὲν δύνασαι, μεταδίδασκε· εἰ δὲ μή, μέμνησο ὅτι πρὸς τοῦτόἡ εὐμένειά σοι δέδοται. καὶ οἱ θεοὶ δὲ εὐμενεῖς τοῖς τοιούτοιςεἰσίν, εἰς ἔνια δὲ καὶ συνεργοῦσιν, εἰς ὑγίειαν, εἰς πλοῦτον, εἰςδόξαν· οὕτως εἰσὶ χρηστοί. ἔξεστι δὲ καὶ σοί· ἢ εἰπέ, τίς ὁ κωλύων;

12. Πόνει μὴ ὡς ἄθλιος μηδὲ ὡς ἐλεεῖσθαι ἢ θαυμάζεσθαι θέλων,ἀλλὰ μόνον ἓν θέλε· κινεῖσθαι καὶ ἴσχεσθαι, ὡς ὁ πολιτικὸςλόγος ἀξιοῖ.

13. Σήμερον ἐξῆλθον πάσης περιστάσεως, μᾶλλον δὲ ἐξέβαλονπᾶσαν περίστασιν· ἔξω γὰρ οὐκ ἦν, ἀλλὰ ἔνδον ἐν ταῖς ὑπολήψεσιν.

14. Πάντα ταὐτά· συνήθη μὲν τῇ πείρᾳ, ἐφήμερα δὲ τῷ χρόνῳ,ρυπαρὰ δὲ τῇ ὕλῃ· πάντα νῦν οἷα ἐπ ἐκείνων οὓς κατεθάψαμεν.

15. Τὰ πράγματα ἔξω θυρῶν ἕστηκεν αὐτὰ ἐφ ἑαυτῶν, μηδὲν μήτεεἰδότα περὶ αὑτῶν μήτε ἀποφαινόμενα. τί οὖν ἀποφαίνεται περὶαὐτῶν; τὸ ἡγεμονικόν.

16. Οὐκ ἐν πείσει ἀλλ ἐνεργείᾳ τὸ τοῦ λογικοῦ πολιτικοῦ ζῴουκακὸν καὶ ἀγαθόν, ὥσπερ οὐδὲ ἡ ἀρετὴ καὶ κακία αὐτοῦ ἐνπείσει ἀλλὰ ἐνεργείᾳ.

17. Τῷ ἀναρριφέντι λίθῳ οὐδὲν κακὸν τὸ κατενεχθῆναι οὐδὲἀγαθὸν τὸ ἀνενεχθῆναι.

18. Δίελθε ἔσω εἰς τὰ ἡγεμονικὰ αὐτῶν καὶ ὄψει τίνας κριτὰςφοβῇ, οἵους καὶ περὶ αὑτῶν ὄντας κριτάς.

19. Πάντα ἐν μεταβολῇ· καὶ αὐτὸς σὺ ἐν διηνεκεῖ ἀλλοιώσει καὶκατά τι φθορᾷ, καὶ ὁ κόσμος δὲ ὅλος.

20. Τὸ ἄλλου ἁμάρτημα ἐκεῖ δεῖ καταλιπεῖν.

21. Ἐνεργείας ἀπόληξις, ὁρμῆς καὶ ὑπολήψεως παῦλα, οἷονθάνατος· οὐδὲν κακόν. μέτιθι νῦν ἐπὶ ἡλικίαν, οἷον τὴν παιδικήν,τὴν τοῦ μειρακίου, τὴν νεότητα, τὸ γῆρας· καὶ γὰρ τούτων πᾶσαμεταβολή, θάνατος· μήτι δεινόν; μέτιθι νῦν ἐπὶ βίον τὸν ὑπὸ τῷπάππῳ, εἶτα τὸν ὑπὸ τῇ μητρί, εἶτα τὸν ὑπὸ τῷ πατρί, καὶ ἄλλαςδὲ πολλὰς διαφθορὰς καὶ μεταβολὰς καὶ ἀπολήξεις εὑρίσκωνἐπερώτα σεαυτόν· μήτι δεινόν; οὕτως τοίνυν οὐδὲ ἡ τοῦ ὅλουσοῦ βίου λῆξις καὶ παῦλα καὶ μεταβολή.

22. Τρέχε ἐπὶ τὸ σεαυτοῦ ἡγεμονικὸν καὶ τὸ τοῦ ὅλου καὶ τὸ τούτου.τὸ μὲν σεαυτοῦ, ἵνα νοῦν δικαϊκὸν αὐτὸ ποιήσῃς· τὸ δὲ τοῦ ὅλου,ἵνα συμμνημονεύσῃς τίνος μέρος εἶ· τὸ δὲ τούτου, ἵνα ἐπιστήσῃςπότερον ἄγνοια ἢ γνώμη, καὶ ἅμα λογίσῃ ὅτι συγγενές.

23. Ὥσπερ αὐτὸς σὺ πολιτικοῦ συστήματος συμπληρωτικὸς εἶ,οὕτως καὶ πᾶσα πρᾶξίς σου συμπληρωτικὴ ἔστω ζωῆς πολιτικῆς.ἥτις ἐὰν οὖν πρᾶξίς σου μὴ ἔχῃ τὴν ἀναφοράν, εἴτε προσεχῶςεἴτε πόρρωθεν, ἐπὶ τὸ κοινωνικὸν τέλος, αὕτη διασπᾷ τὸν βίονκαὶ οὐκ ἐᾷ ἕνα εἶναι καὶ στασιώδης ἐστίν, ὥσπερ ἐν δήμῳ ὁ τὸκαθ αὑτὸν μέρος διιστάμενος ἀπὸ τῆς τοιαύτης συμφωνίας.

24. Παιδίων ὀργαὶ καὶ παίγνια, καὶ "πνευμάτια νεκροὺς βαστάζοντ",ὥστε ἐναργέστερον προσπεσεῖν τὸ τῆς Νεκυίας.

25. Ἴθι ἐπὶ τὴν ποιότητα τοῦ αἰτίου καὶ ἀπὸ τοῦ ὑλικοῦ αὐτὸπεριγράψας θέασαι· εἶτα καὶ τὸν χρόνον περιόρισον, ὅσονπλεῖστον ὑφίστασθαι πέφυκε τοῦτο τὸ ἰδίως ποιόν.

26. Ἀνέτλης μύρια διὰ τὸ μὴ ἀρκεῖσθαι τῷ σῷ ἡγεμονικῷ ποιοῦντιτοιαῦτα, οἷα κατεσκεύασται. ἀλλὰ ἅλις.

27. Ὅταν ἄλλος ψέγῃ σε ἢ μισῇ ἢ τοιαῦτά τινα ἐκφωνῶσιν, ἔρχουἐπὶ τὰ ψυχάρια αὐτῶν, διέλθε ἔσω καὶ ἴδε ποῖοί τινές εἰσιν. ὄψειὅτι οὐ δεῖ σε σπᾶσθαι, ἵνα τούτοις τί ποτε περὶ σοῦ δοκῇ. εὐνοεῖνμέντοι αὐτοῖς δεῖ· φύσει γὰρ φίλοι, καὶ οἱ θεοὶ δὲ παντοίως αὐτοῖςβοηθοῦσι, δἰ ὀνείρων, διὰ μαντειῶν, πρὸς ταῦτα μέντοι, πρὸς ἄἐκεῖνοι διαφέρονται.

28. Ταὐτά ἐστι τὰ τοῦ κόσμου ἐγκύκλια, ἄνω κάτω, ἐξ αἰῶνος εἰςαἰῶνα. καὶ ἤτοι ἐφ ἕκαστον ὁρμᾷ ἡ τοῦ ὅλου διάνοια· ὅπερ εἰἔστιν, ἀποδέχου τὸ ἐκείνης ὁρμητόν· ἢ ἅπαξ ὥρμησε, τὰ δὲ λοιπὰκατ ἐπακολούθησιν, καὶ τί ἐντείνῃ; τὸ δὲ ὅλον - εἴτε θεός, εὐἔχει πάντα· εἴτε τὸ εἰκῇ, τρόπον [γὰρ] τινα ἄτομοι ἢ ἀμερῆ, μὴκαὶ σὺ εἰκῇ Ἤδη πάντας ἡμᾶς γῆ καλύψει, ἔπειτα καὶ αὐτὴμεταβαλεῖ κἀκεῖνα εἰς ἄπειρον μεταβαλεῖ καὶ πάλιν ἐκεῖνα εἰςἄπειρον. τὰς γὰρ ἐπικυματώσεις τῶν μεταβολῶν καὶ ἀλλοιώσεωνἐνθυμούμενός τις καὶ τὸ τάχος παντὸς θνητοῦ καταφρονήσει.

29. Χειμάρρους ἡ τῶν ὅλων αἰτία· πάντα φέρει. ἄνθρωπε, τί ποτε;ποίησον ὃ νῦν ἡ φύσις ἀπαιτεῖ, ὅρμησον, ἐὰν διδῶται, καὶ μὴπεριβλέπου εἴ τις εἴσεται. μὴ τὴν Πλάτωνος πολιτείαν ἔλπιζε,ἀλλὰ ἀρκοῦ, εἰ τὸ βραχύτατον πρόεισι, καὶ τούτου αὐτοῦ τὴνἔκβασιν ὡς οὐ μικρόν τί ἐστι διανοοῦ. ὡς εὐτελῆ δὲ καὶ τἀπολιτικὰ ταῦτα καί, ὡς οἴεται, φιλοσόφως πρακτικὰ ἀνθρώπια·μυξῶν μεστά. δόγμα γὰρ αὐτῶν τίς μεταβαλεῖ; χωρὶς δὲ δογμάτωνμεταβολῆς τί ἄλλο ἢ δουλεία στενόντων καὶ πείθεσθαιπροσποιουμένων; ὕπαγε νῦν καὶ Ἀλέξανδρον καὶ Φίλιππον καὶΔημήτριον τὸν Φαληρέα μοι λέγε. ὄψομαι, εἰ εἶδον, τί ἡ κοινὴφύσις ἤθελε, καὶ ἑαυτοὺς ἐπαιδαγώγησαν· εἰ δὲ ἐτραγῴδησαν,οὐδείς με κατακέκρικε μιμεῖσθαι. ἁπλοῦν ἐστι καὶ αἰδῆμον τὸφιλοσοφίας ἔργον· μή με ἄπαγε ἐπὶ σεμνοτυφίαν.

30. "Ἄνωθεν ἐπιθεωρεῖν" ἀγέλας μυρίας καὶ τελετὰς μυρίας καὶπλοῦν παντοῖον ἐν χειμῶσι καὶ γαλήναις καὶ διαφορὰς γινομένων,συγγινομένων, ἀπογινομένων. ἐπινοεῖν δὲ καὶ τὸν ὑπ ἄλλων πάλαιβεβιωμένον βίον καὶ τὸν μετὰ σὲ βιωθησόμενον καὶ τὸν νῦν ἐντοῖς βαρβάροις ἔθνεσι βιούμενον· καὶ ὅσοι μὲν οὐδὲ ὄνομά σουγινώσκουσιν, ὅσοι δὲ τάχιστα ἐπιλήσονται, ὅσοι δ ἐπαινοῦντεςἴσως νῦν σε τάχιστα ψέξουσι· καὶ ὡς οὔτε ἡ μνήμη ἀξιόλογόν γεοὔτε ἡ δόξα οὔτε ἄλλο τι τὸ σύμπαν.

31. Ἀταραξία μὲν περὶ τὰ ἀπὸ τῆς ἐκτὸς αἰτίας συμβαίνοντα, δικαιότης δὲ ἐν τοῖς παρὰ τὴν ἐκ σοῦ αἰτίαν ἐνεργουμένοις· τουτέστιν, ὁρμὴ καὶ πρᾶξις καταλήγουσα ἐπ αὐτὸ τὸ κοινωνικῶς πρᾶξαι ὡς τοῦτό σοι κατὰ φύσιν ὄν.

32. Πολλὰ περισσὰ περιελεῖν τῶν ἐνοχλούντων σοι δύνασαι ὅλα ἐπὶ τῇ ὑπολήψει σου κείμενα, καὶ πολλὴν εὐρυχωρίαν περιποιήσεις ἤδη σεαυτῷ ‹τῷ› τὸν ὅλον κόσμον περιειληφέναι τῇ γνώμῃ καὶ τὸν ‹ἀ›ίδιον αἰῶνα περινοεῖν καὶ τὴν τῶν κατὰ μέρος ἑκάστου πράγματος ταχεῖαν μεταβολὴν ἐπινοεῖν, ὡς βραχὺ μὲν τὸ ἀπὸ γενέσεως μέχρι διαλύσεως, ἀχανὲς δὲ τὸ πρὸ τῆς γενέσεως, ὡς καὶ τὸ μετὰ τὴν διάλυσιν ὁμοίως ἄπειρον.

33. Πάντα ὅσα ὁρᾷς τάχιστα φθαρήσεται καὶ οἱ φθειρόμενα αὐτὰ ἐπιδόντες τάχιστα καὶ αὐτοὶ φθαρήσονται καὶ ὁ ἐσχατόγηρως ἀποθανὼν εἰς ἴσον καταστήσεται τῷ προώρῳ.

34. Τίνα τὰ ἡγεμονικὰ τούτων καὶ περὶ οἷα ἐσπουδάκασι καὶ δι οἷα φιλοῦσι καὶ τιμῶσι· γυμνὰ νόμιζε βλέπειν τὰ ψυχάρια αὐτῶν. ὅτε δοκοῦσι βλάπτειν ψέγοντες ἢ ὠφελεῖν ἐξυμνοῦντες, ὅση οἴησις.

35. Ἡ ἀποβολὴ οὐδὲν ἄλλο ἐστὶν ἢ μεταβολή. τούτῳ δὲ χαίρει ἡ τῶν ὅλων φύσις, καθ ἣν πάντα καλῶς γίνεται. ἐξ αἰῶνος ὁμοειδῶς ἐγίνετο καὶ εἰς ἄπειρον τοιαῦθ ἕτερα ἔσται. τί οὖν λέγεις ὅτι ἐγίνετό τε πάντα ‹ἀεὶ κακῶς› [ὃ] καὶ πάντα ἀεὶ κακῶς ἔσται καὶ οὐδεμία ἄρα δύναμις ἐν τοσούτοις θεοῖς ἐξευρέθη ποτὲ ἡ διορθώσουσα ταῦτα, ἀλλὰ κατακέκριται ὁ κόσμος ἐν ἀδιαλείπτοις κακοῖς συνέχεσθαι;

36. Τὸ σαπρὸν τῆς ἑκάστῳ ὑποκειμένης ὕλης· ὕδωρ, κόνις, ὀστάρια, γράσος, ἢ πάλιν· πῶροι γῆς τὰ μάρμαρα καὶ ὑποστάθμαι ὁ χρυσός, ὁ ἄργυρος, καὶ τριχία ἡ ἐσθὴς καὶ αἷμα ἡ πορφύρα, καὶ τὰ ἄλλα πάντα τοιαῦτα. καὶ τὸ πνευματικὸν δὲ ἄλλο τοιοῦτον καὶ ἐκ τούτων εἰς ταῦτα μεταβάλλον.

37. Ἅλις τοῦ ἀθλίου βίου καὶ γογγυσμοῦ καὶ πιθηκισμοῦ. - τί ταράσσῃ; τί τούτων καινόν; τί σε ἐξίστησι; τὸ αἴτιον; ἴδε αὐτό. ἀλλ ἡ ὕλη; ἴδε αὐτήν. ἔξω δὲ τούτων οὐδέν ἐστιν· ἀλλὰ καὶ πρὸς τοὺς θεοὺς ἤδη ποτὲ ἁπλούστερος καὶ χρηστότερος γενοῦ.

38. Ἴσον τὸ ἑκατὸν ἔτεσι καὶ τὸ τρισὶ ταῦτα ἱστορῆσαι.

39. Εἰ μὲν ἥμαρτεν, ἐκεῖ τὸ κακόν. τάχα δ οὐχ ἥμαρτεν.

40. Ἤτοι ἀπὸ μιᾶς πηγῆς νοερᾶς πάντα ὡς ἑνὶ σώματι ἐπισυμβαίνεικαὶ οὐ δεῖ τὸ μέρος τοῖς ὑπὲρ τοῦ ὅλου γινομένοις μέμφεσθαι ἢ ἄτομοι καὶ οὐδὲν ἄλλο ἢ κυκεὼν καὶ σκεδασμός· τί οὖνταράσσῃ; τῷ ἡγεμονικῷ λέγειν· τέθνηκας, ἔφθαρσαι, τεθηρίωσαι,ὑποκρίνῃ, συναγελάζῃ, βόσκῃ;

41. Ἤτοι οὐδὲν δύνανται οἱ θεοὶ ἢ δύνανται. εἰ μὲν οὖν μὴδύνανται, τί εὔχῃ; εἰ δὲ δύνανται, διὰ τί οὐχὶ μᾶλλον εὔχῃ διδόναιαὐτοὺς τὸ μήτε φοβεῖσθαί τι τούτων μήτε ἐπιθυμεῖν τινος τούτωνμήτε λυπεῖσθαι ἐπί τινι τούτων, μᾶλλον ἤπερ τὸ μὴ παρεῖναί τιτούτων ἢ τὸ παρεῖναι; πάντως γάρ, εἰ δύνανται συνεργεῖνἀνθρώποις, καὶ εἰς ταῦτα δύνανται συνεργεῖν. ἀλλὰ ἴσως ἐρεῖςὅτι· ἐπ ἐμοὶ αὐτὰ οἱ θεοὶ ἐποίησαν. εἶτα οὐ κρεῖσσον χρῆσθαιτοῖς ἐπὶ σοὶ μετ ἐλευθερίας ἢ διαφέρεσθαι πρὸς τὰ μὴ ἐπὶ σοὶμετὰ δουλείας καὶ ταπεινότητος; τίς δέ σοι εἶπεν ὅτι οὐχὶ καὶ εἰςτὰ ἐφ ἡμῖν οἱ θεοὶ συλλαμβάνουσιν; ἄρξαι γοῦν περὶ τούτωνεὔχεσθαι καὶ ὄψει. οῦτος εὔχεται· πῶς κοιμηθῶ μετ ἐκείνης·σύ· πῶς μὴ ἐπιθυμήσω τοῦ κοιμηθῆναι μετ ἐκείνης. ἄλλος·πῶςστερηθῶ ἐκείνου· σύ· πῶς μὴ χρῄζω τοῦ στερηθῆναι. ἄλλος·πῶς μὴ ἀποβάλω τὸ τεκνίον· σύ· πῶς μὴ φοβηθῶ ἀποβαλεῖν.ὅλως ὧδε ἐπίστρεψον τὰς εὐχὰς καὶ θεώρει τί γίνεται.

42. Ὁ Ἐπίκουρος λέγει ὅτι· "ἐν τῇ νόσῳ οὐκ ἦσάν μοι αἱ ὁμιλίαιπερὶ τῶν τοῦ σωματίου παθῶν οὐδὲ πρὸς τοὺς εἰσιόντας τοιαῦτάτινα, φησίν, ἐλάλουν, ἀλλὰ τὰ προηγούμενα φυσιολογῶν διετέλουνκαὶ πρὸς αὐτῷ τούτῳ ὄν, πῶς ἡ διάνοια συμμεταλαμβάνουσατῶν ἐν τῷ σαρκιδίῳ τοιούτων κινήσεων ἀταρακτεῖ τὸ ἴδιονἀγαθὸν τηροῦσα. οὐδὲ τοῖς ἰατροῖς ἐμπαρεῖχον, φησί, καταφρυάττεσθαιὥς τι ποιοῦσιν, ἀλλὰ ὁ βίος ἤγετο εὖ καὶ καλῶς." ταὐτὰοῦν ἐκείνῳ, ἐν νόσῳ, ἐὰν νοσῇς καὶ ἐν ἄλλῃ τινὶ περιστάσει· τὸγὰρ μὴ ἀφίστασθαι φιλοσοφίας ἐν οἷς δήποτε τοῖς προσπίπτουσιμηδὲ ἰδιώτῃ καὶ ‹ἀ›φυσιολόγῳ συμφλυαρεῖν, πάσης αἱρέσεωςκοινόν. πρὸς μόνῳ τῷ νῦν πρασσομένῳ εἶναι καὶ τῷ ὀργάνῳ, διοῤ πράσσεις.

43. Ὅταν τινὸς ἀναισχυντίᾳ προσκόπτῃς, εὐθὺς πυνθάνου σεαυτοῦ· δύνανται οὖν ἐν τῷ κόσμῳ ἀναίσχυντοι μὴ εἶναι; οὐ δύνανται· μὴ οὖν ἀπαίτει τὸ ἀδύνατον· εἷς γὰρ καὶ οῦτός ἐστινἐκείνων τῶν ἀναισχύντων, οὓς ἀνάγκη ἐν τῷ κόσμῳ εἶναι. τὸ δαὐτὸ καὶ ἐπὶ τοῦ πανούργου καὶ ἐπὶ τοῦ ἀπίστου καὶ παντὸς τοῦὁτιοῦν ἁμαρτάνοντος ἔστω σοι πρόχειρον· ἅμα γὰρ τῷ ὑπομνησθῆναιὅτι τὸ γένος τῶν τοιούτων ἀδύνατόν ἐστι μὴ ὑπάρχειν,εὐμενέστερος ἔσῃ πρὸς τοὺς καθ ἕνα. εὔχρηστον δὲ κἀκεῖνο εὐθὺςἐννοεῖν, τίνα ἔδωκεν ἡ φύσις τῷ ἀνθρώπῳ ἀρετὴν πρὸς τοῦτοτὸ ἁμάρτημα· ἔδωκε γὰρ ὡς ἀντιφάρμακον πρὸς

μὲν τὸν ἀγνώμονατὴν πραότητα, πρὸς δὲ ἄλλον ἄλλην τινὰ δύναμιν, ὅλως δὲ ἔξεστίσοι μεταδιδάσκειν τὸν πεπλανημένον· πᾶς δὲ ὁ ἁμαρτάνωνἀφαμαρτάνει τοῦ προκειμένου καὶ πεπλάνηται. τί δὲ καὶβέβλαψαι; εὑρήσεις γὰρ μηδένα τούτων, πρὸς οὓς παροξύνῃ,πεποιηκότα τι τοιοῦτον ἐξ οῦ ἡ διάνοιά σου χείρων ἔμελλεγενήσεσθαι· τὸ δὲ κακόν σου καὶ τὸ βλαβερὸν ἐνταῦθα πᾶσαντὴν ὑπόστασιν ἔχει. τί δαὶ κακὸν ἢ ξένον γέγονεν, εἰ ὁ ἀπαίδευτοςτὰ τοῦ ἀπαιδεύτου πράσσει; ὅρα μὴ σεαυτῷ μᾶλλον ἐγκαλεῖνὀφείλῃς, ὅτι οὐ προσεδόκησας τοῦτον τοῦτο ἁμαρτήσεσθαι· σὺγὰρ καὶ ἀφορμὰς ἐκ τοῦ λόγου εἶχες πρὸς τὸ ἐνθυμηθῆναι ὅτιεἰκός ἐστι τοῦτον τοῦτο ἁμαρτήσεσθαι, καὶ ὅμως ἐπιλαθόμενοςθαυμάζεις εἰ ἡμάρτηκεν. μάλιστα δέ, ὅταν ὡς ἀπίστῳ ἢ ἀχαρίστῳμέμφῃ, εἰς ἑαυτὸν ἐπιστρέφου· προδήλως γὰρ σὸν τὸ ἁμάρτημα,εἴτε περὶ τοῦ τοιαύτην τὴν διάθεσιν ἔχοντος ἐπίστευσας ὅτι τὴνπίστιν φυλάξει, εἴτε τὴν χάριν διδοὺς μὴ καταληκτικῶς ἔδωκαςμηδὲ ὥστε ἐξ αὐτῆς τῆς σῆς πράξεως εὐθὺς ἀπειληφέναι πάνταντὸν καρπόν. τί γὰρ πλέον θέλεις εὖ ποιήσας, ἄνθρωπε; οὐκ ἀρκεῖτοῦτο, ὅτι κατὰ φύσιν τὴν σήν τι ἔπραξας, ἀλλὰ τούτου μισθὸνζητεῖς; ὡσεὶ ὁ ὀφθαλμὸς ἀμοιβὴν ἀπῄτει, ὅτι βλέπει, ἢ οἱ πόδες,ὅτι βαδίζουσιν. ὥσπερ γὰρ ταῦτα πρὸς τόδε τι γέγονεν, ὅπερκατὰ τὴν ἰδίαν κατασκευὴν ἐνεργοῦντα ἀπέχει τὸ ἴδιον, οὕτωςκαὶ ὁ ἄνθρωπος εὐεργετικὸς πεφυκώς, ὁπόταν τι εὐεργετικὸν ἤἄλλως εἰς τὰ μέσα συνεργητικὸν πράξῃ, πεποίηκε πρὸς ὃ κατεσκεύασται,καὶ ἔχει τὸ ἑαυτοῦ.

BOOK TEN

I. O my soul, the time I trust will be, when thou shalt be good, simple, single, more open and visible, than that body by which it is enclosed. Thou wilt one day be sensible of their happiness, whose end is love, and their affections dead to all worldly things. Thou shalt one day be full, and in want of no external thing: not seeking pleasure from anything, either living or insensible, that this world can afford; neither wanting time for the continuation of thy pleasure, nor place and opportunity, nor the favour either of the weather or of men. When thou shalt have content in thy present estate, and all things present shall add to thy content: when thou shalt persuade thyself, that thou hast all things; all for thy good, and all by the providence of the Gods: and of things future also shalt be as confident, that all will do well, as tending to the maintenance and preser-vation in some sort, of his perfect welfare and happiness, who is perfection of life, of goodness, and beauty; who begets all things, and containeth all things in himself, and in himself doth recollect all things from all places that are dissolved, that of them he may beget others again like unto them. Such one day shall be thy disposition, that thou shalt be able, both in regard of the Gods, and in regard of men, so to fit and order thy conversation, as neither to complain of them at any time, for anything that they do; nor to do anything thyself, for which thou mayest justly be condemned.

II. As one who is altogether governed by nature, let it be thy care to observe what it is that thy nature in general doth require. That done, if thou find not that thy nature, as thou art a living sensible creature, will be the worse for it, thou may-est proceed. Next then thou must examine, what thy nature as thou art a living sensible creature, doth require. And that, whatsoever it be, thou mayest admit of and do it, if thy nature as thou art a reasonable living creature, will not be the worse for it. Now whatsoever is reasonable, is also sociable, Keep thyself to these rules, and trouble not thyself about idle things.

III. Whatsoever doth happen unto thee, thou art naturally by thy natural consti-tution either able, or not able to bear. If thou beest able, be not offended, but bear it according to thy natural constitution, or as nature hath enabled thee. If thou beest not able, be not offended. For it will soon make an end of thee, and itself, (whatsoever it be) at the same time end with thee. But remember, that whatso-ever by the strength of opinion, grounded upon a certain apprehension of both true profit and duty, thou canst conceive tolerable; that thou art able to bear that by thy natural constitution.

IV. Him that offends, to teach with love and meek ness, and to show him his error. But if thou canst not, then to blame thyself; or rather not thyself neither, if thy will and endeavours have not been wanting.

V. Whatsoever it be that happens unto thee, it is that which from all time was appointed unto thee. For by the same coherence of causes, by which thy substance from all eternity was appointed to be, was also whatsoever should happen unto it, destinated and appointed.

VI. Either with Epicurus, we must fondly imagine the atoms to be the cause of all things, or we must needs grant a nature. Let this then be thy first ground, that thou art part of that universe, which is governed by nature. Then secondly, that to those parts that are of the same kind and nature as thou art, thou hast relation of kindred. For of these, if I shall always be mindful, first as I am a part, I shall never be displeased with anything, that falls to my particular share of the common chances of the world. For nothing that is behoveful unto the whole, can be truly hurtful to that which is part of it. For this being the common privilege of all natures, that they contain nothing in themselves that is hurtful unto them; it cannot be that the nature of the universe (whose privilege beyond other particular natures, is, that she cannot against her will by any higher external cause be constrained,) should beget anything and cherish it in her bosom that should tend to her own hurt and prejudice. As then I bear in mind that I am a part of such an universe, I shall not be displeased with anything that happens. And as I have relation of kindred to those parts that are of the same kind and nature that I am, so I shall be careful to do nothing that is prejudicial to the community, but in all my deliberations shall they that are of my kind ever be; and the common good, that, which all my intentions and resolutions shall drive unto, as that which is contrary unto it, I shall by all means endeavour to prevent and avoid. These things once so fixed and concluded, as thou wouldst think him a happy citizen, whose constant study and practice were for the good and benefit of his fellow citizens, and the carriage of the city such towards him, that he were well pleased with it; so must it needs be with thee, that thou shalt live a happy life.

VII. All parts of the world, (all things I mean that are contained within the whole world), must of necessity at some time or other come to corruption. Alteration I should say, to speak truly and properly; but that I may be the better understood, I am content at this time to use that more common word. Now say I, if so be that this be both hurtful unto them, and yet unavoidable, would not, thinkest thou, the whole itself be in a sweet case, all the parts of it being subject to alteration, yea and by their making itself fitted for corruption, as consisting of things different and contrary? And did nature then either of herself thus project and purpose the affliction and misery of her parts, and therefore of purpose so made them, not only that haply they might, but of necessity that they should fall into evil; or did not she know what she did, when she made them? For either of these two to say, is equally absurd. But to let pass nature in general, and to reason of things particular according to their own particular natures; how absurd and ridiculous is it, first to say that all parts of the whole are, by their proper natural constitution, subject to alteration; and then when any such thing doth happen, as when one doth fall sick and dieth, to take on and wonder as though some strange thing had happened? Though this besides might move not so grievously to take on when any such thing doth happen, that whatsoever is dissolved, it is dissolved into those things, whereof it was compounded. For every dissolution is either a mere dispersion, of the elements into those elements again whereof everything did consist, or a change, of that which is more solid into earth; and of that which is pure and subtile or spiritual, into air. So that by this means nothing is lost, but all resumed again into those rational generative seeds of the universe; and this universe, either after a certain period of time to lie consumed by fire, or by continual changes to be renewed, and so for ever to endure. Now that solid and spiritual that we speak of, thou must not conceive it to be that very same, which at first was, when thou wert born. For alas! all this that now thou art in either kind, either for matter of substance, or of life, hath but two or three days ago partly from meats eaten, and partly from air breathed in, received all its influx, being the same then in no other respect, than a running river, maintained by the perpetual influx and new supply of waters, is the same. That therefore which thou hast since received, not that which came from thy mother, is that which comes to change and corruption. But suppose that that for the general substance, and more solid part of it, should still cleave unto thee never so close, yet what is that to the proper qualities and affections of it, by which persons are distinguished, which certainly are quite different?

VIII. Now that thou hast taken these names upon thee of good, modest, true; of emfrwn, sumfrwn, uperfrwn; take heed lest at any times by doing anything that is contrary, thou be but improperly so called, and lose thy right to these appellations. Or if thou do, return unto them again with all possible speed. And remember, that the word emfrwn notes unto thee an intent and intelligent consideration of every object that presents itself unto thee, without distraction. And the word emfrwn a ready and contented acceptation of whatsoever by the appointment of the common nature, happens unto thee. And the word sumfrwn, a super-extension, or a transcendent, and outreaching disposition of thy mind, whereby it passeth by all bodily pains and pleasures, honour and credit, death and whatsoever is of the same nature, as matters of absolute indifferency, and in no wise to be stood upon by a wise man. These then if inviolably thou shalt observe, and shalt not be ambitious to be so called by others, both thou thyself shalt become a new man, and thou shalt begin a new life. For to continue such as hitherto thou hast been, to undergo those distractions and distempers as thou must needs for such a life as hitherto thou hast lived, is the part of one that is very foolish, and is overfond of his life. Whom a man might compare to one of those half-eaten wretches, matched in the amphitheatre with wild beasts; who as full as they are all the body over with wounds and blood, desire for a great favour, that they may be reserved till the next day, then also, and in the same estate to be exposed to the same nails and teeth as before. Away therefore, ship thyself; and from the troubles and distractions of thy former life convey thyself as it were unto these few names; and if thou canst abide in them, or be constant in the practice and possession of them, continue there as glad and joyful as one that were translated unto some such place of bliss and happiness as that which by Hesiod and Plato is called the Islands of the Blessed, by others called the Elysian Fields. And whensoever thou findest thyself; that thou art in danger of a relapse, and that thou art not able to master and overcome those difficulties and temptations that present themselves in thy present station: get thee into any private corner, where thou mayst be better able. Or if that will not serve forsake even thy life rather. But so that it be not in passion but in a plain voluntary modest way: this being the only commendable action of thy whole life that thus thou art departed, or this having been the main work and business of thy whole life, that thou mightest thus depart. Now for the better remembrance of those names that we have spoken of, thou shalt find it a very good help, to remember the Gods as often as may be: and that, the thing which they require at our hands of as many of us, as are by nature reasonable creation is not that with fair words, and outward show of piety and devotion we should flatter them, but that we should become like unto them: and that as all other natural creatures, the fig tree for example; the dog the bee: both do, all of them, and apply themselves unto that which by their natural constitution, is proper unto them; so man likewise should do that, which by his nature, as he is a man, belongs unto him.

IX. Toys and fooleries at home, wars abroad: sometimes terror, sometimes torpor, or stupid sloth: this is thy daily slavery. By little and little, if thou doest not better look to it, those sacred dogmata will be blotted out of thy mind. How many things be there, which when as a mere naturalist, thou hast barely considered of according to their nature, thou doest let pass without any further use? Whereas thou shouldst in all things so join action and contemplation, that thou mightest both at the same time attend all present occasions, to perform everything duly and carefully and yet so intend the contemplative part too, that no part of that delight and pleasure, which the contemplative knowledge of everything according to its true nature doth of itself afford, might be lost. Or, that the true and contemnplative knowledge of everything according to its own nature, might of itself, (action being subject to many lets and impediments) afford unto thee sufficient pleasure and happiness. Not apparent indeed, but not concealed. And when shalt thou attain to the happiness of true simplicity, and unaffected gravity? When shalt thou rejoice in the certain knowledge of every particular object according to its true nature: as what the matter and substance of it is; what use it is for in the world: how long it can subsist: what things it doth consist of: who they be that are capable of it, and who they that can give it, and take it away?

X. As the spider, when it hath caught the fly that it hunted after, is not little proud, nor meanly conceited of herself: as he likewise that hath caught an hare, or hath taken a fish with his net: as another for the taking of a boar, and another of a bear: so may they be proud, and applaud themselves for their valiant acts against the Sarmatai, or northern nations lately defeated. For these also, these famous soldiers and warlike men, if thou dost look into their minds and opinions, what do they for the most part but hunt after prey?

XI. To find out, and set to thyself some certain way and method of contemplation, whereby thou mayest clearly discern and represent unto thyself, the mutual change of all things, the one into the other. Bear it in thy mind evermore, and see that thou be throughly well exercised in this particular. For there is not anything more effectual to beget true magnanimity.

XII. He hath got loose from the bonds of his body, and perceiving that within a very little while he must of necessity bid the world farewell, and leave all these things behind him, he wholly applied himself, as to righteousness in all his actions, so to the common nature in all things that should happen unto him. And contenting himself with these two things, to do all things justly, and whatsoever God doth send to like well of it: what others shall either say or think of him, or shall do against him, he doth not so much as trouble his thoughts with it. To go on straight, whither right and reason directed him, and by so doing to follow God, was the only thing that he did mind, that, his only business and occupation.

XIII. What use is there of suspicion at all? or, why should thoughts of mistrust, and suspicion concerning that which is future, trouble thy mind at all? What now is to be done, if thou mayest search and inquiry into that, what needs thou care for more? And if thou art well able to perceive it alone, let no man divert thee from it. But if alone thou doest not so well perceive it, suspend thine action, and take advice from the best. And if there be anything else that doth hinder thee, go on with prudence and discretion, according to the present occasion and opportunity, still proposing that unto thyself, which thou doest conceive most right and just. For to hit that aright, and to speed in the prosecution of it, must needs be happiness, since it is that only which we can truly and properly be said to miss of, or miscarry in.

XIV. What is that that is slow, and yet quick? merry, and yet grave? He that in all things doth follow reason for his guide.

XV. In the morning as soon as thou art awaked, when thy judgment, before either thy affections, or external objects have wrought upon it, is yet most free and impartial: put this question to thyself, whether if that which is right and just be done, the doing of it by thyself, or by others when thou art not able thyself; be a thing material or no. For sure it is not. And as for these that keep such a life, and stand so much upon the praises, or dispraises of other men, hast thou forgotten what manner of men they be? that such and such upon their beds, and such at their board: what their ordinary actions are: what they pursue after, and what they fly from: what thefts and rapines they commit, if not with their hands and feet, yet with that more precious part of theirs, their minds: which (would it but admit of them) might enjoy faith, modesty, truth, justice, a good spirit.

XVI. Give what thou wilt, and take away what thou wilt, saith he that is well taught and truly modest, to Him that gives, and takes away. And it is not out of a stout and peremptory resolution, that he saith it, but in mere love, and humble submission.

XVII. So live as indifferent to the world and all worldly objects, as one who liveth by himself alone upon some desert hill. For whether here, or there, if the whole world be but as one town, it matters not much for the place. Let them behold and see a man, that is a man indeed, living according to the true nature of man. If they cannot bear with me, let them kill me. For better were it to die, than so to live as they would have thee.

XVIII. Make it not any longer a matter of dispute or discourse, what are the signs and proprieties of a good man, but really and actually to be such.

XIX. Ever to represent unto thyself; and to set before thee, both the general age and time of the world, and the whole substance of it. And how all things particular in respect of these are for their substance, as one of the least seeds that is: and for their duration, as the turning of the pestle in the mortar once about. Then to fix thy mind upon every particular object of the world, and to conceive it, (as it is indeed,) as already being in the state of dissolution, and of change; tending to some kind of either putrefaction or dispersion; or whatsoever else it is, that is the death as it were of everything in his own kind.

XX. Consider them through all actions and occupations, of their lives: as when they eat, and when they sleep: when they are in the act of necessary exoneration, and when in the act of lust. Again, when they either are in their greatest exultation; and in the middle of all their pomp and glory; or being angry and displeased, in great state and majesty, as from an higher place, they chide and rebuke. How base and slavish, but a little while ago, they were fain to be, that they might come to this; and within a very little while what will be their estate, when death hath once seized upon them.

XXI. That is best for every one, that the common nature of all doth send unto every one, and then is it best, when she doth send it.

XXII. The earth, saith the poet, doth often long after the rain. So is the glorious sky often as desirous to fall upon the earth, which argues a mutual kind of love between them. And so (say I) doth the world bear a certain affection of love to whatsoever shall come to pass With thine affections shall mine concur, O world. The same (and no other) shall the object of my longing be which is of thine. Now that the world doth love it is true indeed so is it as commonly said, and acknowledged ledged, when, according to the Greek phrase, imitated by the Latins, of things that used to be, we say commonly, that they love to be.

XXIII. Either thou dost Continue in this kind of life and that is it, which so long thou hast been used unto and therefore tolerable: or thou doest retire, or leave the world, and that of thine own accord, and then thou hast thy mind: or thy life is cut off; and then mayst thou rejoice that thou hast ended thy charge. One of these must needs be. Be therefore of good comfort.

XXIV Let it always appear and be manifest unto thee that solitariness, and desert places, by many philosophers so much esteemed of and affected, are of themselves but thus and thus; and that all things are them to them that live in towns, and converse with others as they are the same nature everywhere to be seen and observed: to them that have retired themselves to the top of mountains, and to desert havens, or what other desert and inhabited places soever. For anywhere it thou wilt mayest thou quickly find and apply that to thyself; which Plato saith of his philosopher, in a place: as private and retired, saith he, as if he were shut up and enclosed about in some shepherd's lodge, on the top of a hill. There by thyself to put these questions to thyself or to enter in these considerations: What is my chief and principal part, which hath power over the rest? What is now the present estate of it, as I use it; and what is it, that I employ it about? Is it now void of reason ir no? Is it free, and separated; or so affixed, so congealed and grown together as it were with the flesh, that it is swayed by the motions and inclinations of it?

XXV. He that runs away from his master is a fugitive. But the law is every man's master. He therefore that forsakes the law, is a fugitive. So is he, whosoever he be, that is either sorry, angry, or afraid, or for anything that either hath been, is, or shall be by his appointment, who is the Lord and Governor of the universe. For he truly and properly is Nomoz, or the law, as the only nemwn (sp.), or distributor and dispenser of all things that happen unto any one in his lifetime— Whatsoever then is either sorry, angry, or afraid, is a fugitive.

XXVI. From man is the seed, that once cast into the womb man hath no more to do with it. Another cause succeedeth, and undertakes the work, and in time brings a child (that wonderful effect from such a beginning!) to perfection. Again, man lets food down through his throat; and that once down, he hath no more to do with it. Another cause succeedeth and distributeth this food into the senses, and the affections: into life, and into strength; and doth with it those other many and marvellous things, that belong unto man. These things therefore that are so secretly and invisibly wrought and brought to pass, thou must use to behold and contemplate; and not the things themselves only, but the power also by which they are effected; that thou mayst behold it, though not with the eyes of the body, yet as plainly and visibly as thou canst see and discern the outward efficient cause of the depression and elevation of anything.

XXVII. Ever to mind and consider with thyself; how all things that now are, have been heretofore much after the same sort, and after the same fashion that now they are: and so to think of those things which shall be hereafter also. Moreover, whole dramata, and uniform scenes, or scenes that comprehend the lives and actions of men of one calling and profession, as many as either in thine own experience thou hast known, or by reading of ancient histories; (as the whole court of Adrianus, the whole court of Antoninus Pius, the whole court of Philippus, that of Alexander, that of Croesus): to set them all before thine eyes. For thou shalt find that they are all but after one sort and fashion: only that the actors were others.

XXVIII. As a pig that cries and flings when his throat is cut, fancy to thyself every one to be, that grieves for any worldly thing and takes on. Such a one is he also, who upon his bed alone, doth bewail the miseries of this our mortal life. And remember this, that Unto reasonable creatures only it is granted that they may willingly and freely submit unto Providence: but absolutely to submit, is a necessity imposed upon all creatures equally.

XXIX. Whatsoever it is that thou goest about, consider of it by thyself, and ask thyself, What? because I shall do this no more when I am dead, should therefore death seem grievous unto me?

XXX. When thou art offended with any man's transgression, presently reflect upon thyself; and consider what thou thyself art guilty of in the same kind. As that thou also perchance dost think it a happiness either to be rich, or to live in pleasure, or to be praised and commended, and so of the rest in particular. For this if thou shalt call to mind, thou shalt soon forget thine anger; especially when at the same time this also shall concur in thy thoughts, that he was constrained by his error and ignorance so to do: for how can he choose as long as he is of that opinion? Do thou therefore if thou canst, take away that from him, that forceth him to do as he doth.

XXXI. When thou seest Satyro, think of Socraticus and Eutyches, or Hymen, and when Euphrates, think of Eutychio, and Sylvanus, when Alciphron, of Tropaeophorus, when Xenophon, of Crito, or Severus. And when thou doest look upon thyself, fancy unto thyself some one or other of the Caesars; and so for every one, some one or other that hath been for estate and profession answerable unto him. Then let this come to thy mind at the same time; and where now are they all? Nowhere or anywhere? For so shalt thou at all time be able to perceive how all worldly things are but as the smoke, that vanisheth away: or, indeed, mere nothing. Especially when thou shalt call to mind this also, that whatsoever is once changed, shall never be again as long as the world endureth. And thou then, how long shalt thou endure? And why doth it not suffice thee, if virtuously, and as becometh thee, thou mayest pass that portion of time, how little soever it be, that is allotted unto thee?

XXXII. What a subject, and what a course of life is it, that thou doest so much desire to be rid of. For all these things, what are they, but fit objects for an understanding, that beholdeth everything according to its true nature, to exercise itself upon? Be patient, therefore, until that (as a strong stomach that turns all things into his own nature; and as a great fire that turneth in flame and light, whatsoever thou doest cast into it) thou have made these things also familiar, and as it were natural unto thee.

XXXIII. Let it not be in any man's power, to say truly of thee, that thou art not truly simple, or sincere and open, or not good. Let him be deceived whosoever he be that shall have any such opinion of thee. For all this doth depend of thee. For who is it that should hinder thee from being either truly simple or good? Do thou only resolve rather not to live, than not to be such. For indeed neither doth it stand with reason that he should live that is not such. What then is it that may upon this present occasion according to best reason and discretion, either be said or done? For whatsoever it be, it is in thy power either to do it, or to say it, and therefore seek not any pretences, as though thou wert hindered. Thou wilt never cease groaning and complaining, until such time as that, what pleasure is unto the voluptuous, be unto thee, to do in everything that presents itself, whatsoever may be done conformably and agreeably to the proper constitution of man, or, to man as he is a man. For thou must account that pleasure, whatsoever it be, that thou mayest do according to thine own nature. And to do this, every place will fit thee. Unto the cylindrus, or roller, it is not granted to move everywhere according to its own proper motion, as neither unto the water, nor unto the fire, nor unto any other thing, that either is merely natural, or natural and sensitive; but not rational for many things there be that can hinder their operations. But of the mind and understanding this is the proper privilege, that according to its own nature, and as it will itself, it can pass through every obstacle that it finds, and keep straight on forwards. Setting therefore before thine eyes this happiness and felicity of thy mind, whereby it is able to pass through all things, and is capable of all motions, whether as the fire, upwards; or as the stone downwards, or as the cylindrus through that which is sloping: content thyself with it, and seek not after any other thing. For all other kind of hindrances that are not hindrances of thy mind either they are proper to the body, or merely proceed from the opinion, reason not making that resistance that it should, but basely, and cowardly suffering itself to be foiled; and of themselves can neither wound, nor do any hurt at all. Else must he of necessity, whosoever he be that meets with any of them, become worse than he was before. For so is it in all other subjects, that that is thought hurtful unto them, whereby they are made worse. But here contrariwise, man (if he make that good use of them that he should) is rather the better and the more praiseworthy for any of those kind of hindrances, than otherwise. But generally remember that nothing can hurt a natural citizen, that is not hurtful unto the city itself, nor anything hurt the city, that is not hurtful unto the law itself. But none of these casualties, or external hindrances, do hurt the law itself; or, are contrary to that course of justice and equity, by which public societies are maintained: neither therefore do they hurt either city or citizen.

XXXIV. As he that is bitten by a mad dog, is afraid of everything almost that he seeth: so unto him, whom the dogmata have once bitten, or in whom true knowledge hath made an impression, everything almost that he sees or reads be it never so short or ordinary, doth afford a good memento; to put him out of all grief and fear, as that of the poet, 'The winds blow upon the trees, and their leaves fall upon the ground. Then do the trees begin to bud again, and by the spring-time they put forth new branches. So is the generation of men; some come into the world, and others go out of it.' Of these leaves then thy children are. And they also that applaud thee so gravely, or, that applaud thy speeches, with that their usual acclamation, axiopistwz, O wisely spoken I and speak well of thee, as on the other side, they that stick not to curse thee, they that privately and secretly dispraise and deride thee, they also are but leaves. And they also that shall follow, in whose memories the names of men famous after death, is preserved, they are but leaves neither. For even so is it of all these worldly things. Their spring comes, and they are put forth. Then blows the wind, and they go down. And then in lieu of them grow others out of the wood or common matter of all things, like unto them. But, to endure but for a while, is common unto all. Why then shouldest thou so earnestly either seek after these things, or fly from them, as though they should endure for ever? Yet a little while, and thine eyes will be closed up, and for him that carries thee to thy grave shall another mourn within a while after.

XXXV. A good eye must be good to see whatsoever is to be seen, and not green things only. For that is proper to sore eyes. So must a good ear, and a good smell be ready for whatsoever is either to be heard, or smelt: and a good stomach as indifferent to all kinds of food, as a millstone is, to whatsoever she was made for to grind. As ready therefore must a sound understanding be for whatsoever shall happen. But he that saith, O that my children might live! and, O that all men might commend me for whatsoever I do! is an eye that seeks after green things; or as teeth, after that which is tender.

XXXVI. There is not any man that is so happy in his death, but that some of those that are by him when he dies, will be ready to rejoice at his supposed calamity. Is it one that was virtuous and wise indeed? will there not some one or other be found, who thus will say to himself; 'Well now at last shall I be at rest from this pedagogue. He did not indeed otherwise trouble us much: but I know well enough that in his heart, he did much condemn us.' Thus will they speak of the virtuous. But as for us, alas I how many things be there, for which there be many that glad would be to be rid of us. This therefore if thou shalt think of whensoever thou diest, thou shalt die the more willingly, when thou shalt think with thyself; I am now to depart from that world, wherein those that have been my nearest friends and acquaintances, they whom I have so much suffered for, so often prayed for, and for whom I have taken such care, even they would have me die, hoping that after my death they shall live happier, than they did before. What then should any man desire to continue here any longer? Nevertheless, whensoever thou diest, thou must not be less kind and loving unto them for it; but as before, see them, continue to be their friend, to wish them well, and meekly, and gently to carry thyself towards them, but yet so that on the other side, it make thee not the more unwilling to die. But as it fareth with them that die an easy quick death, whose soul is soon separated from their bodies, so must thy separation from them be. To these had nature joined and annexed me: now she parts us; I am ready to depart, as from friends and kinsmen, but yet without either reluctancy or compulsion. For this also is according to Nature.

XXXVII. Use thyself; as often, as thou seest any man do anything, presently (if it be possible) to say unto thyself, What is this man's end in this his action? But begin this course with thyself first of all, and diligently examine thyself concerning whatsoever thou doest.

XXXVIII. Remember, that that which sets a man at work, and hath power over the affections to draw them either one way, or the other way, is not any external thing properly, but that which is hidden within every man's dogmata, and opinions: That, that is rhetoric; that is life; that (to speak true) is man himself. As for thy body, which as a vessel, or a case, compasseth thee about, and the many and curious instruments that it hath annexed unto it, let them not trouble thy thoughts. For of themselves they are but as a carpenter's axe, but that they are born with us, and naturally sticking unto us. But otherwise, without the inward cause that hath power to move them, and to restrain them, those parts are of themselves of no more use unto us, than the shuttle is of itself to the weaver, or the pen to the writer, or the whip to the coachman.

ΒΙΒΛΙΟ ΔΕΚΑΤΟ

1. Ἔσῃ ποτὲ ἆρα, ὦ ψυχή, ἀγαθὴ καὶ ἁπλῆ καὶ μία καὶ γυμνή,φανερωτέρα
τοῦ περικειμένου σοι σώματος; γεύσῃ ποτὲ ἆρα τῆςφιλητικῆς καὶ στερκτικῆς
διαθέσεως; ἔσῃ ποτὲ ἆρα πλήρης καὶανενδεὴς καὶ οὐδὲν ἐπιποθοῦσα οὐδὲ
ἐπιθυμοῦσα οὐδενὸς οὔτεέμψύχου οὔτε ἀψύχου πρὸς ἡδονῶν ἀπολαύσεις;
οὐδὲ χρόνου,ἐν ᾧ ἐπὶ μακρότερον ἀπολαύσεις; οὐδὲ τόπου ἢ χώρας ἢ
ἀέρωνεὐκαιρίας; οὐδὲ ἀνθρώπων εὐαρμοστίας; ἀλλὰ ἀρκεσθήσῃ τῇπαρούσῃ
καταστάσει καὶ ἡσθήσῃ τοῖς παροῦσι πᾶσι, καὶσυμπείσεις σεαυτὴν ὅτι πάντα
σοι παρὰ τῶν θεῶν πάρεστι, καὶπάντα σοι εὖ ἔχει καὶ εὖ ἕξει, ὅσα φίλον
αὐτοῖς καὶ ὅσα μέλλουσιδώσειν ἐπὶ σωτηρίᾳ τοῦ τελείου ζῴου, τοῦ ἀγαθοῦ
καὶ δικαίουκαὶ καλοῦ καὶ γεννῶντος πάντα καὶ συνέχοντος καὶ περιέχοντοςκαὶ
περιλαμβάνοντος διαλυόμενα εἰς γένεσιν ἑτέρων ὁμοίων; ἔσῃποτὲ ἆρα τοιαύτη,
οἵα θεοῖς τε καὶ ἀνθρώποις οὕτως συμπολιτεύεσθαιὡς μήτε μέμφεσθαί τι αὐτοῖς
μήτε καταγινώσκεσθαιὑπ᾽ αὐτῶν;

2. Παρατήρει τί σου ἡ φύσις ἐπιζητεῖ ὡς ὑπὸ φύσεως μόνονδιοικουμένου᾿
εἶτα ποίει αὐτὸ καὶ προσίεσο, εἰ μὴ χεῖρον μέλλειδιατίθεσθαί σου ἡ ὡς ζῴου
φύσις. ἑξῆς δὲ παρατηρητέον τίἐπιζητεῖ σου ἡ ὡς ζῴου φύσις, καὶ πᾶν τοῦτο
παραληπτέον, εἰμὴ χεῖρον μέλλει διατίθεσθαι ἡ ὡς ζῴου λογικοῦ φύσις᾿
ἔστι δὲτὸ λογικὸν εὐθὺς καὶ πολιτικόν. τούτοις δὴ κανόσι χρώμενοςμηδὲν
περιεργάζου.

3. Πᾶν τὸ συμβαῖνον ἤτοι οὕτω συμβαίνει ὡς πέφυκας αὐτόφέρειν ἢ ὡς
οὐ πέφυκας αὐτὸ φέρειν. εἰ μὲν οὖν συμβαίνει σοιὡς πέφυκας φέρειν, μὴ
δυσχέραινε, ἀλλ ὡς πέφυκας ‹φέρειν› φέρε.εἰ δὲ ὡς μὴ πέφυκας φέρειν, μὴ
δυσχέραινε᾿ φθήσεται γάρ σεἀπαναλῶσαν. μέμνησο μέντοι ὅτι πέφυκας φέρειν
πᾶν, περὶ οῦἐπὶ τῇ ὑπολήψει ἐστὶ τῇ σῇ φορητὸν καὶ ἀνεκτὸν αὐτὸ ποιῆσαικατὰ
φαντασίαν τοῦ συμφέρειν ἢ καθήκειν σεαυτῷ τοῦτο ποιεῖν.

4. Εἰ μὲν σφάλλεται, διδάσκειν εὐμενῶς καὶ τὸ παρορώμενονδεικνύναι. εἰ δὲ
ἀδυνατεῖς, σεαυτὸν αἰτιᾶσθαι ἢ μηδὲ σεαυτόν.

5. Ὅ τι ἄν σοι συμβαίνῃ, τοῦτό σοι ἐξ αἰῶνος προκατεσκευάζετοκαὶ ἡ ἐπιπλοκὴ
τῶν αἰτίων συνέκλωθε τήν τε σὴν ὑπόστασιν ἐξαιδίου καὶ τὴν τούτου σύμβασιν.

6. Εἴτε ἄτομοι εἴτε φύσις, πρῶτον κείσθω ὅτι μέρος εἰμὶ τοῦ ὅλουὑπὸ φύσεως
διοικουμένου᾿ ἔπειτα, ὅτι ἔχω πως οἰκείως πρὸς τὰὁμογενῆ μέρη. τούτων γὰρ

221

μεμνημένος, καθότι μὲν μέρος εἰμί,οὐδενὶ δυσαρεστήσω τῶν ἐκ τοῦ ὅλου ἀπονεμομένων· οὐδὲν γὰρβλαβερὸν τῷ μέρει ὃ τῷ ὅλῳ συμφέρει. οὐ γὰρ ἔχει τι τὸ ὅλον ὃμὴ συμφέρει ἑαυτῷ, πασῶν μὲν φύσεων κοινὸν ἐχουσῶν τοῦτο,τῆς δὲ τοῦ κόσμου προσειληφυίας τὸ μηδὲ ὑπό τινος ἔξωθεν αἰτίαςἀναγκάζεσθαι βλαβερόν τι ἑαυτῇ γεννᾶν. κατὰ μὲν δὴ τὸμεμνῆσθαι ὅτι μέρος εἰμὶ ὅλου τοῦ τοιούτου, εὐαρεστήσω παντὶτῷ ἀποβαίνοντι, καθόσον δὲ ἔχω πως οἰκείως πρὸς τὰ ὁμογενῆμέρη, οὐδὲν πράξω ἀκοινώνητον, μᾶλλον δὲ στοχάσομαι τῶνὁμογενῶν καὶ πρὸς τὸ κοινῇ συμφέρον πᾶσαν ὁρμὴν ἐμαυτοῦἄξω καὶ ἀπὸ τοὐναντίου ἀπάξω. τούτων δὲ οὕτως περαινομένωνἀνάγκη τὸν βίον εὐροεῖν, ὡς ἂν καὶ πολίτου βίον εὕρουν ἐπινοήσειαςπροϊόντος διὰ πράξεων τοῖς πολίταις λυσιτελῶν καὶὃπερ ἂν ἡ πόλις ἀπονέμῃ, τοῦτο ἀσπαζομένου.

7. Τοῖς μέρεσι τοῦ ὅλου, ὅσα φύσει περιέχεται ὑπὸ τοῦ κόσμου,ἀνάγκη φθείρεσθαι· λεγέσθω δὲ τοῦτο σημαντικῶς τοῦἀλλοιοῦσθαι. εἰ δὲ φύσει κακόν τε καὶ ἀναγκαῖόν ἐστι τοῦτοαὐτοῖς, οὐκ ἂν τὸ ὅλον καλῶς διεξάγοιτο τῶν μερῶν εἰς ἀλλοίωσινἰόντων καὶ πρὸς τὸ φθείρεσθαι διαφόρως κατεσκευασμένων. (πότερον γὰρ ἐπεχείρησεν ἡ φύσις αὐτὴ τὰ ἑαυτῆς μέρη κακοῦνκαὶ περιπτωτικὰ τῷ κακῷ καὶ ἐξ ἀνάγκης ἔμπτωτα εἰς τὸ κακὸνποιεῖν, ἢ ἔλαθεν αὐτὴν τοιάδε τινὰ γινόμενα; ἀμφότερα γὰρἀπίθανα.) εἰ δέ τις καὶ ἀφέμενος τῆς φύσεως κατὰ τὸ πεφυκέναιταῦτα ἐξηγοῖτο, καὶ ὡς γελοῖον ἅμα μὲν φάναι πεφυκέναι τὰμέρη τοῦ ὅλου μεταβάλλειν, ἅμα δὲ ὡς ἐπί τινι τῶν παρὰ φύσινσυμβαίνοντι θαυμάζειν ἢ δυσχεραίνειν, ἄλλως τε καὶ τῆςδιαλύσεως εἰς ταῦτα γινομένης, ἐξ ὧν ἕκαστον συνίσταται. ἤτοιγὰρ σκεδασμὸς στοιχείων, ἐξ ὧν συνεκρίθη, ἢ τροπὴ τοῦ μὲνστερεμνίου εἰς τὸ γεῶδες, τοῦ δὲ πνευματικοῦ εἰς τὸ ἀερῶδες,ὥστε καὶ ταῦτα ἀναληφθῆναι εἰς τὸν τοῦ ὅλου λόγον, εἴτε κατὰπερίοδον ἐκπυρουμένου εἴτε ἀιδίοις ἀμοιβαῖς ἀνανεουμένου. καὶτὸ στερέμνιον δὲ καὶ τὸ πνευματικὸν μὴ φαντάζου τὸ ἀπὸ τῆςπρώτης γενέσεως· πᾶν γὰρ τοῦτο ἐχθὲς καὶ τρίτην ἡμέραν ἐκ τῶνσιτίων καὶ τοῦ ἑλκομένου ἀέρος τὴν ἐπιρροὴν ἔλαβεν· τοῦτοοὖν ὃ ἔλαβε μεταβάλλει, οὐχ ὃ ἡ μήτηρ ἔτεκεν. ὑπόθου δ ὅτιἐκεῖνό σε λίαν προσπλέκει τῷ ἰδίως ποιῷ, οὐδὲν ‹τῷ› ὄντι οἶμαιπρὸς τὸ νῦν λεγόμενον.

8. Ὀνόματα θέμενος ἑαυτῷ ταῦτα· ἀγαθός, αἰδήμων, ἀληθής,ἔμφρων, σύμφρων, ὑπέρφρων, πρόσεχε μήποτε μετονομάζῃ, κἂνἀπολλύῃς ταῦτα τὰ ὀνόματα, [καὶ] ταχέως ἐπάνιθι ἐπ αὐτά.μέμνησο δὲ ὅτι τὸ μὲν ἔμφρων ἐβούλετό σοι σημαίνειν τὴν ἐφ ἑκαστα διαληπτικὴν ἐπίστασιν καὶ τὸ ἀπαρενθύμητον· τὸ δὲσύμφρων τὴν ἑκούσιον ἀπόδεξιν τῶν ὑπὸ τῆς κοινῆς φύσεωςἀπονεμομένων· τὸ δὲ ὑπέρφρων τὴν ὑπέρτασιν τοῦ φρονοῦντοςμορίου ὑπὲρ λείαν ἢ τραχεῖαν κίνησιν τῆς σαρκὸς καὶ τὸ δοξάριονκαὶ τὸν θάνατον καὶ ὅσα τοιαῦτα. ἐὰν οὖν διατηρῇς ἑαυτὸν ἐντούτοις τοῖς ὀνόμασι μὴ γλιχόμενος τοῦ ὑπ ἄλλων κατὰ ταῦταὀνομάζεσθαι, ἔσῃ ἕτερος καὶ εἰς βίον εἰσελεύσῃ ἕτερον. τὸ γὰρἔτι τοιοῦτον εἶναι οἷος μέχρι νῦν γέγονας, καὶ ἐν βίῳ τοιούτῳσπαράσσεσθαι καὶ

μολύνεσθαι, λίαν ἐστὶν ἀναισθήτου καὶφιλοψύχου καὶ ὁμοίου τοῖς ἡμιβρώτοις θηριομάχοις, οἵτινεςμεστοὶ τραυμάτων καὶ λύθρου παρακαλοῦσιν ὅμως εἰς τὴν αὔριονφυλαχθῆναι, παραβληθησόμενοι τοιοῦτοι τοῖς αὐτοῖς ὄνυξι καὶδήγμασιν. ἐμβίβασον οὖν ἑαυτὸν εἰς τὰ ὀλίγα ταῦτα ὀνόματα,κἂν μὲν ἐπ αὐτῶν μένειν δύνῃ, μένε ὥσπερ εἰς μακάρων τινὰςνήσους μετῳ κισμένος· ἐὰν δὲ αἴσθῃ ὅτι ἐκπίπτεις καὶ οὐπερικρατεῖς, ἄπιθι θαρρῶν εἰς γωνίαν τινά, ὅπου κρατήσεις, ἢκαὶ παντάπασιν ἔξιθι τοῦ βίου, μὴ ὀργιζόμενος, ἀλλὰ ἁπλῶς καὶἐλευθέρως καὶ αἰδημόνως, ἕν γε τοῦτο μόνον πράξας ἐν τῷ βίῳτὸ οὕτως ἐξελθεῖν. πρὸς μέντοι τὸ μεμνῆσθαι τῶν ὀνομάτωνμεγάλως συλλήψεταί σοι τὸ μεμνῆσθαι θεῶν καὶ ὅτιπερ οὐκολακεύεσθαι οΡτοι θέλουσιν, ἀλλὰ ἐξομοιοῦσθαι ἑαυτοῖς τὰλογικὰ πάντα καὶ εἶναι τὴν μὲν συκῆν τὰ συκῆς ποιοῦσαν, τὸνδὲ κύνα τὰ κυνός, τὴν δὲ μέλισσαν τὰ μελίσσης, τὸν δὲ ἄνθρωπον τὰ ἀνθρώπου.

9. Μῖμος, πόλεμος, πτοία, νάρκα, δουλεία. καθ ἡμέραν ἀπαλείψεταίσου τὰ ἱερὰ ἐκεῖνα δόγματα, ὁπόσα ἀφυσιολογήτωςφαντάζῃ καὶ παραπέμπεις. δεῖ δὲ πᾶν οὕτω βλέπειν καὶ πράσσεινὥστε καὶ τὸ περιστατικὸν ἅμα συντελεῖσθαι καὶ ἅμα τὸ θεωρητικὸνἐνεργεῖσθαι καὶ τὸ ἐκ τῆς περὶ ἕκαστων ἐπιστήμηςαὔθαδες σῴζεσθαι λανθάνον, οὐχὶ κρυπτόμενον. πότε γὰρἁπλότητος ἀπολαύσεις; πότε δὲ σεμνότητος; πότε δὲ τῆς ἐφἑκάστου γνωρίσεως, τί τε ἐστὶ κατ οὐσίαν καὶ τίνα χώραν ἔχειἐν τῷ κόσμῳ καὶ ἐπὶ πόσον πέφυκεν ὑφίστασθαι καὶ ἐκ τίνωνσυγκέκριται καὶ τίσι δύναται ὑπάρχειν καὶ τίνες δύνανται αὐτὸδιδόναι τε καὶ ἀφαιρεῖσθαι;

10. Ἀράχνιον μυῖαν θηρᾶσαν μέγα φρονεῖ, ἄνθρωπος δὲ λαγίδιον,ἄλλος δὲ ὑποχῇ ἀφύην, ἄλλος δὲ συΐδια, ἄλλος δὲ ἄρκτους, ἄλλοςΣαρμάτας. οΡτοι γὰρ οὐ λῃσταί, ἐὰν τὰ δόγματα ἐξετάζῃς;

11. Πῶς εἰς ἄλληλα πάντα μεταβάλλει, θεωρητικὴν μέθοδονκτῆσαι καὶ διηνεκῶς πρόσεχε καὶ συγγυμνάσθητι περὶ τοῦτο τόμέρος· οὐδὲν γὰρ οὕτως μεγαλοφροσύνης ποιητικόν. ἐξεδύσατοτὸ σῶμα καὶ ἐννοήσας ὅτι ὅσον οὐδέπω πάντα ταῦτα καταλιπεῖνἀπιόντα ἐξ ἀνθρώπων δεήσει, ἀνῆκεν ὅλον ἑαυτὸν δικαιοσύνημὲν εἰς τὰ ὑφ ἑαυτοῦ ἐνεργούμενα, ἐν δὲ τοῖς ἄλλως συμβαίνουσιτῇ τῶν ὅλων φύσει. τί δ ἐρεῖ τις ἢ ὑπολήψεται περὶ αὐτοῦ ἢπράξει κατ αὐτοῦ, οὐδ εἰς νοῦν βάλλεται, δύο τούτοις ἀρκούμενος,εἰ αὐτὸς δικαιοπραγεῖ τὸ νῦν πρασσόμενον καὶ φιλεῖ τὸνῦν ἀπονεμόμενον ἑαυτῷ· ἀσχολίας δὲ πάσας καὶ σπουδὰς ἀφῆκεκαὶ οὐδὲν ἄλλο βούλεται ἢ εὐθεῖαν περαίνειν διὰ τοῦ νόμουκαὶεὐθεῖαν περαίνοντι ἕπεσθαι τῷ θεῷ.

223

12. Τίς ὑπονοίας χρεία παρὸν σκοπεῖν τί δεῖ πραχθῆναι, κἂν μὲνσυνορᾷς, εὐμενῶς, ἀμεταστρεπτὶ ταύτῃ χωρεῖν· ἐὰν δὲ μὴ συνορᾷς, ἐπέχειν καὶ συμβούλοις τοῖς ἀρίστοις χρῆσθαι· ἐὰν δὲ ἕτεράτινα πρὸς ταῦτα ἀντιβαίνῃ, προϊέναι κατὰ τὰς παρούσας ἀφορμὰςλελογισμένως, ἐχόμενον τοῦ φαινομένου δικαίου; ἄριστον γὰρκατατυγχάνειν τούτου, ἐπεί τοι ἥ γε ἀπόπτωσις ἀπὸ τούτου ἐστίν.σχολαῖόν τι καὶ ἅμα εὐκίνητόν ἐστι καὶ φαιδρὸν ἅμα καὶσυνεστηκὸς ὁ τῷ λόγῳ κατὰ πᾶν ἑπόμενος.

13. Πυνθάνεσθαι ἑαυτοῦ εὐθὺς ἐξ ὕπνου γενόμενον· μήτι διοίσεισοι, ἐὰν ὑπὸ ἄλλου ψέγηται τὰ δίκαια καὶ καλῶς ἔχοντα; οὐδιοίσει. μήτι ἐπιλέλησαι ὅτι οΡτοι οἱ ἐν τοῖς περὶ ἄλλων ἐπαίνοικαὶ ψόγοις φρυαττόμενοι τοιοῦτοι μὲν ἐπὶ τῆς κλίνης εἰσί, τοιοῦτοιδὲ ἐπὶ τῆς τραπέζης, οἷα δὲ ποιοῦσιν, οἷα δὲ φεύγουσιν, οἷα δεδιώκουσιν, οἷα δὲ κλέπτουσιν, οἷα δὲ ἁρπάζουσιν, οὐ χερσὶ καὶποσίν, ἀλλὰ τῷ τιμιωτάτῳ ἑαυτῶν μέρει, ᾧ γίνεται, ὅταν θέλῃ,πίστις, αἰδώς, ἀλήθεια, νόμος, ἀγαθὸς δαίμων;

14. Τῇ πάντα διδούσῃ καὶ ἀπολαμβανούσῃ φύσει ὁ πεπαιδευμένοςκαὶ αἰδήμων λέγει· δὸς ὃ θέλεις· ἀπόλαβε ὃ θέλεις. λέγει δὲτοῦτο οὐ καταθρασυνόμενος, ἀλλὰ πειθαρχῶν μόνον καὶ εὐνοῶναὐτῇ.

15. Ὀλίγον ἐστὶ τὸ ὑπολειπόμενον τοῦτο. ζῆσον ὡς ἐν ὄρει· οὐδὲνγὰρ διαφέρει ἐκεῖ ἢ ὧδε, ἐὰν τις πανταχοῦ ὡς ἐν πόλει τῷκόσμῳ. ἰδέτωσαν, ἱστορησάτωσαν οἱ ἄνθρωποι ἄνθρωπονἀληθινὸν κατὰ φύσιν ζῶντα. εἰ μὴ φέρουσιν, ἀποκτεινάτωσαν·κρεῖττον γὰρ ἢ οὕτως ζῆν.

16. Μηκέθ' ὅλως περὶ τοῦ οἷόν τινα εἶναι τὸν ἀγαθὸν ἄνδραδιαλέγεσθαι, ἀλλὰ εἶναι τοιοῦτον.

17. Τοῦ ὅλου αἰῶνος καὶ τῆς ὅλης οὐσίας συνεχῶς φαντασία ‹ἔστω›καὶ ὅτι πάντα τὰ κατὰ μέρος, ὡς μὲν πρὸς οὐσίαν, κεγχραμίς, ὧςδὲ πρὸς χρόνον, τρυπάνου περιστροφή.

18. Εἰς ἕκαστον τῶν ὑποκειμένων ἐφιστάντα ἐπινοεῖν αὐτὸ ἤδηδιαλυόμενον καὶ ἐν μεταβολῇ καὶ οἷον σήψει ἢ σκεδάσειγινόμενον ἢ καθότι ἕκαστον πέφυκεν ὥσπερ θνήσκειν.

19. Οἷοί εἰσιν ἐσθίοντες, καθεύδοντες, ὀχεύοντες, ἀποπατοῦντες,τὰ ἄλλα· εἶτα οἷοι ἀνδρονομούμενοι καὶ γαυρούμενοι ἢ χαλεπαίνοντεςκαὶ ἐξ ὑπεροχῆς ἐπιπλήττοντες, πρὸ ὀλίγου δὲ ἐδούλευονπόσοις καὶ δἰ οἷα· καὶ μετ ὀλίγον ἐν τοιούτοις ἔσονται.

20. Συμφέρει ἑκάστῳ ὃ φέρει ἑκάστῳ ἡ τῶν ὅλων φύσις, καὶ τότεσυμφέρει ὅτε ἐκείνη φέρει.

21. Ἐρᾷ μὲν ὄμβρου γαῖα, ἐρᾷ δὲ ὁ σεμνὸς αἰθήρ, ἐρᾷ δὲ ὁ κόσμοςποιῆσαι ὃ ἂν μέλλῃ γίνεσθαι. λέγω οὖν τῷ κόσμῳ ὅτι σοὶ συνερῶ.μήτι δὲ οὕτω κἀκεῖνο λέγεται, ὅτι· φιλεῖ τοῦτο γίνεσθαι;

22. Ἤτοι ἐνταῦθα ζῇς καὶ ἤδη εἴθικας· ἢ ἔξω ὑπάγεις καὶ τοῦτοἤθελες· ἢ ἀποθνήσκεις καὶ ἀπελειτούργησας. παρὰ δὲ ταῦταοὐδέν. οὐκοῦν εὐθύμει.

23. Ἐναργὲς ἔστω ἀεὶ τὸ ὅτι τοιοῦτο ἐκεῖνος ὁ ἀγρός ἐστι καὶ πῶςπάντα ἐστὶ τὰ αὐτὰ ἐνθάδε τοῖς ἐν ἄκρῳ τῷ ὄρει ἢ ἐπὶ τοῦ αἰγιαλοῦἢ ὅπου θέλεις. ἄντικρυς γὰρ εὑρήσεις τὰ τοῦ Πλάτωνος· "σηκὸνἐν ὄρει, φησί, περιβαλλόμενος καὶ βδάλλων βληχήματα."

24. Τί ἐστί μοι τὸ ἡγεμονικόν μου καὶ ποῖόν τι αὐτὸ ἐγὼ ποιῶ νῦνκαὶ πρὸς τί ποτε αὐτῷ νῦν χρῶμαι; μήτι κενὸν νοῦ ἐστι; μήτιἀπόλυτον καὶ ἀπεσπασμένον κοινωνίας; μήτι προστετηκὸς καὶἀνακεκραμένον τῷ σαρκιδίῳ, ὥστε τούτῳ συντρέπεσθαι;

25. Ὁ τὸν κύριον φεύγων δραπέτης· κύριος δὲ ὁ νόμος καὶ ὁπαρανομῶν ‹ἄρα› δραπέτης. ἅμα καὶ ὁ λυπούμενος ἢ ὀργιζόμενοςἢ φοβούμενος οὐ βούλεταί τι γεγονέναι ἢ γίνεσθαι ἢ γενήσεσθαιτῶν ὑπὸ τοῦ τὰ πάντα διοικοῦντος τεταγμένων, ὅς ἐστι νόμος,νέμων ὅσα ἑκάστῳ ἐπιβάλλει. ὁ ἄρα φοβούμενος ἢ λυπούμενοςἢ ὀργιζόμενος δραπέτης.

26. Σπέρμα εἰς μήτραν ἀφεὶς ἀπεχώρησε καὶ λοιπὸν ἄλλη αἰτίαπαραλαβοῦσα ἐργάζεται καὶ ἀποτελεῖ βρέφος· ἐξ οἵου οἷον; πάλιν· τροφὴν διὰ φάρυγγος ἀφῆκε καὶ λοιπὸν ἄλλη αἰτία παραλαβοῦσααἴσθησιν καὶ ὁρμὴν καὶ τὸ ὅλον ζωὴν καὶ ῥώμην καὶ ἄλλα, ὅσακαὶ οἷα, ποιεῖ. ταῦτα οὖν ἐν τοιαύτῃ ἐγκαλύψει γινόμενα θεωρεῖνκαὶ τὴν δύναμιν οὕτως ὁρᾶν, ὡς καὶ τὴν βρίθουσαν καὶ τὴνἀνωφερῆ ὁρῶμεν, οὐχὶ τοῖς ὀφθαλμοῖς, ἀλλ οὐχ ἧττον ἐναργῶς.

225

27. Συνεχῶς ἐπινοεῖν πῶς πάντα τοιαῦτα, ὁποῖα νῦν γίνεται, καὶπρόσθεν ἐγίνετο, καὶ ἐπινοεῖν γενησόμενα· καὶ ὅλα δράματα καὶσκηνὰς ὁμοειδεῖς, ὅσα ἐκ πείρας τῆς σῆς ἢ τῆς πρεσβυτέραςἱστορίας ἔγνως, πρὸ ὀμμάτων τίθεσθαι, οἷον αὐλὴν ὅληνἈδριανοῦ καὶ αὐλὴν ὅλην Ἀντωνίνου καὶ αὐλὴν ὅλην Φιλίππου,Ἀλεξάνδρου, Κροίσου· πάντα γὰρ ἐκεῖνα τοιαῦτα ἦν, μόνον διέτέρων.

28. Φαντάζου πάντα τὸν ἐφ ᾡτινιοῦν λυπούμενον ἢ δυσαρεστοῦνταὅμοιον τῷ θυομένῳ χοιριδίῳ καὶ ἀπολακτίζοντι καὶ κεκραγότι· ὅμοιος καὶ ὁ οἰμώζων ἐπὶ τοῦ κλινιδίου μόνος σιωπῇ. τὴν ἔνδεσινἡμῶν, καὶ ὅτι μόνῳ τῷ λογικῷ ζῴῳ δέδοται τὸ ἑκουσίως ἕπεσθαιτοῖς γινομένοις, τὸ δὲ ἕπεσθαι ψιλὸν πᾶσιν ἀναγκαῖον.

29. Κατὰ μέρος ἐφ ἑκάστου ὧν ποιεῖς ἐφιστάνων ἐπερώτα σεαυτὸνεἰ ὁ θάνατος δεινὸν διὰ τὸ τούτου στέρεσθαι.

30. Ὅταν προσκόπτῃς ἐπί τινος ἁμαρτίᾳ, εὐθὺς μεταβὰς ἐπιλογίζουτί παρόμοιον ἁμαρτάνεις· οἷον, ἀργύριον ἀγαθὸν εἶναι κρίνων‹ἢ› τὴν ἡδονὴν ἢ τὸ δοξάριον καὶ κατ εἶδος. τούτῳ γὰρ ἐπιβάλλωνταχέως ἐπιλήσῃ τῆς ὀργῆς, συμ‹προσ›πίπτοντος τοῦ ὅτι βιάζεται· τί γὰρ ποιήσει; ἤ, εἰ δύνασαι, ἄφελε αὐτοῦ τὸ βιαζόμενον.

31. Σατυρίωνα ἰδὼν Σωκρατικὸν φαντάζου ἢ Εὐτύχην ἢ Ὑμένα,καὶ Εὐφράτην ἰδὼν Εὐτυχίωνα ἢ Σιλουανὸν φαντάζου, καὶἈλκίφρονα Τροπαιοφόρον φαντάζου, καὶ Σεῦρον ἰδὼν Κρίτωναἢ Ξενοφῶντα φαντάζου, καὶ εἰς ἑαυτὸν ἀπιδὼν τῶν Καισάρωντινὰ φαντάζου, καὶ ἐφ ἑκάστου τὸ ἀνάλογον. εἶτα συμπροσπιπτέτωσοι· ποῦ οὖν ἐκεῖνοι; οὐδαμοῦ ἢ ὁπουδή. οὕτως γὰρσυνεχῶς θεάσῃ τὰ ἀνθρώπινα καπνὸν καὶ τὸ μηδέν, μάλισταἐὰν συμμνημονεύσῃς ὅτι τὸ ἅπαξ μεταβαλὸν οὐκέτι ἔσται ἐν τῷἀπείρῳ χρόνῳ. τί οὖν ἐντείνῃ; τί δ οὐκ ἀρκεῖ σοι τὸ βραχὺτοῦτο κοσμίως διαπερᾶσαι;

32. Οἵαν ὕλην καὶ ὑπόθεσιν φεύγεις· τί γάρ ἐστι πάντα ταῦταἄλλο πλὴν γυμνάσματα λόγου ἑωρακότος ἀκριβῶς καὶ φυσιολόγωςτὰ ἐν τῷ βίῳ; μένε οὖν, μέχρι ἐξοικειώσῃς σεαυτῷ καὶταῦτα, ὡς ὁ ἐρρωμένος στόμαχος πάντα ἐξοικειοῖ, ὡς τὸ λαμπρὸνπῦρ, ὅ τι ἂν ‹ἐμ›βάλῃς, φλόγα ἐξ αὐτοῦ καὶ αὐγὴν ποιεῖ.

33. Μηδενὶ ἐξέστω εἰπεῖν ἀληθεύοντι περὶ σοῦ ὅτι οὐχ ἁπλοῦς ἢὅτι οὐκ ἀγαθός, ἀλλὰ ψευδέσθω, ὅστις τούτων τι περὶ σοῦὑπολήψεται. πᾶν δὲ τοῦτο ἐπὶ σοί· τίς γὰρ ὁ κωλύων ἀγαθὸνεἶναί σε καὶ ἁπλοῦν; σὺ μόνον κρῖνον μηκέτι ζῆν, εἰ μὴ τοιοῦτοςἔσῃ· οὐδὲ γὰρ αἱρεῖ λόγος μὴ τοιοῦτον ὄντα.

34. Τί ἐστι τὸ ἐπὶ ταύτης τῆς ὕλης δυνάμενον κατὰ τὸ ὑγιέστατονπραχθῆναι ἢ ῥηθῆναι; ὅ τι γὰρ ἂν τοῦτο ᾖ, ἔξεστιν αὐτὸ πρᾶξαιἢ εἰπεῖν καὶ μὴ προφασίζου ὡς κωλυόμενος. Οὐ πρότερον παύσῃστένων πρὶν ἢ τοῦτο πάθῃς, ὅτι οἷόν ἐστι τοῖς ἡδυπαθοῦσιν ἡτρυφή, τοιοῦτό σοι τὸ ἐπὶ τῆς ὑποβαλλομένης καὶ ὑποπιπτούσηςὕλης ποιεῖν τὰ οἰκεῖα τῇ τοῦ ἀνθρώπου κατασκευῇ· ἀπόλαυσινγὰρ δεῖ ὑπολαμβάνειν πᾶν ὃ ἔξεστι κατὰ τὴν ἰδίαν φύσιν ἐνεργεῖν.πανταχοῦ δὲ ἔξεστι. τῷ μὲν οὖν κυλίνδρῳ οὐ πανταχοῦ δίδοταιφέρεσθαι τὴν ἰδίαν κίνησιν οὐδὲ τῷ ὕδατι οὐδὲ πυρὶ οὐδὲ τοῖςἄλλοις ὅσα ὑπὸ φύσεως ἢ ψυχῆς ἀλόγου διοικεῖται· τὰ γὰρδιείργοντα καὶ ἐνιστάμενα πολλά· νοῦς δὲ καὶ λόγος διὰ παντὸςτοῦ ἀντιπίπτοντος οὕτως πορεύεσθαι δύναται ὡς πέφυκε καὶ ὡςθέλει. ταύτην τὴν ῥᾳστώνην πρὸ ὀμμάτων τιθέμενος, καθ᾽ ἣνἐνεχθήσεται ὁ λόγος διὰ πάντων (ὡς πῦρ ἄνω, ὡς λίθος κάτω, ὡςκύλινδρος κατὰ πρανοῦς), μηκέτι μηδὲν ἐπιζήτει· τὰ γὰρ λοιπὰἐγκόμματα ἤτοι τοῦ σωματίου ἐστὶ τοῦ νεκροῦ, ἢ χωρὶςὑπολήψεως καὶ τῆς αὐτοῦ τοῦ λόγου ἐνδόσεως οὐ θραύει οὐδέποιεῖ κακὸν οὐδ᾽ ὁτιοῦν. ἐπεί τοι καὶ ὁ πάσχων αὐτὸς κακὸς ἂνεὐθὺς ἐγίνετο· ἐπὶ γοῦν τῶν ἄλλων κατασκευασμάτων πάντων, ὅτι ἂν κακόν τινι αὐτῶν συμβῇ, παρὰ τοῦτο χεῖρον γίνεται αὐτὸτὸ πάσχον· ἐνταῦθα δέ, εἰ δεῖ εἰπεῖν, καὶ κρείττων γίνεταιὁ ἄνθρωπος καὶ ἐπαινετώτερος, ὀρθῶς χρώμενος τοῖς προσπίπτουσιν.ὅλως δὲ μέμνησο ὅτι τὸν φύσει πολίτην οὐδὲν βλάπτειὃ πόλιν οὐ βλάπτει, οὐδέ γε πόλιν βλάπτει ὃ νόμον οὐ βλάπτει·τούτων δὲ τῶν καλουμένων ἀκληρη μάτων οὐδὲν βλάπτει νόμον.ὃ τοίνυν νόμον οὐ βλάπτει, οὔτε πόλιν οὔτε πολίτην.

35. Τῷ δεδηγμένῳ ὑπὸ τῶν ἀληθῶν δογμάτων ἀρκεῖ καὶ τὸβραχύτατον καὶ ἐν μέσῳ κείμενον εἰς ὑπόμνησιν ἀλυπίας καὶἀφοβίας, οἷον· φύλλα τὰ μέν τ᾽ ἄνεμος χαμάδις χέει· ὣς ἀνδρῶνγενεή. φυλλάρια δὲ καὶ τὰ τεκνία σου, φυλλάρια δὲ καὶ ταῦτατὰ ἐπιβοῶντα ἀξιοπίστως καὶ ἐπευφημοῦντα ἢ ἐκ τῶνἐναντίωνκαταρώμενα ἢ ἡσυχῇ ψέγοντα καὶ χλευάζοντα, φυλλάρια δὲὁμοίως καὶ τὰ διαδεξόμενα τὴν ὑστεροφημίαν. πάντα γὰρ ταῦτα"ἔαρος ἐπιγίγνεται ὥρῃ"· εἶτα ἄνεμος καταβέβληκεν· ἔπειθ᾽ ὕλη ἕτερα ἀντὶ τούτων φύει. τὸ δὲὀλιγοχρόνιον κοινὸν πᾶσιν, ἀλλὰσὺ πάντα ὡς αἰώνια ἐσόμενα φεύγεις καὶδιώκεις. μικρὸν καὶκαταμύσεις, τὸν δὲ ἐξενεγκόντα σε ἤδη ἄλλος θρηνήσει.

36. Τὸν ὑγιαίνοντα ὀφθαλμὸν πάντα ὁρᾶν δεῖ τὰ ὁρατὰ καὶ μὴλέγειν· τὰ χλωρὰ θέλω· τοῦτο γὰρ ὀφθαλμιῶντός ἐστιν. καὶ τὴνὑγιαίνουσαν ἀκοὴν καὶ ὄσφρησιν εἰς πάντα δεῖ τὰ ἀκουστὰ καὶὀσφραντὰ ἑτοίμην εἶναι, καὶ τὸν ὑγιαίνοντα στόμαχον πρὸς πάντατὰ τρόφιμα ὁμοίως ἔχειν ὡς μύλην πρὸς πάντα ὅσα ἀλέσουσακατεσκεύασται. καὶ τοίνυν τὴν ὑγιαίνουσαν διάνοιαν πρὸς πάνταδεῖ τὰ συμβαίνοντα ἑτοίμην εἶναι, ἡ δὲ λέγουσα· τὰ τεκνία σῳζέσθω, καί· πάντες ὅ τι ἂν πράξω ἐπαινείτωσαν, ὀφθαλμός ἐστιτὰ χλωρὰ ζητῶν ἢ ὀδόντες τὰ ἁπαλά.

⁙ Marcus Aurelius ⁙

37. Οὐδείς ἐστιν οὕτως εὔποτμος ᾧ ἀποθνήσκοντι οὐ παρεστήξονταίτινες ἀσπαζόμενοι τὸ συμβαῖνον κακόν. σπουδαῖοςκαὶ σοφὸς ἦν· μὴ τὸ πανύστατον ἔσται τις ὁ καθ αὑτὸν λέγων ἀναπνεύσομέν ποτε ἀπὸ τούτου τοῦ παιδαγωγοῦ; χαλεπὸς μὲνοὐδενὶ ἡμῶν ἦν, ἀλλὰ ᾐσθανόμην ὅτι ἡσυχῇ καταγινώσκει ἡμῶν. ταῦτα μὲν οὖν ἐπὶ τοῦ σπουδαίου, ἐφ ἡμῶν δὲ πόσα ἄλλα ἐστί,δἰ ἃ πολὺς ὁ ἀπαλλακτιῶν ἡμῶν. τοῦτο οὖν ἐννοήσεις ἀποθνήσκων καὶ εὐκολώτερον ἐξελεύσῃ, λογιζόμενος· ἐκ τοιούτου βίουἀπέρχομαι, ἐν ᾧ αὐτοὶ οἱ κοινωνοί, ὑπὲρ ὧν τὰ τοσαῦτα ἠγωνισάμην,ηὐξάμην, ἐφρόντισα, αὐτοὶ ἐκεῖνοι θέλουσί με ὑπάγειν,ἄλλην τινὰ τυχὸν ἐκ τούτου ῥαστώνην ἐλπίζοντες. τί ἂν οὖν τιςἀντέχοιτο τῆς ἐνταῦθα μακροτέρας διατριβῆς; μὴ μέντοι διὰ τοῦτοἔλαττον εὐμενὴς αὐτοῖς ἄπιθι, ἀλλὰ τὸ ἴδιον ἔθος διασῴζων,φίλος καὶ εὔνους καὶ ἵλεως· καὶ μὴ πάλιν ὡς ἀποσπώμενος, ἀλλ ὥσπερ ἐπὶ τοῦ εὐθανατοῦντος εὐκόλως τὸ ψυχάριον ἀπὸ τοῦσώματος ἐξειλεῖται, τοιαύτην καὶ τὴν ἀπὸ τούτων ἀποχώρησινδεῖ γίνεσθαι· καὶ γὰρ τούτοις ἡ φύσις συνῆψε ‹σε› καὶ συνέκρινεν,ἀλλὰ νῦν διαλύει. διαλύομαι ὡς ἀπὸ οἰκείων μέν, οὐ μὴνἀνθελκόμενος ἀλλ ἀβιάστως· ἓν γὰρ καὶ τοῦτο τῶν κατὰ φύσιν.

38. Ἔθισον ἐπὶ παντός, ὡς οἷόν τε, τοῦ πρασσομένου ὑπό τινοςἐπιζητεῖν κατὰ σαυτόν· οῦτος τοῦτο ἐπὶ τί ἀναφέρει; ἄρχου δὲἀπὸ σαυτοῦ καὶ σαυτὸν πρῶτον ἐξέταζε.

39. Μέμνησο ὅτι τὸ νευροσπαστοῦν ἐστιν ἐκεῖνο τὸ ἔνδον ἐγκεκρυμμένον· ἐκεῖνο ἐνέργεια, ἐκεῖνο ζωή, ἐκεῖνο, εἰ δεῖ εἰπεῖν,ἄνθρωπος. μηδέποτε συμπεριφαντάζου τὸ περικείμενον ἀγγειῶδεςκαὶ τὰ ὀργάνια ταῦτα τὰ περιπεπλασμένα· ὅμοια γάρ ἐστισκεπάρνῳ, μόνον διαφέροντα, καθότι προσφυῆ ἐστιν. ἐπεί τοιοὺ μᾶλλόν τι τούτων ὄφελός ἐστι τῶν μορίων χωρὶς τῆς κινούσηςκαὶ ἰσχούσης αὐτὰ αἰτίας, ἢ τῆς κερκίδος τῇ ὑφαντρίᾳ καὶ τοῦκαλάμου τῷ γράφοντι καὶ τοῦ μαστιγίου τῷ ἡνιόχῳ.

BOOK ELEVEN

I. The natural properties, and privileges of a reasonable soul are: That she seeth herself; that she can order, and compose herself: that she makes herself as she will herself: that she reaps her own fruits whatsoever, whereas plants, trees, unreasonable creatures, what fruit soever (be it either fruit properly, or analogically only) they bear, they bear them unto others, and not to themselves. Again; whensoever, and wheresoever, sooner or later, her life doth end, she hath her own end nevertheless. For it is not with her, as with dancers and players, who if they be interrupted in any part of their action, the whole action must needs be imperfect: but she in what part of time or action soever she be surprised, can make that which she hath in her hand whatsoever it be, complete and full, so that she may depart with that comfort, 'I have lived; neither want I anything of that which properly did belong unto me.' Again, she compasseth the whole world, and penetrateth into the vanity, and mere outside (wanting substance and solidity) of it, and stretcheth herself unto the infiniteness of eternity; and the revolution or restoration of all things after a certain period of time, to the same state and place as before, she fetcheth about, and doth comprehend in herself; and considers withal, and sees clearly this, that neither they that shall follow us, shall see any new thing, that we have not seen, nor they that went before, anything more than we: but that he that is once come to forty (if he have any wit at all) can in a manner (for that they are all of one kind) see all things, both past and future. As proper is it, and natural to the soul of man to love her neighbour, to be true and modest; and to regard nothing so much as herself: which is also the property of the law: whereby by the way it appears, that sound reason and justice comes all to one, and therefore that justice is the chief thing, that reasonable creatures ought to propose unto themselves as their end.

II. A pleasant song or dance; the Pancratiast's exercise, sports that thou art wont to be much taken with, thou shalt easily contemn; if the harmonious voice thou shalt divide into so many particular sounds whereof it doth consist, and of every one in particular shall ask thyself; whether this or that sound is it, that doth so conquer thee. For thou wilt be ashamed of it. And so for shame, if accordingly thou shalt consider it, every particular motion and posture by itself: and so for the wrestler's exercise too. Generally then, whatsoever it be, besides virtue, and those things that proceed from virtue that thou art subject to be much affected with, remember presently thus to divide it, and by this kind of division, in each particular to attain unto the contempt of the whole. This thou must transfer and apply to thy whole life also.

III. That soul which is ever ready, even now presently (if need be) from the body, whether by way of extinction, or dispersion, or continuation in another place and estate to be separated, how blessed and happy is it! But this readiness of it, it must proceed, not from an obstinate and peremptory resolution of the mind, violently and passionately set upon Opposition, as Christians are wont; but from a peculiar judgment; with discretion and gravity, so that others may be persuaded also and drawn to the like example, but without any noise and passionate exclamations.

IV. Have I done anything charitably? then am I benefited by it. See that this upon all occasions may present itself unto thy mind, and never cease to think of it. What is thy profession? to be good. And how should this be well brought to pass, but by certain theorems and doctrines; some Concerning the nature of the universe, and some Concerning the proper and particular constitution of man?

V. Tragedies were at first brought in and instituted, to put men in mind of worldly chances and casualties: that these things in the ordinary course of nature did so happen: that men that were much pleased and delighted by such accidents upon this stage, would not by the same things in a greater stage be grieved and afflicted: for here you see what is the end of all such things; and that even they that cry out so mournfully to Cithaeron, must bear them for all their cries and exclamations, as well as others. And in very truth many good things are spoken by these poets; as that (for example) is an excellent passage: 'But if so be that I and my two children be neglected by the Gods, they have some reason even for that,' &c. And again, 'It will   but little avail thee to storm and rage against the things themselves,' &c. Again, 'To reap one's life, as a ripe ear of corn;' and whatsoever else is to be found in them, that is of the same kind. After the tragedy, the ancient comedy was brought in, which had the liberty to inveigh against personal vices; being therefore through this her freedom and liberty of speech of very good use and effect, to restrain men from pride and arrogancy. To which end it was, that Diogenes took also the same liberty. After these, what were either the Middle, or New Comedy admitted for, but merely, (Or for the most part at least) for the delight and pleasure of curious and excellent imitation? 'It will steal away; look to it,' &c. Why, no man denies, but that these also have some good things whereof that may be one: but the whole drift and foundation of that kind of dramatical poetry, what is it else, but as we have said?

VI. How clearly doth it appear unto thee, that no other course of thy life could fit a true philosopher's practice better, than this very course, that thou art now already in?

VII. A branch cut off from the continuity of that which was next unto it, must needs be cut off from the whole tree: so a man that is divided from another man, is divided from the whole society. A branch is cut off by another, but he that hates and is averse, cuts himself off from his neighbour, and knows not that at the same time he divides himself from the whole body, or corporation. But herein is the gift and mercy of God, the Author of this society, in that, once cut off we may grow together and become part of the whole again. But if this happen often the misery is that the further a man is run in this division, the harder he is to be reunited and restored again: and however the branch which, once cut of afterwards was graffed in, gardeners can tell you is not like that which sprouted together at first, and still continued in the unity of the body.

VIII. To grow together like fellow branches in matter of good correspondence and affection; but not in matter of opinions. They that shall oppose thee in thy right courses, as it is not in their power to divert thee from thy good action, so neither let it be to divert thee from thy good affection towards them. But be it thy care to keep thyself constant in both; both in a right judgment and action, and in true meekness towards them, that either shall do their endeavour to hinder thee, or at least will be displeased with thee for what thou hast done. For to fail in either (either in the one to give over for fear, or in the other to forsake thy natural affection towards him, who by nature is both thy friend and thy kinsman) is equally base, and much savouring of the disposition of a cowardly fugitive soldier.

IX. It is not possible that any nature should be inferior unto art, since that all arts imitate nature. If this be so; that the most perfect and general nature of all natures should in her operation come short of the skill of arts, is most improbable. Now common is it to all arts, to make that which is worse for the better's sake. Much more then doth the common nature do the same. Hence is the first ground of justice. From justice all other virtues have their existence. For justice cannot be preserved, if either we settle our minds and affections upon worldly things; or be apt to be deceived, or rash, and inconstant.

X. The things themselves (which either to get or to avoid thou art put to so much trouble) come not unto thee themselves; but thou in a manner goest unto them. Let then thine own judgment and opinion concerning those things be at rest; and as for the things themselves, they stand still and quiet, without any noise or stir at all; and so shall all pursuing and flying cease.

233

XI. Then is the soul as Empedocles doth liken it, like unto a sphere or globe, when she is all of one form and figure: when she neither greedily stretcheth out herself unto anything, nor basely contracts herself, or lies flat and dejected; but shineth all with light, whereby she does see and behold the true nature, both that of the universe, and her own in particular.

XII. Will any contemn me? let him look to that, upon what grounds he does it: my care shall be that I may never be found either doing or speaking anything that doth truly deserve contempt. Will any hate me? let him look to that. I for my part will be kind and loving unto all, and even unto him that hates me, whom-soever he be, will I be ready to show his error, not by way of exprobation or ostentation of my patience, but ingenuously and meekly: such as was that famous Phocion, if so be that he did not dissemble. For it is inwardly that these things must be: that the Gods who look inwardly, and not upon the outward appearance, may behold a man truly free from all indignation and grief. For what hurt can it be unto thee whatsoever any man else doth, as long as thou mayest do that which is proper and suitable to thine own nature? Wilt not thou (a man wholly appointed to be both what, and as the common good shall require) accept of that which is now seasonable to the nature of the universe?

XIII. They contemn one another, and yet they seek to please one another: and whilst they seek to surpass one another in worldly pomp and greatness, they most debase and prostitute themselves in their better part one to another.

XIV. How rotten and insincere is he, that saith, I am resolved to carry myself hereafter towards you with all ingenuity and simplicity. O man, what doest thou mean! what needs this profession of thine? the thing itself will show it. It ought to be written upon thy forehead. No sooner thy voice is heard, than thy countenance must be able to show what is in thy mind: even as he that is loved knows presently by the looks of his sweetheart what is in her mind. Such must he be for all the world, that is truly simple and good, as he whose arm-holes are offensive, that whosoever stands by, as soon as ever he comes near him, may as it were smell him whether he will or no. But the affectation of simplicity is nowise laudable. There is nothing more shameful than perfidious friendship. Above all things, that must be avoided. However true goodness, simplicity, and kindness cannot so be hidden, but that as we have already said in the very eyes and countenance they will show themselves.

XV. To live happily is an inward power of the soul, when she is affected with indifferency, towards those things that are by their nature indifferent. To be thus affected she must consider all worldly objects both divided and whole: remembering withal that no object can of itself beget any opinion in us, neither can come to us, but stands without still and quiet; but that we ourselves beget, and as it were print in ourselves opinions concerning them. Now it is in our power, not to print them; and if they creep in and lurk in some corner, it is in our power to wipe them off. Remembering moreover, that this care and circumspection of thine, is to continue but for a while, and then thy life will be at an end. And what should hinder, but that thou mayest do well with all these things? For if they be according to nature, rejoice in them, and let them be pleasing and acceptable unto thee. But if they be against nature, seek thou that which is according to thine own nature, and whether it be for thy credit or no, use all possible speed for the attainment of it: for no man ought to be blamed, for seeking his own good and happiness.

XVI. Of everything thou must consider from whence it came, of what things it doth consist, and into what it will be changed: what will be the nature of it, or what it will be like unto when it is changed; and that it can suffer no hurt by this change. And as for other men's either foolishness or wickedness, that it may not trouble and grieve thee; first generally thus; What reference have I unto these? and that we are all born for one another's good: then more particularly after another consideration; as a ram is first in a flock of sheep, and a bull in a herd of cattle, so am I born to rule over them. Begin yet higher, even from this: if atoms be not the beginning of all things, than which to believe nothing can be more absurd, then must we needs grant that there is a nature, that doth govern the universe. If such a nature, then are all worse things made for the better's sake; and all better for one another's sake. Secondly, what manner of men they be, at board, and upon their beds, and so forth. But above all things, how they are forced by their opinions that they hold, to do what they do; and even those things that they do, with what pride and self-conceit they do them. Thirdly, that if they do these things rightly, thou hast no reason to be grieved. But if not rightly, it must needs be that they do them against their wills, and through mere ignorance. For as, according to Plato's opinion, no soul doth willingly err, so by consequent neither doth it anything otherwise than it ought, but against her will. Therefore are they grieved, whensoever they hear themselves charged, either of injustice, or unconscionableness, or covetousness, or in general, of any injurious kind of dealing towards their neighbours. Fourthly, that thou thyself doest transgress in many things, and art even such another as they are. And though perchance thou doest forbear the very act of some sins, yet hast thou in thyself an habitual disposition to them, but that either through fear, or vainglory, or some such other ambitious foolish respect, thou art restrained. Fifthly, that whether they have sinned or no, thou doest not understand perfectly. For many things are done by way of discreet policy; and generally a man must know many things first, before he be able truly and judiciously to judge of another man's action. Sixthly, that whensoever thou doest take on grievously, or makest great woe, little doest thou remember then that a man's life is but for a moment of time, and that within a while we shall all be in our graves. Seventhly, that it is not the sins and transgressions themselves that trouble us properly; for they have their existence in their minds and understandings only, that commit them; but our own opinions concerning those sins. Remove then, and be content to part with that conceit of thine, that it is a grievous thing, and thou hast removed thine anger. But how should I remove it? How? reasoning with thyself that it is not shameful. For if that which is shameful, be not the only true evil that is, thou also wilt be driven whilest thou doest follow the common instinct of nature, to avoid that which is evil, to commit many unjust things, and to become a thief, and anything, that will make to the attainment of thy intended worldly ends. Eighthly, how many things may and do oftentimes follow upon such fits of anger and grief; far more grievous in themselves, than those very things which we are so grieved or angry for. Ninthly, that meekness is a thing unconquerable, if it be true and natural, and not affected or hypocritical. For how shall even the most fierce and malicious that thou shalt conceive, be able to hold on against thee, if thou shalt still continue meek and loving unto him; and that even at that time, when he is about to do thee wrong, thou shalt be well disposed, and in good temper, with all meekness to teach him, and to instruct him better? As for example; My son, we were not born for this, to hurt and annoy one another; it will be thy hurt not mine, my son: and so to show him forcibly and fully, that it is so in very deed: and that neither bees do it one to another, nor any other creatures that are naturally sociable. But this thou must do, not scoffingly, not by way of exprobation, but tenderly without any harshness of words. Neither must thou do it by way of exercise, or ostentation, that they that are by and hear thee, may admire thee: but so always that nobody be privy to it, but himself alone: yea, though there be more present at the same time. These nine particular heads, as so many gifts from the Muses, see that thou remember well: and begin one day, whilest thou art yet alive, to be a man indeed. But on the other side thou must take heed, as much to flatter them, as to be angry with them: for both are equally uncharitable, and equally hurtful. And in thy passions, take it presently to thy consideration, that to be angry is not the part of a man, but that to be meek and gentle, as it savours of more humanity, so of more manhood. That in this, there is strength and nerves, or vigour and fortitude: whereof anger and indignation is altogether void. For the nearer everything is unto unpassionateness, the nearer it is unto power. And as grief doth proceed from weakness, so doth anger. For both, both he that is angry and that grieveth, have received a wound, and cowardly have as it were yielded themselves unto their affections.

If thou wilt have a tenth also, receive this tenth gift from Hercules the guide and leader of the Muses: that is a mad man's part, to look that there should be no wicked men in the world, because it is impossible. Now for a man to brook well enough, that there should be wicked men in the world, but not to endure that any should transgress against himself, is against all equity, and indeed tyrannical.

XVII. Four several dispositions or inclinations there be of the mind and understanding, which to be aware of, thou must carefully observe: and whensoever thou doest discover them, thou must rectify them, saying to thyself concerning every one of them, This imagination is not necessary; this is uncharitable: this thou shalt speak as another man's slave, or instrument; than which nothing can be more senseless and absurd: for the fourth, thou shalt sharply check and upbraid thyself; for that thou doest suffer that more divine part in thee, to become subject and obnoxious to that more ignoble part of thy body, and the gross lusts and concupiscences thereof.

XVIII. What portion soever, either of air or fire there be in thee, although by nature it tend upwards, submitting nevertheless to the ordinance of the universe, it abides here below in this mixed body. So whatsoever is in thee, either earthy, or humid, although by nature it tend downwards, yet is it against its nature both raised upwards, and standing, or consistent. So obedient are even the elements themselves to the universe, abiding patiently wheresoever (though against their nature) they are placed, until the sound as it were of their retreat, and separation. Is it not a grievous thing then, that thy reasonable part only should be disobedient, and should not endure to keep its place: yea though it be nothing enjoined that is contrary unto it, but that only which is according to its nature? For we cannot say of it when it is disobedient, as we say of the fire, or air, that it tends upwards towards its proper element, for then goes it the quite contrary way. For the motion of the mind to any injustice, or incontinency, or to sorrow, or to fear, is nothing else but a separation from nature. Also when the mind is grieved for anything that is happened by the divine providence, then doth it likewise forsake its own place. For it was ordained unto holiness and godliness, which specially consist in an humble submission to God and His providence in all things; as well as unto justice: these also being part of those duties, which as naturally sociable, we are bound unto; and without which we cannot happily converse one with another: yea and the very ground and fountain indeed of all just actions.

XIX. He that hath not one and the self-same general end always as long as he liveth, cannot possibly be one and the self-same man always. But this will not suffice except thou add also what ought to be this general end. For as the general conceit and apprehension of all those things which upon no certain ground are by the greater part of men deemed good, cannot be uniform and agreeable, but that only which is limited and restrained by some certain proprieties and conditions, as of community: that nothing be conceived good, which is not commonly and publicly good: so must the end also that we propose unto ourselves, be common and sociable. For he that doth direct all his own private motions and purposes to that end, all his actions will be agreeable and uniform; and by that means will be still the same man.

XX. Remember the fable of the country mouse and the city mouse, and the great fright and terror that this was put into.

XXI. Socrates was wont to call the common conceits and opinions of men, the common bugbears of the world: the proper terror of silly children.

XXII. The Lacedaemonians at their public spectacles were wont to appoint seats and forms for their strangers in the shadow, they themselves were content to sit anywhere.

XXIII. What Socrates answered unto Perdiccas, why he did not come unto him, Lest of all deaths I should die the worst kind of death, said he: that is, not able to requite the good that hath been done unto me.

XXIV. In the ancient mystical letters of the Ephesians, there was an item, that a man should always have in his mind some one or other of the ancient worthies.

XXV. The Pythagoreans were wont betimes in the morning the first thing they did, to look up unto the heavens, to put themselves in mind of them who constantly and invariably did perform their task: as also to put themselves in mind of orderliness, or good order, and of purity, and of naked simplicity. For no star or planet hath any cover before it.

XXVI. How Socrates looked, when he was fain to gird himself with a skin, Xanthippe his wife having taken away his clothes, and carried them abroad with her, and what he said to his fellows and friends, who were ashamed; and out of respect to him, did retire themselves when they saw him thus decked.

XXVII. In matter of writing or reading thou must needs be taught before thou can do either: much more in matter of life. 'For thou art born a mere slave, to thy senses and brutish affections;' destitute without teaching of all true knowledge and sound reason.

XXVIII. 'My heart smiled within me.' 'They will accuse even virtue herself; with heinous and opprobrious words.'

XXIX. As they that long after figs in winter when they cannot be had; so are they that long after children, before they be granted them.

XXX. 'As often as a father kisseth his child, he should say secretly with himself' (said Epictetus,) 'tomorrow perchance shall he die.' But these words be ominous. No words ominous (said he) that signify anything that is natural: in very truth and deed not more ominous than this, 'to cut down grapes when they are ripe.' Green grapes, ripe grapes, dried grapes, or raisins: so many changes and mutations of one thing, not into that which was not absolutely, but rather so many several changes and mutations, not into that which hath no being at all, but into that which is not yet in being.

XXXI. 'Of the free will there is no thief or robber:' out of Epictetus; Whose is this also: that we should find a certain art and method of assenting; and that we should always observe with great care and heed the inclinations of our minds, that they may always be with their due restraint and reservation, always charitable, and according to the true worth of every present object. And as for earnest longing, that we should altogether avoid it: and to use averseness in those things only, that wholly depend of our own wills. It is not about ordinary petty matters, believe it, that all our strife and contention is, but whether, with the vulgar, we should be mad, or by the help of philosophy wise and sober, said he. XXXII. Socrates said, 'What will you have? the souls of reasonable, or unreasonable creatures? Of reasonable. But what? Of those whose reason is sound and perfect? or of those whose reason is vitiated and corrupted? Of those whose reason is sound and perfect. Why then labour ye not for such? Because we have them already. What then do ye so strive and contend between you?'

ΒΙΒΛΙΟ ΕΝΔΕΚΑΤΟ

1. Τὰ ἴδια τῆς λογικῆς ψυχῆς· ἑαυτὴν ὁρᾷ, ἑαυτὴν διαρθροῖ,ἑαυτὴν ὁποίαν ἂν βούληται ποιεῖ, τὸν καρπὸν ὃν φέρει αὐτὴκαρποῦται (τοὺς γὰρ τῶν φυτῶν καρποὺς καὶ τὸ ἀνάλογον ἐπὶτῶν ζῴων ἄλλοι καρποῦνται), τοῦ ἰδίου τέλους τυγχάνει, ὅπουἂν τὸ τοῦ βίου πέρας ἐπιστῇ, οὐχ ὥσπερ ἐπὶ ὀρχήσεως καὶὑποκρίσεως καὶ τῶν τοιούτων ἀτελὴς γίνεται ἡ ὅλη πρᾶξις, ἐάντι ἐγκόψῃ, ἀλλ ἐπὶ παντὸς μέρους καὶ ὅπου ἂν καταληφθῇ, πλῆρεςκαὶ ἀπροσδεὲς ἑαυτῇ τὸ προτεθὲν ποιεῖ, ὥστε εἰπεῖν· ἐγὼ ἀπέχωτὰ ἐμά. ἔτι δὲ περιέρχεται τὸν ὅλον κόσμον καὶ τὸ περὶ αὐτὸνκενὸν καὶ τὸ σχῆμα αὐτοῦ καὶ εἰς τὴν ἀπειρίαν τοῦ αἰῶνοςἐκτείνεται καὶ τὴν περιοδικὴν παλιγγενεσίαν τῶν ὅλων ἐμπεριλαμβάνεικαὶ περινοεῖ καὶ θεωρεῖ ὅτι οὐδὲν νεώτερον ὄψονταιοί μεθ ἡμᾶς οὐδὲ περιττότερον εἶδον οἱ πρὸ ἡμῶν, ἀλλὰ τρόπουτινὰ ὁ τεσσαρακοντούτης, ἐὰν νοῦν ὁποσονοῦν ἔχῃ, πάντα τὰγεγονότα καὶ τὰ ἐσόμενα ἑώρακε κατὰ τὸ ὁμοειδές. ἴδιον δὲλογικῆς ψυχῆς καὶ τὸ φιλεῖν τοὺς πλησίον καὶ ἀλήθεια καὶ αἰδὼςκαὶ τὸ μηδὲν ἑαυτῆς προτιμᾶν, ὅπερ ἴδιον καὶ νόμου· οὕτως ἄρʼοὐδὲν διήνεγκε λόγος ὀρθὸς καὶ λόγος δικαιοσύνης.

2. Ὠιδῆς ἐπιτερποῦς καὶ ὀρχήσεως καὶ παγκρατίου καταφρονήσεις,ἐὰν τὴν μὲν ἐμμελῆ φωνὴν καταμερίσῃς εἰς ἕκαστον τῶνφθόγγων καὶ καθ ἕνα πύθῃ σεαυτοῦ, εἰ τούτου ἥττων εἶʼ διατραπήσῃ γάρʼ ἐπὶ δὲ ὀρχήσεως τὸ ἀνάλογον ποιήσας καθἑκάστην κίνησιν ἢ σχέσιν, τὸ δ αὐτὸ καὶ ἐπὶ τοῦ παγκρατίου.ὅλως οὖν, χωρὶς ἀρετῆς καὶ τῶν ἀπ ἀρετῆς, μέμνησο ἐπὶ τὰ κατὰμέρος τρέχειν καὶ τῇ διαιρέσει αὐτῶν εἰς καταφρόνησιν ἰέναι,τὸ δ αὐτὸ καὶ ἐπὶ τὸν βίον ὅλον μεταφέρειν.

3. Οἷα ἐστὶν ἡ ψυχὴ ἡ ἕτοιμος, ἐὰν ἤδη ἀπολυθῆναι δέῃ τοῦσώματος, [καὶ] ἤτοι σβεσθῆναι ἢ σκεδασθῆναι ἢ συμμεῖναι. τὸδὲ ἕτοιμον τοῦτο ἵνα ἀπὸ ἰδικῆς κρίσεως ἔρχηται, μὴ κατὰ ψιλὴνπαράταξιν ὡς οἱ Χριστιανοί, ἀλλὰ λελογισμένως καὶ σεμνῶς καὶὥστε καὶ ἄλλον πεῖσαι, ἀτραγῴδως.

4. Πεποίηκά τι κοινωνικῶς; οὐκοῦν ὠφέλημαι. τοῦτο ἵνα ἀεὶπρόχειρον ἀπαντᾷ καὶ μηδαμοῦ παύου.

5. Τίς σου ἡ τέχνη; ἀγαθὸν εἶναι. τοῦτο δὲ πῶς ἄλλως γίνεται ἢἐκ θεωρημάτων, τῶν μὲν περὶ τῆς τοῦ ὅλου φύσεως, τῶν δὲ περὶτῆς ἰδίας τοῦ ἀνθρώπου κατασκευῆς.

6. Πρῶτον αἱ τραγῳδίαι παρήχθησαν ὑπομνηστικαὶ τῶν συμβαινόντωνκαὶ ὅτι ταῦτα οὕτως πέφυκε γίνεσθαι καὶ ὅτι, οἷς ἐπὶτῆς σκηνῆς ψυχαγωγεῖσθε, τούτοις μὴ ἄχθεσθε ἐπὶ τῆς μείζονοςσκηνῆς· ὁρᾶτε γὰρ ὅτι οὕτως δεῖ ταῦτα περαίνεσθαι καὶ ὅτιφέρουσιν αὐτὰ καὶ οἱ κεκραγότες· "ἰὼ Κιθαιρών." καὶ λέγεται δέτινα ὑπὸ τῶν τὰ δράματα ποιούντων χρησίμως· οἷόν ἐστιν ἐκεῖνομάλιστα· εἰ δ ἠμελήθην ἐκ θεῶν καὶ παῖδ ἐμώ, ἔχει λόγον καὶτοῦτο· καὶ πάλιν· τοῖς πράγμασιν γὰρ οὐχὶ θυμοῦσθαι ‹χρεών›.καί· βίον θερίζειν ὥστε κάρπιμον στάχυν· καὶ ὅσα τοιαῦτα. μετὰδὲ τὴν τραγῳδίαν ἡ ἀρχαία κωμῳδία παρήχθη, παιδαγωγικὴνπαρρησίαν ἔχουσα καὶ τῆς ἀτυφίας οὐκ ἀχρήστως δι αὐτῆς τῆςεὐθυρρημοσύνης ὑπομιμνήσκουσα· πρὸς οἷόν τι καὶ Διογένηςταυτὶ παρελάμβανεν. μετὰ ταῦτα τίς ἡ μέση κωμῳδία καὶ λοιπὸνἡ νέα πρὸς τί ποτε παρείληπται, ἢ κατ ὀλίγον ἐπὶ τὴν ἐκ μιμήσεωςφιλοτεχνίαν ὑπερρύη, ἐπίστησον. ὅτι μὲν γὰρ λέγεται καὶ ὑπότούτων τινὰ χρήσιμα οὐκ ἀγνοεῖται, ἀλλὰ ἡ ὅλη ἐπιβολὴ τῆςτοιαύτης ποιήσεως καὶ δραματουργίας πρὸς τίνα ποτὲ σκοπὸνἀπέβλεψεν;

7. Πῶς ἐναργὲς προσπίπτει τὸ μὴ εἶναι ἄλλην βίου ὑπόθεσιν εἰςτὸ φιλοσοφεῖν οὕτως ἐπιτήδειον ὡς ταύτην, ἐν ᾗ νῦν ὢν τυγχάνεις.

8. Κλάδος τοῦ προσεχοῦς κλάδου ἀποκοπεὶς οὐ δύναται μὴ καὶτοῦ ὅλου φυτοῦ ἀποκεκόφθαι. οὕτω δὴ καὶ ἄνθρωπος ἑνὸςἀνθρώπου ἀποσχισθεὶς ὅλης τῆς κοινωνίας ἀποπέπτωκεν. κλάδονμὲν οὖν ἄλλος ἀποκόπτει· ἄνθρωπος δὲ αὐτὸς ἑαυτὸν τοῦ πλησίονχωρίζει μισήσας καὶ ἀποστραφείς, ἀγνοεῖ δὲ ὅτι καὶ τοῦ ὅλουπολιτεύματος ἅμα ἀποτέτμηκεν ἑαυτόν. πλὴν ἐκεῖνό γε δῶροντοῦ συστησαμένου τὴν κοινωνίαν Διός· ἔξεστι γὰρ ἡμῖν πάλινσυμφῦναι τῷ προσεχεῖ καὶ πάλιν τοῦ ὅλου συμπληρωτικοῖςγενέσθαι. πλεονάκις μέντοι γινόμενον τὸ κατὰ τὴν τοιαύτηνδιαίρεσιν δυσένωτον καὶ δυσαποκατάστατον ‹τὸ› ἀποχωροῦνποιεῖ. ὅλως τε οὐχ ὅμοιος ὁ κλάδος ὁ ἀπ ἀρχῆς συμβλαστήσαςκαὶ σύμπνους συμμείνας τῷ μετὰ τὴν ἀποκοπὴν αὖθις ἐγκεντρισθέντι,ὅ τι ποτὲ λέγουσιν οἱ φυτουργοί. Ὁμοθαμνεῖν μέν, μὴὁμοδογματεῖν δέ.

9. Οἱ ἐνιστάμενοι προϊόντι σοι κατὰ τὸν ὀρθὸν λόγον ὥσπερ ἀπότῆς ὑγιοῦς πράξεως ἀποτρέψαι σε οὐ δυνήσονται, οὕτως μηδὲτῆς πρὸς αὐτοὺς εὐμενείας ἐκκρουέτωσαν, ἀλλὰ φύλασσε σεαυτὸνἐπ ἀμφοτέρων ὁμοίως, μὴ μόνον ἐπὶ τῆς εὐσταθοῦς κρίσεως καὶπράξεως, ἀλλὰ καὶ ἐπὶ τῆς πρὸς τοὺς κωλύειν ἐπιχειροῦντας ἢἄλλως δυσχεραίνοντας πραότητος. καὶ γὰρ τοῦτο ἀσθενές, τὸχαλεπαίνειν αὐτοῖς, ὥσπερ τὸ ἀποστῆναι τῆς πράξεως καὶἐνδοῦναι καταπλαγέντα· ἀμφότεροι γὰρ ἐπίσης λιποτάκται, ὁ μὲνὑποτρέσας, ὁ δὲ ἀλλοτριωθεὶς πρὸς τὸν φύσει συγγενῆ καὶ φίλον.

10. Οὐκ ἔστι χείρων οὐδεμία φύσις τέχνης· καὶ γὰρ αἱ τέχναι τὰςφύσεις μιμοῦνται. εἰ δὲ τοῦτο, ἡ πασῶν τῶν ἄλλων τελεωτάτηκαὶ περιληπτικωτάτη φύσις οὐκ ἂν ἀπολείποιτο τῆς τεχνικῆςεὐμηχανίας. πᾶσαι δέ γε τέχναι τῶν κρειττόνων ἕνεκεν τὰ χείρωποιοῦσιν· οὐκοῦν καὶ ἡ κοινὴ φύσις. καὶ δὴ ἔνθεν μὲν γένεσιςδικαιοσύνης, ἀπὸ δὲ ταύτης αἱ λοιπαὶ ἀρεταὶ ὑφίστανται· οὐγὰρ τηρηθήσεται τὸ δίκαιον, ἐὰν ἤτοι διαφερώμεθα πρὸς τὰ μέσαἢ εὐεξαπάτητοι καὶ προπτωτικοὶ καὶ μεταπτωτικοὶ ὦμεν.

11. [Εἰ μὲν] Οὐκ ἔρχεται ἐπὶ σὲ τὰ πράγματα ὧν αἱ διώξεις καὶφυγαὶ θορυβοῦσί σε, ἀλλὰ τρόπον τινὰ αὐτὸς ἐπ᾽ ἐκεῖνα ἔρχῃ· τόγοῦν κρῖμα τὸ περὶ αὐτῶν ἡσυχαζέτω κἀκεῖνα μενεῖ ἀτρεμοῦντακαὶ οὔτε διώκων οὔτε φεύγων ὀφθήσῃ.

12. Σφαῖρα ψυχῆς αὐτοειδής, ὅταν μήτε ἐκτείνηται ἐπί τι μήτεἔσω συντρέχῃ μήτε σπείρηται μήτε συνιζάνῃ, ἀλλὰ φωτὶ λάμπηταιᾧ τὴν ἀλήθειαν ὁρᾷ τὴν πάντων καὶ τὴν ἐν αὑτῇ.

13. Καταφρονήσει μού τις; ὄψεται. ἐγὼ δὲ ὄψομαι ἵνα μή τικαταφρονήσεως ἄξιον πράσσων ἢ λέγων εὑρίσκωμαι. μισήσει;ὄψεται. ἀλλὰ ἐγὼ εὐμενὴς καὶ εὔνους παντὶ καὶ τούτῳ αὐτῷἕτοιμος τὸ παρορώμενον δεῖξαι, οὐκ ὀνειδιστικῶς οὐδὲ ὡςκατεπιδεικνύμενος ὅτι ἀνέχομαι, ἀλλὰ γνησίως καὶ χρηστῶς, οἷοςὁ Φωκίων ἐκεῖνος, εἴ γε μὴ προσεποιεῖτο. τὰ ἔσω γὰρ δεῖ τοιαῦταεἶναι καὶ ὑπὸ τῶν θεῶν βλέπεσθαι ἄνθρωπον πρὸς μηδὲνἀγανακτικῶς διατιθέμενον μηδὲ δεινοπαθοῦντα. τί γάρ σοι κακόν,εἰ αὐτὸς νῦν ποιεῖς τὸ τῇ φύσει σου οἰκεῖον καὶ δέχῃ τὸ νῦν τῇτῶν ὅλων φύσει εὔκαιρον, ἄνθρωπος τεταμένος πρὸς τὸ γίνεσθαιδὶ ὅτου δὴ τὸ κοινῇ συμφέρον;

14. Ἀλλήλων καταφρονοῦντες ἀλλήλοις ἀρεσκεύονται καὶἀλλήλων ὑπερέχειν θέλοντες ἀλλήλοις ὑποκατακλίνονται.

15. Ὡς σαπρὸς καὶ κίβδηλος ὁ λέγων· ἐγὼ προῄρημαι ἁπλῶς σοιπροσφέρεσθαι. τί ποιεῖς, ἄνθρωπε; τοῦτο οὐ δεῖ προλέγειν. αὐτὸφανήσεται· ἐπὶ τοῦ μετώπου γεγράφθαι ὀφείλει· εὐθὺς ἡ φωνὴτοιοῦτον ἠχεῖν, εὐθὺς ἐν τοῖς ὄμμασιν ἐξέχειν, ὡς τῶν ἐραστῶνἐν τῷ βλέμματι πάντα εὐθὺς γνωρίζει ὁ ἐρώμενος. τοιοῦτονὅλως δεῖ τὸν ἁπλοῦν καὶ ἀγαθὸν εἶναι, οἷον γράσωνα, ἵνα ὁ παραστὰςἅμα τῷ προσελθεῖν, θέλει οὐ θέλει, αἴσθηται. ἐπιτήδευσις δὲἁπλότητος σκάλμη ἐστίν. οὐδέν ἐστιν αἴσχιον λυκοφιλίας· πάντωνμάλιστα τοῦτο φεῦγε. ὁ ἀγαθὸς καὶ ἁπλοῦς καὶ εὐμενὴςἐν τοῖς ὄμμασιν ἔχει ταῦτα καὶ οὐ λανθάνει.

16. Κάλλιστα διαζῆν, δύναμις αὕτη ἐν τῇ ψυχῇ, ἐὰν πρὸς τὰἀδιάφορά τις ἀδιαφορῇ. ἀδιαφορήσει δέ, ἐὰν ἕκαστον αὐτῶνθεωρῇ διηρημένως καὶ ὁλικῶς καὶ μεμνημένος ὅτι οὐδὲν αὐτῶνὑπόληψιν περὶ αὐτοῦ ἡμῖν ἐμποιεῖ οὐδὲ ἔρχεται ἐφ ἡμᾶς, ἀλλὰτὰ μὲν ἀτρεμεῖ, ἡμεῖς δέ ἐσμεν οἱ τὰς περὶ αὐτῶν κρίσεις γεννῶντεςκαὶ οἷον γράφοντες ἐν ἑαυτοῖς, ἐξὸν μὲν μὴ γράφειν, ἐξὸν δέ, κἄνπου λάθῃ, εὐθὺς ἐξαλεῖψαι· ὅτι ὀλίγου χρόνου ἔσται ἡ τοιαύτηπροσοχὴ καὶ λοιπὸν πεπαύσεται ὁ βίος. τί μέντοι δύσκολον ἔχειταῦτα; εἰ μὲν γὰρ κατὰ φύσιν ἐστί, χαῖρε αὐτοῖς καὶ ῥᾴδια ἔσταισοι· εἰ δὲ παρὰ φύσιν, ζήτει τί ἐστί σοι κατὰ τὴν σὴν φύσιν καὶἐπὶ τοῦτο σπεῦδε κἂν ἄδοξον ᾖ· παντὶ γὰρ συγγνώμη τὸ ἴδιονἀγαθὸν ζητοῦντι.

17. Πόθεν ἐλήλυθεν ἕκαστον καὶ ἐκ τίνων ἕκαστον ὑποκειμένωνκαὶ εἰς τί μεταβάλλει καὶ οἷον ἔσται μεταβαλὸν καὶ ὡς οὐδὲνκακὸν πείσεται.

18. [Καὶ] Πρῶτον, τίς ἡ πρὸς αὐτούς μοι σχέσις καὶ ὅτι ἀλλήλωνἕνεκεν γεγόναμεν καὶ καθ ἕτερον λόγον προστησόμενος αὐτῶνγέγονα ὡς κριὸς ποίμνης ἢ ταῦρος ἀγέλης. ἄνωθεν δὲ ἔπιθι ἀπὸτοῦ· εἰ μὴ ἄτομοι, φύσις ἡ τὰ ὅλα διοικοῦσα· εἰ τοῦτο, τὰ χείρονατῶν κρειττόνων ἕνεκεν, ταῦτα δὲ ἀλλήλων.Δεύτερον δέ, ὁποῖοί τινες εἰσιν ἐπὶ τῆς τραπέζης, ἐν τῷ κλιναρίῳ,τἆλλα· μάλιστα δέ, οἵας ἀνάγκας δογμάτων κειμένας ἔχουσι·καὶ αὐτὰ δὲ ταῦτα, μεθ οἵου τύφου ποιοῦσιν.Τρίτον, ὅτι, εἰ μὲν ὀρθῶς ταῦτα ποιοῦσιν, οὐ δεῖ δυσχεραίνειν· εἰ δ οὐκ ὀρθῶς, δηλονότι ἄκοντες καὶ ἀγνοοῦντες· - πᾶσα γὰρψυχὴ ἄκουσα στέρεται, ὥσπερ τοῦ ἀληθοῦς, οὕτως καὶ τοῦ κατάξίαν ἑκάστῳ προσφέρεσθαι - ἄχθονται γοῦν ἀκούοντες ἄδικοικαὶ ἀγνώμονες καὶ πλεονέκται καὶ καθάπαξ ἁμαρτητικοὶ περὶτοὺς πλησίον. Τέταρτον, ὅτι καὶ αὐτὸς πολλὰ ἁμαρτάνεις καὶ ἄλλος τοιοῦτοςεἶ· καὶ εἴ τινων δὲ ἁμαρτημάτων ἀπέχῃ, ἀλλὰ τήν γε ἕξινἐποιστικὴν ἔχεις, εἰ καὶ διὰ δειλίαν ἢ δοξοκοπίαν ἢ τοιοῦτό τικακὸν ἀπέχῃ τῶν ὁμοίων ἁμαρτημάτων.Πέμπτον, ὅτι οὐδὲ εἰ ἁμαρτάνουσι κατείληφας· πολλὰ γὰρ κατοἰκονομίαν γίνεται καὶ ὅλως πολλὰ δεῖ πρότερον μαθεῖν, ἵνα τιςπερὶ ἀλλοτρίας πράξεως καταληπτικῶς τι ἀποφήνηται.Ἕκτον, ὅτι, ὅταν λίαν ἀγανακτῇς ἢ καὶ δυσπαθῇς, ἀκαριαῖόςὁ ἀνθρώπινος βίος καὶ μετ ὀλίγον πάντες ἐξετάθημεν.Ἕβδομον, ὅτι οὐχ αἱ πράξεις αὐτῶν ἐνοχλοῦσιν ἡμῖν· ἐκεῖναιγάρ εἰσιν ἐν τοῖς ἐκείνων ἡγεμονικοῖς· ἀλλὰ αἱ ἡμέτεραιὑπολήψεις. ἆρον γοῦν καὶ θέλησον ἀφεῖναι τὴν ὡς περὶ δεινοῦκρίσιν καὶ ἀπῆλθεν ἡ ὀργή. πῶς οὖν ἀρεῖς; λογισάμενος ὅτι οὐκαἰσχρόν· ἐὰν γὰρ μὴ μόνον ᾖ τὸ αἰσχρὸν κακόν, ἀνάγκη καὶ σὲπολλὰ ἁμαρτάνειν καὶ λῃστὴν καὶ παντοῖον γίνεσθαι.Ὄγδοον, ὅσῳ χαλεπώτερα ἐπιφέρουσιν αἱ ὀργαὶ καὶ λῦπαι αἱἐπὶ τοῖς τοιούτοις, ἤπερ αὐτά ἐστιν ἐφ οἷς ὀργιζόμεθα καὶλυπούμεθα.Ἔνατον, ὅτι τὸ εὐμενὲς ἀνίκητον, ἐὰν γνήσιον ᾖ καὶ μὴ σεσηρὸςμηδὲ ὑπόκρισις. τί γάρ σοι ποιήσει ὁ ὑβριστικώτατος, ἐὰν διατελῇςεὐμενὴς αὐτῷ καί, εἰ οὕτως ἔτυχε, πράως παραινῇς καὶμεταδιδάσκῃς εὐσχολῶν παρ αὐτὸν ἐκεῖνον τὸν καιρὸν ὅτεκακοποιεῖν σε ἐπιχειρεῖ· "μή, τέκνον· πρὸς ἄλλο πεφύκαμεν· ἐγὼμὲν οὐ μὴ

βλαβῶ, σὺ δὲ βλάπτῃ, τέκνον." καὶ δεικνύναι εὐαφῶςκαὶ ὁλικῶς ὅτι τοῦτο οὕτως ἔχει, ὅτι οὐδὲ μέλισσαι αὐτὸ ποιοῦσινοὐδ᾽ ὅσα συναγελαστικὰ πέφυκε. δεῖ δὲ μήτε εἰρωνικῶς αὐτὸποιεῖν μήτε ὀνειδιστικῶς, ἀλλὰ φιλοστόργως καὶ ἀδήκτως τῇ ψυχῇκαὶ μὴ ὡς ἐν σχολῇ μηδὲ ἵνα ἄλλος παραστὰς θαυμάσῃ, ἀλλ᾽ ἤτοι πρὸς μόνον καὶ ἐὰν ἄλλοι τινὲς περιεστήκωσι.τούτων τῶν ἐννέα κεφαλαίων μέμνησο ὡς παρὰ τῶν Μουσῶνδῶρα εἰληφὼς καὶ ἄρξαι ποτὲ ἄνθρωπος εἶναι, ἕως ζῇς. φυλακτέονδὲ ἐπίσης τῷ ὀργίζεσθαι αὐτοῖς τὸ κολακεύειν αὐτούς· ἀμφότεραγὰρ ἀκοινώνητα καὶ πρὸς βλάβην φέρει. πρόχειρον δὲ ἐν ταῖςὀργαῖς ὅτι οὐχὶ τὸ θυμοῦσθαι ἀνδρικόν, ἀλλὰ τὸ πρᾷον καὶἥμερον ὥσπερ ἀνθρωπικώτερον, οὕτως καὶ ἀρρενικώτερον, καὶἰσχύος καὶ νεύρων καὶ ἀνδρείας τούτῳ μέτεστιν, οὐχὶ τῷἀγανακτοῦντι καὶ δυσαρεστοῦντι· ὅσῳ γὰρ ἀπαθείᾳ τοῦτοοἰκειότερον, τοσούτῳ καὶ δυνάμει, ὥσπερ τε ἡ λύπη ἀσθενοῦς,οὕτως καὶ ἡ ὀργή· ἀμφότεροι γὰρ τέτρωνται καὶ ἐνδεδώκασιν.εἰ δὲ βούλει, καὶ δέκατον παρὰ τοῦ Μουσηγέτου δῶρον λάβε,ὅτι τὸ ἀξιοῦν μὴ ἁμαρτάνειν τοὺς φαύλους μανικόν· ἀδυνάτουγὰρ ἐφίεται. τὸ δὲ συγχωρεῖν ‹εἰς› ἄλλους μὲν εἶναι τοιούτους,ἀξιοῦν δὲ μὴ εἰς σὲ ἁμαρτάνειν, ἄγνωμον καὶ τυραννικόν.

19. Τέσσαρας μάλιστα τροπὰς τοῦ ἡγεμονικοῦ παραφυλακτέονδιηνεκῶς καὶ ἐπειδὰν φωράσῃς ἀπαλειπτέον, ἐπιλέγοντα ἐφ᾽ ἑκάστου οὕτως· τοῦτο τὸ φάντασμα οὐκ ἀναγκαῖον· τοῦτο λυτικὸνκοινωνίας· τοῦτο οὐκ ἀπὸ σαυτοῦ μέλλεις λέγειν· τὸ γὰρ μὴ ἀφ᾽ἑαυτοῦ λέγειν ἐν τοῖς ἀτοπωτάτοις νόμιζε. τέταρτον δέ ἐστι καθὸ σεαυτῷ ὀνειδιεῖς, ὅτι τοῦτο ἡττωμένου ἐστὶ καὶ ὑποκατακλινομένουτοῦ ἐν σοὶ θειοτέρου μέρους τῇ ἀτιμοτέρᾳ καὶ θνητῇμοίρᾳ, τῇ τοῦ σώματος καὶ ταῖς τούτου παχείαις ἡδοναῖς.

20. Τὸ μὲν πνευματικόν σου καὶ τὸ πυρῶδες πᾶν, ὅσον ἐγκέκραται,καίτοι φύσει ἀνωφερῆ ὄντα, ὅμως πειθόμενα τῇ τῶν ὅλων διατάξειπαρακρατεῖται ἐνταῦθα ἐπὶ τοῦ συγκρίματος. καὶ τὸ γεῶδες δὲτὸ ἐν σοὶ πᾶν καὶ τὸ ὑγρόν, καίτοι κατωφερῆ ὄντα, ὅμως ἐγήγερταικαὶ ἕστηκε τὴν οὐχ ἑαυτῶν φυσικὴν στάσιν. οὕτως ἄρα καὶ τὰστοιχεῖα ὑπακούει τοῖς ὅλοις, ἐπειδάν που καταταχθῇ, βίασυμμένοντα μέχρις ἂν ἐκεῖθεν πάλιν τὸ ἐνδόσιμον τῆς διαλύσεωςσημήνῃ. οὐ δεινὸν οὖν μόνον τὸ νοερόν σου μέρος ἀπειθὲς εἶναικαὶ ἀγανακτεῖν τῇ ἑαυτοῦ χώρᾳ; καίτοι οὐδέν γε βίαιον τούτῳἐπιτάσσεται, ἀλλὰ μόνα ὅσα κατὰ φύσιν ἐστὶν αὐτῷ· οὐ μέντοιἀνέχεται, ἀλλὰ τὴν ἐναντίαν φέρεται. ἡ γὰρ ἐπὶ τὰ ἀδικήματακαὶ τὰ ἀκολαστήματα καὶ τὰς ὀργὰς καὶ τὰς λύπας καὶ τοὺςφόβους κίνησις οὐδὲν ἄλλο ἐστὶν ἢ ἀφισταμένου τῆς φύσεως.καὶ ὅταν δέ τινι τῶν συμβαινόντων δυσχεραίνῃ τὸ ἡγεμονικόν,καταλείπει καὶ τότε τὴν ἑαυτοῦ χώραν· πρὸς ὁσιότητα γὰρ καὶθεοσέβειαν κατεσκεύασται οὐχ ἧττον ἢ πρὸς δικαιοσύνην. καὶγὰρ ταῦτα ἐν εἴδει ἐστὶ τῆς εὐκοινωνησίας, μᾶλλον δὲ πρεσβύτερατῶν δικαιοπραγημάτων.

21. "Ὧι μὴ εἷς καὶ ὁ αὐτός ἐστιν ἀεὶ τοῦ βίου σκοπός, οῬτος εἷςκαὶ ὁ αὐτὸς δἰ ὅλου τοῦ βίου εἶναι οὐ δύναται." οὐκ ἀρκεῖ τὸεἰρημένον, ἐὰν μὴ κἀκεῖνο προσθῇς, ὁποῖον εἶναι δεῖ τοῦτον τὸνσκοπόν. ὥσπερ γὰρ οὐχ ἡ πάντων τῶν ὁπωσοῦν τοῖς πλείοσιδοκούντων ἀγαθῶν ὑπόληψις ὁμοία ἐστίν, ἀλλ ἡ τῶν τοιῶνδέτινων, τουτέστι τῶν κοινῶν, οὕτω καὶ τὸν σκοπὸν δεῖ τὸνκοινωνικὸν καὶ πολιτικὸν ὑποστήσασθαι. ὁ γὰρ εἰς τοῦτον πάσαςτὰς ἰδίας ὁρμὰς ἀπευθύνων πάσας τὰς πράξεις ὁμοίας ἀποδώσεικαὶ κατὰ τοῦτο ἀεὶ ὁ αὐτὸς ἔσται.

22. Τὸν μῦν τὸν ὀρεινὸν καὶ τὸν κατοικίδιον καὶ τὴν πτοίαν τούτουκαὶ διασόβησιν.

23. ‹Ὁ› Σωκράτης καὶ τὰ τῶν πολλῶν δόγματα Λαμίας ἐκάλει,παιδίων δείματα.

24. ‹Οἱ› Λακεδαιμόνιοι τοῖς μὲν ξένοις ἐν ταῖς θεωρίαις ὑπὸ τῇσκιᾷ τὰ βάθρα ἐτίθεσαν, αὐτοὶ δὲ οῬ ἔτυχεν, ἐκαθέζοντο.

25. Τῷ Περδίκκᾳ ὁ Σωκράτης περὶ τοῦ μὴ ἔρχεσθαι παρ αὐτόν·"ἵνα, ἔφη, μὴ τῷ κακίστῳ ὀλέθρῳ ἀπόλωμα", τουτέστι, μὴ εὐπαθὼν οὐ δυνηθῶ ἀντευποιῆσαι.

26. Ἐν τοῖς τῶν Ἐπικουρείων γράμμασι παράγγελμα ἔκειτο συνεχῶςὑπομιμνήσκεσθαι τῶν παλαιῶν τινος τῶν ἀρετῇ χρησαμένων.

27. Οἱ Πυθαγόρειοι· ἔωθεν εἰς τὸν οὐρανὸν ἀφορᾶν, ἵν ὑπομιμνησκώμεθα τῶν ἀεὶ κατὰ τὰ αὐτὰ καὶ ὡσαύτως τὸ ἑαυτῶν ἔργονδιανυόντων καὶ τῆς τάξεως καὶ τῆς καθαρότητος καὶ τῆςγυμνότητος· οὐδὲν γὰρ προκάλυμμα ἄστρου.

28. Οἷος ὁ Σωκράτης τὸ κῴδιον ὑπεζωσμένος, ὅτε ἡ Ξανθίππηλαβοῦσα τὸ ἱμάτιον ἔξω προῆλθεν· καὶ ἃ εἶπεν ὁ Σωκράτης τοῖςἑταίροις αἰδεσθεῖσι καὶ ἀναχωρήσασιν, ὅτε αὐτὸν εἶδον οὕτωςἐσταλμένον.

29. Ἐν τῷ γράφειν καὶ ἀναγινώσκειν οὐ πρότερον ἄρξεις πρὶνἀρχθῇς. τοῦτο πολλῷ μᾶλλον ἐν τῷ βίῳ.

30. Δοῦλος πέφυκας, οὐ μέτεστί σοι λόγου.

31. Ἐμὸν δ ἐγέλασσε φίλον κῆρ.

32. Μέμψονται δ ἀρετὴν χαλεποῖς βάζοντες ἔπεσσιν.

33. Σῦκον χειμῶνος ζητεῖν μαινομένου· τοιοῦτος ὁ [τὸ] παιδίονζητῶν, ὅτε οὐκέτι δίδοται.

34. Καταφιλοῦντα τὸ παιδίον δεῖν, ἔλεγεν ὁ Ἐπίκτητος, ἔνδονἐπιφθέγγεσθαι· "αὔριον ἴσως ἀποθανῇ." - "δύσφημα ταῦτα." -"οὐδὲν δύσφημον", ἔφη, "φυσικοῦ τινος ἔργου σημαντικόν· ἦκαὶ τὸ τοὺς στάχυας θερισθῆναι δύσφημον."

35. Ὄμφαξ, σταφυλή, σταφίς, πάντα μεταβολαί, οὐκ εἰς τὸ μὴ ὄν,ἀλλὰ εἰς τὸ νῦν μὴ ὄν.

36. Λῃστὴς προαιρέσεως οὐ γίνεται· τὸ τοῦ Ἐπικτήτου.

37. "Τέχνην", ἔφη, "δεῖ περὶ τὸ συγκατατίθεσθαι εὑρεῖν καὶ ἐν τῷπερὶ τὰς ὁρμὰς τόπῳ τὸ προσεκτικὸν φυλάσσειν, ἵνα μεθὑπεξαιρέσεως ‹ὦσιν,› ἵνα κοινωνικαί, ἵνα κατ ἀξίαν, καὶ ὀρέξεωςμὲν παντάπασιν ἀπέχεσθαι, ἐκκλίσει δὲ πρὸς μηδὲν τῶν οὐκ ἐφήμῖν χρῆσθαι."

38. "Οὐ περὶ τοῦ τυχόντος οὖν", ἔφη, "ἐστὶν ὁ ἀγών, ἀλλὰ περὶτοῦ μαίνεσθαι ἢ μή."

39. Ὁ Σωκράτης ἔλεγεν· "τί θέλετε; λογικῶν ψυχὰς ἔχειν ἢ ἀλόγων;""λογικῶν." "τίνων λογικῶν; ὑγιῶν ἢ φαύλων;" "ὑγιῶν." "τί οὖνοὐ ζητεῖτε;" "ὅτι ἔχομεν." "τί οὖν μάχεσθε καὶ διαφέρεσθε;"

BOOK TWELVE

I. Whatsoever thou doest hereafter aspire unto, thou mayest even now enjoy and possess, if thou doest not envy thyself thine own happiness. And that will be, if thou shalt forget all that is past, and for the future, refer thyself wholly to the Divine Providence, and shalt bend and apply all thy present thoughts and intentions to holiness and righteousness. To holiness, in accepting willingly whatsoever is sent by the Divine Providence, as being that which the nature of the universe hath appointed unto thee, which also hath appointed thee for that, whatsoever it be. To righteousness, in speaking the truth freely, and without ambiguity; and in doing all things justly and discreetly. Now in this good course, let not other men's either wickedness, or opinion, or voice hinder thee: no, nor the sense of this thy pampered mass of flesh: for let that which suffers, look to itself. If therefore whensoever the time of thy departing shall come, thou shalt readily leave all things, and shalt respect thy mind only, and that divine part of thine, and this shall be thine only fear, not that some time or other thou shalt cease to live, but thou shalt never begin to live according to nature: then shalt thou be a man indeed, worthy of that world, from which thou hadst thy beginning; then shalt thou cease to be a stranger in thy country, and to wonder at those things that happen daily, as things strange and unexpected, and anxiously to depend of divers things that are not in thy power.

II. God beholds our minds and understandings, bare and naked from these material vessels, and outsides, and all earthly dross. For with His simple and pure understanding, He pierceth into our inmost and purest parts, which from His, as it were by a water pipe and channel, first flowed and issued. This if thou also shalt use to do, thou shalt rid thyself of that manifold luggage, wherewith thou art round about encumbered. For he that does regard neither his body, nor his clothing, nor his dwelling, nor any such external furniture, must needs gain unto himself great rest and ease. Three things there be in all, which thou doest consist of; thy body, thy life, and thy mind. Of these the two former, are so far forth thine, as that thou art bound to take care for them. But the third alone is that which is properly thine. If then thou shalt separate from thyself, that is from thy mind, whatsoever other men either do or say, or whatsoever thou thyself hast heretofore either done or said; and all troublesome thoughts concerning the future, and whatsoever, (as either belonging to thy body or life:) is without the jurisdiction of thine own will, and whatsoever in the ordinary course of human chances and accidents doth happen unto thee; so that thy mind (keeping herself loose and free from all outward coincidental entanglements; always in a readiness to depart:) shall live by herself, and to herself, doing that which is just, accepting whatsoever doth happen, and speaking the truth always; if, I say, thou shalt separate from thy mind, whatsoever by sympathy might adhere unto it, and all time both past and future, and shalt make thyself in all points and respects, like unto Empedocles his allegorical sphere, 'all round and circular,' &c., and shalt think of no longer life than that which is now present: then shalt thou be truly able to pass the remainder of thy days without troubles and distractions; nobly and generously disposed, and in good favour and correspondency, with that spirit which is within thee.

III. I have often wondered how it should come to pass, that every man loving himself best, should more regard other men's opinions concerning himself than his own. For if any God or grave master standing by, should command any of us to think nothing by himself but what he should presently speak out; no man were able to endure it, though but for one day. Thus do we fear more what our neighbours will think of us, than what we ourselves.

IV. how come it to pass that the Gods having ordered all other things so well and so lovingly, should be overseen in this one only thing, that whereas then hath been some very good men that have made many covenants as it were with God and by many holy actions and outward services contracted a kind of familiarity with Him; that these men when once they are dead, should never be restored to life, but be extinct for ever. But this thou mayest be sure of, that this (if it be so indeed) would never have been so ordered by the Gods, had it been fit otherwise. For certainly it was possible, had it been more just so and had it been according to nature, the nature of the universe would easily have borne it. But now because it is not so, (if so be that it be not so indeed) be therefore confident that it was not fit it should be so for thou seest thyself, that now seeking after this matter, how freely thou doest argue and contest with God. But were not the Gods both just and good in the highest degree, thou durst not thus reason with them. Now if just and good, it could not be that in the creation of the world, they should either unjustly or unreasonably oversee anything.

V. Use thyself even unto those things that thou doest at first despair of. For the left hand we see, which for the most part lieth idle because not used; yet doth it hold the bridle with more strength than the right, because it hath been used unto it.

VI. Let these be the objects of thy ordinary meditation: to consider, what manner of men both for soul and body we ought to be, whensoever death shall surprise us: the shortness of this our mortal life: the immense vastness of the time that hath been before, and will he after us: the frailty of every worldly material object: all these things to consider, and behold clearly in themselves, all disguisement of external outside being removed and taken away. Again, to consider the efficient causes of all things: the proper ends and references of all actions: what pain is in itself; what pleasure, what death: what fame or honour, how every man is the true and proper ground of his own rest and tranquillity, and that no man can truly be hindered by any other: that all is but conceit and opinion. As for the use of thy dogmata, thou must carry thyself in the practice of them, rather like unto a pancratiastes, or one that at the same time both fights and wrestles with hands and feet, than a gladiator. For this, if he lose his sword that he fights with, he is gone: whereas the other hath still his hand free, which he may easily turn and manage at his will.

VII. All worldly things thou must behold and consider, dividing them into matter, form, and reference, or their proper end.

VIII. How happy is man in this his power that hath been granted unto him: that he needs not do anything but what God shall approve, and that he may embrace contentedly, whatsoever God doth send unto him?

IX. Whatsoever doth happen in the ordinary course and consequence of natural events, neither the Gods, (for it is not possible, that they either wittingly or unwittingly should do anything amiss) nor men, (for it is through ignorance, and therefore against their wills that they do anything amiss) must be accused. None then must be accused.

X. How ridiculous and strange is he, that wonders at anything that happens in this life in the ordinary course of nature!

XI. Either fate, (and that either an absolute necessity, and unavoidable decree; or a placable and flexible Providence) or all is a mere casual confusion, void of all order and government. If an absolute and unavoidable necessity, why doest thou resist? If a placable and exorable Providence, make thyself worthy of the divine help and assistance. If all be a mere confusion without any moderator, or governor, then hast thou reason to congratulate thyself; that in such a general flood of confusion thou thyself hast obtained a reasonable faculty, whereby thou mayest govern thine own life and actions. But if thou beest carried away with the flood, it must be thy body perchance, or thy life, or some other thing that belongs unto them that is carried away: thy mind and understanding cannot. Or should it be

255

so, that the light of a candle indeed is still bright and lightsome until it be put out: and should truth, and righteousness, and temperance cease to shine in thee whilest thou thyself hast any being?

XII. At the conceit and apprehension that such and such a one hath sinned, thus reason with thyself; What do I know whether this be a sin indeed, as it seems to be? But if it be, what do I know but that he himself hath already condemned himself for it? And that is all one as if a man should scratch and tear his own face, an object of compassion rather than of anger. Again, that he that would not have a vicious man to sin, is like unto him that would not have moisture in the fig, nor children to welp nor a horse to neigh, nor anything else that in the course of nature is necessary. For what shall he do that hath such an habit? If thou therefore beest powerful and eloquent, remedy it if thou canst.

XIII. If it be not fitting, do it not. If it be not true, speak it not. Ever maintain thine own purpose and resolution free from all compulsion and necessity.

XIV. Of everything that presents itself unto thee, to consider what the true nature of it is, and to unfold it, as it were, by dividing it into that which is formal: that which is material: the true use or end of it, and the just time that it is appointed to last.

XV. It is high time for thee, to understand that there is somewhat in thee, better and more divine than either thy passions, or thy sensual appetites and affections. What is now the object of my mind, is it fear, or suspicion, or lust, or any such thing? To do nothing rashly without some certain end; let that be thy first care. The next, to have no other end than the common good. For, alas! yet a little while, and thou art no more: no more will any, either of those things that now thou seest, or of those men that now are living, be any more. For all things are by nature appointed soon to be changed, turned, and corrupted, that other things might succeed in their room.

XVI. Remember that all is but opinion, and all opinion depends of the mind. Take thine opinion away, and then as a ship that hath stricken in within the arms and mouth of the harbour, a present calm; all things safe and steady: a bay, not capable of any storms and tempests: as the poet hath it.

XVII. No operation whatsoever it he, ceasing for a while, can be truly said to suffer any evil, because it is at an end. Neither can he that is the author of that operation; for this very respect, because his operation is at an end, be said to suffer any evil. Likewise then, neither can the whole body of all our actions (which is our life) if in time it cease, be said to suffer any evil for this very reason, because it is at an end; nor he truly be said to have been ill affected, that did put a period to this series of actions. Now this time or certain period, depends of the determination of nature: sometimes of particular nature, as when a man dieth old; but of nature in general, however; the parts whereof thus changing one after another, the whole world still continues fresh and new. Now that is ever best and most seasonable, which is for the good of the whole. Thus it appears that death of itself can neither be hurtful to any in particular, because it is not a shameful thing (for neither is it a thing that depends of our own will, nor of itself contrary to the common good) and generally, as it is both expedient and seasonable to the whole, that in that respect it must needs be good. It is that also, which is brought unto us by the order and appointment of the Divine Providence; so that he whose will and mind in these things runs along with the Divine ordinance, and by this concurrence of his will and mind with the Divine Providence, is led and driven along, as it were by God Himself; may truly be termed and esteemed, or divinely led and inspired.

XVIII. These three things thou must have always in a readiness: first concerning thine own actions, whether thou doest nothing either idly, or otherwise, than justice and equity do require: and concerning those things that happen unto thee externally, that either they happen unto thee by chance, or by providence; of which two to accuse either, is equally against reason. Secondly, what like unto our bodies are whilest yet rude and imperfect, until they be animated: and from their animation, until their expiration: of what things they are compounded, and into what things they shall be dissolved. Thirdly, how vain all things will appear unto thee when, from on high as it were, looking down thou shalt contemplate all things upon earth, and the wonderful mutability, that they are subject unto: considering withal, the infinite both greatness and variety of things aerial and things celestial that are round about it. And that as often as thou shalt behold them, thou shalt still see the same: as the same things, so the same shortness of continuance of all those things. And, behold, these be the things that we are so proud and puffed up for.

XIX. Cast away from thee opinion, and thou art safe. And what is it that hinders thee from casting of it away? When thou art grieved at anything, hast thou forgotten that all things happen according to the nature of the universe; and that him only it concerns, who is in fault; and moreover, that what is now done, is that which from ever hath been done in the world, and will ever be done, and is now done everywhere: how nearly all men are allied one to another by a kindred not of blood, nor of seed, but of the same mind. Thou hast also forgotten that every man's mind partakes of the Deity, and issueth from thence; and that no man can properly call anything his own, no not his son, nor his body, nor his life; for that they all proceed from that One who is the giver of all things: that all things are but opinion; that no man lives properly, but that very instant of time which is now present. And therefore that no man whensoever he dieth can properly be said to lose any more, than an instant of time.

XX. Let thy thoughts ever run upon them, who once for some one thing or other, were moved with extraordinary indignation; who were once in the highest pitch of either honour, or calamity; or mutual hatred and enmity; or of any other fortune or condition whatsoever. Then consider what's now become of all those things. All is turned to smoke; all to ashes, and a mere fable; and perchance not so much as a fable. As also whatsoever is of this nature, as Fabius Catulinus in the field; Lucius Lupus, and Stertinius, at Baiae Tiberius at Caprem: and Velius Rufus, and all such examples of vehement prosecution in worldly matters; let these also run in thy mind at the same time; and how vile every object of such earnest and vehement prosecution is; and how much more agreeable to true philosophy it is, for a man to carry himself in every matter that offers itself; justly, and moderately, as one that followeth the Gods with all simplicity. For, for a man to be proud and high conceited, that he is not proud and high conceited, is of all kind of pride and presumption, the most intolerable.

XXI. To them that ask thee, Where hast thou seen the Gods, or how knowest thou certainly that there be Gods, that thou art so devout in their worship? I answer first of all, that even to the very eye, they are in some manner visible and apparent. Secondly, neither have I ever seen mine own soul, and yet I respect and honour it. So then for the Gods, by the daily experience that I have of their power and providence towards myself and others, I know certainly that they are, and therefore worship them.

XXII. Herein doth consist happiness of life, for a man to know thoroughly the true nature of everything; what is the matter, and what is the form of it: with all his heart and soul, ever to do that which is just, and to speak the truth. What then remaineth but to enjoy thy life in a course and coherence of good actions, one upon another immediately succeeding, and never interrupted, though for never so little a while?

XXIII. There is but one light of the sun, though it be intercepted by walls and mountains, and other thousand objects. There is but one common substance of the whole world, though it be concluded and restrained into several different bodies, in number infinite. There is but one common soul, though divided into innumerable particular essences and natures. So is there but one common intellectual soul, though it seem to be divided. And as for all other parts of those generals which we have mentioned, as either sensitive souls or subjects, these of themselves (as naturally irrational) have no common mutual reference one unto another, though many of them contain a mind, or reasonable faculty in them, whereby they are ruled and governed. But of every reasonable mind, this the particular nature, that it hath reference to whatsoever is of her own kind, and desireth to be united: neither can this common affection, or mutual unity and correspondency, be here intercepted or divided, or confined to particulars as those other common things are.

XXIV. What doest thou desire? To live long. What? To enjoy the operations of a sensitive soul; or of the appetitive faculty? or wouldst thou grow, and then decrease again? Wouldst thou long be able to talk, to think and reason with thyself? Which of all these seems unto thee a worthy object of thy desire? Now if of all these thou doest find that they be but little worth in themselves, proceed on unto the last, which is, in all things to follow God and reason. But for a man to grieve that by death he shall be deprived of any of these things, is both against God and reason.

XXV. What a small portion of vast and infinite eternity it is, that is allowed unto every one of us, and how soon it vanisheth into the general age of the world: of the common substance, and of the common soul also what a small portion is allotted unto us: and in what a little clod of the whole earth (as it were) it is that thou doest crawl. After thou shalt rightly have considered these things with thyself; fancy not anything else in the world any more to be of any weight and moment but this, to do that only which thine own nature doth require; and to conform thyself to that which the common nature doth afford.

XXVI. What is the present estate of my understanding? For herein lieth all indeed. As for all other things, they are without the compass of mine own will: and if without the compass of my will, then are they as dead things unto me, and as it were mere smoke.

XXVII. To stir up a man to the contempt of death this among other things, is of good power and efficacy, that even they who esteemed pleasure to be happiness, and pain misery, did nevertheless many of them contemn death as much as any. And can death be terrible to him, to whom that only seems good, which in the ordinary course of nature is seasonable? to him, to whom, whether his actions be many or few, so they be all good, is all one; and who whether he behold the things of the world being always the same either for many years, or for few years only, is altogether indifferent? O man! as a citizen thou hast lived, and conversed in this great city the world. Whether just for so many years, or no, what is it unto thee? Thou hast lived (thou mayest be sure) as long as the laws and orders of the city required; which may be the common comfort of all. Why then should it be grievous unto thee, if (not a tyrant, nor an unjust judge, but) the same nature that brought thee in, doth now send thee out of the world? As if the praetor should fairly dismiss him from the stage, whom he had taken in to act a while. Oh, but the play is not yet at an end, there are but three acts yet acted of it? Thou hast well said: for in matter of life, three acts is the whole play. Now to set a certain time to every man's acting, belongs unto him only, who as first he was of thy composition, so is now the cause of thy dissolution. As for thyself; thou hast to do with neither. Go thy ways then well pleased and contented: for so is He that dismisseth thee.

ΒΙΒΛΙΟ ΔΩΔΕΚΑΤΟ

1. Πάντα ἐκεῖνα, ἐφ ἃ διὰ περιόδου εὕχῃ ἐλθεῖν, ἤδη ἔχεινδύνασαι, ἐὰν μὴ σαυτῷ φθονῇς. τοῦτο δέ ἐστιν, ἐὰν πᾶν τὸπαρελθὸν καταλίπῃς καὶ τὸ μέλλον ἐπιτρέψῃς τῇ προνοίᾳ καὶ τὸπαρὸν μόνον ἀπευθύνῃς πρὸς ὁσιότητα καὶ δικαιοσύνην. ὁσιότητα μέν, ἵνα φιλῇς τὸ ἀπονεμόμενον· σοὶ γὰρ αὐτὸ ἡ φύσιςἔφερεν καὶ σὲ τούτῳ· δικαιοσύνην δέ, ἵνα ἐλευθέρως καὶ χωρὶςπεριπλοκῆς λέγῃς τε τάληθῆ καὶ πράσσῃς τὰ κατὰ νόμον καὶκατ ἀξίαν· μὴ ἐμποδίζῃ δέ σε μήτε κακία ἀλλοτρία μήτε ὑπόληψιςμήτε φωνὴ μηδὲ μὴν αἴσθησις τοῦ περιτεθραμμένου σοισαρκιδίου· ὄψεται γὰρ τὸ πάσχον. ἐὰν οὖν, ὅτε δήποτε πρὸςἐξόδῳ γίνῃ, πάντα τὰ ἄλλα καταλιπὼν μόνον τὸ ἡγεμονικόν σουκαὶ τὸ ἐν σοὶ θεῖον τιμήσῃς καὶ μὴ τὸ παύσασθαί ποτε ‹τοῦ› ζῆνφοβηθῇς, ἀλλὰ τό γε μηδέποτε ἄρξασθαι κατὰ φύσιν ζῆν, ἔσῃἄνθρωπος ἄξιος τοῦ γεννήσαντος κόσμου καὶ παύσῃ ξένος ὢντῆς πατρίδος καὶ θαυμάζων ὡς ἀπροσδόκητα τὰ καθ ἡμέρανγινόμενα καὶ κρεμάμενος ἐκ τοῦδε καὶ τοῦδε.

2. Ὁ θεὸς πάντα τὰ ἡγεμονικὰ γυμνὰ τῶν ὑλικῶν ἀγγείων καὶφλοιῶν καὶ καθαρμάτων ὁρᾷ· μόνῳ γὰρ τῷ ἑαυτοῦ νοερῷ μόνωνἅπτεται τῶν ἐξ ἑαυτοῦ εἰς ταῦτα ἐρρυηκότων καὶ ἀπωχετευμένων.ἐὰν δὲ καὶ σὺ τοῦτο ἐθίσῃς ποιεῖν, τὸν πολὺν περισπασμὸνσεαυτοῦ περιαιρήσεις· ὁ γὰρ μὴ τὰ περικείμενα κρεάδια ὁρῶν, ἦπού γε ἐσθῆτα καὶ οἰκίαν καὶ δόξαν καὶ τὴν τοιαύτην περιβολὴνκαὶ σκηνὴν θεώμενος ἀσχολήσεται.

3. Τρία ἐστὶν ἐξ ὧν συνέστηκας· σωμάτιον, πνευμάτιον, νοῦς.τούτων τἆλλα μέχρι τοῦ ἐπιμελεῖσθαι δεῖν σά ἐστι, τὸ δὲ τρίτονμόνον κυρίως σόν. ‹διὸ ἐὰν χωρίσῃς ἀπὸ σεαυτοῦ, τουτέστινἀπὸ τῆς σῆς διανοίας, ὅσα ἄλλοι ποιοῦσιν ἢ λέγουσιν ἢ ὅσααὐτὸς ἐποίησας ἢ εἶπας καὶ ὅσα ὡς μέλλοντα ταράσσει σε καὶὅσα τοῦ περικειμένου σοι σωματίου ἢ τοῦ συμφύτου πνευματίουἀπροαίρετα πρόσεστιν καὶ ὅσα ἡ ἔξωθεν περιρρέουσα δίνηἑλίσσει, ὥστε τῶν συνειμαρμένων ἐξῃρημένην, καθαρὰν ‹τε› τὴννοερὰν δύναμιν ‹καὶ› ἀπόλυτον ἐφ ἑαυτῆς ζῆν, ποιοῦσαν τὰδίκαια καὶ θέλουσαν τὰ συμβαίνοντα καὶ λέγουσαν τάληθῆ· ἐὰνχωρίσῃς, φημί, τοῦ ἡγεμονικοῦ τούτου τὰ προσηρτημένα ἐκπροσπαθείας καὶ τοῦ χρόνου τὰ ἐπέκεινα ἢ τὰ παρῳχηκότα,ποιήσῃς τε σεαυτόν, οἷος ὁ Ἐμπεδόκλειος σφαῖρος κυκλοτερὴςμονίῃ περιγηθεῖ γαίαν, μόνον τε ζῆν ἐκμελετήσῃς ὃ ζῇς,τουτέστιτὸ παρόν, δυνήσῃ τό γε μέχρι τοῦ ἀποθανεῖν ὑπολειπόμενονἀταράκτως καὶ εὐμενῶς καὶ ἵλεως τῷ σαυτοῦ δαίμονι διαβιῶναι.

4. Πολλάκις ἐθαύμασα πῶς ἑαυτὸν μὲν ἕκαστος μᾶλλον πάντωνφιλεῖ, τὴν δὲ ἑαυτοῦ περὶ αὐτοῦ ὑπόληψιν ἐν ἐλάττονι λόγῳ τίθεταιἢ τὴν τῶν ἄλλων.

ἐὰν γοῦν τινα θεὸς ἐπιστὰς ἢ διδάσκαλοςἔμφρων κελεύσῃ μηδὲν καθ αὑτὸν ἐνθυμεῖσθαι καὶ διανοεῖσθαιὃ μὴ ἅμα καὶ γεγωνίσκων ἐξοίσει, οὐδὲ πρὸς μίαν ἡμέραν τοῦτούπομενεῖ. οὕτως τοὺς πέλας μᾶλλον αἰδούμεθα, τί ποτε περὶἡμῶν φρονήσουσιν, ἢ ἑαυτούς.

5. Πῶς ποτε πάντα καλῶς καὶ φιλανθρώπως διατάξαντες οἱ θεοὶτοῦτο μόνον παρεῖδον, τὸ ἐνίους τῶν ἀνθρώπων καὶ πάνυχρηστοὺς καὶ πλεῖστα πρὸς τὸ θεῖον ὥσπερ συμβόλαια θεμένουςκαὶ ἐπὶ πλεῖστον δὶ ἔργων ὁσίων καὶ ἱερουργιῶν συνήθεις τῷθείῳ γενομένους, ἐπειδὰν ἅπαξ ἀποθάνωσι, μηκέτι αὖθις γίνεσθαι,ἀλλ εἰς τὸ παντελὲς ἀπεσβηκέναι; τοῦτο δὲ εἴπερ ἄρα καὶ οὕτωςἔχει, εὖ ἴσθι ὅτι, εἰ ὡς ἑτέρως ἔχειν ἔδει, ἐποίησαν ἄν· εἰ γὰρδίκαιον ἦν, ἦν ἂν καὶ δυνατόν, καὶ εἰ κατὰ φύσιν, ἤνεγκεν ἂναὐτὸ ἡ φύσις. ἐκ δὴ τοῦ μὴ οὕτως ἔχειν, εἴπερ οὐχ οὕτως ἔχει,πιστούσθω σοι τὸ μὴ δεῆσαι οὕτως γίνεσθαι· ὁρᾶς γὰρ καὶ αὐτὸςὅτι τοῦτο παραζητῶν δικαιολογῇ πρὸς τὸν θεόν· οὐκ ἂν δ οὕτωςδιελεγόμεθα τοῖς θεοῖς, εἰ μὴ ἄριστοι καὶ δικαιότατοι ἦσαν. εἰδὲ τοῦτο, οὐκ ἄν τι περιεῖδον ἀδίκως καὶ ἀλόγως ἠμελημένῶν ἐν τῇ διακοσμήσει.

6. Ἔθιζε καὶ ὅσα ἀπογινώσκεις. καὶ γὰρ ἡ χεὶρ ἡ ἀριστερὰ πρὸςτὰ ἄλλα διὰ τὸ ἀνέθιστον ἀργὸς οὖσα τοῦ χαλινοῦ ἐρρωμενέστερονἢ ἡ δεξιὰ κρατεῖ· τοῦτο γὰρ εἴθισται.

7. Ὁποῖον δεῖ καταληφθῆναι ὑπὸ τοῦ θανάτου καὶ σώματι καὶψυχῇ· τὴν βραχύτητα τοῦ βίου· τὴν ἀχάνειαν τοῦ ὀπίσω καὶπρόσω αἰῶνος· τὴν ἀσθένειαν πάσης ὕλης.

8. Γυμνὰ τῶν φλοιῶν θεάσασθαι τὰ αἰτιώδη· τὰς ἀναφορὰς τῶνπράξεων· τί πόνος· τί ἡδονή· τί θάνατος· τί δόξα· τίς οὐχ ἑαυτῷἀσχολίας αἴτιος· πῶς οὐδεὶς ὑπ ἄλλου ἐμποδίζεται· ὅτι πάνταὑπόληψις.

9. Ὅμοιον εἶναι [δεῖ] ἐν τῇ τῶν δογμάτων χρήσει παγκρατιαστῇ,οὐχὶ μονομάχῳ· ὁ μὲν γὰρ τὸ ξίφος ᾧ χρῆται ἀποτίθεται καὶἀναιρεῖται· ὁ δὲ τὴν χεῖρα ἀεὶ ἔχει καὶ οὐδὲν ἄλλο ἢ συστρέψαιαὐτὴν δεῖ.

10. Αὐτὰ τὰ πράγματα ὁρᾶν, διαιροῦντα εἰς ὕλην, αἴτιον,ἀναφοράν.

11. Ἡλίκην ἐξουσίαν ἔχει ἄνθρωπος μὴ ποιεῖν ἄλλο ἢ ὅπερ μέλλειὁ θεὸς ἐπαινεῖν, καὶ δέχεσθαι πᾶν ὃ ἂν νέμῃ αὐτῷ ὁ θεός, ‹ὡς›τὸ ἑξῆς τῇ φύσει.

12. Μήτε θεοῖς μεμπτέον· οὐδὲν γὰρ ἑκόντες ἢ ἄκοντες ἁμαρτάνουσι·μήτε ἀνθρώποις· οὐδὲν γὰρ οὐχὶ ἄκοντες. ὥστε οὐδενὶμεμπτέον.

13. Πῶς γελοῖος καὶ ξένος ὁ θαυμάζων καὶ ὁτιοῦν τῶν ἐν τῷ βίῳγινομένων.

14. Ἤτοι ἀνάγκη εἱμαρμένης καὶ ἀπαράβατος τάξις ἢ πρόνοιαἱλάσιμος ἢ φυρμὸς εἰκαιότητος ἀπροστάτητος. εἰ μὲν οὖνἀπαράβατος ἀνάγκη, τί ἀντιτείνεις; εἰ δὲ πρόνοια ἐπιδεχομένητὸ ἱλάσκεσθαι, ἄξιον ἑαυτὸν ποίησον τῆς ἐκ τοῦ θείου βοηθείας.εἰ δὲ φυρμὸς ἀνηγεμόνευτος, ἀσμένιζε ὅτι ἐν τοιούτῳ τῷκλύδωνι αὐτὸς ἔχεις ἐν ἑαυτῷ τινα νοῦν ἡγεμονικόν, κἂν παραφέρῃσε ὁ κλύδων, παραφερέτω τὸ σαρκίδιον, τὸ πνευμάτιον,

15. τἆλλα· τὸν γὰρ νοῦν οὐ παροίσει. ἢ τὸ μὲν τοῦ λύχνου φῶς,μέχρι σβεσθῇ, φαίνει καὶ τὴν αὐγὴν οὐκ ἀποβάλλει, ἡ δὲ ἐν σοὶἀλήθεια καὶ δικαιοσύνη καὶ σωφροσύνη προαποσβήσεται;

16. Ἐπὶ τοῦ φαντασίαν παρασχόντος ὅτι ἥμαρτε· τί δαὶ οἶδα εἰτοῦτο ἁμάρτημα; εἰ δὲ καὶ ἥμαρτεν, ὅτι ‹οὐ› κατέκρινεν αὐτὸςἑαυτόν, καὶ οὕτως ὅμοιον τοῦτο τῷ καταδρύπτειν τὴν ἑαυτοῦὄψιν;Ὅτι ὁ μὴ θέλων τὸν φαῦλον ἁμαρτάνειν ὅμοιος τῷ μὴ θέλοντιτὴν συκῆν ὀπὸν ἐν τοῖς σύκοις φέρειν καὶ τὰ βρέφη κλαυθμυρίζεσθαικαὶ τὸν ἵππον χρεμετίζειν καὶ ὅσα ἄλλα ἀναγκαῖα. τίγὰρ πάθῃ τὴν ἕξιν ἔχων τοιαύτην; εἰ οὖν γοργὸς εἶ, ταύτην θεράπευσον.

17. Εἰ μὴ καθήκει, μὴ πράξῃς· εἰ μὴ ἀληθές ἐστι, μὴ εἴπῃς. ἡ γὰρόρμή σου ἔστω εἰς τὸ πάν‹τως› ἀεὶ ὁρᾶν, τί ἐστιν αὐτὸ ἐκεῖνο τὸτὴν φαντασίαν σοι ποιοῦν, καὶ ἀναπτύσσειν διαιροῦντα εἰς τὸαἴτιον, εἰς τὸ ὑλικόν, εἰς τὴν ἀναφοράν, εἰς τὸν χρόνον ἐντὸς οὗπεπαῦσθαι αὐτὸ δεήσει.

18. Αἴσθου ποτὲ ὅτι κρεῖττόν τι καὶ δαιμονιώτερον ἔχεις ἐν σαυτῷτῶν τὰ πάθη ποιούντων καὶ καθάπαξ τῶν νευροσπαστούντωνσε. τί μου νῦν ἐστιν ἡ διάνοια; μὴ φόβος; μὴ ὑποψία; μὴ ἐπιθυμία;μὴ ἄλλο τι τοιοῦτον;

19. Πρῶτον τὸ μὴ εἰκῇ μηδὲ ἄνευ ἀναφορᾶς. δεύτερον τὸ μὴ ἐπ‘ἄλλο τι ἢ ἐπὶ τὸ κοινωνικὸν τέλος τὴν ἀναγωγὴν ποιεῖσθαι.

20. Ὅτι μετ οὐ πολὺ οὐδεὶς οὐδαμοῦ ἔσῃ οὐδὲ τούτων τι ἃ νῦνβλέπεις οὐδὲ τούτων τις τῶν νῦν βιούντων· ἅπαντα γὰρμεταβάλλειν καὶ τρέπεσθαι καὶ φθείρεσθαι πέφυκεν, ἵνα ἕτεραἐφεξῆς γίνηται.

21. Ὅτι πάντα ὑπόληψις καὶ αὕτη ἐπὶ σοί. ἆρον οὖν ὅτε θέλειςτὴν ὑπόληψιν καὶ ὥσπερ κάμψαντι τὴν ἄκραν γαλήνη, σταθερὰπάντα καὶ κόλπος ἀκύμων.

22. Μία καὶ ἡτισοῦν ἐνέργεια κατὰ καιρὸν παυσαμένη οὐδὲν κακὸνπάσχει, καθὸ πέπαυται· οὐδὲ ὁ πράξας τὴν πρᾶξιν ταύτην καταὐτὸ τοῦτο, καθὸ πέπαυται, κακόν τι πέπονθεν. ὁμοίως οὖν τὸἐκ πασῶν τῶν πράξεων σύστημα, ὅπερ ἐστὶν ὁ βίος, ἐὰν ἐν καιρῷπαύσηται, οὐδὲν κακὸν πάσχει κατ αὐτὸ τοῦτο, καθὸ πέπαυται· οὐδὲ ὁ καταπαύσας ἐν καιρῷ τὸν εἱρμὸν τοῦτον κακῶς διετέθη.τὸν δὲ καιρὸν καὶ τὸν ὅρον δίδωσιν ἡ φύσις, ποτὲ μὲν καὶ ἡ ἰδία,ὅταν ἐν γήρᾳ, πάντως δὲ ἡ τῶν ὅλων, ἧς τῶν μερῶν μεταβαλλόντωννεαρὸς ἀεὶ καὶ ἀκμαῖος ὁ σύμπας κόσμος διαμένει. καλὸν δὲἀεὶ πᾶν καὶ ὡραῖον τὸ συμφέρον τῷ ὅλῳ. ἡ οὖν κατάπαυσις τοῦβίου ἑκάστῳ οὐ κακὸν μὲν ὅτι οὐδὲ αἰσχρόν, εἴπερ καὶἀπροαίρετον καὶ οὐκ ἀκοινώνητον· ἀγαθὸν δὲ εἴπερ τῷ ὅλῳκαίριον καὶ συμφέρον καὶ συμφερόμενον. οὕτως γὰρ καὶθεοφόρητος ὁ φερόμενος κατὰ ταὐτὰ θεῷ καὶ ἐπὶ ταὐτὰ τῇ γνώμῃφερόμενος.

23. Τρία ταῦτα δεῖ πρόχειρα ἔχειν· ἐπὶ μὲν ὧν ποιεῖς, [εἰ] μήτεεἰκῇ μήτε ἄλλως ἢ ὡς ἂν ἡ Δίκη αὐτὴ ἐνήργησεν· ἐπὶ δὲ τῶνἔξωθεν συμβαινόντων, ὅτι ἤτοι κατ ἐπιτυχίαν ἢ κατὰ πρόνοιαν·οὔτε δὲ τῇ ἐπιτυχίᾳ μεμπτέον οὔτε τῇ προνοίᾳ ἐγκλητέον. δεύτερόντό· ὁποῖον ἕκαστον ἀπὸ σπέρματος μέχρι ψυχώσεως καὶἀποψυχώσεως μέχρι τοῦ τὴν ψυχὴν ἀποδοῦναι καὶ ἐξ οἵων ἡσύγκρισις καὶ εἰς οἷα ἡ λύσις. τρίτον εἰ ἄφνω μετέωρος ἐξαρθεὶςκατασκέψαιο τὰ ἀνθρώπεια καὶ τὴν πολυτροπίαν [ὅση]κατανοήσαις, ὅτι καταφρονήσεις συνιδὼν ἅμα καὶ ὅσον τὸπεριοικοῦν ἐναερίων καὶ ἐναιθερίων· καὶ ὅτι, ὁσάκις ἂν ἐξαρθῇς,ταὐτὰ ὄψῃ· τὸ ὁμοειδές, τὸ ὀλιγοχρόνιον· ἐπὶ τούτοις ὁ τῦφος.

24. Βάλε ἔξω τὴν ὑπόληψιν· σέσωσαι. τίς οὖν ὁ κωλύων ἐκβάλλειν;

25. Ὅταν δυσφορῇς ἐπί τινι, ἐπελάθου τοῦ, ὅτι πάντα κατὰ τὴντῶν ὅλων φύσιν γίνεται, καὶ τοῦ, ὅτι τὸ ἁμαρτανόμενον ἀλλότριον,καὶ ἐπὶ τούτοις τοῦ, ὅτι πᾶν τὸ γινόμενον οὕτως ἀεὶ ἐγίνετο καὶγενήσεται καὶ νῦν πανταχοῦ γίνεται· τοῦ, ὅση ἡ συγγένειαἀνθρώπου πρὸς πᾶν τὸ ἀνθρώπειον γένος· οὐ γὰρ αἱματίουἢσπερματίου, ἀλλὰ νοῦ κοινωνία. ἐπελάθου δὲ καὶ τοῦ, ὅτι ὁ ἑκάστου νοῦς θεὸς καὶ ἐκεῖθεν ἐρρύηκεν· τοῦ, ὅτι οὐδὲν ἴδιονοὐδενός, ἀλλὰ καὶ τὸ τεκνίον καὶ τὸ σωμάτιον καὶ αὐτὸ τὸψυχάριον ἐκεῖθεν ἐλήλυθεν· τοῦ, ὅτι πάνθ ὑπόληψις· τοῦ,

ὅτιτὸ παρὸν μόνον ἕκαστος ζῇ καὶ τοῦτο ἀποβάλλει.

26. Συνεχῶς ἀναπολεῖν τοὺς ἐπί τινι λίαν ἀγανακτήσαντας, τοὺςἐν μεγίσταις δόξαις ἢ συμφοραῖς ἢ ἔχθραις ἢ ὁποιαισοῦν τύχαιςἀκμάσαντας· εἶτα ἐφιστάνειν· ποῦ νῦν πάντα ἐκεῖνα; καπνὸςκαὶ σποδὸς καὶ μῦθος ἢ οὐδὲ μῦθος. συμπροσπιπτέτω δὲ καὶ τὸτοιοῦτο πᾶν, οἷον· Φάβιος Κατουλλῖνος ἐπ᾽ ἀγροῦ καὶ ΛούσιοςΛοῦπος ἐν τοῖς κήποις καὶ Στερτίνιος ἐν Βαίαις καὶ Τιβέριος ἐνΚαπρέαις καὶ Οὐήλιος Ῥοῦφος καὶ ὅλως ἡ πρὸς ὁτιοῦν μετοιήσεως διαφορά· καὶ ὡς εὐτελὲς πᾶν τὸ κατεντεινόμενον καὶὅσῳ φιλοσοφώτερον τὸ ἐπὶ τῆς δοθείσης ὕλης ἑαυτὸν δίκαιον,σώφρονα, θεοῖς ἑπόμενον ἀφελῶς παρέχειν· ὁ γὰρ ἐπὶ ἀτυφίᾳτῦφος τυφόμενος πάντων χαλεπώτατος.

27. Πρὸς τοὺς ἐπιζητοῦντας· ποῦ γὰρ ἰδὼν τοὺς θεοὺς ἢ πόθενκατειληφὼς ὅτι εἰσὶν οὕτω σέβεις; πρῶτον μὲν καὶ ὄψει ὁρατοίεἰσιν· ἔπειτα μέντοι οὐδὲ τὴν ψυχὴν τὴν ἐμαυτοῦ ἑώρακα καὶὅμως τιμῶ· οὕτως οὖν καὶ τοὺς θεούς, ἐξ ὧν τῆς δυνάμεως αὐτῶνἑκάστοτε πειρῶμαι, ἐκ τούτων ὅτι τε εἰσὶ καταλαμβάνω καὶαἰδοῦμαι.

28. Σωτηρία βίου ἕκαστον δι᾽ ὅλου αὐτὸ τί ἐστιν ὁρᾶν, τί μὲναὐτοῦ τὸ ὑλικόν, τί δὲ τὸ αἰτιῶδες· ἐξ ὅλης τῆς ψυχῆς τὰ δίκαιαποιεῖν καὶ τἀληθῆ λέγειν. τί λοιπὸν ἢ ἀπολαύειν τοῦ ζῆνσυνάπτοντα ἄλλο ἐπ᾽ ἄλλῳ ἀγαθόν, ὥστε μηδὲ τὸ βραχύτατονδιάστημα ἀπολείπειν;

29. Ἓν φῶς ἡλίου, κἂν διείργηται τοίχοις, ὄρεσιν, ἄλλοις μυρίοις.μία οὐσία κοινή, κἂν διείργηται ἰδίως ποιοῖς σώμασι μυρίοις.μία ψυχή, κἂν φύσεσι διείργηται μυρίαις καὶ ἰδίαις περιγραφαῖς.μία νοερὰ ψυχή, κἂν διακεκρίσθαι δοκῇ. τὰ μὲν οὖν ἄλλα μέρητῶν εἰρημένων, οἷον πνεύματα καὶ ὑποκείμενα ἀναίσθητα, καὶἀνοικείωτα ἀλλήλοις· καίτοι κἀκεῖνα τὸ ἑνοῦν συνέχει καὶ τὸἐπὶ τὰ αὐτὰ βρῖθον. διάνοια δὲ ἰδίως ἐπὶ τὸ ὁμόφυλον τείνεταικαὶ συνίσταται καὶ οὐ διείργεται τὸ κοινωνικὸν πάθος.

30. Τί ἐπιζητεῖς; τὸ διαγίνεσθαι; ἀλλὰ τὸ αἰσθάνεσθαι; τὸ ὁρμᾶν;τὸ αὔξεσθαι; τὸ λήγειν αὖθις; τὸ φωνῇ χρῆσθαι; τὸ διανοεῖσθαι;τί τούτων πόθου σοι ἄξιον δοκεῖ; εἰ δὲ ἕκαστα εὐκαταφρόνητα,πρόιθι ἐπὶ τελευταῖον τὸ ἕπεσθαι τῷ λόγῳ καὶ τῷ θεῷ. ἀλλὰμάχεται τὸ τιμᾶν ταῦτα, τὸ ἄχθεσθαι εἰ διὰ τοῦ τεθνηκέναιστερήσεταί τις αὐτῶν.

31. Πόστον μέρος τοῦ ἀπείρου καὶ ἀχανοῦς αἰῶνος ἀπομεμέρισταιἑκάστῳ· τάχιστα γὰρ ἐναφανίζεται τῷ ἀιδίῳ· πόστον δὲ τῆς ὅληςοὐσίας· πόστον δὲ τῆς ὅλης ψυχῆς· ἐν πόστῳ δὲ βωλαρίῳ τῆςὅλης γῆς ἕρπεις. πάντα ταῦτα ἐνθυμούμενος μηδὲν μέγα φαντάζουἦ τό, ὡς μὲν ἡ σὴ φύσις ἄγει ποιεῖν, πάσχειν δὲ ὡς ἡ κοινὴ φύσιςφέρει.

32. Πῶς ἑαυτῷ χρῆται τὸ ἡγεμονικόν; ἐν γὰρ τούτῳ τὸ πᾶν ἐστι.τὰ δὲ λοιπὰ ἢ προαιρετικά ἐστιν ἢ ἀπροαίρετα, νεκρὰ καὶ καπνός.

33. Πρὸς θανάτου καταφρόνησιν ἐγερτικώτατον ὅτι καὶ οἱ τὴνἡδονὴν ἀγαθὸν καὶ τὸν πόνον κακὸν κρίνοντες ὅμως τούτουκατεφρόνησαν.

34. Ὧι τὸ εὔκαιρον μόνον ἀγαθὸν καὶ ᾧ τὸ πλείους κατὰ λόγονὀρθὸν πράξεις ἀποδοῦναι τῷ ὀλιγωτέρας ἐν ἴσῳ ἐστὶ καὶ ᾧ τὸνκόσμον θεωρῆσαι πλείονι ἢ ἐλάσσονι χρόνῳ οὐ διαφέρει, τούτῳοὐδὲ ὁ θάνατος φοβερόν.

35. Ἄνθρωπε, ἐπολιτεύσω ἐν τῇ μεγάλῃ ταύτῃ πόλει· τί σοιδιαφέρει, εἰ πέντε ἔτεσιν ‹ἢ πεντήκοντα›; τὸ γὰρ κατὰ τοὺς νόμουςἴσον ἑκάστῳ. τί οὖν δεινόν, εἰ τῆς πόλεως ἀποπέμπει σε οὐτύραννος οὐδὲ δικαστὴς ἄδικος, ἀλλ ἡ φύσις ἡ εἰσαγαγοῦσα,οἷον εἰ κωμῳδὸν ἀπολύοι τῆς σκηνῆς ὁ παραλαβὼν στρατηγός;- "ἀλλ οὐκ εἶπον τὰ πέντε μέρη, ἀλλὰ τὰ τρία." - "καλῶς εἶπας·ἐν μέντοι τῷ βίῳ τὰ τρία ὅλον τὸ δρᾶμά ἐστι." τὸ γὰρ τέλειονἐκεῖνος ὁρίζει ὁ τότε μὲν τῆς συγκρίσεως, νῦν δὲ τῆς διαλύσεωςαἴτιος· σὺ δὲ ἀναίτιος ἀμφοτέρων. ἄπιθι οὖν ἵλεως· καὶ γὰρ ὁἀπολύων ἵλεως.

Erebus Society

Made in the USA
Columbia, SC
17 March 2023

13918714R00164